A
history
OF
WESTERN
LITERATURE

A history OF WESTERN LITERATURE

FROM MEDIEVAL EPIC TO MODERN POETRY

John M. Cohen

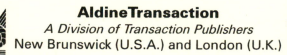

AldineTransaction
A Division of Transaction Publishers
New Brunswick (U.S.A.) and London (U.K.)

First paperback publishing 2008
Copyright © 1963 by J. M. Cohen

This book is printed on acid-free paper that meets the American National Standard for Permanence of Paper for Printed Library Materials.

Library of Congress Catalog Number: 2008002631
ISBN: 978-0-202-36185-7
Printed in the United States of America

Library of Congress Cataloging-in-Publication Data

Cohen, J. M. (John Michael), 1903-1989
    A history of Western literature : from Medieval epic to modern poetry /
J. M. Cohen.
        p. cm.
    Originally published: Chicago : Aldine Pub., 1963.
    Includes bibliographical references and index.
    ISBN 978-0-202-36185-7 (alk. paper)
    1. Literature, Modern—History and criticism. 2. Literature, Medieval—
History and criticism. I. Title.

PN701.C57 2008
809—dc22   2008002631

TO AUDREY

CONTENTS

FOREWORD 9

1 Epic Tales and Romances of Adventure 11
2 The Theme of Courtly Love 25
3 The Rebirth of Italy 45
4 Mysticism, Mannerism, and Popular Poetry 65
5 The Birth of the Drama 84
6 The Later Italian Renaissance 95
7 Reformation in Germany and Renaissance in France 109
8 The Great Age of Spain and Portugal 130
9 Italian Epic, Spanish Drama, and German Poetry 145
10 The Great Age of France 172
11 The Early Novel, The Reign of Reason, and The Birth of Sensibility 198
12 Italian Revival and the Age of Goethe 218
13 The Romantics 241
14 The Novel in its Prime 264
15 Poetry after the Romantics 290
16 The Great Scandinavians and the Modern Theatre 323
17 The Novel Loses Focus, and a Hope for Poetry 339

A NOTE ON TRANSLATIONS 357
LIST OF DATES 360
INDEX 373

FOREWORD

WESTERN Literature, from the birth of vernacular poetry in France to the present age in which similar fashions prevail over an area extending from Buenos Aires to Moscow, from Athens to San Francisco, can be thought of as a single expanding tradition. It is the history of this tradition that I have set out to write, excluding, however, all direct reference to English writers, since my viewpoint is that of one who looks across the Channel for similarities and contrasts, but is nevertheless conscious of the—admittedly subjective—differences separating his own literature from that written in other languages.

English literature—and consequently American also—is excluded from this survey, as is all writing in Latin which, although closely related to medieval writing in the vernacular, has an academic flavour that prevents its being read today.

For my especial purpose is to act as a guide to what is living and readable, either in the original or in translation. I have avoided all reference to dead works, important only for historical reasons, and have deliberately refrained from providing a bibliography of books on literary history and criticism. It is the poetry, the plays, the novels and the works of speculation, of the great authors of the past that I would urge my readers to turn to, and in respect of these anyone can extract his own reading-list from my text.

There are, however, a few books which have strongly influenced my way of looking at literature, and the chief of these are Ernst Robert Curtius's *European Literature and the Latin Middle Ages* (translation, Routledge), C. S. Lewis's *Allegory of Love* (Oxford Univ. Press), and various works by Ramón Menéndez Pidal. The translation of Curtius's book originated as Bollinger series XXVI published in 1953 by Pantheon Books Inc. for the Bollinger Foundation.

FOREWORD

I have had much help, and from many people, in the writing of this book; and I am particularly grateful to Miss G. R. Levy for her careful reading of my typescript, for her many suggestions, and for the initial inspiration which I drew from her study of the epic, *The Sword from the Rock* (Faber 1953); also to Mr Colin Hardie for the loan of two scripts on Dante, entitled *A Spiritual Autobiography,* read by him in the Third Programme in October, 1954, and so far, I believe, unprinted; to Mrs H. A. Frankfort for reading some Dutch poetry with me; to Professor L. W. Forster for information concerning Dutch and Flemish authors; to my son Mark for criticism, interest, and the drawing of the Time Chart, and finally to my wife, with whom so much that I have read during nearly thirty years has been fruitfully discussed.

Quotations are given in English where a satisfactory translation exists: otherwise in the original, followed by a plain prose rendering.

For the present edition I have made a few necessary corrections and expanded or otherwise altered several paragraphs towards the end of the book, to account for a few important works published in the last few years.

J.M.C.

Chapter One

EPIC TALES AND ROMANCES
OF ADVENTURE

EUROPEAN Literature was born fully mature towards the beginning of the twelfth century. It was contemporary with the Crusades, and it was the product of the same conflict of forces. It arose, that is to say, from the impact of the non-Christian upon the Christian world. On the one side the Romance languages had developed so far as to be virtually independent of the debased Latin from which they had evolved; on the other hand the Dark Ages had not themselves produced from the relics of classical culture any fresh myths which could be the subject of poetry in the vernacular. Priests and monks continued to compose epics and treatises, chronicles and hymns, in Medieval Latin, but their inspiration had run dry. What is more, a new public had appeared, that had little or no Latin. The feudal princes who were leading the great counter-offensive against the infidels had leisure. They had furthermore contact in many places with these same infidels, whose level of civilization was higher than theirs. Their courts – perhaps in imitation of the more cultured Moslem – were becoming more luxurious, and they demanded entertainment. Some of their ladies, indeed, quickly set themselves up as patronesses of the almost non-existent literary arts. The lords of the Frankish world wanted to hear their own praises sung; not by way of personal adulation, however, for this was not an age of personality worship. What they asked of their *jongleurs* or minstrels was an idealized picture of the Christian mission which they had assumed. They demanded a presentation of the Christian way of life that they were defending, and their own age offered them no compelling idea. So from outside the narrow Latin world were called in the heroic sagas of the Teutons, the romantic legends of the Celts, and that spiritualized cult of courtship, which was probably taught them by the infidels themselves, but which came to its second and

European birth in the courts of Central and Southern France.

Now the *jongleur* could sing of knightly virtues, of beauty in women, of constancy in love, and of adventure in strange lands to grasping feudal chieftains, who saw themselves, as they listened, making a last stand with Roland in the pass of Roncesvalles, or – more realistically – reconquering the Spanish peninsula piecemeal with the Cid, and loading an ungrateful king with the spoils – of which however, sufficient remained in the conqueror's hands to make him a rich man. Alternatively, at one degree farther from reality, some young knight in the draughty hall of a Norman castle might set out, in his imagination, with Lancelot or Percival in search of that mysterious Graal, the bringing of which to King Arthur's court would usher in a new age; or, in a more private dream, he might see himself glorified in the shape of Tristan, mad for the love of Queen Iseult, or as Lancelot martyred by the triumph and shame of his passion for Guenevere. The new literature supplied living myths for the emergent knightly caste. The *chansons de geste* (Songs of the great Deeds of old) presented the pettiest baron to himself as a Christian hero; the poems that told of the 'Matter of Britain', the central theme of which was the history of King Arthur and his knights, transformed him into a romantic adventurer; and the lyrical poetry, which arose contemporaneously with the epic, showed him to himself in the light of a lover, approaching his mistress with mingled awe and desire. Here, for the first time in Western poetry, sexual feeling was raised to the level of a transcendent emotion, and the theme of ideal love, unknown to the poets of Greece and Rome, was added to those of great poetry. The poetry of the twelfth century, indeed, contained from the outset four of the five principal ingredients of the European poetic tradition. Heroism, love, the worship of God and the search for the unknown, were all treated by the epic and lyric poets of France and Spain, while the fifth ingredient, the analysis of the poet's own feelings and motives, and the dramatization of his own personality, though on the whole missing until the Renaissance began to stress the importance of the individual and his private vision, appeared sporadically even at that time among the lyricists of the West, and most recognizably in the Danube valley, among the Minnesänger, the German poets of courtly love.

Twelfth-century poetry, nevertheless, is on the whole virtually anonymous. Just as we hardly know the names of the architects who, in the same age, were building the great Cathedrals, so we know very little about the *troubadours* or *trouvères* – as they were called in Provence and Northern France respectively – who made the songs which the *joglars* or *jongleurs* sang. Even the name which they assumed suggests that the composers of the *chansons de geste* thought of themselves as nameless craftsmen rather than as poets to compare with the almost legendary ancients, Homer, Virgil, and their favourite Statius. For the word *trouvère* means no more than finder, or at best inventor. The *troubadour* of the South, on the other hand, though the name makes no greater claim to poetic individuality, leaves on his songs the imprint of a personal mannerism, if not of a fully independent style; and we have at least some anecdotes, if no very full biographical information, about the chief poets of Provence. But most often such stories as can be extracted from his work have little reference to the composer's own life.

The vernacular literature of the twelfth century was not designed for reading. The epic poems were composed for recitation to the simple music of a primitive fiddle, and the lyrics for singing to more complicated tunes, sometimes with refrains, or as a voice and fiddle accompaniment to a dance. There was, consequently, a very close relationship between the metres used and the traditional dance steps; and since most of the dances were popular in origin it was at this point that the cultivated lyric touched the folk-song, with the result that in some districts, in Northern France and Spain in particular, poems began to be devised on less sophisticated subjects by the *jongleurs* themselves, independently of the *trouvères*, to be sung at the festivities of the common people. It was the dance that bridged the gap between the art-forms proper to each caste.

The *jongleur*, who recited the *trouvère*'s poetry at the feudal courts, or at stages on the much frequented pilgrimage roads to Jerusalem, to St James of Compostela, and to the shrines of the many lesser saints, was probably a cleric. For, in this age, only a cleric was able to read and write; and his poem was almost certainly not recited out of his head, but learnt from a parchment copy. In the earliest days he may well have been a decent monk, entrusted with the job of entertaining passing pilgrims for the benefit of his monastery funds. But by the twelfth century his activities were by no means confined within institutional walls, or to the mere recitation of poetry. He was by then a general wandering entertainer, a singer, a conjuror, an acrobat, and even an actor in crude knock-about farces, for the amusement either of gentlemen and their ladies in their castles or of the crowd in the market place. Originally, the chief items in his repertory had been poems on the lives of saints and miracle stories, of which some fragments have survived which predate the *chansons de geste*. These were the only form of religious literature then circulating, for the Church discouraged its priests from giving readings from the Bible, and such partial translations into the vernacular as existed were rare. Among these miracle stories one of the favourites in all countries was the story of St Alexis, a verse rendering of which, attributed to a canon of Rouen Cathedral, is one of the oldest monuments of Northern French literature; it dates from the eleventh century, but begins with a characteristically backward glance to a golden age, long years before that:

> The world was good in the times of old,
> For then there was faith and justice and love.

Those were the days in which wealthy Christians like Alexis would abandon the secular life and wander the pagan world, begging crusts from the tables of the great and taking beatings from their servants, amidst an efflorescence of miracles. Legends of the Saints, Bible stories, and apocryphal tales about the Virgin Mary, whose cult was then rapidly spreading, made up the *jongleur*'s early repertory, and these continued to be written until well on into the thirteenth century. But, as has been suggested, to the extent that the *jongleur*'s repertory extended his reputation declined: and soon ecclesiastical dignitaries began to protest against the disgrace which he brought on the clergy; soon his ranks came to be recruited only from among unfrocked or disreputable priests, or from laymen who had somehow managed to pick up a clerk's education.

The *jongleur*, however, was not – as has been noted – usually the composer of the poems or stories that he recited. The composer, the *troubadour* or *trouvère*, was either a respectable cleric or a landed nobleman or, at worst, the rackety younger son of some aristocratic house. It is true that, especially in Southern France, the *troubadour* might sink so far as to recite his compositions himself, which would bring his status down to that of a mere baron's retainer. But he was divided by the widest of social cleavages from the disreputable *jongleur*, who wandered like St Alexis, sometimes as far abroad as Hungary or Cyprus, though for less laudable reasons than that blessed saint and martyr.

The first *trouvère* whose name we find attached to an important work signs with the Latinized form of his name, Turoldus: 'Here ends the *geste*, for Turoldus grows weak'. The obvious interpretation of this last line of the *Chanson de Roland* is that one Théroulde, to give his Norman name its French form, claims to be its author. Scholarship, however, is by no means unanimous in accepting this reading: nor can any of the Thé rouldes living in England or Normandy in the first half of the twelfth century be associated with any certainty with this first great work of Romance literature. The general assumption is that he was a cleric of some eminence and of wide reading, and some have gone so far as to see in the *Chanson* parallels to various passages in the *Aeneid*. The poem indubitably bears evidence of at least some acquaintance with Virgil, an author very little read at that time and known chiefly for his reputation, mysteriously acquired in the Dark Ages, as a practitioner in magic.

The version that we have is certainly not the first treatment of the story. We learn, indeed, from a verse chronicle that a *jongleur* named Taillefer recited a song of Roland and Oliver before William the Conqueror on the field of Hastings. But this is not our poem, which we know from a copy made in England about the middle of the twelfth century from an original probably quite recent. For though the *jongleur*'s practice was, no doubt, to graft new material on old, and himself to alter the poem in the course of memorizing it, or even to adapt it to the particular local interests of his hearers, this poem bears every sign of being a completely new version retelling the old story, but supplemented by new material drawn from a history of the Franks (*Gesta Francorum*) which is several times mentioned in the text. It is of these *gesta* that some scholars believe Théroulde to have been the author; the meaning of the line quoted would then be, Here ends the *geste* for Théroulde (my authority) gives out.

The basis of the *Chanson* is unhistorical. Charlemagne made only a very perfunctory show of fighting the Saracens; he did not succeed in taking Saragossa, a Moslem town, but did sack Pamplona, a Christian one; and the rearguard action in the pass of Roncesvalles, in which a certain knight Hruoland – Count of the Breton marches – fell, was in fact fought against the local Basques, not against the infidel at all. However, the legend of Charlemagne's Saracenic wars was by the eleventh century firmly established, and the Roland poem had a great topical appeal. For now once more all the knights of Christendom were gathering to fight the infidel, this time in defence of the newly reconquered Holy Places. There is even a theory that Théroulde's *Chanson* was composed as recruiting propaganda at a moment when the nobles of France and England were losing interest in the Eastern war.

The tale tells of the heroic defence of Roncesvalles by Charlemagne's headstrong nephew Roland and his more sober comrade Oliver, of their death after the slaughter of countless foes, of Charlemagne's tardy arrival on the battlefield and of his revenge upon the enemy. It is a story of battle and treachery, of honour, loyalty, and superhuman endurance; and its passages of deepest feeling are those which record the friendship of Roland and Oliver, and lament their successive deaths. Apart from the mutual loyalty of these two knights, the theme of love occurs only once, at the end, when the fair Alde falls dead on learning that Roland will never return to marry her; and there are few supernatural incidents except for Charlemagne's prophetic dreams, for Gabriel's appearance at the moment of Roland's death, and for the moment when the sun stands still in the sky for him as it did for Joshua. But the numbers of the slain and the prodigious valour of Roland's rearguard are hugely, if not supernaturally, exaggerated.

The poem's religious angle is that of a combative Christianity of the most unspiritual kind. Archbishop Turpin, who shares the hero's rôle with Roland and Oliver, is the most vigorous of chaplains, who gives absolution to his own side with the same wholesale efficiency as he devotes to the slaughter of the Saracens. The *Chanson* is, in fact, though written by a priest, deliberately addressed to the knightly caste, and is concerned not with the good life in general, but with certain specific problems of feudal obligation. At what point, it asks, does disinterested duty end and the desire for personal glory begin? Roland willingly agrees to take charge of the fatally weak rearguard when his treacherous stepfather proposes that it shall be entrusted to him, for it would be dishonourable to protest. Nor will he take the large reinforcements which Charlemagne, suspecting treachery, offers him as he departs. Destiny is not portrayed as blind; here Roland is given two chances of saving himself. But he could not have accepted either without appearing as a coward in his own eyes. Then, when at the pass of Roncesvalles he sees the Saracens' strength and knows that his men will be overwhelmed, he refuses yet again to purchase safety, this time by blowing his marvellous horn, the olifant, to summon Charlemagne with his great army to his aid.

Now this is *desmesure* or rashness. Roland displays an over-fidelity to his obligations which bears the taint of pride, and he must atone for it, as Oliver reminds him, by his death. At this point, says the poet, in effect, the selflessness of a true vassal passes over into headstrong worship of his own image. That is the poem's central theme. Its ethics, in fact, are based on the ideal of disinterested action, as exemplified by Achilles in the *Iliad* or by Krishna's counsel to Arjuna in the *Bhagavadgita*.

But in the end Roland atones for his sin, as he lies dying beneath a pine, his face turned towards Spain. '"True Father," he prays, "who hast never lied, who raised Lazarus from the

dead, and protected Daniel from the lions, protect my soul
from all perils from the sins I have committed in my life."
Then he stretched his right gauntlet towards God, and
Gabriel grasped it in his hand.' The theme of feudal obligation
is for a moment transcended for that of personal destiny. But
Roland's death and atonement are but one incident in the
Chanson and we return to the greater question: 'Will the true
God in the end be vanquished by Mahomet?'

The poem tells its story in a straightforward way, with
copious declamations by each character, who is endowed with
a rough-and-ready individuality. But there is little figurative
language, hardly more, indeed, than a single simile throughout. The landscape is barely indicated, by the frequent
refrain-like repetition – inserted, no doubt, as an aid to the
reciter's memory – of such occasional and magical lines as:

> High are the mountains, tall and dark

or,

> Roland gazed at the mountains, and over the plain;
> So many of the Frankish army lay there slain,
> And like a noble knight he wept for them.

All the poem's colour lies in its martial descriptions, of
armies on the move, of the heroes in action, of their weapons
and of the blows they strike. It is built up in stanzas or
laisses, normally of fourteen lines, all of which end on the
same assonance. Each *laisse*, moreover, is devoted to a single
incident, and many of them rise to some sort of climax,
sometimes to a sententious speech, sometimes to words of
foreboding. These *laisses* are frequently connected by the
repetition of phrases, but the assonance of each differs from
the last. The general effect is one of roughness. It has even
been suggested that the poem's author was deliberately
writing in an archaic style. Moreover to modern ears the
Chanson's music is somewhat monotonous, as indeed it would
have been to its original audience. For the *jongleur* had only
two tunes for his accompaniment, one for the odd and one for
the even lines, and these he endlessly repeated, twanging
them on his fiddle or on its successor the *cifoine*, which was a
kind of hurdy-gurdy. This at least is the usual scholar's

theory. The tunes were no doubt taught orally, for they are not noted down on the manuscript.

The *Chanson de Roland* is the best of the *chansons de geste* that have survived, but there were many others. One tells of Charlemagne's legendary journey to Constantinople and Jerusalem, and a whole group is concerned with the historical figure of Count William of Orange and his exploits against the Saracens. Here, as in the *Chanson de Roland*, events are seen from the standpoint of the vassal rather than of his overlord. Most of Count William's deeds are more fantastic than those of Roland and Oliver, and are interrupted by much discursive matter, among it an attempt to explain the Roman cemeteries around Arles as the burial places of a whole people slaughtered in battle.

The epic tradition in France is hard to account for. Heroic songs had been traditional among the Germanic peoples since pre-Christian times, and it is possible that it was the Viking invaders of Normandy or the Germans of the Holy Roman Empire who gave the French *trouvères* their first impetus. But in default of documents, any attempt to trace the genealogy of the *chansons de geste* must be speculative.

There can be no doubt, however, that its emergence in Spain, a country then far removed from Teutonic influences, was directly due to French examples. The Spanish heroic poems must in the first instance have been imitations or even translations of the French *gestes*. But soon they acquired qualities and technical forms of their own. One of the earliest, indeed, the *cantar de gesta* concerning Bernardo del Carpio, evidence for the existence of which is based on passages in later prose chronicles which are clearly verses reduced to prose, was very far from being a Crusader's poem. For its hero fought on the Moslem side, and owed his popularity as a Spanish hero to his defiance of the French, whose interference in the petty kingdoms beyond the Pyrenees was resented far more than was the existence of the Moorish emirates of Al-andalus, or Andalusia. The Cid, too, the hero of the only one of these epics to survive in its entirety, actually derived his title from the Arabic Sidi, meaning 'My Lord', and had on at least one occasion fought on the Moslem side against the Christian Count of Barcelona. But this irregularity is glossed over in the poem.

El Cantar de mío Cid, which dates from about 1140, shows us the Spanish epic at the height of its powers, and now completely independent of French models. The Cid, Rodrigo Díaz de Vivar, unlike Roland, or William of Orange, was no hero drawn out of the legendary past, but a local Castilian leader who had died only some forty years before the making of the poem. The poem was consequently realistic in its details and unexaggerated in its narration. The Cid displays neither phenomenal loyalty nor overweening pride. He is merely a soldier who has offended his king, and whose aims are wealth and rehabilitation. He fights the Moors, but in no crusading spirit, and on conquering a town makes no attempt forcibly to convert its inhabitants. Nor are the Moors of the poem the sooty-faced bogey-men imagined by the Norman poet of the *Chanson de Roland*; the Cid in fact treats the Moors whom he conquers with such kindness that they weep on his departure. When he fights he kills his enemy, and when he is insulted he takes stern revenge, but here there are no oceans of blood. The Spanish hero is comparatively humane and shows a great respect for law. He is more interested too in the capture of booty than in the conversion or slaughter of the infidel, also far more sparing than Roland in his declamations. He and the other characters in the poem speak succinctly and to the point, and there is a real lyricism in their brevity. Seven lines are enough to describe the Cid's arrival at the monastery of St Peter on the first stage of his ride into exile, and one only for his wife's prayer for his safety:

> The cocks had started crowing – and day was about to break
> when the good knight Ruy Díaz – rode up to St Peter's gate.
> Don Sancho the abbot, a credit – to God who did him create
> was just reciting the matins – in thanks for a new day.
> And there was Doña Jiména – five ladies in her train,
> praying to good St Peter – and God who did us create:
> 'Lord, who art guide to all men – to my Cid, the knight, give aid.'

The *Cantar del Cid* is a far more economical poem than the *Chanson de Roland*, but it is less well constructed. It falls, in fact, into two barely related halves, the first concerning the Cid's exile, his campaigns, his rehabilitation and the betrothal of his daughters to the Princes of Carrión, and the second relating the insult offered to the ladies by these princes and their father's revenge. The incidents follow the events of history as they are told in the prose chronicles, though we have no other evidence than the poem for the Cid's quarrel with the Princes of Carrión. We do know, however, that he was at feud with their family. The characters of the poem are none of them drawn above life size; indeed they are most lively and convincing. Such realistic details as the scurvy swindling of two Jews at a moment when the hero's coffers are empty, and his pride at taking his wife and daughters on to the walls of Valencia so that they can have a good view of the battle that he is just going to fight and see how he earns his bread and butter, make him an entirely credible figure: no Christian knight, it is true, but a feudal chieftain trying to push himself up in the world at the expense of Christian and Moslem alike; and when, after the incident with the Princes of Carrión, the Kings of Navarre and Aragon send to sue for his daughters' hands, we feel that now the Cid has finally achieved the success he was aiming at.

Worldly success, in fact, together with humour and tough endurance, is the highest quality envisaged by the poem's author. His conception of feudal duty is a far more workaday one than that of the *Chanson de Roland*, and no questions of destiny or atonement even arise. Within its limits the *Cantar del Cid* is, perhaps, a more appealing poem than the *Chanson*, which has its longueurs, but it would be impossible to compare it in any way, as one can the *geste* of Roland, to the *Iliad* or the *Gita*.

The poem of the Cid is written in *laisses* like those of the *Chanson de Roland* and assonanced in the same way, though they are less regular in length. The line is longer, and rather resembles the English alliterative line of *Piers Plowman*. Indeed it would probably have been accepted by Gerard Manley Hopkins as in *sprung rhythm*.

The epic, both in France and in Spain, quickly decayed. But

its successor, the courtly romance, was already in existence by the time when that manuscript of *Roland* which has come down to us left the hands of the scribe. This heroic, fantastic, adventurous, sentimental, and digressive kind of tale, which was written in a smooth rhymed verse, appealed first, no doubt, to the court ladies, who in the middle of the twelfth century could pretend to rather more culture than their warring, hunting, and sporting husbands. Eleanor of Aquitaine indeed, the domineering queen of our own Henry II, was a particular patroness of the *trouvères*, and it was at the Plantagenet court that much of this new poetry was first recited. At first the favourite subjects were classical: the legends of Alexander, of Thebes, of Troy, of Aeneas, and of Julius Caesar were drawn from various late Latin sources, and retold in terms of the new chivalry. Some of the *trouvères*, like the author of *Roland,* may have known Virgil: many of them had undoubtedly read Ovid's *Ars amatoria*, from which they stole with and without acknowledgement. But there was a general failure to distinguish good Latin poetry from bad. The romancers exploited all ancient material alike as a quarry for modern constructions, many of which were so overlaid with decorative embellishments as to be, for a modern reader, somewhat too long and rather tedious. The most successful purveyor of these fictions was CHRÉTIEN DE TROYES (*fl. c.*1170), who specialized in Arthurian themes and revelled in descriptions.

The 'Matter of Britain', a series of interrelated tales probably emanating from different Celtic sources, Welsh, Irish, and Cornish, had made its first known appearance in Geoffrey of Monmouth's Latin *History of the Kings of Britain*. In origin, the figure of Arthur was, perhaps, based on that of a certain Artus, a minor Romano-British chieftain who had put up a successful defence against the Saxon invaders in the sixth century. But the Arthur whom the shadowy Welsh bard Bledhri introduced to the poets at the French ducal courts about the middle of the twelfth century, was a legendary and mighty king, and the patron of an order of knights who were engaged on a mysterious quest. The quest of the Grail is central to the Arthurian legend almost from the moment of its arrival in France, although in Celtic lore it was an entirely independent story.

The theme of both tales is of decay and renewal. The knight Percival glimpses the Grail, in the form of a shining dish, in the castle of the dying Fisher King, in the midst of the Waste Land. Had he asked the questions aright, 'Who is served by the Grail?' and 'With what is he served?' the king would have been cured and the fertility of his kingdom restored. We seem to be confronted with a death and resurrection story belonging to some pre-Christian faith: and this theme is reinforced by the parallel story of Arthur himself, who seems, in origin, to have been a dying king also, for he takes no part in the quests of his knights or the rescue of his queen, but is betrayed by his nephew Mordred, and by that same queen Guenevere. Furthermore, in Arthur as in the Fisher King is symbolized not only the death of an old world but also its possible rebirth. For after his last battle he does not die, but is transported to the enchanted kingdom of Avalon, whence in due time he will return.

Upon this material, which still contained religious significance for the Welshman who brought it, Chrétien de Troyes and the other poets who composed tales of Arthur in French and in German, superimposed the themes of courtly love and of knightly adventure, while at the same time interpreting its details in terms of Christianity. For them the Grail, which had originally been a dish bringing supersubstantial food, became a communion dish in the form of that from which Christ ate at the Last Supper, or the chalice in which His blood had been caught when the Roman soldier's spear pierced His side; in fact it became one of these holy relics which the first Crusaders were bringing back from Palestine.

The Grail quest too was transformed. No longer was it a purely subjective adventure, the search for the redemption of a man's own soul, for which the Grail provided magical nourishment. It now became a militarized exploit, the purpose of an order of knights who met at the Round Table, which had originally been a symbol of the same significance as the Grail itself. Now, in so far as the story at all retained its old meaning, the individual knight's quest conflicted with his duty to his order; a clash of two irreconcilable ideas, never thought of as such by any of the poets, reduced the whole legend to a dreamlike unreality, and as a romantic dream it came to be treated.

But no sooner were these symbolic Celtic stories taken over and transformed for the edification of those Frankish knights who loved the epics, than yet another element was introduced, the courtly one which pleased their ladies. Thus in the story of Lancelot and Guenevere, a late accretion, we see the conflict between love and duty superimposed on the original conflict between military duty and the quest for personal fulfilment. But this second situation can best be studied in the next chapter, in a story of different origin which runs parallel with that of Arthur's queen, the story of Tristan and Iseult.

Chapter Two

THE THEME OF COURTLY LOVE

THE Arthurian legend has a greater beauty and significance than is to be found in any single treatment of it. No poet who handled it presented its issues with a dramatic power equal to that of the *Chanson de Roland*. Potentially epic though the material was, it found no epic writer. Chrétien de Troyes, the first to turn it into courtly poems, missed its symbolism. He could not see it as an inheritance from an alien civilization to another, which was itself beginning to change its ideals from those of the battlefield to those of ideal love. The action of his poems, therefore, passes as if in a magic mirror. Neither mystery, heroism, nor love moves him to quicken the pleasant patter of his verse.

Chrétien de Troyes' treatment of the second great Celtic love-story, *Tristan and Iseult,* which was only loosely attached to the Arthurian cycle, has not survived. But we know from references to these lovers in others of his poems that he did not find their 'unreasoning' love a theme to his taste.

No complete poem of Tristan and Iseult written in French has survived. But it is clear from fragments that at least three versions of their tale were in circulation in the twelfth century, and with the help of contemporary translations into German it is possible to piece together quite satisfactorily the tale as it was then told. Arriving from its unknown Celtic source – which was probably Cornwall – into a society which placed obligation above personal happiness or grief, it was presented by the French poets as the story of an overwhelming and guilty passion.

Passion, to the eleventh- or twelfth-century moralist – even a man's passion for his own wife – was sinful. The sexual relation was an obligation, subject to the laws of contract and physical pleasure: it must not involve emotion. To violate an obligation out of an obsession for a woman, therefore, was as much *desmesure* as Roland's refusal to blow his horn on the

field of Roncesvalles. But it was less heroic. The love of
Tristan and Iseult, therefore, which violated her duty to her
husband and his to his uncle and feudal superior, could not be
thought of as an act of freewill. The romancers attributed it
solely to the drinking of the magic love potion – a familiar
Celtic motif – aboard the ship on which Tristan was bringing
Iseult from Ireland as his uncle's bride.

'We have lost the world and the world has lost us. How
does it seem to you, Tristan my love?' asks Iseult in a later
prose rendering of the tale. 'When I have you with me, beloved,' he replies, 'then what do I lack? If all the worlds were
with us here and now, I should have eyes for nothing but you
alone.' By the time that the lovers had become the hero and
heroine of this prose account the theme of *all for love and the
world well lost* seemed a less guilty one. The laws of adulterous
love had been codified and, outside the field of feudal and
religious obligation, a man and a woman might love one another in defiance of the jealous husband. But what remained
illegitimate was what we now think of as an honourable passion
ending in marriage. Here the Middle Ages still paid some
respect to the Christian doctrine that love was reserved for
God alone. Adulterous love was subject to other laws: to
those of the god Amor, who was permitted, by an early
exercise of what George Orwell called 'double-think', to
exercise authority in a limited enclave within Christian
territory. But marriage was subject to the laws of God and
society. By the code of Amor, a knight owed fealty and undying service to his lady. By the Christian and feudal codes,
the wife owed unquestioning duty and obedience to her
husband. Therefore a love affair leading to marriage was
theoretically an impossibility. For if the wife served Amor it
then became her duty to accept a lover; if she served God her
passion for her husband was a sin.

The code of the god Amor was introduced by the Provençal
poets, probably from Arabic sources. In its inception, it was
not, in the vulgar sense, Platonic. It, however, reversed the
habitual relations of the sexes, and for the first time in Europe
since matriarchal days, set up the image of divine womanhood
as an object to be selflessly worshipped, though not without

hope of reward, by every true knight. Parallel with it arose the cult of the Virgin, which raised the passive element at the expense of the active in the practice of Christianity itself. Between St Bernard's return to the imagery of the *Song of Songs*, in which the love of man for woman was used as a metaphor for the love of the soul for God, and the Provençal poets' theory of service to the lady, there was no doubt a connexion at a deep level in what one can think of as the guided evolution of human thought.

The first considerable body of lyrical poetry to be written in any Western vernacular, the Provençal, dates from the beginning of the twelfth century, when a highly developed and conventionalized school of poets was working in South-West France, between the Loire and the Garonne. This poetry appears to have had little preparation and no ancestry in its own tongue beyond a minor folk-poetry, common to the whole Western Mediterranean, and known only from traces which are to be found in the form of refrains, generally put into the mouth of a girl. These have been found attached to the Hebrew and Arabic poems of Southern Spain, which are invariably spoken by a male voice. Developed from such minor sources, the new poetry seems to have arisen in Southern France in an almost perfect state, and then to have rapidly deteriorated. Technically, no doubt, the development was assisted by the existence of a considerable bulk of popular poetry in Latin, including hymns and student-songs, also popular snatches, extemporary satires, and mnemonic rhymes. What was new was the lyrical impulse, which rapidly raised this small body of poetry to the very high level already attained by the old established epic and the new courtly romance.

The language used by the new poetry, which was intended to be sung to an instrumental accompaniment, was an artificial one, based, not as later Italian theorists supposed, on the tongue of Provence, but on that of the Limousin, far further north, and not far from where the first known Provençal *troubadour*, WILLIAM, COUNT OF POITIERS (1071–1126), lived and ruled. His contacts with the fertilizing East are well-established. His father had brought back captive dancing girls from Spain, who would have known and sung the Moorish songs on which the earliest verse-forms seem to have been modelled. He had himself been on a Crusade in Syria. and again in Aragon, whence he had brought back a wife.

In the earliest poems themselves, moreover, not only is the form similar to the Moorish *zejel*, a variant of which was, as has already been noted, common to the whole Western Mediterranean, but there was also a similarity to the Arabic poets' imagery, which was purely Eastern; in the *troubadours'* songs, as in those of Moorish Spain, the nightingale sings its accompaniment to lovers, and the flowers open for their delight. The Christian poet seems to be imitating the Arab also in his preliminary flourish of self-advertisement. It has even been suggested – though I do not think very feasibly – that the root *trobar*, despite its apparently sound Latin etymology, should be associated with the popular Arabic *tarab*, which signifies the excitement of love. Count William, moreover, was not the only one of the early *troubadours* who was acquainted with the Muslim poetic tradition at first hand. MARCABRU (*fl.c.*1130–48), a man of humbler birth, whose love poems delighted, and whose satires or *sirventes* exasperated, the courts of France, had also travelled widely in Spain.

These origins of the European lyric seem now reasonably well proved. But at the moment when the style emerges in the few surviving poems of the gay, sensual, fantastic, and unfortunate William of Poitiers, the main themes were not yet fixed. It was a later generation of *troubadours*, who lived in the Limousin itself, at the court of the Vicomte de Ventadour, who settled the forms of Provençal poetry. BERNART DE VENTADOUR, ARNAUT DE MAREUIL, BERTRAN DE BORN, and GIRAUT DE BORNEIL (second half of twelfth century) were for the most part impoverished gentlemen, dependent upon the feudal courts, who led wandering lives and carried their songs into far corners of France and beyond, into the Spanish kingdoms and into Italy. They sang of courtly love, of the love of the poor minstrel for the high-born lady, of her beauty, of her scorn, and of the lover's persistence.

Despite the wealth of their apparent self-revelations,

however, we know very little about them. Even when we read
that Bernart de Ventadour was exiled by the Vicomte for carrying on an intrigue with the Vicomtesse, it is impossible to be
certain that this corresponds to a historical fact. The poet
exults and rages, grieves and curses the nature of women by
turns. But the situations are by now all conventional. Only
occasionally, as in the case of Marcabru, do we find a personal
viewpoint expressed; and with him, very often, it was a most
uncourtly and satirical contempt for the whole female sex. But
on the whole the *troubadour* concealed his own feelings and
was as ready to write from a woman's standpoint as from a
man's. An *alba*, or dawn piece, for instance, is always put into
the mouth of the girl, never into that of her lover, with what
success one of the most famous of all Provençal poems, an
anonymous *alba*, will show:

> In a leafy orchard, underneath a thorn,
> the lady clasps her lover in her arms
> until the watchman cries he's seen the dawn.
> Oh God! Oh God! How quickly dawn comes round!
>
> 'Oh would to God night might for ever stay,
> and my friend never again be far away,
> and the watchman never spy the dawn of day!
> Oh God! Oh God! How quickly dawn comes round!
>
> 'Dear sweet friend, let us join our lips again,
> down in the meadow. Hark, the birds begin!
> Let's do it just to spite that jealous man!
> Oh God! Oh God! How quickly dawn comes round!
>
> 'Dear sweet friend, let's enjoy another bout,
> while in the garden the birds sing and shout,
> before the watchman's warning horn rings out.
> Oh God! Oh God! How quickly dawn comes round!'
>
> On the soft breeze that blows from that far place
> where my friend is, fair, gay and courteous,
> a soft puff of his breath has caught my face.
> Oh God! Oh God! How quickly dawn comes round!
>
> She is a charming and most gracious lady,
> and many men admire her for her beauty,
> but only love possesses her heart's loyalty.
> Oh God! Oh God! How quickly dawn comes round!

So fresh is this little poem that it is difficult to remind oneself that the orchard and the watchman, the jealous husband and even the thorn-bush, are all stock properties; and that the poet is not writing from any experience of his own.

The subjects of Provençal poetry are by no means limited to that of courtly love; while Bertran de Born sings in praise of war, others indulge in satirical argument in dialogue form, or in political debate. Apart from its idealization of sexual love, this school's chief contribution to the European poetic tradition lies in its fixing of the forms in which lyrics were to be written, in all languages, almost until the nineteenth century. *Aubade, sestina, pastourelle, chanson or canzone, ballade, virelai, rondel,* and the Spanish *copla,* were all the invention of these poets of Southern France. Indeed, such masters of form were they that the content of their poetry frequently became almost hermetic during the two centuries in which they flourished. Theirs was a courtly art, addressed to a very restricted audience who followed them in their obscurities with the delight of so many solvers of acrostics. So when Arnaut Daniel sang them his new Sestina – a form which he had himself originated – in which the repeating rhymes were the Limousin equivalents of *enters, pail, soul, rod, uncle* and *chamber,* they no doubt applauded him for his virtuosity and forgave him the line and a half in which he claimed: 'I never loved my uncle's sister more, or even so much.'

Troubadour poetry quickly ran into this obscurity, never entirely to emerge from it before it met its death, with the whole civilization of which it was the flower, in the Albigensian Crusades. The religion of the Bogomils, a faith of Asiatic origin, of which we know little except from hostile accounts, had spread by way of Northern Italy to the Southern parts of France, bringing with it a new call for humility and a deep hostility among the poor towards the dignitaries of the Church. Failing to convince these heretics of their errors, even after forming a new order of Friars, the Dominicans, to preach to them, the Pope unleashed the envious and less prosperous noblemen of Northern France upon the rich and heretical Southern cities, under the pretext of a Crusade. Among the first victims of this war, which incidentally also saw the foundation of the Holy Inquisition, was the school of Provençal poetry. Some *troubadours*, however, migrated to Italy and other countries, carrying their poetic skill with them. But, except for a factitious revival in the nineteenth century, the literary language of Southern France fell into complete disuse at the beginning of the thirteenth.

The *trouvères* of Northern France, who seem to have arisen independently of their Southern brothers, were more light-hearted than those of Provence, and served a larger audience. Their language too was closer to popular speech than the conventional Limousin, which steadfastly refused to expand its vocabulary. The Southerners' love-themes, therefore, received far more realistic treatment north of the line that divided the two main areas of French speech, separating those who said *oui* for yes from those who said *oc*. The poet CONON DE BÉTHUNE, a nobleman and crusader (*c.*1150–1219 or 1220), approached the themes of the men of *oc* in a vigorous mood, and wrote poems of the Crusade, deploring his separation from his lady, while COLIN MUSET (early thirteenth century), a minstrel of humbler birth, could not sing of love without bringing in the theme of good food, and THIBAUT, COUNT OF CHAMPAGNE (1201–53), perhaps the first French poet strongly to betray his individual feelings, while boasting an undying passion for Princess Blanche of Castile, sang cheerfully and unforcedly enough, even when pleading that the sole purpose of his song was to dry his own tears.

Poetry in Northern France soon ceased to be exclusively composed by *trouvères*; and *jongleurs*, such as Colin Muset, were already taking a considerable hand. There was indeed a little school of composition at Arras, on the borders of Flanders, and in the centre of the weaving industry, where a characteristically middle-class poetry, entertaining and often scurrilous, was beginning to evolve. But the Northern French lyric as a whole has a somewhat popular air; it seems from the start to have been crossed with folksong. The Northern *pastourelle*, for instance, has far easier rhythms than the Provençal *pastorela*, and the shepherdesses – truer to life perhaps – prove far more accommodating to the advances of the roving knight than their Southern sisters. But the *pastourelle* is really less concerned with the theme of the seduction of shepherdesses than with the pranks and dances of the shepherds.

The most characteristic poetry of Northern France, however, which had sprung up in the twelfth century, took the form of spinning or weaving songs (*chansons de toile*), which were sung by the women at their work. These were, in the words of a French critic, 'epic in subject, lyrical in their rhythms, and dramatic in the manner of their telling'; they were in fact close in feeling to our own much later ballads, though the incidents are always seen from the woman's point of view. Gayette and Orieur go down to the brook one evening, hand in hand, to bathe, and there the young knight Gérard meets them on his way back from the tilting-yard. He bears Gayette off to the town to marry him, leaving poor Orieur without a lover and much perturbed for her sister.

> The breeze blows, the branches sway;
> may all true lovers sleep in peace.

runs the refrain that follows each of its six verses. In another of these weaving songs the fair Doette sits at her window waiting for news of her husband, who is at the wars. A squire rides up and tells her of his death, and she swears in her grief that she will take the veil. In a third, Érembor, the Emperor's daughter, protests her love for the knight Reynaut, who believes that she has been false to him. She swears that she has been true, and he 'broad of shoulder, slender of waist', mounts the steps to her tower, where their early love is renewed. In a fourth *chanson*, the king's daughter, married to a cruel husband, prays for her lover's return. Her petition is answered; the Count Guy appears and comforts her in the conventional leafy arbour of the Limousins.

This last weaving song is close in theme to another popular form of lyric, the unhappy bride's song (*chanson de mal-mariée*), which makes rather less play of the lady's unhappiness than of her means of consolation. Not only shepherdesses but knights' ladies also are more accommodating in the North than in Provence, where the theme of the *mal-mariée* originated.

But what most distinguishes the poetry of the North is its great variety. Not only are there the *chansons de geste*, the rhymed romances, the variations on Provençal themes, the weaving songs and the light-hearted, satirical poetry of Arras. There is the first great adumbration of the theme of mortality in vernacular poetry, *Le Mort, reine du Monde* (*Death, Queen of the World*), written in the last decade of the twelfth century by HÉLINANT DE FROIDMONT (late twelfth century), a *troubadour* who had become a Cistercian monk. There is also the satirical, rumbustious, anecdotal poetry of the Parisian RUTEBEUF (1250–85), a thirteenth-century Villon, who had more luck in keeping out of the hands of the police than his more famous successor. A *jongleur*, whose talent was for hire to the king or great noble who could pay for it, he wrote recruiting poems for the Crusades, took part in the feuds around the University of Paris, championing the old scholars against the new friars, composed miracle plays, and put so firm a personal signature on all that he wrote that not only was he the first French satirist, but also the first French poet who emerges with a recognizable personality.

Rutebeuf was a producer also of yet one more new type of poetry, the *fabliau*, a more or less disreputable tale, cheerful and irreverent, and aimed indifferently against priests, doctors, pretentious ladies, usurers, and other butts of the middle-class satirist. Chaucer's *Pardoner's Tale* is a developed example, but the supreme practitioner in this medium was La Fontaine who, four hundred years later, was also the final master of another type of poem first written in France in the twelfth century, the fable or *isopet*, as it was called after its Greek originator, Aesop. Under this title five collections of fables circulated in France at the end of the twelfth century, the first of which had been composed from Latin models by the poetess MARIE DE FRANCE, who probably lived at the court of our own Henry II. On account of these fables and of her *lais*, which retell the Arthurian and other romantic stories with less elaboration than Chrétien de Troyes, but with a true feeling for their magic, she has been called the greatest poetess of the Middle Ages. Her poetry, however, is a little thin. She has a certain feminine charm, but none of the power to wake an old myth into living reality. If she deserves the title, it is only owing to lack of other claimants. Even her *isopets* are neither better nor worse than those in the other four collections.

Le Roman de Renard, blended of the *isopet* and the *fabliau*, of the fable and the racy story, is a loose-knit series of tales by various hands, and one of the masterpieces of medieval French poetry, a book which though constantly imitated, even by such masters as Chaucer and Goethe in their different centuries, is still readable to-day. Renard the fox, Isengrin the wolf, Chantecler the cock, Tibert the cat, and Tiercelin the crow started as animals, perhaps deriving from those of the Indian allegories and fables, and endowed with the powers of speech necessary for purposes of narration. Soon, however, these beasts became the vehicle for wholesale satire, and turned into so many men and women in wolves' and foxes' clothing.

This cycle contains tales that have become part of our nursery heritage. Two priests quarrel over the skin of the cat which they have not caught, and which succeeds in throwing one of them to the ground and riding off on his horse. Sly Master Fox starts an intrigue with the wolf's lady, and Isengrin summons him before the court of King Lion. Here Master Camel, the Papal Legate, demands the fox's punishment in a mixed jargon of Latin, French, and Italian. But the interference of this foreigner annoys the gentlemen, who are all for a composition, on the solid bourgeois ground that since there were no witnesses except the prosecutor nothing of serious importance could really have occurred. Isengrin and his friend Roonel, the sheepdog, however, decide to take a private revenge, but Renard gets wind of their plan and bolts. The pitting of wits against wits, trickery, national pride, and a ready anticlericalism are hall-marks of this middle-class literature, which spread from town to town, especially in the woollen districts of France and Flanders. In its origins the Renard story would appear to have been Flemish, for the animals' names are certainly Teutonic. But it was in France that they were most successfully elaborated before returning, together with the scurrilous *fabliau*, to the lands which first gave them birth.

The literature of Northern France in the thirteenth century continued to be the richest in Europe. For alongside the middle-class poetry of Paris and Arras, court writing took a fresh turn about the year 1230 with two works in which the Provençal theme of passionate love was divorced from that of adultery.

Aucassin and Nicolette, described by its unknown author as a *chantefable*, tells a love-story with a happy ending. It is written in a charming dramatic prose, and the interpolated verses have a decorative lightness that fits the highly romantic plot. Aucassin, the son of a Provençal count, falls hopelessly in love with Nicolette, the captive servant and god-daughter of a neighbouring nobleman, who eventually turns out to be the daughter of the King of Carthage. The Count opposes his son's infatuation, but after sundry escapes, pursuits, and pinings, which culminate in an idyllic sojourn in the green-wood, followed by further separations, the lovers are honour-ably united.

Now this radical break with the courtly convention, this dispensing with the usual concomitants of an intrigue – the jealous husband, the violation of duty, the need for conceal-ment – marks a very great advance in the medieval attitude to love, so violent an advance indeed that it is generally thought that the plot derived, like so much else in these early centuries, in the first place from Arabic or at least from Spanish sources. True, the names of the characters and the local setting are Provençal, and the short scene at the court of Carthage suggests no acquaintance by its author with Moslem ways. Yet the story's freedom from the normal conventions, its occasional lapses into satire, even into cynicism, the strange puppet-like unreality of its action and its alternations between prose and verse, relate it far more closely to an Eastern story than to anything that was then being written by the school of Arras, of which its author was probably a member. *Aucassin and Nicolette,* because of its modern concession to the happy ending, has been a popular work ever since its first printing in the eighteenth century, and this pair of lovers have come to rank with Romeo and Juliet and Paul and Virginie. It is with surprise therefore that one finds in the work a delightful,

Rabelaisian description of a mock battle, and a most eccentric scene in which Aucassin assaults a local ruler who is practising the primitive custom of *couvade* and has taken to his bed during his wife's confinement. It is really a very strange story.

Le Roman de la Rose, the first part of which was written at much the same time as *Aucassin and Nicolette*, also developed the Provençal love theme in a new direction, bringing it however rather into the field of abstract psychology than into that of realism and marriage. It is an allegory of a love-affair, the consummation of which is symbolized by the winning or plucking of a rose, which grows in the centre of a magic garden. Here there is no Romeo or Juliet; neither the man nor the girl appear in their own persons, but are represented by a number of voices which stand for their qualities. It is as if the poet believes his characters to consist not of a single ego but of a variety of personalities, who fight out among themselves the issue of the wooing. How the poem's first author, GUILLAUME DE LORRIS (*fl. c.*1235), a very young man, intended it to end we do not know. For he died, leaving a poem little more than four thousand lines long to be completed forty years later by JEAN DE MEUN (*d.* before 1305), who differed from him in every possible way and who, having chosen to complete the poem because it was a popular success, proceeded to add to de Lorris's neat and fresh allegory a huge, coarse, digressive, philosophical work, at least four times as long, which was as satirical as its original had been serious, and as bourgeois as the first poem had been courtly. Whatever de Lorris's intended ending was – and Professor C. S. Lewis, the chief English authority on the *Roman*, thinks that de Lorris was really an enemy of the god Amor·and that the lover would have been denied his rose – de Meun perfunctorily threw it to him in the end, perhaps as a consolation for his having been crowded out of the poem.

Guillaume de Lorris's *Roman* opens, like many medieval poems, with a dreamer, a dream, and a garden.

> Within my twenty yere of age,
> Whan that love taketh his corage
> Of yonge folk, I wente sone
> To bedde, as I was wont to done,

> And fast I sleep; and in sleeping,
> Me mette such a *swevening,**
> That lykede me wonders wel:
> But in that *sweven** is never a del
> That it nis afterward befelle . . .†

This dream is prophetic, the time is May, the birds are singing, and the stream is rippling. These are so many *troubadour* clichés, but they are used for a new purpose. Outside the wall of a garden hang the effigies of all those qualities that can never be allowed admittance: Hate, Felonye, Vilanye, Coveityse, Avarice, Envye, and with them, less expectedly, Sorowe, Elde (old age), Time, and a figure of hypocrisy called Pope-holy. At the garden gate sits Ydelnesse. For the garden is the world of courtly society, in which the dreamer meets in allegory the noble qualities, Sir Mirthe, Gladnesse, Curtesye, etc., and among them Cupid the love-god. But within this courtly garden lies a more private rose garden, and within that garden a particular rose, to whom the dreamer is brought by Bialacoil (the ordinary welcome of good manners), only to be chased away by Danger (the snub direct, according to Professor Lewis), by Malebouche (gossip), by Shame, Fear and Jealousy. Bialacoil is then thrown into prison as a traitor, the lady is given a duenna, and the lover casts one despairing look behind him as Guillaume de Lorris's part of the poem ends.

Allegory was no new medium; it had already been fully worked out in Latin and had antecedents going back as far as Plato: nor did the subject of courtly love seem to offer aspects that had not already been treated by Chrétien de Troyes and many others. Yet the *Roman de la Rose* immediately found great favour, and dictated the form which much poetry was to assume, especially in England and France, for the next two centuries. True, the religion of Christ and that of Cupid still remained unreconciled. But allegory lifted the contradiction on to the plane of philosophy or fantasy. Love did not seem to menace the social or religious structure so long as it was only to be found in the narrow garden of the poet's mind, whose gate-keeper was idleness. It was a mere leisure product.

* dream.   † Trans. attributed to G. Chaucer.

Moreover, courtly poetry, henceforth, came to be confined to the narrowest idle circles. Despite the perfection of de Lorris's poem, the future was with de Meun and the poets of the *Roman de Renard*.

Jean de Meun took the world at its face value, paying some lip-service to allegory and almost none to courtly love. For he treated womankind with as little idealism as he and his fellow satirists meted out to fat friars, dishonest merchants, and the variegated population of the market place, in which he was at home.

Our own Chaucer owes an almost equal debt to him and to de Lorris. Starting in the high allegorical tradition, he attempted to make the behaviour of his lovers Troilus and Criseyde conform to the idea of gentleness prescribed by the first *Roman de la Rose*. Their tale had already been told in the eleventh-century epic of Troy. But in the interval it had been rehandled by Boccaccio, who had made the pair of them straightforward sexual creatures with the simplest of motives. Chaucer, as a disciple of de Lorris, raised the tale's morality and made its psychology more subtle. But when he came to write the *Canterbury Tales* he showed that he had read de Meun with attention also. For the wife of Bath's opinions on marriage were very like Jean de Meun's, and much of the incidental philosophical discussion in one *Tale* and another reminds one forcibly of the continuation of the *Roman*. But Chaucer derived much more than this from the bourgeois stream in Northern French literature. His Chauntecleer and Pertelote owe much to the *Renard*, and such tales as the Miller's and the Reve's are in essence *fabliaux*, while the Frankleyne's Tale belongs to a yet older stream, and is related to the *lais* of Marie de France. In fact the first of English poets learnt everything that the French poets from the time of Chrétien de Troyes could teach him, and by his own subtlety of mind and lightness of touch surpassed them in every medium except the lyric.

While Northern France remained, on account of the deeper cultural basis of its literature, the leader of fashion from the disaster of the Albigensian war to the emergence of the new poetry in Italy, three smaller centres of literary production were active in the thirteenth century, none of which depended entirely on French examples for its inspiration. The first, which was in Norway and Iceland, had sprung up outside the bounds of Christendom; the second, on the Rhine and in the upper Danube valley, owed a great deal to France, but something also to the pagans beyond the border, while the third, in the North-West corner of the Iberian peninsula, was centred on one of Christendom's most holy shrines, the alleged tomb of St James at Compostella.

Some of the oldest vernacular poetry, which stands somewhat apart from the main current of European development – though it is related to such Anglo-Saxon poems as *Beowulf* and *The Song of Maldon* – survived in oral form from a very early date among the Norsemen of Iceland and Norway, and was first written down in the twelfth or thirteenth century. The Elder Edda tells the stories of the ancient Norse gods, but in the form that has survived show evidence of the impact of Christianity. Some of these lays take the form of dialogues between the gods, and some tell of the heroes. Of this last group the tales of the Volsungs and the Nibelungs were later treated by an unknown German epic writer, and so became a Germanic counterpart to the 'Matter of Britain'. But the rest present a world rapidly being forgotten when the Edda was written down, with its great cosmological legends and its contrasted moments when the great gods behaved with comic bombast and lack of dignity.

In the thirteenth century this verse Edda was succeeded by a recapitulation in prose, written by one S N O R R I S T U R L U S O N (*d.*1241) as a compendium of tales for the use of future *scalds* or bards. Sturluson also wrote down the *Heimskringla*, a prose collection of biographies of Norway's early kings.

The saga is, in essence, a form of historical novel, told with great economy and with the immediacy of an eyewitness, by its anonymous composers. The first and best tales, those of *Grettir the Strong* and *Njal's Saga* tell of feuds dating back to the first settlement of Iceland, which were conducted according to a harsh conception of family honour comparable to that of seventeenth-century Spain. The characters are closely modelled from the life, and the incidents are those of a rough heroic age; high lights being such moments as that in which the roof is dragged off Gunnar's house, or when all but one of Njal's kin are burnt to death in a deed of revenge. Here, in Iceland, the highest values were attached to human endurance and the valour of pioneers. Later, tales from the Eddas, such as that of the Volsungs, were retold in saga form, and even later, when some commerce of ideas had been opened with the South, the deeds of Alexander and Charlemagne were adapted for Norse ears.

As has been said, the sung epic, which attained sudden popularity in Western Europe at the time of the Crusades, was perhaps an inheritance from the Germanic peoples, who had composed the Edda and brought such songs as that of *Beowulf* to the lands which they had invaded. It is impossible, however, to plot the possible stages in the epic's underground development between the sixth century and the twelfth. We know that Charlemagne himself had some of the old songs – lays perhaps like the Edda – collected and written down, and it is reasonable to assume that the memory of them persisted more strongly on Germanic soil than on French.

Though they contributed the great legend of Siegfried and the Nibelungen – the Germanic counterpart of the Celtic 'Matter of Britain' – to the Western heritage, it was not Iceland nor yet Scandinavia that set off the revival of the German epic. If there were native German *chansons de geste* corresponding to those of *Roland* and the *Cid*, they have not survived. When we first meet German poetry in the twelfth century it is strongly under the influence of Chrétien de Troyes; it is in fact a court poetry. HARTMANN VON AUE (*c.*1170–1215), the first of the German epic writers, has contributed to the world's stock of familiar tales at least one subject of his own, that of *Der arme Heinrich* (*Poor Henry*), the knight stricken with leprosy who refuses the peasant girl's offer to give her own life to work his cure. As a reward for his self-sacrifice, a miracle occurs; his disease suddenly leaves him, and out of gratitude he marries the girl. The incident is said to be based on some event of this sort in the poet's own family; it bears, however, every mark of being descended rather from some religious myth similar to the tale of the sacrifice of Isaac.

WOLFRAM VON ESCHENBACH'S *Parzival* and GOTT-FRIED VON STRASSBURG'S *Tristan,* both of the early thirteenth century, are very closely based on French poems, and if their German authors contribute any individual touches they are a certain over-exaltation of the knightly ideal and a greater realism of detail. However, the anonymous *Nibelungen-lied*, the principal German epic, the earliest-known version of which is contemporary with these, contains elements which are not only German, but true to the Germanic ideal even to this day. For in it the frenzy of heroism is raised to a tragic plane, and Kriemhild, its heroine, with Hitlerian intensity, revenges the murder of her beloved Siegfried by bringing the whole world, friend and foe alike and even her own son, down in bloody destruction. The *Niebelungenlied* indeed, with its appended *Lament*, is both in technique and content more primitive and more decadent than any of its French or Spanish counterparts.

The German love-lyric, on the other hand, preserves a pleasing freedom from the Provençal convention that inspired it. Here the nightingales seem to sing less mechanically than in the South, the trees and bushes to grow more freely than in the formal fields of Provence, and the maidens to behave more realistically than the hard taskmistresses of the Provençal courts. In one of the poems of WALTHER VON DER VOGELWEIDE (*c*.1170–1230), indeed, the lady is so simple as to give her man the most ordinary of glass rings as a pledge. He speaks to her too not of *Minne*, or courtly love, but of *Liebe*, the commoner sort. Walther, though the most famous of the Minnesänger – the German equivalent of the *troubadours* – was not the first. The few surviving lyrics of HEINRICH VON MORUNGEN (?–1222) tell, again with German intensity, of love as a sacred yet unholy power that drives its victim into sickness, madness, and death. But he, like the epic writers, has also an eye for landscape, for sunlight, and for the passing shadows of joy or sadness over his beloved's face.

With Hartmann von Aue, Heinrich von Morungen, and Walther von der Vogelweide, the German lyric took on an original character. Unfortunately, however, its inspiration dried up, and no middle-class poetry developed to succeed it. All that Germany produced thereafter were collections of *Sprüche* or apophthegms of no great poetic value. There is little German lyrical poetry of importance between the thirteenth and the seventeenth century.

Chief among the roads travelled by the *jongleurs* of the North and the *joglars* of Provence was the pilgrim route to St James of Compostella in Galicia: and here, when the Provençal epoch was over, came a sudden little flowering of poetry written in a courtly language based on the Spanish of Galicia, by gentlemen at the courts of Alfonso the Wise of Castile and of his nephew King Dinis of Portugal. The selection of this dialect as a basis for the poet's language was arbitrary. It was accepted, however, that Castilian was a fitting medium for the prose chronicle, but that Galician alone suited the lyric. Of Castilian poems of this age we have only two or three examples, though it is possible that many more of a semi-popular sort were written, in the tradition of that oldest of lyrical romance forms, the *zejel* or refrain, to which this Galician poetry also is closely akin. It would seem, indeed, that the Iberian peninsula remained the centre of older types of writing in an age when new styles were rapidly developing. King Alfonso himself, who wrote his songs in praise of the Virgin in Galician, seems to have been profoundly influenced by the old folk-poetry.

The poems in the Galician song-books are of various strictly conventional types. Taking the situations familiar from the Provençal lyrics, the Galicians isolated a single moment from each, and dwelt on it with subtle and musical variations of language. In the *cantiga de amigo*, a much practised form, the girl deplores the absence of her lover; in the *pastorela* the shepherd maid sends her wooer away after a single word; in the *barcarola*, an original contribution from this sea-faring people, the girl asks a returned sailor for news of her lover. The most popular form was the *cosante*, or round dance, a pattern of repetitions and variations in which word-music counts for more than meaning, and in which the play of a half-rhyme is far more important than originality of phrase or presentation.

None of the Galician poets stands out, still less does any one of them speak in his own character. Most of the poems, indeed, are put into the mouths of women, who must have sung them at their work, or in time to the dance. Though this is courtly poetry, it lies very close to folk-song. For owing to the lack of feudal organization in that backward corner of Christendom, there was little more than a farming class for the *jogral*, as he was there called, to appeal to; certainly no audience for poetry whose sophistication lay on the surface. The sophistication of the Galician lyric lies in its conscious closeness to the people's own songs and its deliberate adaptations to their dance tunes. The girls are no high ladies, but are presented to us washing their shifts at the fountain or arguing with their mothers at the door; and their lovers are no questing knights, but the farmers and fishermen of that bleak country.

Perfect in their wispish melancholy, the Galician songs seem, after King Dinis's time, to have melted back again into the popular tradition. The song-books lay in gentlemen's libraries, and after a very short while were forgotten, not to be rediscovered until the nineteenth century. For Castilian, the language of the Cid's tough, practical descendants who were reconquering the land from the Moors, had now become the Peninsula's literary language. It has few early monuments, however, except the epic of the Cid, and the most perfect of miracle tales written by the priest GONZALO DE BERCEO in the first half of the thirteenth century. This is popular poetry, written in the jogging *cuaderna via*, with its sets of four rhyming lines. But, rough though it is, there are no pleasanter tales in medieval literature than Berceo's *Milagros de Nuestra Señora* (*Miracles of our Lady*), with their mixture of freshness and credulity, their sweetness, gravity, and monotony, and their charmingly pedestrian use of the French convention of dream, allegory, and heavenly vision. Berceo, like the author of *El Cantar del Cid*, was a realist; and though he was willing to violate every law of probability in the narration of his miracles, he would not leave a single homely detail out in describing the simple Spanish countryside in which they took place.

The first two centuries of vernacular literature display great developments in poetry designed for singing or reciting, or to accompany a dance. But there was little progress in the writing of prose, intended for the study or library. Chroniclers such as Joinville and Villehardouin composed their accounts of the Crusades, of which they had been eye-witnesses: there were also prose romance, moralities, satires, and works on legal or theological subjects. But the main vehicle for prose was still Latin.

Chapter Three

THE REBIRTH OF ITALY

ITALY was slower than other European countries in developing a vernacular literature, partly owing to her political weakness – since throughout the eleventh and twelfth centuries she had been the battle-ground of Popes and Emperors – and partly owing to the difficulty of disentangling a literary idiom from a popular speech which men of education considered to be no more than a debased form of the ancient language of Rome. In the Italian courts of the twelfth century the conventional idiom of the poets was Provençal, and even in the thirteenth the Mantuan *troubadour* Sordello, celebrated by Dante and the hero of Browning's poem, wrote entirely in that tongue. There was, furthermore, in Northern Italy, a French influence which fostered poetry in a mixture of French and the Venetian dialect, and which persisted well past the end of the fourteenth century.

The Italian revival, when it came, originated in that distant province of Italy which had been for some centuries most subject to alien influences. Sicily had been conquered by the Normans, who had entertained Provençal *troubadours* at their courts. But in the more remote past it had been held by the Arabs and, at the moment when Italian poetry was born, Palermo, its capital, was the seat of a German emperor, Frederick the Second, whom Dante afterwards placed among the arch-heretics in the sixth circle of Hell. Frederick's sin – though from the standpoint of literature it must count as a great merit – was that he attempted to blend at his court all the conflicting cultural influences predominant in this island where two faiths and two continents met. For it was in Sicily that the first school of Italian poetry arose, and it was there that poetic forms first gained their independence of music. Henceforth a *chanson* or *canzone*, despite its name, was not a piece composed for singing, but merely a poem which followed a pattern originally invented for that purpose.

Italy's new poets were not predominantly Sicilians; nor were the dialects on which they drew for the making of a literary Italian even predominantly southern. They wrote, on the whole, in the language of Central Italy. Also, unlike the *troubadours*, the poets at the court of Frederick II were not professionals. So, though they used the now hackneyed Provençal verse forms, they used them with a freshness which was heightened by the novelty – and sometimes by the awkwardness – of their language. Their subject was love, and their favourite measure the *canzone*. But the principal figure among them, the lawyer JACOPO DA LENTINI (*c*.1195–*c*.1240) seems to have been the originator of a new form, suitable for the poetry of reflexion, which demanded a greater compression of poetic thought than the longer Provençal verses. This was the sonnet, of which he left twenty-five examples.

Whether or no Jacopo da Lentini was actually the first man to write a sonnet is not certain. In his hands the new measure was already perfect. Indeed, his sonnet to his Lady in Heaven is technically a great deal more accomplished than the first of Sir Thomas Wyatt's attempts to give the form an English dress, more than three centuries later.

The Sicilian poets, however, soon lost their freshness; and within fifty years a mannerism had grown up which concealed any emotion that may have been present in their addresses to their conventionally beautiful mistresses, kind and unkind. This school, however, did not survive to lapse into the tiresome obscurities of the last *troubadours*. With the death of Frederick's heir, Manfred, and the break-up of the Palermo court in 1265, the centre of Italian poetry moved abruptly northwards.

There had grown up a school of didactic and religious poetry in Lombardy, which attempted to develop a literary language based on the dialects of the Po valley, and which drew its inspiration not from the main Provençal stream, but out of the literature of popular piety. This had emanated from the Franciscan order and the religious revival which it stimulated. ST FRANCIS himself (1182–1226) had left only one poem in Italian, a canticle couched in Biblical language.

But the new order stimulated a poetry of devotion, largely in Latin, and produced various books of sermons, lives of its founder, and collections of the legends that had grown up around him. The poetry was modelled on the Latin hymns and on folk-songs, and had little in common with the cultured writings of the Sicilian court. The Franciscan movement, like the Albigensian heresy which it came to replace, made its appeal directly to the people.

The one considerable poet to emerge in Northern Italy before the rise of the Tuscan school had been nurtured on this humble fare. J ACOPONE DA TODI (*c.*1230–1306), a friar from St Francis's native Umbria, composed many canticles in Italian, and is also the reputed author of the Latin *Stabat mater*, as we know it. These *laude*, which are largely in dialogue form, were possibly intended for dramatic recitation. Jacopone had all the dramatist's quick changes of mood, and none of the sonneteer's reflectiveness. He moves from the lyrical to the sententious, from violence to ecstasy, with a gnomic simplicity that is often close to that of the oldest poetry of the *zejel*, which may have survived in the north of Italy as well as in Spain. Always he seems to have a direct vision of those events of which Mary was the heroine and centre and Christ the suffering hero.

> *Socorri Donna ajuta*
> *Ch'al tuo figlio si sputa*
> *E la gente lo muta:*
> *Hanlo dato a Pilato.*

cries the messenger, who has witnessed the Passion. (Bring help, lady, for they are spitting on your son. And the people have changed their minds. They have handed him over to Pilate.) There is an immediacy about Jacopone da Todi's poetry that is absolutely lacking in that of the *troubadours*, and with it a peculiar sense of rejoicing, which hall-marks all the poetry of this group.

The new poetry of Italy, however, was destined to be not religious in basis but philosophical, not emotional but intellectual, not Umbrian but Tuscan; these Northern schools quickly faded into obscurity and merely local significance.

The Tuscan cities, chief among them Florence, had already by the thirteenth century developed an urban civilization which, like that of Northern France, had not entirely fallen under the spell either of chivalry or of the *troubadours*. Each of them was a centre of crafts and trading, all had their painters working on altar pieces and wall-paintings in colour and gold, and Bologna in particular had a university, which was famous for law, rhetoric, and philosophy. The achievement of the Tuscan poets, who grew up in this expanding culture, was in the first place to take over the Sicilian tradition, secondly to develop and intellectualize it, and thirdly to reconcile it with Latin writing, the centre of which remained in Rome, a city unable, owing to its tradition, to play any part in the making of a new vernacular literature.

The first of the new poets, the Bolognese, GUIDO GUINI-ZELLI (1230/40–76) was to Dante, if for one poem only, 'the father of me and others, my betters, who always wrote of love with sweetness and elegance.' Guinizelli was the first poet to relate love to nobility (*gentilezza*), to expand an idea which was, perhaps, latent in the poems of the later *troubadours*. Love was now thought of not only as a sentiment to be expressed in service of the lady desired; it had become a quality of the spirit. Only the noble-minded could love, and love implied a nobility of mind. The adulterous implications of courtly love fell away, and the lady herself began to assume abstract qualities that disguise her circumstances and physical features. She is little more than 'the fair unknown'. A certain Platonism, circulating in the university of Bologna, deriving from the Arab philosophers, and read in translation, re-inforced – or perhaps produced – this tendency to see the spiritual *idea* or reality underlying the 'appearance', which was the aspect of things that preoccupied the Aristotelian school-men of the Middle Ages.

Guido Guinizelli was succeeded, as Dante wrote in the *Purgatorio*, by a second and greater Guido, who carried Tuscan poetry farther along the path of abstraction, and greatly increased its technical perfection. GUIDO CAVALCANTI (*c.*1260–1300) was a Florentine to whom love was a testing and an agony, an intellectual whose philosophizing inflamed, rather than comforted, his introspective passion. Some of his poetry is abstruse, the expression of a speculative mind familiar with the Arab philosophers, with Albertus Magnus and perhaps with Roger Bacon, but many of his fifty surviving pieces are as direct, though not as light-hearted, as their troubadour models. His *pastorella*,

> Within a copse I met a shepherd-maid,
> More fair, I said, than any star to see . . .

and his *ballata* written from exile, to appear before his lady as from one already dead, have, even in D. G. Rossetti's rather too wordy translation, a beauty which makes it plain why Cavalcanti is held to be the best poet of the Tuscan school after Dante.

The two Guidos were the first practitioners of what became known as the *dolce stil nuovo* (the melifluous new style). But the third precursor of Italy's great age wrote in a middle-class realistic vein, reminiscent of Lombardy or of Arras, sardonic sonnets against his parents for keeping him on a short allowance, for and against his wife and his mistress, and against Dante himself, that 'pinchbeck florin', as he called him, for rebuking him on the triviality of his themes. CECCO ANGIOLERI (*c*.1260–*c*.1312) turned the sonnet to uses which would have surprised its Sicilian inventor. Trivial he may have been, but there is a crisp matter-of-factness about his peevishness and his self-mockery.

> I am enamoured and yet not so much
> But that I'd do without it easily . . .

Rossetti makes him say in one of his translations. Angioleri seems to be writing a sardonic epitaph on the ideal of courtly love; he knew just what it cost, in florins and small town jealousies. Trivial he may have been, and a precursor of Boccaccio rather than of Dante, yet the precise imagery of the *Divina Commedia* had roots rather in his middle-class realism than in Cavalcanti's high-flown imprecisions.

DANTE ALIGHIERI (1265–1321) is more than the perfecter of the *dolce stil nuovo*, more even than the supreme poet of Italy. His poetry, indeed, transcends the mere limits of language. Like the Gospels, though in the realm of art not of revelation, the *Divina Commedia* demands of a reader not so much a knowledge of Italian as an understanding of a great symbolism, that of the Middle Ages: the world picture shading down from the heavenly light to the murky hells of man's sinful heart. This picture Dante was able to draw with greater realism than the theologians because he had had, at certain intense moments in his life, direct mystical apprehensions. Indeed, his poem derives from deeper and more consistent levels of experience than almost any other poetry of the West, and the evidence for this rests in its organic shape. It is conceived as a whole, with each part firmly, almost mathematically related to the rest. Compared with it the organization of most other long poems appears haphazard. But it is as a poet, not as a visionary – though the two cannot be divorced – that Dante must be considered here, and in that capacity his greatness is equally incontestable.

Dante received as his inheritance from his age two stock themes of poetry: that of courtly love – wearing a little shabby by now – and that of moral allegory which had been carried into its final, digressive, and satirical morass by Jean de Meun while the Tuscan poet was only a boy. It was on this double foundation, reinforced by the Platonic influence of his friend and senior Guido Cavalcanti, that he constructed first the allegorized tale of his devotion to the unknown beloved, whom he called by the name of Beatrice, and then, in his maturity, the universal allegory of Hell, Purgatory, and Heaven, into which he was led by the thread of his devotion to Beatrice, and compared with which de Lorris's Garden of the Rose was a cold, intellectual fancy.

When Dante put together his *Vita nuova*, the poems dealing with his 'new life', he was a young man of about twenty-six, who had taken some part in the affairs of his native city, who who had written some poetry in the *troubadour* convention, and who was the friend of all the poets and scholars of his native Florence. It is useless to inquire whether the Beatrice whom he addressed as his first love was in fact the wife of Simone Bardi, who had died a year or more before. It is even more useless to ask whether, as the poem's prose commentary appears to state, Dante had seen her first when he was only nine, and had been moved to such emotion by this meeting that his whole life began anew. Numbers played such a part in Dante's symbolism that nine cannot be read as a simple indication of age. For a second vision is described, and attributed to a date nine years after the first, which second vision led Dante to a preliminary exchange of sonnets with Guido Cavalcanti, to whom he dedicated the *Vita nuova*. In his first sonnet Dante asks the meaning of a vision in which love plucked out his heart and gave it to his lady to eat. Cavalcanti replied with a courtly and Platonic interpretation based on the assurance that dreams go by contraries. But Dante's vision, as we can now see, had a deeper and a plainer significance. His love was to consume his outward corporeal being, and to lead him to higher states in which he would have experience even of paradise.

Guido Cavalcanti may have been far behind his younger friend in spiritual apprehension. As a poet, however, he led Dante, to his profit, towards the new vernacular and the new style. But whereas the platonic convention suited Cavalcanti, who was more concerned with the theory of love than with his amorous situation, which may have been largely fictional, Dante had to stretch it to cover a relationship that existed on several planes at once. In the first place, it could be used simply, as a form of compliment addressed to other ladies whom Love had bidden him place as a screen before the figure of Beatrice, that none might know of his adoration. Love was for Dante a private aspiration, but for Cavalcanti it was a public gesture. Yet Dante's relationship to these other ladies cannot have been a mere pretence. For, when he committed himself too deeply to it, Beatrice denied him her salutation, and mocked him at the mysterious wedding feast, which may have been her own to Simone Bardi. Here she seems to be showing Dante that the love of creatures is only a means to the love of something higher, and warning him that too deep a commitment to worldly love – that of other women – will cause the higher love to disappear. This does not mean, however, that Beatrice is a mere figment, a maiden from the Garden of the Rose. The *Vita nuova*, like the *Commedia* after it, is founded on reality, on real vision and true emotion, though for a girl with whom his actual contact may have been far less even than Cavalcanti's for his maiden of Toulouse. But Beatrice dies, or Dante loses his vision of her, and in his acceptance of her death the young poet reconciles himself with death.

There are many layers of meaning in the *Vita nuova,* and only the outermost of them are concerned with this actual Beatrice. Dante has taken up from his 'father' Guinizelli the notion that love and nobility of mind are one, that a man is, in fact, what he gives out: and Beatrice remains, right through the *Commedia,* the figure to whom the poet can give out this love, which is to him the clue leading from Hell to Paradise, the force which 'moves the sun and the other stars'.

In his thirties Dante was once more actively engaged in Florentine politics, attempting to preserve the peace between two warring factions. This caused him to send his extremist friend Guido Cavalcanti, with others, into exile. But with the defeat of the White or imperialist party, of which he was a moderate member, by the Blacks, who favoured the Pope, Dante was himself banished from Florence, never to return. From the age of thirty-eight he was a homeless man, crying in vain, though sometimes hopefully, for justice. In a little while he drifted to the university city of Bologna, where he began to write controversially in Latin.

His first important work, which he did not finish, was the treatise *De vulgari eloquentia,* in which he examined the contemporary state of literature. After a preliminary survey of the history of language, in so far as he knew it, and of the Italian dialects, he reached the conclusion that the ideal language for poetry was that vulgar tongue which belonged to every Italian city and yet seemed to belong to none, and in which the poems of Cino da Pistoia 'and his friend' (Dante himself) were written. He did not realize at this point that this standard Italian was in fact based on Tuscan. From here he went on to examine the various verse forms, all lyrical and, in his opinion, demanding a musical accompaniment, and analysed examples of all these drawn from the works of the *troubadours.* In passing, he stated that there are only three subjects deserving poetic treatment: the conduct of arms, the fire of love, and *rectitudo* or direction of the will. He places himself in the class of those who have written on the third theme. So, clearly he did not look back on the *Vita nuova* as a work concerned primarily with love or the loss of love. In a second Latin treatise, the *De Monarchia*, he dealt with his ideal of kingship and with his hopes that Henry of Luxemburg, the Holy Roman Emperor, would bring peace to Italy.

Meanwhile Dante continued to write poems which he embedded, after the manner of the *Vita nuova*, in a prose commentary. The *Convivio* or Banquet, is entirely allegorical, but for the mention of Beatrice, his first love, the memory of whom is challenged by a new love, that for the lady Philosophy, addressed as 'you who by understanding move the third heaven (*Voi che intendendo il terzo ciel movete*). The *rime* included in the *Convivio* and others of the time divide sharply into poems of intellectual speculation and poems concerned with the poet's love for flesh-and-blood women, the chief of whom, said to be a Paduan, he addresses as Pietra, the stony one. These last are full of winter imagery, and follow forms invented by that late *troubadour* Arnaut Daniel, whom Dante thought of as the poet of love, in contrast to Girault de Borneil, a poet, like himself, of *rectitudo*.

In his early exile, Dante has clearly lost his vision; intellect and emotion have sprung apart. He remains, nevertheless, in these *canzoni*, a supreme poet. For despite this fissure there is no confusion. Beatrice has become Truth, has become the dear image in which the poet clothes his speculations, has become the lovely face of wisdom. But Dante knows what he has lost; and the moment will come when Beatrice will return in her own form, and will assume as well the qualities that now seem separate from her. The Beatrice of the *Commedia* is both the figure of the *Vita nuova* and the maid Philosophy of the *Convivio*, for in that great work intellect and emotion are drawn together again.

The *Commedia* is a work of perfect symmetry in content balanced between allegorical exposition and visionary experience, in form made up of a hundred cantos – the square of the *perfect number* of Pythagoras and the astrologers – divided into three sections of thirty-four, thirty-three, and thirty-three cantos respectively. The cantos in their turn are of roughly equal length, and written in a continuous measure of eleven-syllabled lines, woven together in groups of three by the rhymes of their middle lines in a measure invented by Dante himself and based on imperfect Provençal examples; it is known as *terza rima* or triple rhyme.

The *Commedia* bears every mark of having been conceived as a whole, and premeditated in all its details before the first lines of the *Inferno* were written. For every detail corresponds to every other: there are no loose ends. The complete poem is both a vision and an allegory. It is a vision of the state after death, seen by the poet on Good Friday, 1300, in his thirty-fifth year, half-way on the journey of his own life, as he saw it, though in fact he had hardly more than twenty years to live. But it is also an allegory of man's state on earth, and in this life. In the same way his vision of Hell, Purgatory, and Paradise corresponds both to the common ideas then circulating and, in many of its details, to very special doctrines Classical, Moslem and even Irish. Dante had very wide reading. But the *Commedia* is not eclectic. If he drew details for his poem from Aquinas, Ibn-Arabi, Tundal the Irishman, and Virgil, they were fused in the heat of his vision. But the *Commedia* was not only a vision and an allegory; it was also an autobiography. Dante knew the circles of Hell and Purgatory because he had himself lingered in them. He had glimpsed the light of Paradise in his first love for Beatrice, in his later devotion to the lady Philosophy and at other moments when he had been granted access to higher states of experience. In this Dante's enlightenment can be compared to that of his German contemporary Meister Eckhart. But whereas Dante embodied his vision in a poem that is throughout on a higher level both of insight and organic unity than other poems, Eckhart used his to write plain sermons in downright German prose for the benefit of the nuns under his care.

In the *Commedia* many levels of vision coincide. Virgil, Dante's guide, is in the first place the Latin poet who himself described his hero Aeneas's descent into Hell, and so was counted a forerunner of Christ, a Baptist of the pagan world. But he stands also for human reason which is capable of taking a man only so far on the way to Paradise or self-transcendence. Beatrice again represents the girl whom Dante had loved, and with whom he was now reunited in vision, but she also embodies divine Philosophy, which becomes man's guide when human reason fails: and the figures too whom Dante met in each of the three spheres he visited stood not for themselves – for who but God could judge them? – but for qualities which Dante saw both in mankind and in himself, and which he ranged there in their order of heinousness.

The story of Paolo and Francesca, as the poet and his guide met them in the Second Circle of Hell, will serve as an example of Dante's judgement and of its psychological accuracy.

> To and fro, down, up, driven in helpless flight,
>   Comforted by no hope ever to lie
>   At rest, nor even to bear a pain more light,
> And as the cranes in long line streak the sky
>   And in procession chant their mournful call,
> So I saw come with sound of wailing by
>   The shadows fluttering in the tempest's brawl.*

Clearly the winds that toss the damned are here their own passions. But Dante's judgement is an objective, a compassionate one. He sees there the lovers of legend, Cleopatra, Helen, Paris, Tristan, and then at closer view Francesca, who tells how, as she and Paolo bent over a book of courtly love, their eyes met, their colour changed, and they kissed. He is not condemning them for adultery, but for falling into the trap of wilful love, for neglecting, as Tristan and Iseult had done, all duty to God and man in favour of the pleasure they took in each other. To Dante, they represented his own danger of exclusive love for Beatrice, which would have led perhaps to possession, but certainly not to vision. There were for him three levels of love, the lower and the higher carnal love, symbolized by his love for Beatrice living and for Beatrice dead; and finally there was his love for the heavenly Beatrice, which was man's love for his own spirit, that relationship which gave rise to poetry of yet another sort in Crashaw and St John of the Cross.

*This, and subsequent quotations from the *Commedia* are of Laurence Binyon's translation.

In the *Purgatorio*, Dante and his guide meet the artists, a class who, like lovers, are wont to be content with the gifts of this world. But those whom he found there, on the way to Paradise, were only such as had learnt the vanity of fame. Omberto Oderisi,

> honour of that art
> The illuminators famed in Paris ply,

who was himself with all his kinsfolk mastered by the sin of pride, possessed with the desire to overmaster the rest, had attained Purgatory instead of Hell only because, although having 'the power of sinful doing', he yet turned to God. Into his mouth Dante puts his own renunciation even of poetic fame:

> O idle glory of all human dower!
>   How short a time, save a dull age succeed,
>   Its flourishing fresh greenness doth devour!
> In painting Cimabue thought indeed
>   To hold the field: now Giotto has the cry,
>   So that the fame of the other few now heed.
> So our tongue's glory from one Guido by
>   The other is taken: and from their nest of fame
>   Perchance is born one who shall make both fly.
> Naught but a wind's breath is the world's acclaim...

This is no conventional tribute to the destructive passage of time, no plaintive plea for last year's roses. Guido Cavalcanti succeeds Guido Guinizelli, and in his turn is succeeded in the popular acclaim by Dante himself. But mere pride, even in the highest achievement, is a trap, even as carnal love is. Again Dante is warning himself of the dangers of taking proud pleasure in the craft that he exercises so superlatively well.

But in Paradise itself the poet found some whose names were glorious on earth: Judas Maccabaeus, Charlemagne, Roland, William of Orange (the hero of the *chansons de geste*), the Crusader Godfrey de Bouillon and Robert Guiscard, who reconquered Sicily from the Arabs. These were God's knights who had performed selfless duty in the cause of Christendom, but who had attained a lower circle of Paradise than was reserved for the contemplatives, though a higher place than the theologians.

Everyone in the *Commedia* is assigned to his just place, and everyone has, in addition to his symbolic significance for Dante, his personal value. It is possible to read the poem indeed – the *Inferno* especially – with an eye solely to the worldly history of Italy in that day. Everything is there: feuds, rivalries, riches, poverty, ostentation, romance, lechery, cheating, crime, all awaiting the coming of a redeemer, whom some critics have supposed to be that Henry of Luxembourg in whom Dante once put his hopes. It is reasonable, however, raising the whole issue to a higher plane, to see this country which is outspread before the reader in the light of Dante's vision, as awaiting its own moment of vision – perhaps thought of as the Second Coming – to redeem it.

Dante's style is not a *great style* in the Miltonic sense, nor is it what Professor Lewis calls a *drab style*, that hovers monotonously just above the conversational level. It is, as the word *Commedia* signifies, a homely style, sparing of imagery and only occasionally rising to grandeur of statement. Such images as there are are clear visual images, such as are essential, as T. S. Eliot has said, to an allegory. The cranes in long line streaking across the sky, the dead crowding round Virgil and Dante in the underworld, and peering at them

> as men are wont to do
> At dusk, when a new moon is in the sky:
> And at us puckering their brows, they pried
> Like an old tailor at his needle's eye.

– a comparison singled out for praise by Matthew Arnold: such pictures have a clear impact, and are for ever memorable. Outstanding passages are few in the *Commedia*, and these occur for the most part in the *Inferno*. Such are the meetings with Ulysses and with Bertran de Born, and that with Arnaut, the poet of love, in the *Purgatorio*, in which Arnaut speaks in his native Provençal:

> I am Arnald, and I weep and singing go.
> I think on my past folly and see the stain,
> And view with joy the day that I hope to know.

> I pray you by that Goodness which doth deign
>   To guide you to the summit of this stair.
>   Bethink you in due season of my pain.
>   Then he shrank back in the refining fire.

He shrank back voluntarily since the fires of Purgatory could burn away his sin, and permit him finally to enter Paradise.

This first great poem in the vernacular literature set a standard which may have been equalled, even surpassed, by parts of other great poems and dramas, but which has never been equalled or surpassed as a whole. The effect of the *Commedia* on Italian literature was not immediate. The poem was quickly dubbed 'divine', and duly embellished with commentaries as serious and as fundamental as those lavished on Aristotle or on Holy Writ. But though it gave to the Tuscan vernacular the standing of a tongue that had produced a masterpiece, it did not lead to the linguistic unification of Italy. Latin was still considered by the next generation to be the most suitable tongue for a work of great scope.

The chief poem written under the influence of the *Commedia*, the *Dittamondo* of FAZIO DEGLI UBERTI (c.1305–c.1368) was a discursive and unfinished allegory in *terza rima*, with an autobiographical basis. The direction which Italian poetry took, however, was rather that of the *Vita nuova*, and the principal intermediary between Dante and Tuscany's next great poet, Francesco Petrarca, was that friend whom Dante had described in *De vulgari eloquentia* as the best of love poets. CINO DA PISTOIA (c.1270–1336) was the most prolific writer in the 'new style'. A lawyer, who had been educated at the university of Bologna, he might have been expected to share the intellectualism of Guido Cavalcanti, but Guido's influence he expressly denied:

> No artist I, – all men may gather it
>   Nor do I work in ignorance of pride
> Though the world reach alone the coarser sense;
> But am a certain man of humble wit
>   Who journeys with his sorrow at his side,
> For a heart's sake, alas! that is gone hence.*
>   *Trans. D. G. Rossetti.

Cino's poems in memory of his mistress Selvaggia, and his celebration of her in her life, are sad and tender, though perhaps a little monotonous. He was incapable of understanding the *Commedia* and addressed a sonnet to its author rebuking him for 'fixing folk's nearness to the Fiend their foe' in the *Inferno*, as if Dante's chief purpose in writing the poem had been to pay off old scores and put everyone in his place. But Cino, the humble man who did not deny his acquaintance with pride, wrote from a vein of genuine experience. It was for that reason that he, rather than Dante, was an immediate inspiration to Petrarch.

FRANCESCO PETRARCA, commonly called Petrarch (1304–74) knew pride also, and was not humble. He was, as Cavalcanti had been and as Cino claimed not to be, consciously an artist; and he was also, as no writer had been before him, a man of contradictions who placed his private imprint upon his poetry, who used it as a confessional.

Petrarch's originality lay not in his theme, for love had been the chief subject of European poetry since its *troubadour* beginnings; nor in his philosophical standpoint, which was loosely Platonic, though he had probably not read Plato; nor yet in the strength of his feelings. What is new in Petrarch's *Canzoniere* is that the subjective view prevails over the objective; the poet writes of his love for Laura with all the Provençal hyperbole of service, and of his loss of her in the conventionally exaggerative language of grief. But the light is thrown not outwards but inwards. What we see is the nature of his love, which was not a joy but an agony; a passionate reality but one that he could not accept until, after Laura's death, he could receive her back as a ghost, as the purified figure of a dream. For Petrarch, as he related in his Latin dialogue with St Augustine, was half captivated by the world and its glories, half impelled to renounce it, and with it his own pride. He was in the tortured position of Augustine, in the years before the Saint accepted Christianity. But for him there was no possible solution by religious conversion. Petrarch saw in his brother the effects of the monastic call; he learnt, safe in his French retreat, of Laura's death from plague;

he was himself drawn to the inner, contemplative life, but not
to the monastery. His vocation was not a religious one. It was
rather to turn life experience into art; he was, in fact, the first
dedicated artist.

Petrarch saw the world pass as in a mirror:

> Zephyr returns and brings us in fair weather,
> Sweet retinue of leaves and flowers as well,
> With Spring in white and scarlet blent together,
> And chattering Progne and sad Philomel . . . *

The features of Laura, his glimpses of Nature, of woods and
fields and fountains, are conventionally reflected in the glass of
his memory; even while she lived he saw her more clearly
in his dreams than in waking reality. Yet one has no doubt
that he was writing of an actual mistress, not of a feigned
object of courtly love.

Petrarch's influence on European literature was far more
immediate than Dante's. In the first place he established a
refined poetic language, which was followed by later Italian
poets even as late as the nineteenth century, and which was
also a model for poetic norms in English, in French, and in
other languages, when they came to be fixed a century and a
half after his death.

This power of moulding the vernacular Petrarch owed to
the freshness with which he read Latin. An avid explorer of
ancient writing, he was the first to see how far medieval Latin
had departed from classical standards. He was, in fact, the
first to think of his own times, the Middle Ages, as an interval
of barbarism, and to demand a return to Augustan perfection.
His one large-scale poetic work, his epic *Africa*, was a deliberate attempt to write in the Latin of Virgil; and into this
work, which tells the tale of Scipio Africanus and his campaigns, Petrarch put even more originality than into his
Canzoniere. In his prose too, he tried to return to the purity
and rhythms of Seneca and Cicero.

In his public life, Petrarch was primarily a scholar and man
of affairs, who travelled widely in Europe in search of classical
manuscripts, which had suddenly become objects of great

*Trans. J. Heath-Stubbs.

value and importance, not only to scholars but to princes. In his journeys from one monastery library to another in search of treasures, which he frequently discovered, Petrarch would meet and converse with his fellow-scholars, who were newly infected with the same enthusiasms. Thus a renewed interest in Latin stimulated the new writing in the vernacular; and writing in Latin itself, perhaps partly out of rivalry, became increasingly self-conscious. Standards of artistry acquired an importance in both fields that they had not possessed since the collapse of the Roman Empire.

Petrarch, therefore, with his patriotism, which he expressed in that first of patriotic odes *All'Italia*, and his ideal of translating life experience into terms not of theology or of philosophy, but of art, was widely imitated in Italy, first in his humanism, or concern for classical learning, and afterwards in his attitude to his passion and his art. But this second development did not take place till almost a hundred years after his death. For it was not until then that the poet's inner life, his private feelings and fluctuations of emotion and insight, became the common subject of poetry, as they have remained ever since.

Petrarch was, therefore, the first of modern poets. For whatever his ostensible subject, when writing in the vernacular, he was in fact describing his own relations to it, seen on a scale which excluded Hell and Paradise, which ignored the high philosophical implications of Cavalcanti, and confined itself to the narrow Purgatory of an artist's consciousness, torn between the love of fame and beauty, and gnawed by the worm of self-doubt.

> La vita fugge e non s'arresta un'ora,
>   E la morte vien dietro a gran giornate,
>   E le cose presenti e le passate
>   Mi danno guerra, e le future ancora ...

(Life flies and never stays an hour, and death comes fast, in long stages, and the present and the past make war upon me, and the future too.) With Petrarch and the exclusion from poetry of the element of eternity, a classical melancholy reigns once more, as in the age before Christianity.

Just as Petrarch had his doubts about the spiritual safety of his life as a man of letters, so his friend BOCCACCIO (1313–75), who was nine years his junior, after a long devotion first to the art of narrative poetry in the school of Ovid and of Chrétien de Troyes, and then to the art of prose narrative, was struck with sudden fear and revulsion, and decided to burn the manuscript of his *Decameron*. It was Petrarch, who knew that art was its own justification, that prevented him. But Boccaccio thereafter forswore profane literature and wrote in Latin.

Hitherto the great writers of Tuscany had drawn their education from the university of Bologna; Boccaccio, on the other hand, a merchant's son, acquired his training in the mercantile world. Soon, however, when visiting Virgil's tomb it is said, he became convinced that poetry, not trade, was his vocation. At the licentious court of Naples, he fell in love with the natural daughter of King Robert of Anjou, and wrote of his mistress, after the convention of courtly love, as Fiametta. He admired Dante and set out to interpret him, but he was too well acquainted with carnal love to understand Dante's worship of Beatrice. He was more at home with French romances. Dante's use of the Tuscan language impressed him, as did his allegory, and the scale of his achievement. He was excited too by the new interest in Latin literature, and stuffed his own first work, the prose *Filocolo*, full of classical mythology, though its subject was the Provençal theme of the love of Floire and Blancheflor, and its setting was in pagan Spain. Here, in fact, Boccaccio's native sense of reality, his greatest virtue, was overlaid by his dominant vice of rhetoric. But ambition drove him on, and his next work, the verse romance *Teseida*, which Chaucer later shortened and adapted to make his *Knight's Tale*, was actually intended to resemble the *Aeneid*. In fact, it marks a connecting link between Chrétien de Troyes and the epics of the Renaissance. For in it Boccaccio employed for the first time the *ottava rima*, or octave, a vehicle for leisurely verse narrative, which was to be used by Ariosto, by Tasso, and by Camões. But Boccaccio's powers of storytelling were still undeveloped, and a leisurely medium tempted him into piling up detail upon detail. Every battlefield was described weapon by weapon, every fight blow by blow, and the heroine Emilia was portrayed inch by inch, from her golden hair to her little feet. Yet still she failed to come to life.

The *Filostrato*, Boccaccio's next verse narrative, which Chaucer used for his *Troilus and Criseyde*, was a rehandling of an incident from the Troy legend, beloved of the French romancers. This was far more successful, since here, without implications classical, chivalrous, or philosophical, was a tale of love and betrayal such as might have taken place beneath the poet's own eyes at the court of Naples itself. Here, as in Petrarch's *Canzoniere*, though far more openly, we are shown the pleasures and pains of love divorced from ideals of duty and honour, and from religion; platonic love has yielded to the love of the senses.

Boccaccio's *Amorosa Visione*, therefore, his imitation of the *Commedia* written in *terza rima*, has almost the air of a parody: all values are reversed. A psychological romance, a pastoral idyll, a satire against women: all these experiments of Boccaccio's fail through an excess of rhetoric and classical learning. He is a master only when he is content to tell a direct story. Then he produces the human comedy to match Dante's divine one.

The *Decameron* is the intelligent man's caricature of things and people on a lower intellectual level than himself. It is a picture of the passing show by a man whose standards are worldly, yet who can imagine a better behaved world than the one he sees. Corrupt priests, false saints, bold students, deceived husbands, romantic young ladies who long to offer the pleasures of their beds to any personable young man: such are the characters whom Boccaccio's imaginary narrators – a group of wealthy people who have retired to a country place to avoid the plague – love best to conjure up. Many of the plots were not of Boccaccio's invention: a bourgeois literature of this sort had existed for a long time as a disreputable counterpoint to the high poetry of the nobles and churchmen. All the stories are short and their stings are all in the tail. Boccaccio is a master of the unexpected *dénouement*. Caring less for character and motive than for the turn of event, he can afford to make his people behave arbitrarily.

When they are serious they are mere eccentrics. When most lively they are broadly comical. His world is divided between the sly and the simpletons, and he keeps his readers guessing which will in the end prove to be which. The hermit in that most indelicate tale about putting the devil in hell deceives the girl, only to find that he has taken on more than he can manage; the priest who is only able to win the lady's favours at the expense of his new cloak finds a way of getting his cloak back and of keeping the lady's favour. Some of the tales are romantic, but the best are delightfully realistic, and hinge on the most worldly of worldly points: the possession of wealth, a wife or the favours of another man's.

After his religious crisis Boccaccio fell increasingly under the influence of his friend Petrarch and wrote, as has been said, only in Latin. For many years it was the Latin works of both men that were most admired. They had, nevertheless, together founded not only Italy's national literature, but a new literature of the Renaissance. Dante was great but inimitable; Petrarch and Boccaccio had set examples for the new writers of all Europe, Petrarch in his verse forms, his language and his personal confession within a strict convention, Boccaccio in the choice prose of his tales, in his use of mythology and his willingness to attempt every medium, and both in their devotion to art as their highest ideal seem now to be the first, in time and in talents, of the professional writers of the coming age.

Chapter Four

MYSTICISM, MANNERISM, AND
POPULAR POETRY

THE twelfth and thirteenth centuries contain the complete flowering of medieval poetry, culminating in the one multi-foliate rose, the *Divina Commedia* in which all the age's themes, of carnal love, of ideal love, and of social criticism lie one above the other, petal above petal, in organic unity, and are transcended. In the next hundred and fifty years, up to the discovery of printing and Columbus's voyage, writing fell back again into multiplicity, and no literature of comparable scope was produced.

Europe itself was falling apart. The Papacy, once a world-power which had challenged the Empire for the supremacy of the world, was driven even out of the city of Rome. The Avignonese captivity and the rivalries of Pope and anti-Pope; the ossification of the once creative orders of friars; the over-throw of the great imperial dynasty of the Hohenstaufen; the Black Death; the long and devastating wars between England and France, which laid waste the civilization of the North even as the Albigensian wars had destroyed that of the South; the rivalries and commercialism of the Italian cities: these disasters tended to drive the art of letters in on itself, to reduce it to a new mannerism, comparable with that of the later *troubadours*. For the French poets of the fourteenth century, technique was everything, as it had been for Arnaut Daniel and the men of his generation: their poetry was the poetry of a reduced, sometimes fugitive, court intent on pre-serving its standards in face of the crude and illiterate English, but content to keep their writing on the level of a polite pastime.

With the decay of the Church too, of which there is ample evidence in the almost universal anti-clericalism among popu-lar writers, there arose a restricted school of mystical writers whose perhaps unconscious task was to preserve the essence

of Christianity, despite the discouragement or active persecu-
tion of the worldly ecclesiastical authorities.

The birth of medieval Christian mysticism took place, in
all probability in the convent of St Victor, near Paris, at the
beginning of the twelfth century. First Hugh of St Victor, a
German, then Richard, a Scot, did for theology what Dante
was to do for poetry: they subordinated all learning to the
direct experience of God. Their writings, which were in
Latin, circulated in the next century among the monasteries
and convents of Europe, together with Latin versions of those
of a Byzantine mystic of the fifth century, the pseudo-Dionysius. To what extent this Northern mysticism was reinforced
by influences from across the Mediterranean is uncertain. The
Moslem sufis stressed the same central theme, of man's direct
relationship with God; and their teachings were well known
to such Christian mystics as Ramón Lull, a Catalan contemporary of Dante's, who not only read but wrote in Arabic, for
the avowed purpose of discovering arguments with which to
convert the infidel. Many Arabic works had been translated
also at the court of ALFONSO X OF CASTILE (1221–49),
who himself wrote some 400 *Cantigas de Santa Maria*, poetic
legends about the Blessed Virgin, in Galician. In the field of
religion as in that of literature the two apparently hostile
faiths appear to have drawn closer during this age of active
hostility.

The first mystical writer in the vernacular was MECHTILD
VON MAGDEBURG (*c*.1212–80), who wrote in the Low
German dialect a collection of rhapsodic prose and rhymed
prayers, which owe something to the language of the *Song of
Songs*, and something to the Minnesänger. But her original
work has not survived; only translations into Latin and into
High German are still to be read. It was the nunneries of
Germany and of Flanders, however, that gave the impetus to
mystical writing in the vernacular. For these nuns had insufficient knowledge of Latin to allow of their listening to
Latin sermons: and while their sisters in the Romance
countries might manage to follow the argument by the light
of the still great resemblance between the Latin of the day and
their everyday vernacular, German nuns required the friars

who visited them to speak to them in their own tongue. Mechtild von Magdeburg had a Dominican confessor, and it was a Dominican, the head of the whole Saxon province, who was the most important figure in the history of German religion and literature during the later Middle Ages.

MEISTER ECKHART (c.1260–c.1328) studied at Cologne, where Albertus Magnus, the first theologian to accept the new currents of Graeco-Arabic science and philosophy, and also Thomas Aquinas, had taught; and from there he was sent to Paris. Eckhart was a man of the highest intellectuality who in his sermons and tractates spoke directly of the inner life. For him man's soul was a spark of the divine fire, and Christ was less a figure in history than a potentiality existing in every man's heart. His sermons, requiring as they do the exposition of the most abstruse philosophy in the simplest language, greatly expanded the capacities of High German as a vehicle for exact expression. Such a tractate as that of Sister Katrei, his Strasbourg 'daughter' who proved so much further advanced in the way of the spirit than her spiritual father, is already remarkable for beauty of language as well as for profundity of thought.

Eckhart was first accused by his more worldly brothers of dealing with matters too abstruse for his audience's understanding. Later he was summoned before an archiepiscopal court to answer charges of heresy, and in due course he travelled to Avignon to defend himself before the Pope. He died before the final verdict, dismissing his appeal, was pronounced.

Eckhart firmly asserted throughout that he had never been guilty of preaching false doctrine. There were, however, heretical sects in the Rhineland which held views in many ways similar to his. For in his sermons he so stripped away the commonplace of dogma as to expose a level of understanding on which Christian and non-Christian could have met. Although he was in no sense what the Nazis claimed him to be, a representative of 'German Christianity', he was, in his insistence on the direct relationship between man and God, a forerunner of Protestantism, and even of the non-dogmatic cult of mysticism prevailing to-day.

HEINRICH SEUSE or Suso (*c*.1295–1366), Eckhart's first important follower, was a Dominican from Swabia who lived most of his life on the shores of Lake Constance. After studying at Cologne, he defended Eckhart's views in his first treatise, the *Little Book of Truth*. This seems to have earned him the charge of being a heretical writer, and although the language of his defence was deliberately cautious, he was probably dismissed from his office of lector in the friary school. This can only have been a temporary set-back, however. For he was, in due course elected prior, and afterwards travelled widely, visiting convents, preaching, taking confessions, and meeting with much opposition from those who misunderstood him.

His *Little Book of Eternal Wisdom*, which he rewrote in Latin as *Horologium Sapientiae*, is a paean in praise of suffering and its purgative powers. In style far less abstruse than Eckhart's, Suso's writing is, nevertheless, much less universal; his experience being based on a kind of physical asceticism which is difficult to understand to-day. He abandoned his ascetic practices, however, in middle life, and in his old age put together his autobiography, *The Life of the Servant*, which contains magnificent passages and incidents. With Suso, as with Mechtild before him, the influence of the Minnesänger's lyricism invades the field of mystical theology.

JOHANNES TAULER (*c*.1300–71), also a Dominican, was most probably a pupil of Eckhart's. In parts his sermons echo his master's, though with considerable caution. He did not speak of the 'spark', as Eckhart had done, but of the 'ground' of the soul. Often in his sermons he repeated his master's injunction that God must be born in the soul, but he took care to make it clear that the soul is not God, thus protecting himself from the charge of heresy. Tauler, living in an age when an Emperor had been excommunicated, when the country had been ravaged by plague and civil war, and when morals were in decline, frequently struck an apocalyptic note, calling his hearers to repentance. In his language he was homely; he spoke less esoterically than Eckhart, drawing his imagery from the humble trades and pursuits, and explaining his doctrinal points by popular analogies. So it was not only because Eckhart's works were hard to find that his pupil's achieved a wide circulation. Tauler spoke directly to his age, an age of disaster: and Luther looking back on him a hundred years later regarded him too as a spiritual ancestor.

A mystic of profound influence on later schools, who stood somewhat apart from Eckhart's tradition, was the Fleming JAN VAN RUYSBROECK (1293–1381), who was prior of a convent not far from Brussels. His writings are consistently addressed to monks following the way of purgation, and his masterpiece, *The Adornment of the Spiritual Life*, plots the three main stages of this road. Ruysbroeck is sparing of imagery, and concentrates on the accurate description of psychological states. His works circulated widely, nevertheless, and were much translated. His influence, therefore, spread, and can be detected – as that of the school of Eckhart cannot – in the next group of mystics to spring up in Europe, the Spanish school of the sixteenth century.

Around these main figures among the German and Flemish mystics of the fourteenth century there existed a loose society called 'the Friends of God', at the centre of which stood an inner group 'The Secret Sons of God'. These included members of the two antagonistic Orders, Franciscan and Dominican, and numbered amongst them supporters both of the Pope and the Emperor. It is possible that they were also in touch with the heretical Waldensians, though Ruysbroeck, in particular, was a fervent enemy both of quietism and of heresy. Their connexions, indeed, were wide, and are hard to trace. For, in addition to these who wrote in the vernacular, they appear to have stimulated Thomas A Kempis and the author of the *Theologia Germanica*, who used Latin, also a cognate group in England comprising Richard Rolle, Walter Hilton, Julian of Norwich, and the unknown author of *The Cloud of Unknowing*.

Whilst the countries beside the Rhine reacted in a religious way to the worsening state of society, in France, where the situation was as desperate, the tendency was towards an aesthetic preciosity. Here, while the Universities merely strove to keep scholarship alive, at court a poetry was evolved, full of learned allusions and allegories, largely derived from the *Roman de la Rose*, and written in such strict forms as the *ballade*, with its *envoi*, the *rondeau*, the *chant royal*, and the *virelai*: forms which had grown out of the old *troubadour* conventions, and which, all except the last, were widely divorced from the measures of popular poetry. The most fertile inventor in the new techniques was GUILLAUME DE MACHAUT (*c*.1300–77), a cleric who attached himself to a number of noblemen in succession, who followed a crusading war into the wilds of Lithuania and who was present at the capture of Breslau from the heathen Poles. Machaut was both poet and musician, and composed, in addition to his copious poetry and the tunes to which it was to be sung, several motets, also a Mass for the coronation of King Charles V. He was an extremely facile but very polished craftsman, much of whose work is a variation on a single theme, the lover's complaint.

EUSTACHE DESCHAMPS (*c*.1346–*c*.1406) was equally prolific, and left behind him 1,175 *ballades*, also 171 *rondeaux*, on the most diverse subjects. Fortunately, although the pupil of Machaut, he did not imprison himself in his convention, but allowed his life's experience to colour some of his poems. His double *ballade* dedicated to Machaut, *le noble rhétorique*, his *ballade* against the evils of his time, his farewell to Paris, his *ballade* of the signs of death and other pieces celebrate man's mortality with a solemnity, a realism, and a rhetorical use of famous names that look forward to Villon, or across the North Sea to William Dunbar.

> *Ou est Nembroth le grant jayant*
> *Qui premier obtint seigneurie*
> *Sur Babiloine?* . . .

(Where is Nimrod, the great giant who first won lordship over Babylon?)

Deschamps sent many of his poems to Chaucer, who looted him, Machaut, and the *Roman de la Rose* for the stuff and the metres of his own early poetry.

Both Deschamps and his master continued a debate begun in the second part of the *Roman de la Rose*, on the nature of women; and in this they were joined by a most accomplished poetess, who boldly took the feminist side. CHRISTINE DE PISAN (1365–*c*.1429), the daughter of Charles V's Italian astrologer and physician, married one of the king's secretaries and, after his death, supported herself and her family by the profession of letters, offering finely penned and luxurious editions of her works to wealthy amateurs. As a balladist, she followed Deschamps in allowing real feeling to emerge, especially in the *ballades* of her widowhood, written immediately after her husband's early death. Among her works is a life of her king and a poem in honour of Joan of Arc. Alone among the French poets of her time, she seems to have been aware of the new Petrarchan style, which was developing in her father's country. Another balladist, ALAIN CHARTIER (*c*.1385–1429) was a follower of Joan's Dauphin, who ate his heart out at the shadowy court of Bourges before Joan led her self-distrustful master to victory. His writing, though rather over-rhetorical, carries a genuine flavour of despair and thwarted love. His best-known poem, *La Belle Dame sans merci*, a dialogue between a pair of unhappy lovers, presented this phrase to Keats and to later poets. Chartier is, perhaps, happiest in his light and charming *rondeaux*.

Another victim of the Hundred Years War, the prince CHARLES D'ORLÉANS (1394–1465) succeeded in writing with some freshness in a courtly convention which was now finally becoming outworn. His subject is love, but into his later poems a certain bitterness seems to creep. He had worked all his life for the reconciliation of France and England, and suffered a captivity of twenty-five years after the battle of Agincourt. This long sojourn in England made him sufficient master of the language to write some poems in English, but the bulk of his work is in French. There is a prevailing melancholy about all that he wrote; often his imagery is fresh, but he seems always to be lost in his *forest d'ennuyeuse Tristesse* (forest of tedious sadness).

JEAN FROISSART (*c*.1337–*c*.1405), the most important writer of this epoch, was only secondarily a poet, being the author of an Arthurian romance and of a large number of lyrics written in the style of Machaut, though with a somewhat lighter touch. His Chronicles, however, which cover the events in Western Europe from 1325 to 1400, are on a much greater scale. They are one long celebration in dramatic prose of the vanishing glories of chivalry. Froissart did not see that the nobility was in its decadence; he did not see that wars were not a matter only of knights and challenges, campaigns and sieges; that wealth lay in trade and wool, in banking and agriculture rather than in plate and fine armour. It was not for nothing that Froissart had served his apprenticeship to the legends of King Arthur; for him that age had not entirely passed, any more than it had in the next century, in the midst of the Wars of the Roses, for Sir Thomas Malory, nor yet a hundred and fifty years later for Cervantes' creature Don Quixote. Froissart was not unwilling to falsify history in the interests of good narration; he was an artist before he was a historian, as his successor PHILIPPE DE COMMYNES (1447–1511) was not. Though he lived at a time when the Middle Ages were dying, it is to Froissart that one must turn if one wishes to understand the medieval soldier's idea of himself and his achievement.

FRANÇOIS VILLON (1431–c.1463), the last great figure of the Middle Ages in France, was completely objective about himself and the age he lived in. A cleric of dissolute life, he was guilty of at least one murderous assault, of one robbery and of participation in a brawl which earned him the death sentence, later commuted to banishment. Much of his life he seems to have spent in prison, and the rest, until his departure for an unknown place of exile, in the low quarters of Paris. His poetry consists of two ribald, cynical Testaments, interspersed with ballades sometimes jocose and sometimes of melancholy beauty. At his best, he was a poet of true feeling who watched the passing of all loveliness, lamenting the kings and queens of olden times, and who could offer a simple prayer to the Virgin at his mother's request. But he was capable too of a harsh realism as in his Ballade of the Hanged, and his regrets for an old courtesan. These ballades are connected by the main body of the Testaments, which is made up of whole strings of minor and major bequests to old friends and enemies. These verses are riddled with private jokes and barbs of malice the point of which has worn down with time. Nevertheless, there emerges from them in more than flashes an authentic picture of the Paris that Villon knew:

> Item, I leave to Begging Friars,
> God's Daughters and devout Béguines,
> Morsels to tickle their desires,
> Cakes, capons and rich galantines.
> And leave to preach the Fifteen Signs
> And on their recompense grow fat.
> (These Carmelites make concubines
> Of our goodwives – but what of that?)*

Often when he seems to be illustrating his poems with incidents from his life, François Villon is in fact making great poetry out of the commonplaces of his age. The Fifteen Signs of the approaching Day of Judgement were visible not only to him and the Paris friars, but to all Western Europe. Villon was born in the year of Joan of Arc's martyrdom. During his lifetime France slowly recovered from the depredations of the English, only to plunge itself into further civil wars. The theme of *Ubi sunt* – 'Where are the snows of yesteryear?' – was common to him, to Deschamps before him, to Dunbar in Scotland, to Skelton in his elegy on King Edward IV, and to the poets of Spain. 'Vanity of vanities' was the motto of a dying world-order, for which Villon could speak with profound authority, since the lesson of his age exactly matched his personal experience.

The middle of the fifteenth century is rich in well-turned *ballades* by minor poets, many of whom were men and women of high station, whose favourite theme seems to have been a consideration of the married state, a topic seemingly capable of interminable development. Among single poems of this time one alone seems to demand special mention: Catherine d'Amboise's *Chant Royal de la plus belle qui jamais fut au monde* (*Chant Royal of the most beautiful woman ever born into the world*) in which she turns the grandeur that Villon used in his laments to purposes of praise. But some of the most charming pieces of these sad years are to be found in the anonymous song-books,

*Trans. Norman Cameron.

Av'ous veu la Peronelle
Que les gendarmes ont emmenée?

Ils l'ont abillée comme ung paige:
C'est pour passer la Dauphiné . . .

(Have you seen the Peronelle whom the soldiers have taken away? They have dressed her as a page, to pass her through Dauphine).

In its unforced way this song tells us more about fifteenth-century France, infested with wandering bands of mercenaries, than do the more solemn trumpetings of doom among the poems by court poets.

The poetry of Spain followed a different evolution from that of France, only to arrive, in Jorge Manrique's famous elegy on the death of his father, at a point identical with that reached by Villon in his lament for the Ladies of the Olden Times.

The earliest developed poetry of the Peninsula, that of the Galician school, had left a thin trickle of influence only on the poets of Castile and Aragon. The rival Arabic tradition, on the other hand, which had grafted oriental elaborations on the simple kernel of traditional Mediterranean refrains, and which had been flourishing for centuries at the courts of the Moorish emirs, tempted the sober poets of the Castilian plateau to ornate forms utterly foreign to the unknown author of the *Cantar del Cid*, to the French-influenced adapters of the tales of Troy, of Alexander, and the rest, or to the simple and credulous biographer of the saints, Gonzalo de Berceo.

JUAN RUIZ, the archpriest of Hita (? –*c*.1350), Spain's first great poet, was a worldly cleric who, like Villon and Manrique after him, embodied the commonplaces of his day in individual poetry. He purports to be telling his life-story in order to warn men of the dangers of carnal love and to encourage them to love of God. *El libro de buen amor* (*The Book of True Love*) is, however, chiefly concerned with love of the commonplace sort. Its incidents may be largely fictional, for many of them follow those which its author may have found in a certain minor Latin comedy of the twelfth century. The poem tells of three unsuccessful love affairs, which are

narrated with great realism, with a peculiar blend of shameless-
ness and piety, and with a novelist's sense of character.
Trotaconventos, a hag who plays the part of a professional
procuress, is as living a figure as Juliet's nurse, and Doña
Endrina's excuses and tergiversations have all the appearance
of being studied from the life. The *Libro de buen amor*, however,
is a great deal more than a disguised autobiography. It contains lyrics, some of them parodies of popular motives, an
allegorical battle between Carnival and Lent, a poem in praise
of small women, religious verses of a rather perfunctory
nature, and a satire against the priests of a neighbouring town.
It is as if the archpriest had assembled all the items in his considerable and varied minstrel's repertory. Some of his characters narrate fables; others indulge in typical fourteenth-century
disquisitions on human nature, and the whole book is informed with a pleasantly dry and unmalicious humour. There
is endless variety in it, held together on the thread of a single
ironic temperament. A satirist, a novelist, a master of pithy
allegory, Juan Ruiz was at the same time the forerunner of the
author of *La Celestina*, of the Cervantes of the *Exemplary
Novels*, and of Spain's greatest satirist, the equally fantastic
though more bitter Quevedo.

Spanish court poetry of the fourteenth century, a large
collection of which survives in a single song-book, the *Cancionero de Baena* of 1445, was quite uninfluenced by the *Libro de
buen amor*. Some of the poems were written by cultured
gentlemen, among whom were a prince or two, a chancellor,
and a high admiral; others by professional minstrels who
recited their poems without music, being the first generation
to do so. Their subjects derived for the most part from the
troubadour repertory. Their *serranas*, the counterpart of the
French *pastourelles*, tell of encounters with amorous cow-
girls among the hills, a situation from which Juan Ruiz had
derived some coarse fun. Others tell of the love of a constant
Moorish maiden, who forsakes her people and turns Christian,
caring not whether her knight take her for wife or mistress.

The best of the poets of this generation was ALFONSO
ÁLVAREZ DE VILLASANDINO (*c.*1345–*c.*1425), a professional *trovador*, who made his poems for money, composing an

annual Christmas panegyric for the town of Seville for a fee of a hundred gold crowns. Satire, panegyric, and social criticism were coming into fashion; courtly love – never a well-established theme in Spain – was going out. Indeed one of the most charming pieces in the *Cancionero* is a *Love's Farewell* by Garcí Fernández de Jerena, a *trovador* rather older than Villasandino, in which the little god is seen leaving Castile, and complaining that he is not honoured there.

Most of the types of poetry current in France were also written in Spain at this time. There is the anonymous Dance of Death, a familiar medieval subject treated as a poem for several voices; there is the dignified and solemn treatment of the *Ubi sunt* theme by Ferrant Sánchez Calavera, who asks, where are the emperors, popes, kings, and great nobles, what has become of science, learning, and the masters of poetry, even as Villon and Manrique were to do in the next century; and there are also, the gnomic moral proverbs of the rabbi Sem Tob (early fourteenth century).

But Spain differs from France not only by the presence of its Moorish and Jewish element, which had more effect on its poetry than influence from over the Pyrenees or the dying memory of the Galician *troubadours,* though echoes from them can still be heard in the poems of Fernández de Jerena and of Villasandino. Spain was also the first to undergo an Italian influence, from Dante and Petrarch, though no poets succeeded in successfully acclimatizing the new style until the sixteenth century.

The first would-be Italianizer was FRANCISCO IMPERIAL (early fifteenth century), a Genoese jeweller living in Seville, whose clumsy attempt to imitate the *Divinae Commedia* made much of the *Baena* song-book, in which it appeared, look thin. So little did the Spaniards understand his intention, and so great was the contrast between the fluid verse of Italy and the heavily accented Spanish 'sprung rhythms', however, that the copyist of his *Dezir a las siete Virtudes* (*Address to the seven Virtues*) produced what is obviously an inaccurate version of the poem. From his father's country, Imperial brought a taste for symbolism, if an imperfect mastery of the eleven-syllabled line; and his voice carried a distant echo of Dante's, which alone was enough to start Spanish poetry in fresh directions.

The next poet to attempt the rhythms of the new poetry was a rhetorical Andalusian, JUAN DE MENA (1411–56), whose allegory, *El Laberinto de la Fortuna* (*The Labyrinth of Fortune*) presents a highly descriptive and apocalyptic survey of history, heavily latinized in vocabulary. Juan de Mena is at his best when narrating the details of a siege or writing a grand pane-gyric of a hero, but his affinities to Dante are as slight as Imperial's. He is in fact no more than an accomplished Andalusian poet who has added an Italian trick or two to his repertory.

The MARQUIS DE SANTILLANA (1398–1458) also at-tempted to naturalize Italian measures, and even wrote a few sonnets 'made in the Italian style'. But it was in the convention of the Galicians and the *troubadours* that he wrote the handful of poems by which he will always be remembered. When a boy he had found an old Galician song-book in his grand-mother's house, and although in later life he had collected and read contemporary poetry in Latin, French, Italian, and Catalan, it is as a poet in the old tradition that the Marquis excelled.

> I don't think the roses
> of springtime could ever
> have seemed half so lovely,
> or looked so good either –
> I put the case baldly –
> if I'd known beforehand
> of that pretty cowgirl
> of La Finojosa.

The *serranillas* of La Finojosa and of Bores, with their seeming effortlessness, as of folk-songs – a medium that the Marquis despised – are only surpassed by his delicate *villancico* or carol to his three daughters, which tells how he surprised them singing in a garden. Tenderly they inform him that it is not he they are singing of, but their lovers; and here reality breaks right through the *troubadour* convention, and we see the poet as he must have seen himself: a father getting old and sad to find his children growing away from him. The Marquis's melancholy is a little like that of his contemporary

Charles d'Orléans. But he is the robuster figure of the two: his verses lack the 'dying fall' of the French prince's. For they stand not so much at the end of a medieval culture as at the beginning of new things. In the introduction to his poems, he praised the poets of Italy, and placed the French a good second, though rather for their metrical mastery than for the content of their poems.

The last considerable poet of the Spanish Middle Ages, JORGE MANRIQUE (c.1440–79) died in battle in the course of a civil war, leaving behind him his magnificent *Coplas* and a handful of neat trivialities. In this world-famous elegy on the death of his father, he treated the favourite theme of the age – the omnipresence of death and the vanity of worldly things – with a great and solemn dignity; his is the supreme poetic treatment of the time's most solemn commonplace, the contrast between the spirit and the flesh, which was soon to yield to the new Petrarchan commonplace of the ideal world in which the contradiction is reconciled. Manrique writes in a simple almost colloquial style, raised to emotional heights by the constant repetition of its simple three line pattern of sound, by its frequent Biblical echoes, and by the roll call of princely names it invokes, of those who have now gone to join the illustrious dead.

> What has become of the king, Don John?
> And the princes of Aragon,
>   Where are they now?
> Where is that host of gallant men?
> The feats of arms that they did then,
>   Where are they now?

The medieval tradition struggled on into the sixteenth century, still challenging the new ideas from Italy, and finally succeeded in acclimatizing some of its forms to the new Latinate manner and language. But Manrique's *Coplas* were the last and the greatest statement of a medieval theme in Spanish poetry.

Side by side with the court and the *troubadours'* poetry in the fourteenth and fifteenth centuries, there was in Spain a great flowering of folk-songs and ballads. The tradition of Spanish folk-poetry had been a long one, stretching back, like that of the court-poetry, from which it was not so far divorced as were these two species in France, to the old Galician song-books, and also to the Arabic poetry of Andalusia. As we first meet it in Spanish song-books it clearly partakes of both Northern and Southern influences. From the Galicians it has learnt their remarkable condensation of narrative, and it is their themes that predominate. A song may tell of a girl waiting for her lover, or confiding in her mother: or she may not be presented directly, but symbolized as a heron, or even as a flower or a herb: a device which was copied and developed by the sophisticated poets of later centuries. The kernel of the song lies in its refrain – the old Mediterranean refrain – and in the repetition of its sonorities; it tells no story, but weaves variations of metaphor and of music around a single state-ment. All that was asked of it was an incantatory rhythm, generally evocative of a gentle melancholy, which was no doubt counterpointed by the steady beating of the dancers' feet. But the Galician was not the only thread in the delicate tissue of these songs; the hotter and more direct sensuality of the Arab also contributed motifs as elusive in their sym-bolism but more sanguine in mood. Similar folk-poetry probably existed in most countries of Europe; we have seen examples of it from the France of the Hundred Years' War. But it owes its especial survival in Spain to the enthusiasm of sixteenth-century collectors, who gathered the songs and printed them for the pleasure of the upper classes, who were addicts of chamber music, and sang these *estribillos* – or *villancicos* as they later came to be called – to the accompani-ment of a variety of guitar.

But, by the fifteenth century, the *villancicos* had been partially replaced in the popular favour by the *romances* or ballads. These too were highly repetitive in sound, being constructed like the *laisse* of the ancient *chansons de geste* on a single assonance: their metres, in fact, were very close to those of the old epics, late versions of which undoubtedly persisted into the fourteenth century, though none has survived in its entirety.

The first *romances* may very possibly have been composed for local entertainments by travelling *juglares*. Their subjects were drawn from incidents either in the civil wars of the North or in the border forays against the Moors. They were in fact a kind of political poetry, and there are records of King Pedro the Cruel having actually commissioned a *romance* to be composed in celebration of a victory. Like other popular Spanish poetry these ballads were both economical of incident and objective, so objective that those of the Moorish border often relate a Moorish defeat with compassion and from the Moorish point of view. Like front line soldiers, these Christian *juglares* see that their enemy's case is the same as their own.

Soon, however, other less local themes came to be treated by the *romances*; dramatic passages were taken from the decaying epics and suitably embellished. King Roderick the Goth's betrayal, the deeds of the Cid, the murder of the seven princes of Lara, each formed the subject for whole ballad-cycles; and to these were added, perhaps for a rather more sophisticated audience, *romances* based on the prose stories of Charlemagne, Tristan, and Lancelot, and even on incidents from more recent tales of adventure. The majority of these poems are short, and could have been sung by the villagers themselves, though a small number extend to a few hundred lines, and seem to postulate a professional reciter.

The *romances* are, for the most part, matter-of-fact in tone, and a little monotonous in rhythm. Many of their lines too are the crudest conventional padding; the rhythm counting for a great deal more to their original audience than did the sense. In the sheer bareness of their narration, however, they are highly dramatic; and sometimes, though much more rarely than our own border ballads, they rise into rare and mysterious regions of poetry. On the whole, the Spaniard was far less touched by the supernatural than was the inhabitant of the misty Cheviot border. Yet occasionally, as in the famous fragment concerning Count Arnaldos, there are poignant suggestions of mystery. Coming to the seashore, the knight hears a sailor singing aboard a ship with silken shrouds; and when he asks for the words of the song the sailor replies: 'I only tell my song to those who sail away with me.' But this ballad was not a deliberate exercise in the mysterious. It was in fact part of a far longer and rather dull story, the whole of which was gathered in the nineteenth century from a version preserved among the Jews of Morocco. With a sure feeling for essentials, derived from the tradition of Galicia, successive singers must have omitted the pedestrian development of this ballad, preserving only its supreme moment.

The Spanish Jews of Morocco, also those of Turkey, and of Salonica before their massacre by the Nazis, preserved many of the *romances*, which have been forgotten in the Peninsula. Expelled by the Inquisition, their ancestors carried with them their native language and culture, much as did the *poor whites* of Kentucky and Tennessee, from whom our own collectors have gathered versions of our folk-songs and ballads.

The poetry of Portugal developed along similar lines to that of Spain, though its level remained consistently lower than that of the major partner. After the middle of the fourteenth century, the Galician love-poem quickly declined into a courtly exercise, yielding to more Spanish forms, sometimes written in the dominant language itself. Possessing no epics, the Portuguese developed independent ballad subjects and, following the differences in national mood, tended both to be more elaborate than their neighbours, and to be melancholy where the Spaniard was vigorous. Portugal's most considerable literary figure prior to the Renaissance was GARCIA DE RESENDE (c.1470–1536?), a prose chronicler and the collector of a large song-book, the *Cancionero geral*, from which anything reminiscent of folk-poetry was rigorously excluded. The book contains, among many conventionalities both lyrical and satiric on a lower level than those of the *Baena* song-book, a few original poems, among them his own verses on the death of Dona Inés de Castro, a complaint put into the mouth of the murdered lady, a prince's mistress, who possesses for the Portuguese something of the martyred glamour of Mary, Queen of Scots. These *Trovas* are Portugal's equivalent to Manrique's *Coplas*, with which, in their straightforward solemnity, they almost challenge comparison. But though Resende's pathos is greater than Manrique's, his orchestration is not so strong, nor does he awaken the same universal echoes. Some other pieces in the book show a dilute Italian influence derived from the Marquis de Santillana, and an occasional *serranilho* or *vilancete*, such as those of Francisco de Sousa, a fine poet of whom nothing is known, compares favourably even with the Marquis's own.

A single poet writing in Catalan, AUZIÀS MARCH (*c*.1397–1458), promises a literature in that language which did not develop owing to Castile's predominance in the Peninsula. March is in one aspect the last of the *troubadours,* to whose language Catalan is closely akin; but in another he is the first successful Italianizer in the whole of Europe. With a complexity only comparable with that of Arnaut Daniel, whose metres he followed, he was at the same time one of the first poets outside Italy to make his poetry out of his own experience. His recurrent theme is the struggle between carnal and spiritual love, which led him into indecisions, and made him equally unhappy in the attainment of his pleasures and in their thwarting. He was, in this respect, a poet who looked forward rather than backward and, as such, had his influence on the Spanish poets of the Renaissance, one of whom translated his works into Castilian.

Spanish prose in the late Middle Ages largely takes the form of chronicles, which tell a story well enough, but which on the whole lack both Froissart's sweep and de Commynes' accuracy. So very deficient were these chroniclers in historical sense that quite often they reduced the old epics to prose, and incorporated them in their tale, treating them as adequate authority for the deeds of the days of old. Indeed, recent scholars have found it possible to reconstruct parts of these lost poems, or at least to acquire positive proof of their existence, by picking out the poetic rhythms and assonances from the passages in which they have been roughly embedded.

The first readable book in Spanish prose is roughly contemporary in date with the *Decameron,* though not so advanced in the technique of story telling. *El Conde Lucanor* by the prince JUAN MANUEL (1282–1349?) is a collection of exemplary tales, told by an imaginary steward to his noble young master, and each pointing an elementary moral. The incidents are ironical and worldly, but a little repetitive; and many of them come from Arab sources.

The second Spanish story teller, Alfonso Martínez de Toledo, better known as the ARCHPRIEST OF TALAVERA (1398?–1470) was a more immediate pupil of Boccaccio's, who wrote some racy satires full of snapshots from low life and of those pungent Spanish proverbs which Sancho Panza was to quote with such effect. 'Women prefer a bird in the hand,' he remarks, 'to a vulture on the wing, or an ass that carries them to a horse that throws them,' and 'The fool is wiser in his own house than a sane man in another's.' This archpriest, who is in the true line of descent from his brother of Hita to the author of *La Celestina* and Cervantes himself, compiled, in addition to these stories, a historical chronicle and the lives of two saints, all in a lively prose.

Another important prose work, much read in its day, derives from that most western of sources, the Arthurian legend. *Amadis de Gaula*, the first of those sixteenth-century chivalrous tales that turned Don Quixote's head, must originally have been written in the early fourteenth century, but whether in Castilian or Portuguese remains uncertain. The unbroken victories of its hero, the unsullied virtues of its heroine, and the regularity with which the villains' machinations are foiled, together with a rather monotonous style, may make a modern reader wonder why this book was not burnt with the rest in the holocaust of Don Quixote's library.

In Spain the transition from medievalism to the Renaissance proceeded more smoothly than in the rest of Western Europe. For here there was no catastrophic decline in morality; no break up of the feudal system, which had never taken root beyond the Pyrenees; no such disease and no such devastation as that occasioned by the Hundred Years' War and the Black Death; no such disillusionment as had overcome those nations that had taken leading parts in the wrangling about St Peter's disputed throne. The Peninsula consequently lacked both the mystical literature and the developed preciosity that go with bad times: here was still vigour and expansion at the expense of the last remaining Moorish princes. In a buoyant culture, the literary tradition uniting court and people remained alive, and each stimulated the other.

Chapter Five

THE BIRTH OF THE DRAMA

IT had been the Church that had put an end to the decadent classical drama, first by excommunicating all actors in the fifth century, and then by finally closing all the theatres in the sixth. By a stroke of irony, however, the very emperor Justinian, who forbade the last indelicate and blasphemous performances of the mimes, himself married an actress and raised her to the Imperial throne.

It is possible that irregular companies of actors continued to defy the imperial ban and the Church's hostility. Simple types of drama or farce may have continued to be presented by strolling players throughout the Dark Ages; the minstrels who carried the *troubadours'* songs to the hall and the market square may have been the lineal descendants of the last Roman actors. But a gap of five centuries, interrupted by barbarian invasions, migrations of peoples, imperial revivals, and doctrinal quarrels, can hardly have allowed any real dramatic tradition to persist. Certainly the new drama did not owe its beginnings to the strolling players, though within the first century of its new existence professional entertainers may well have taken over some of its comic parts. The new drama, the 'mystery', was the creation of the Church itself, and its avowed purpose was 'the strengthening of faith in the unlearned vulgar and in neophytes'. Its beginnings were liturgical; it grew, as did Western sung music, out of the Mass. The earliest *trope*, or additional and interpolated melody, seems to have been introduced into the Easter morning Mass; and then to have developed into a little mimed scene, in which different voices represented the three Marys coming to the Tomb, and the Angel whom they found guarding it.

This *Quem quaeritis* (*Whom seek ye*), as it was called, in the first place followed the Latin words of the Gospel. At some time, probably in the eleventh century, however, this embryo drama was detached from the Mass and acted separately at

Matins on Easter morning. About the same time the acting, which had been highly stylized, became more free; the action moved out of the choir into the nave of the church, and a small structure was erected there to represent the Tomb. Simultaneously additional scenes were devised, one in the garden and one at the spice-seller's from whom the Marys bought unguents with which to anoint the corpse. These necessitated fresh dialogue, and more structures in other parts of the church, for the presentation was processional, never static. The spicer seller's scene, moreover, led to the introduction of comedy.

In addition to these Easter performances, others were staged at Christmas, in which the Magi or the three shepherds came to visit the Mother and Child, led by a movable star; and this again led to comedy and character acting. At the same time, a third dramatic subject was presented by the stock sermon concerning the prophecies that foretold the Messiah. Here the priest delivering the oration would be reinforced by voices representing each of the Old Testament prophets and quoting their words. Soon characters were added who were not strictly prophets, and the whole wealth of the Old Testament was added to the Passion story of the New, as material from which this Church drama could develop.

This growth appears to have taken place simultaneously throughout Western Europe, with the Northern French and Anglo-Normans leading the fashion. There can be no doubt of the popularity of this liturgical drama. The medieval peasant and townsman was starved for entertainment, for the travelling *jongleur* could have touched a fraction only of his potential audience, and his courtly convention and stylized language, Limousin or French, must have seemed far more difficult to the average illiterate man or woman than the familiar Bible story, presented in the Latin of the familiar Church Service. The Church, with its painting and window glass, had already begun to speak to him through his eyes, and now to his eyes and ears was presented this new drama, which made the Bible a living reality to him.

The first-known dramatic script on a large scale is the twelfth-century *Adam*, written partly in Anglo-Norman and partly in Latin, for presentation, not in the church itself, but on a platform erected outside the West door, upon which the garden scene was acted, and another erection intended to represent hell, the open space between being available for the general action, with the whole square before the church for the audience. A copy of *Adam* survives complete with its stage directions, from which we learn that God – here called the *Figura* – wears a dalmatic, in contrast to Adam's red tunic, and that he retires into the church after giving his commands to Adam and Eve, only to re-emerge after the eating of the apple. The primal pair, meanwhile, paraded upon the Paradise platform, which was hung round with silk curtains, so that they were only visible from the shoulders upwards. The temptation scene is written with great subtlety, the devil pouring quiet scorn for Adam into the frivolous Eve's willing ear, and recommending the fatal fruit as 'heavenly food'. The expulsion scene is followed by the murder of Abel, and then by a grand procession of the Prophets, which concludes with a vision of the Redeemer.

The drama had now, in emerging from the Church itself, escaped from a priestly monopoly. For clearly the clergy could not have provided the large cast required, nor would they willingly have impersonated the hordes of devils who ran about the open ground in front of the stage, and who bundled Adam and Eve into Hell with a great clatter of pans and kettles. Already there were townsfolk acting the chief parts, with small boys to play the devils; and this side of the production was undertaken in England by the merchant guilds, in France by special local fraternities or *Confréries*, and in Italy by companies of youths devoted to particular saints. The writing of the plays too was entrusted to laymen, the school of Arras, with its strong vein of satire and its broad humour, providing pieces on various subjects, some of which could only by courtesy be described as sacred.

Throughout the thirteenth century the scope of drama broadened. The admission of stories from the lives of saints, acted for the first time, perhaps, on their festivals, allowed a considerable choice of subjects; and prominent among these 'miracle plays' emanating from the school of Arras were *Le*

Jeu de Saint Nicholas (*c*.1200) by Jean Bodel, a romantic play of
the Crusades, and *Le Miracle de Théophile* (*c*.1284) by Rutebeuf,
an early treatment of the tale of the man who sold his soul to
the devil, and had it stolen back for him by the Virgin Mary.
Here the devil is presented as a poor fool very much afraid of
being outwitted. Indeed, he is full of suspicions and claims to
have had rather bad experience of men. In this play too, as in
many others, the miraculous element is entirely swamped by
secular byplay: in one or two it is omitted altogether.

The original 'mystery play', which had sprung out of the
Easter *trope* and was now supposed to set out the dogmas of
the Faith, also underwent a large development, or expansion,
and came to be broken up, first into a number of acts, each
requiring a different stage, as for the *Conversion de l'Apôtre
Paul*, a play of the twelfth century, and then into a series of
different plays, acted on a number of platforms. These performances were eventually spread over several consecutive
days, for the cycles grew too long to be presented in one. The
technique of production varied from country to country. In
France and Southern Europe the platforms remained fixed in
the main squares, but in England and Flanders they were
mounted on great wagons, and spectators gathered at any
part of the town saw a number of them which were brought
round in succession.

This great development of the drama took some three
centuries to be complete, and it was not till the fifteenth
century that the fraternities, now reinforced by the craft
guilds, presented their cycles in all their perfection. The great
occasion for dramatic performances was Corpus Christi, a
feast established in 1311 in honour of the Blessed Sacrament;
for since there was nothing about this day to attract the
imagination to any particular scene in Scripture or the Lives of
the Saints, the dramatist then felt free to wander very far into
the field of romance or of satire to find a subject.

Secular literature provided, however, a medium neither
romantic nor satirical, to enrich the dramatist's repertory and
at the same time to point a religious moral. This offshoot from
the all-popular allegory of the fourteenth century, the 'morality' play, brought on to the stage the familiar vices and virtues,

even the most abstract of which, in the best examples, such as the Dutch *Everyman* – familiar to us in its English translation – succeeded in throwing off their bonds of symbolism and becoming human. The Devil and Old Vice provided the humour. The 'morality', therefore, which may have looked like a somewhat retrograde development in the history of drama, did not prove so. Thanks to its unity, indeed, it lies closer to the main line of ancestry of modern drama than the more diffuse 'mystery' and 'miracle' plays with their multiple stages.

The growth of drama varied little from country to country. Europe was more uniform in its plays than in its poetry. Nor was there a perpetual succession of novelties: a piece, having found its way into one of the cycles, remained there, though probably subject to alterations and expansions, for many years. The majority of these plays are, of course, lost; and, as is natural, it is from the fifteenth century, the last and most vigorous age of the old drama, that the finest specimens have come down to us. In France the 'mystery' had by that time attracted some of the best poets, poets with the metrical accomplishment of the *ballade* writers who were not content to be confined to so narrow a poetic medium.

The *Mystère du Vieux Testament*, a comprehensive and collective work, seems to have occupied a number of hands, possibly including the Gréban brothers of Le Mans, who were princes of the craft. Such a scene as that of the building of the Tower of Babel, in which men of the various building trades quarrel amongst themselves, bully the apprentice boys, flatter Nemroth, who has commanded the project, and finally fall to babbling in strange tongues, has a delightful urban reality, while Arnoul Gréban's *Mystère de la Passion*, which played for four days, contains everything from delicate verse, given to the shepherds on their way to Bethlehem, to a metaphysical discussion between Judas and Despair – a figure borrowed from the 'morality' – prior to the Betrayer's self-destruction.

By 1500 all the cycles had been built up, and were beginning to decay. The sixteenth century, however, saw the emergence of the individual dramatist, and the growth of a new form of drama which, though it had medieval antecedents, was not

directly derived from the religious play. The principal ancestor of the Interlude was the *farce*, a knock-about entertainment, presented by a company of fools, and usually
exercising its fun at the expense of the respectable citizen. In
Germany, Nuremberg, and perhaps other towns, had their
Shrovetide Plays, at first anonymous, but composed towards
the middle of the sixteenth century by the prolific and accomplished HANS SACHS (1494–1576). The stuff of these
plays is very similar to that of the old *fabliaux*. A wandering
student tricks a housewife into giving him a bundle of her
second husband's clothes, on the excuse that he is just on his
way back from Paradise where he has met her first husband in
a sorry plight, clad in no more than the sheet and the hat he
was buried in. A horse thief cheats the peasants who have
caught him, and who are unwilling to hang him immediately
for fear that the crowd around the gibbet may trample down
their crops. He insists that they keep him in comfort until they
are ready to deal with him, and ends by stealing right and left,
and setting his captors at odds.

Similar plays were performed in the Netherlands, where the
Rederijker, middle-class guilds of drama and poetry lovers,
produced such serious moralities as *Everyman*, and organized
literary competitions and pageants. In England and France,
meanwhile, there grew up companies of interlude players
whose repertory was entirely made up of short farces. John
Heywood was the chief playwright in this genre in England,
while in France the anonymous author of *Maître Pierre
Pathelin* scored such a success that his rascally lawyer was still a
proverbial figure fifty years after the play's first presentation,
when Rabelais was writing his *Pantagruel*. For there are several
references in that book to Pathelin and his roll of cloth, of
which he had defrauded a tailor. Delighted at his easy victory,
Pathelin had then set up to give other men lessons in rascality,
but found himself cheated out of his fee by a wily shepherd
who proved too apt a pupil.

In its form *Maître Pierre Pathelin* (1464) lies half way between
the *sottie* – a playlet for a company of fools in cap and bells –
and the developed comedy of the seventeenth century. But so
rich is its simple humour, so well-contrived are its situations,

and so spare is its dialogue, that it must rank as the most entertaining French play before Molière. It is from this play that all Europe has drawn the phrase – repeated by Rabelais – 'But let us return to our muttons'.

But most interludes were far more fragmentary than this French masterpiece. They were, literally, plays suitable for performance between the courses of a banquet, at wedding festivities or, as in Italy, between the acts of a more serious, classical drama.

While drama in Italy made fresh beginnings under the influence of the revival in knowledge of the classics – and will therefore be considered in the next chapter – the Iberian peninsula remained the last stronghold of the old forms, from which the new drama developed without any radical break, the *auto* or religious play written by Lope or Calderón for the Corpus Christi festival linking directly on to the 'miracle' play and 'morality'.

The first of these Spanish primitives, JUAN DE ENCINA (1469–1529), was a writer of eclogues, the atmosphere of which will be familiar to anyone who remembers the sad and protracted story of the shepherd Grisóstomo and the cruel Marcela in the first part of *Don Quixote*. Encina mingled paganism and piety, and in his masterpiece presented a new version of the temptation of St Antony, in which the would-be saint abandoned his hermit's life for the pleasures of carnal love. Perhaps Encina himself felt the rival claims of the two worlds, which he saw so splendidly reconciled in Rome, at the worldly court of Pope Leo X, under whose patronage he lived for some time. From Italy he made a pilgrimage to Jerusalem and, having taken holy orders, there sang his first Mass. But he found Palestine a 'sterile and very stony' country, and was more at home in his native Salamanca, whose university was a humanist stronghold.

Encina's plays lack theatrical construction; passionate love-poetry, rustic humours, pastoral, parody, courtly gallantry, and a spice of anti-clericalism may have made a good Christmas entertainment for the Duke of Alba's household, but did not seriously advance the growth of a native drama.

Encina noted that there were more good shepherds than good priests in the world, and his successor, the second of the Spanish primitives, TORRES NAHARRO (*c.*1480–*c.*1532), though he also enjoyed the patronage of the Medici pope, was a great deal more bitter in his anti-clericalism than Encina. For him Rome was 'the fortress of evil'. His plays are more concentrated, and come nearer to attaining a real dramatic form, than do those of his predecessor in the school of Salamanca. His best comedy, *Himenea,* presents many of the features that were afterwards to be developed in the 'cloak and sword drama' of Lope de Vega and Calderón; the point of honour, the dialogue between servants which doubles the scene between their masters, the nocturnal serenade; all are present in embryo in Naharro's plays. But this early Spanish drama is essentially poetic, though with a satirical bite, and it is remarkable to-day rather for its detached lyrics in traditional measures than for its theatrical effectiveness.

The supreme master in this intermediate dramatic form, and the most important poet to concern himself with the stage before Shakespeare's time was the Portuguese, GIL VICENTE (*c.*1465–1539). About his life very little is known. He is generally identified with a court-goldsmith of that name, who flourished in Lisbon at the time when the plays were written, but it is not absolutely certain that this is the man. When Vicente began to write, the Portuguese language was in decay, and there was every possibility that with the next dynastic marriage the kingdom itself would be joined to that of Castile and Aragon. For the moment, however, Lisbon possessed a parvenu court which flourished on the growing sea- power of this little state. Vicente's earliest dramatic pieces were imitations of Encina's pastoral comedies, written in Castilian, but even from the first he displayed great individuality. His peasants were studied from the life; his impoverished gentlemen, crooked judges, and grasping friars were real characters, faithfully observed. Furthermore the poetry that informed his plays achieved for them a unity that his Spanish models had never attained; it lyricized the whole of the action. Vicente entitled his pieces farces, comedies, tragi-comedies, and *autos*, but there is no strict dividing line between one form and the other. All are lyrical and satirical by turns, yet without internal disharmonies; and all alike draw their themes from pastoral, mystery, morality, and farce, uniting them in a form as redolent of the Portuguese village as are Shakespeare's comedies of the forest of Arden.

As he developed Vicente began to write in Portuguese as well as in Spanish, on the whole reserving his own tongue for scenes of low life, and writing his grander scenes in Castilian. His two *autos* – or sacred plays – in the latter tongue, that of the *Four Seasons*, and that of *Sibila Cassandra*, show him at his most poetic and delicate. In the latter Cassandra, a village maid, refuses to marry despite the entreaties of Solomon, her suitor, of her three aunts and of her three uncles, Abraham, Isaiah, and Moses. First she excuses herself by offering a satirical picture of the miseries of marriage. Then she reveals her true reason. She has heard that one day God is to be incarnated in the womb of a virgin, and feels herself fitted to be the chosen maid. Now the play which has hitherto seemed to be a village comedy in a Portuguese setting, but for the strangely Biblical names of the heroine's relatives, shows itself to be a Nativity; and her peasant aunts and uncles begin to prophesy as these personages did in that primitive twelfth-century drama which grew out of the Messianic sermon. First her uncle Isaiah, after rebuking her for her conceit, announces in a lovely poetic passage that all nature's beauties are but heralds and prefigurations of the Virgin's. Then a Sibyllic aunt proclaims that the moment has now come, when justice is perverted, and faith cold, when the Church is the prisoner of greed, when the poor are oppressed, and shame and reason in eclipse. A curtain is then drawn back, and a cradle is revealed with four angels standing round it singing a lullaby. All the peasants worship the babe, and the *auto* ends with a song in praise of the maiden's beauty, which recalls the first of Galician love-songs.

> *Digas tú, el marinero*
> *que en las naves vivías,*
> *si la nave o la vela o la estrella*
> *es tan bella.*

(Tell me, sailor, who dwells in ships, if ship or sail or star are as beautiful.)

The play mingles lyricism and satire, reconciles the Jewish prophets with the pagan sibyls, and turns a peasant Cassandra into a prefiguration of Mary the Virgin, all in verse as sensitive to changes in tempo and feeling as an orchestral score.

Vicente's most important work, a trilogy on the subject of the Dance of Death, the first two pieces in Portuguese and the third in Spanish, derives directly from the 'morality' and gives the poet scope both for his anti-clerical satire and for some sinister humour; qualities which caused some of his work to be roughly handled, or even banned, by the Inquisition.

Typical of another vein in which Vicente excelled is the *Triunfo do Inverno* (*Winter's triumph*) a lyrical allegory designed for presentation at court, and somewhat resembling an English masque of the next century. Dancing, music, satire, and sheer farce are strung together on a thread of delicate fancy. Always Vicente is primarily a poet. Poetical too, and slightly ironic in their treatment of their material are his two romantic plays on themes from the *romances* of chivalry, *Dom Duardos* and *Amadís de Gaula*, while his loosely knit farces have wit, good humour, and some excellent character sketches.

Most of Gil Vicente's forty-four pieces have come down to us in corrupt texts. It is clear too that the primitive technique of his theatre limited his resources to those of a charade in costume. Yet no one with anything like his combination of talents appeared in the Peninsula before Lope de Vega, nor was any poet of that day so close to the popular imagination, so successful in welding the courtly and the rural, the medieval and the new, into something fresh and original. The great humanist Erasmus is said to have wished to learn Portuguese solely for the pleasure of reading Vicente's plays; and even to-day such a labour might seem sufficiently rewarding.

The intermediate drama of the Peninsula is, in all European literature, the truest link between the Middle Ages, whose dramatic and poetic inheritance Gil Vicente, in particular, used to the full, and the new writing of the Renaissance. There, it seems, behind the protective rampart of the Pyrenees, the transition from one world to another was less abrupt than in France, Italy or England. Poetic form underwent no violent changes; court and village were not suddenly rent apart; the pastoral convention was grafted naturally on to a poetry whose roots had always been in the countryside; gods and goddesses, nymphs and swains, all were transplanted to the bare Spanish uplands, to appear at real fountains and tend real flocks. So it is that the connexion between these lyrical dramatists and the great masters of the next century, Cervantes and Lope de Vega, is a close one. The break came later, when the Spanish Empire decayed, when satire at the expense of Church and State was no longer safe, and when lyrical conventions, founded on the reconciliation between medieval and renaissance practice, themselves hardened into mannerisms.

Chapter Six

THE LATER ITALIAN RENAISSANCE

For fifty years after the death of Petrarch and Boccaccio, Italian scholars continued to unearth the Latin past and, with the aid of such teachers of Greek as were available, to explore the largely unknown literature of Greece. The immediate results lay, however, rather in the improved and more Ciceronian form of their Latin writing than in any developments in the realm either of Greek scholarship or of the *latino volgare*, the common language of the Peninsula. During this time more centres of learning grew up to challenge Florence and Bologna. Now Rome, Naples, Ferrara, and Padua competed for the services of scholars. But, though the reputation of the Tuscan poets slowly grew there was no movement towards imitating them. At best their idiom came to be recognized as the literary language of Italy and other dialects yielded before it. The one outstanding name in the Tuscan writing of this interregnum is that of FRANCO SACCHETTI (*c*.1330–1400) a follower of Boccaccio, and the author of a collection of vigorous popular tales, the *Trecento Novelle* (300 *Tales*), also of much light poetry which was set to music by the composers of the new Florentine school.

The next century, however, saw a development, centred on Florence, which not only carried the rebirth of culture a great stage forward in Italy itself, but which also had a transforming effect on the rest of Western Europe. In the year 1438, faced by the certainty that what remained of his empire would speedily be overrun by the Turkish invader, the Byzantine Emperor sent a deputation of Greek churchmen to Italy, to call for help. At the Council of Florence in the next year the union of the two churches was proclaimed. Even if it was too late to rescue any material relics of the Byzantine world from the Turk, at least the cultural and religious heritage would be saved. The projected union, however, did not mature; nevertheless the *mysteria platonica*, the central core of Byzantine learning, was effectually transplanted to Italy.

Cosimo de Medici, the head of a great banking family whose fortune had been founded on the financing of the papacy, had recently returned from exile, to become the effectual ruler of the Florentine republic. Listening, it was said, to the lectures of George Gemistus Plethon, a member of the Byzantine delegation, he was so inspired by this scholar's interpretation of Plato that he decided, at the earliest opportunity, himself to found a Platonic Academy at Florence. The story is, perhaps, an over-simplification. What is certain is that Cosimo was discontented with the old humanistic learning of Petrarch's day and that he was looking for a more direct contact with the Greek tradition.

Little was heard of Cosimo's intentions for a full twenty years, until in 1459 he installed MARSILIO FICINO (1433–99), the son of his physician, in a villa at Careggi, close to the city, with a volume of Plato to translate into Latin. But the task entrusted to the young man was not merely a scholarly one. Cosimo, as he came near to death, was more closely drawn to the 'platonic mystery', and used Careggi as a country retreat in which to study the ancient learning. The 'sanctuary of contemplation' which he founded for Ficino soon came to be spoken of as the Academy, and there for some years after Cosimo's death Ficino continued with his work of translation, collecting around him many young men, but leaving the official *Studio*, or school of Florence to the orthodox humanists. It was not until the *Studio* broke up in violent quarrels between Platonists and Aristotelians that Ficino gained intellectual dominance in the city, and that his friends obtained the chief teaching posts.

The Platonism which Ficino brought to Florence could not by its very nature be a cold intellectual discipline. It was a way of life in which both contemplation and the arts played a part; a way of life neither wilfully pagan, nor hostile to Christianity, but one which was founded on mysteries that had survived in the East from a far earlier day. Cosimo's teacher, Gemistus Plethon, was a strange and impressive person who had made contact not only with Islam, but also with Zoroastrianism, with the teaching transmitted under the name of Hermes Trismegistus, and with the work of Plotinus. In his exposition of Plato, he invoked the traditions of Greece and of Christianity, of Persia, and of Egypt; and Ficino, in the direct line of descent from him, aimed at a reconciliation between religion and philosophy, between learning and morals, between the East and the West. Until 1489 he taught and worked without incurring the Church's hostility, and on one occasion even spoke from the pulpit of Santa Maria degli Angeli. His teaching, indeed, attracted Churchmen as well as representatives of the older generation of humanists and appears to have had wide connexions. He was linked, for instance, with what seems to have been a parallel organization, called the Brotherhood of the Magi, which met in the sacristy of San Marco.

The work of the Academy was not confined to the exposition of the Greeks, or of Dante, whom they placed on a level with them. Medicine, natural science, the astrology of planetary influences, the Pythagorean science of numbers: all were studied and expounded. Humanists visited the Academy from Oxford, Paris, and Cologne, and among its pupils was a group of young men who were to be the intellectual *élite* of Italy in the next generation: PICO DELLA MIRANDOLA (1463–94), who continued Ficino's efforts to reconcile religion and philosophy and who met with imprisonment, exile, and death by poisoning as his reward; ANGELO POLIZIANO a poet in both Latin and Italian, who filled the chair of classical rhetoric in the *Studio*; and LORENZO DE MEDICI, Cosimo's grandson and successor both as ruler of Florence and protector of the Academy, himself a poet, a patron of the arts and of Michelangelo in particular.

The Academy in due course disintegrated under the stress of wars and of the death of its original members; and the golden age of Florence, the age of its last great painters, sculptors, and architects, of L. B. Alberti, a member of the Accademia who was all three and a poet as well, of Botticelli, Gozzoli, and Pollaiuolo, ended with it. But as Burckhardt, the great historian of the Renaissance, recognized, the Florentine Academy contributed motive power to almost every important development of the next century. After its break-up, many of its members supported Savonarola in his attempts to purify the Church from within, even though this popular preacher was a declared enemy of the Arts.

But by now the alliance between Platonism and Christianity had broken down. The sensuality, the luxury, and the immorality of the papal court were blamed on the philosophy to which the Borgias and Medicis paid lip-service. 'Plato teaches arrogance and Aristotle godlessness', was now the cry; and violent hostility to the gross extravagance of the Roman court, which squandered much of what it gained by the sale of Indulgences and like practices on such buildings as the new St Peter's and on the commissioning of works of art, reinforced the puritanical aspect of the growing Reformation movement.

Nevertheless the critics and reformers north of the Alps themselves owed a great debt to the Academy. For through the agency of Johann Reuchlin, who had been its guest at Florence, it certainly contributed both to the thought of Reuchlin's friend Erasmus, who did not go so far as to join Luther, and to Luther's movement also, which was so firmly founded on a new reading of the Bible.

The direct influence of the Academy in Italy waned, and by the next century the tradition which Plethon had preached was to be discovered in some of its purity only in the thought of one or two eccentrics upon whom the Church waged pitiless war. TOMMASO CAMPANELLA (1568–1639), a heretical friar, a political idealist, and the author of some interesting poetry, and GIORDANO BRUNO (1548–1600) the remorseless enemy of medieval philosophy, who spent most of his life in exile, who during his stay in England gained the friendship and support of Sir Philip Sidney, and who was betrayed on venturing to return to Italy, where after nine years in the prisons of the Church he was burnt at the stake.

While it is impossible to register all the more important influences that the Academy may have had on the movements of the sixteenth century, its immediate effect on Italian poetry was to raise the prestige of Dante and of the Tuscan idiom, and to encourage the growth of Petrarchism.

Outstanding among the new writers was ANGELO POLIZIANO (1454–94) a poet of great originality, who wrote in Italian, in Latin, and even in Greek. He composed love lyrics of great but fragile beauty, and a pastoral idyll on the subject of Orpheus, in the form of a play as loosely constructed and as variously lyrical as those of Gil Vicente were to be in the next century. The legend of Orpheus was a story pregnant with symbolism for the Florentine school. For in his person was embodied the Renaissance's own myth, of the divine inspiration of art. Orpheus with his music moved all nature and the animal kingdom to follow him; by its power he was able to penetrate even to the realm of the shades, there to bargain with the infernal powers themselves for the return of his Eurydice. In this last act, despite its final failure, the Greek enchanter took on at least one aspect of the Saviour himself. For had not Christ, after the Crucifixion, descended into Hell, there to preach to the shades of the famous dead? And had He not brought back with Him the Old Testament worthies?

In the previous, Gothic phase of civilization, the arts had existed as the handmaids of theology. The painter's, sculptor's, and architect's task had been to build and beautify the Church, the musician's to write and sing its anthems, and the poet's to praise the divine creation and expound the mysteries of doctrine. But now art seemed itself to be of divine inspiration; and the true artist stood, like Orpheus, as a mediator between the upper and lower worlds, capable of descending into the realm of unredeemed Nature, and of endowing what he found there with divine shape: an office, incidentally, which Rilke still claimed for himself when he wrote his *Duineser Elegien* four hundred years later. Man was now drawn in the centre of the Universe, and life on earth assumed the importance that Dante had given to the Eternal. 'When I investigate,' wrote that Florentine paragon Leon Battista Alberti, who was at the same time architect, sculptor, and painter, poet, prose-writer and Academician, and a master both in Latin and in Italian, 'and when I discover that the forces of the heavens and the planets are within ourselves, then truly I seem to be living among the gods.'

The best of Poliziano's poetry is the poetry of one dwelling amongst the gods. Godlike is the prowess of his hero Giuliano de Medici, and enchanting the beauty of the divine Simonetta Vespucci in his unfinished masterpiece written in their honour. In these *Stanzas for the Joust* the popular *ottava rima* used by Boccaccio for honest narrative, is polished till each stanza sparkles like a diamond: in the *Orfeo*, where he turned the mystery play to profane use, Poliziano not only advanced half way towards the secular drama, but in its lyrical passages achieved a pagan lightness in which few poets of the Renaissance were his equals; and in his love lyrics he combined a classical purity of form with an apparent spontaneity derived from the popular Florentine poetry of the day.

Poliziano dwelt, if only for fleeting moments, on these godlike heights. But LORENZO DE MEDICI the Magnificent (1449–92) his patron, and the protector of the Academy, lingered below in the world of Nature, and never rose into the realm of the ideal at all. A poet of great skill and imitative powers, he wrote parodies of Dante and of Petrarch, and also poems that showed their serious influence. He composed a religious play, for presentation in his own palace, and even short stories. But at his best, in his love-poetry, he showed himself as a simpler successor to Petrarch, a poet of carnal love and of natural beauty, who used the mythological imagery, now coming into fashion, with taste and delicacy. One feels in his sonnets that long familiarity with Platonic scholars has rather reinforced than diminished his commonplace pleasure in the things of this life. He may betray some shame at his lowly preoccupations, but honesty will out; and when in his *canzonetta* on madness he talks of both wanting and not wanting a woman, we recognize that, though he may pay some service to the idealisms of the *dolce stil nuovo*, he is bound by all his bourgeois ancestry quite as closely to Angiolieri of the 'trivial themes'. Perhaps what he loved best in the Academic retreat of Careggi was not the discussions, but that rural ease celebrated by Petrarch before him; for the flowers and trees, the brooks and birds of his sonnets have the enchanting freshness of gardens visible in the backgrounds of the Crucifixions and Annunciations of the painters whom he supported. He was more at home in a gay city crowd, as so many of his Carnival poems prove, than in the conclaves of scholars.

This second phase of Petrarchism crystallized also in the poetry of PIETRO BEMBO (1470–1547), the son of a member of Ficino's Academy, who was himself a great defender of the Tuscan tongue against Latin and against theorists who held that literary Italian ought to draw on other dialects, and even to borrow from foreign tongues. Bembo was a traditionalist who made Petrarch's *Rime* a model for his own and who, by exercising virtual dictatorship over vernacular literature, was largely responsible for hardening the Petrarchan form and themes into a rigid convention. With him begins a new mannerism which was to culminate in the purely decorative style of Marino. Bembo was in his life a typical Renaissance churchman who combined scholarship, wealth, good taste, and paternity with the highest honours that the Church could bestow: a bishopric and a cardinal's hat.

Poliziano, Lorenzo de Medici, and Bembo were agreed, as were Tasso, Spenser, Camões, and Milton after them, in their belief in the divine inspiration of art. Horatian rationalism was not to reappear as an aesthetic theory for a full two centuries. Not all the poets of Lorenzo's time, however, subscribed to this exalted view of poetry. LUIGI PULCI (1432–84) was a close friend of Lorenzo's, and no lover of the Academy, whose chief he caricatured as the enchanter Malazzi in his epic *Morgante*. The poem is a racy treatment of the Charlemagne stories in *ottava rima*, and in a style inherited from Boccaccio and Sacchetti. Pulci is a master of burlesque; his principal characters are comic, and his broad picture of the age of chivalry a mockery. Pulci took the tales as he found them on the streets. What we see is a little bourgeois world in which the heroes have come down from their pedestals, and the poet guys his own craft – as did Rabelais after him, though in prose – by making mock invocations and quoting mock authorities. Even the death of Orlando, which might have tempted him to write a serious passage, is a piece of buffoonery. Pulci makes death ridiculous. For him battlefields are mere scenes of grotesque butchery, and Hell is a kitchen scarcely capable of coping with the multitude of souls that are expected to descend when Christian meets Saracen.

The popular tradition was stronger in Florence than elsewhere in Italy, for here popular institutions survived. The Florentine constitution was in many ways too elaborate to be workable, and the Medici family possessed virtual control of the state. But the middle class of bankers, merchants, and craftsmen preserved their rights, at the expense of both nobles and poor; and popular forms of art consequently flourished. The strength of the somewhat experimental literature, of which it was a centre in the fifteenth century, lay therefore in the cross-fertilization of the new Platonism with a sound and humorous local tradition; there was a compensating weakness, however, in the failure of its poets to commit themselves entirely to writing in Tuscan. Their best work was never long sustained.

The two Italian poets of the fifteenth century who worked on a large scale, and whose poems stood as examples to their greater successors in the age to come, were neither of them Florentines, nor was either close to any popular tradition of vernacular writing.

MATTEO MARIA BOIARDO (1441–94), whose unfinished romantic epic *Orlando innamorato* was a serious treatment of the popular stories which had given Pulci a theme for his buffoonery, was from Emilia, and throughout his life served the noble family of Este, who rewarded him with posts at their court and with governorships. In this brief golden age, before the irruption of the French into Italy turned the country into a battleground, fought over by Frenchmen and Spaniards to the ruin of the Italians themselves, the Estes' court at Ferrara was one of many humanistic centres, and Boiardo one of many talented amateurs, writing sometimes in Latin, sometimes in Italian, with one eye on patrons and preferment and the other on the possibilities of a country retreat, away from the intriguing and competitive life of the court. For if there was one thing that most poets of this day shared, it was a nostalgia for rural peace, which even the poorest of them painted with a certain freshness. It was this yearning that lent force to the pastoral convention.

The second serious poet of this late fifteenth century, JACOPO SANNAZARO (*c.*1457–1530), though also the servant of princes, constructed out of his regrets for the loss of a juvenile and rural Eden, an Arcadia, based on those of Theocritus and Virgil, which became the model for the many Arcadias of the next century. 'If Pope was able to take it for granted that "Pastoral is an image of what they call the Golden Age",' wrote C. S. Lewis, 'this was largely the result of Sannazzaro's *Arcadia*.' It is a narrative, told in a prose enriched with echoes of epic, and with connecting poems put into the mouths of singing shepherds, whose world is painted as the ideal alternative to that of city and camp. It is the world which Poussin later illustrated with his vision of slow-moving pastoral dances, of stately ruins and grave sojourners in a landscape of unvarying fair weather.

Sannazaro's *Arcadia*, like that of Philip Sidney, which followed it, is no longer readable, except for an occasional passage; nor did it seem so even to the generation that succeeded him, for it was speedily rewritten with comic relief inserted by Francesco Berni, and its original text remained unknown until the nineteenth century.

A greater poet than Boiardo, in the same tradition, LUDOVICO ARIOSTO (1474–1533) was, like him, attached to the Este court at Ferrara, which he served successfully as statesman and administrator, as director of court entertainments and as governor of a province, until he retired to revise for yet a second time his *Orlando furioso*. This was a continuation of Boiardo's poem, which he had begun nine years after Boiardo's death, and which he had published in its first form in 1516. Like Boiardo, the servant of a court where aristocratic chivalry was admired if not practised, Ariosto stood midway between an acceptance of these ideals, of which Malory had celebrated the passing forty years before, and the contemptuous disbelief of a Pulci. His tale, therefore, varies in tone from romance to irony, from picturesque heroics to mere descriptiveness. Discursively, in the *ottava rima*, Ariosto retells the tale of Roland, with greater mastery of language and construction than Boiardo, and with a greater sense of character. The story is episodic, one set of persons yielding to another – as in a Dickens novel – and reappearing in the narrative a canto or two farther on. But underlying the whole of this fast-moving story of infinite ramifications, is a spirit of slight mockery, only half-conscious perhaps, which emerges most fruitfully in such a description as that of Astolfo's journey to the moon in search of Orlando's wits. But there is another side to Ariosto's achievement: his power of developing character and situation, of showing the stages of the amazon Bradamante's passion for Ruggiero, in portraying the loves of Isabella and Zerbino. If he lacks the high seriousness of the epic poet, he has at least a zest for the pageant of life, which makes him readable as a fantastic novelist.

Ariosto was a poet who wrote entirely from an artist's standpoint, without thought for philosophy or religion. At a time when no one dared to proclaim himself independent of his forerunners, Latin or Tuscan, Ariosto boldly continued Boiardo's story in his own way, deliberately electing to be first among the Italians rather than a poor second among the writers of Latin, with such results that he made himself the most accomplished poet between Dante and Tasso.

Contemporary with Ariosto and with the wars of invasion which reduced Italy to an economically depressed battle-ground, whose princes became clients to one nation of barbarians or the other, to France or to Spain, two prose writers endeavoured to give the country a sense of her past, and of her national destiny. One of them, moreover, NICCOLÒ MACHIAVELLI (1469–1527), went so far as to advocate new and better methods of government, which he outlined in *Il Principe*, his book of advice to a non-existent ideal prince. Machiavelli had been in the service of the Florentine republic, which he had vainly striven to defend both from mercenary armies and from the Medicis, who had again been driven into exile. A year after their return to power, after being tortured and finally acquitted on a charge of conspiracy, Machiavelli employed the enforced idleness of a sentence of house-arrest in the writing of this book, which he addressed to a minor member of the Medici family. His attitude was one of unashamed realism; things must be looked at as they are, without reference to any ideal possibilities. To him experience and intellect counted for everything, and by their light alone a proper constitution must be devised. This is the basic doctrine of the Middle Ages turned upside down: and it bears no relation either to the theories of the Renaissance, with their desire for a return to pure spirituality. The decay of Italy had gone too far for reform: medieval theology was now repeated mechanically by self-interested and worldly princes of the Church; and the wisdom of the Academy had been perverted into a doctrine of art for art's sake – or was preserved by a few men, who were looked upon by all sides as heretics.

So the science of man was born, and with it came the call to Italian nationalism. Machiavelli wrote a history of Florence, and FRANCESCO GUICCIARDINI (1483–1540), the Florentine ambassador to Spain, embarked on his history of contemporary Italy, whose birth he dated from the French invasions. Impatient of all theory, Guicciardini was even more of a realist than Machiavelli, with whom he held discussions.

The chief theorist of this science of man, however, which was born from the ebb of Platonic idealism, was a writer whose influence was to be as potent for good as Machiavelli's was for evil and crude power-politics, far beyond the borders of Italy. BALDASSARE CASTIGLIONE (1478–1529) defined the Renaissance gentleman. The ideal courtier, of whom he drew a portrait in the book of that name, must combine learning and good manners, must subscribe to a code of chivalry and also of courtly love. His book is far from being a mere directive, as was *The Prince*, for those anxious for political success. Castiglione does not only praise a prince for his strength, but rather for his power of attracting gentlemen to his court. Man is no longer seen as created in the image of God, but he is encouraged to exercise the highest human qualities: to behave with charm, naturalness, and dignity, to exercise his virtues as patron, philosopher, and poet. It was to this high ideal that Sir Philip Sidney aspired, and it was as the ideal courtier that he was respected in his life and almost worshipped after his death.

As the early sixteenth century progressed, many ladies and gentlemen wrote charming poetry in the Petrarchan mode, which had become the accepted mode of all amateurs after its codification by Pietro Bembo. The sonnets of MICHELANGELO (1475–1564), written in his old age, of VITTORIA COLONNA (1492–1525), and of GASPARA STAMPA (1523–54) show how this medium could be used by a poet who had known real experience, to convey something more than well-turned platitudes.

In addition to the Petrarchan convention there also persisted in Italy the tradition of the *Decameron*, and many volumes of tales were printed in which ingenuity of plot, sudden changes of fortune, magical transformations, and surprising methods of winning wealth or women prevailed over any interest in character or motive. These tales, which won more than a passing popularity, proved splendid quarries to our Elizabethan dramatists and even to Molière at the end of the seventeenth century, who found them a perfect source for ready-made plots.

The Italian Theatre of this period can best be considered here, in relation to the literature of the age. For it was an entirely literary production unconnected with the drama of the Middle Ages. It is important, moreover, not for its own achievement, which was small, but rather for its influence on more substantial developments in England, Spain, and France, and for its effect on the history of music. At its birth, it was hampered by too close a respect for classical models – Plautus and Terence for comedy, Seneca for tragedy – and for its unquestioning adherence to the rule of the Three Unities – of plot, of time, and of scene – a law which theorists based on their reading of Aristotle's *Poetics*. The new Italian theatre was a court theatre, which played indoors to a small audience; which imitated a classical stage in the form of a classical façade, pierced by a number of doors representing the houses of various characters; and which made some early experiments in lighting. The plots of the new court comedies followed stereotyped lines; identical twins, romantic young ladies in male disguise, duped husbands, bawds, cheats, and misers provided the expected humours, though with a little greater variety than that of Roman comedy. For, from Boccaccio and other story-tellers, these early dramatists derived romantic detail that they did not find in their crisper and more single-minded Latin models.

Ariosto, whose four comedies are some of the best of the time, forestalled Jonson in the plot and the leading character of *Il Negromante* (*The Necromancer*) a play as rich in quacks and astrologers as *Volpone*. Again in *La Scolastica* (*The Academic Comedy*) he drew on contemporary student life and, placing his scene in Ferrara itself, produced something both hilarious and slap up to date. Macchiavelli too, wrote one comedy *La Mandragola* (*The Mandrake*) on the subject of credulity, with a plot akin to that of one of Boccaccio's more salacious stories. It tells of a husband so gullible that he connives at his own cuckolding, in the belief that only by compelling a stranger to make love to his wife can he save himself from the evil effects of the mandrake, a drug which has been administered to her to remedy her barrenness.

Derivatives of these Italian comedies can be seen in *The Comedy of Errors*, *The Taming of the Shrew*, and in *Much Ado about Nothing*. But, in the two latter at least, Shakespeare derives great advantage from the fact that he is writing for a live theatre and an audience far more various and far larger than that of a single Italian city. He cannot rely either on the humour of the past; he is providing entertainment for men without knowledge of Latin, for whom an allegedly Italian setting must be heavily coloured with English detail.

For the Italian Senecan tragedy *Titus Andronicus* may serve as an example. There is the same plethora of blood. For a tragedy, by the Senecan definition, was a play concerned with the bloody overthrow of some great character, 'Enter Demetrius and Chiron, with Lavinia, ravished; her hands cut off, and her tongue cut out', might as easily come from Giraldi Cinthio's *Orbecche* as from this least successful of Shakespearian tragedies. Cinthio, in presenting his play to the Ferrarese court, promised them 'tears, sighs, anguish, terrors, and frightsome deaths', and threw in an incest and a ghost for good measure. Trissino's *Sofonisba*, rated in its time above the *Oedipus* of Sophocles, is less horrific but somewhat dull.

Italy's principal contribution to European drama lay rather in the pastoral or lyrical play, a development from Poliziano's *Orfeo* which reached its culmination in Torquato Tasso's *Aminta* and Guarini's *Pastor fido* (*Faithful Shepherd*), both of which belong to the end of the sixteenth century. After this, in the hands of a first-class musical genius, Claudio Monteverde, the pastoral drifted out of the field of the drama altogether into that of opera. For, with its singing shepherds and its Arcadian background, it had already come to depend rather on the tunes of its songs and on its orchestral *intermezzi* than on its dramatic dialogue.

This mixed form of art steadily gained the favour of the Italian courts at the expense of the drama proper. But, in the principal cities of Italy, the sixteenth century saw the growth of a popular theatre, the *Commedia dell' Arte* with companies of professional players, and a stock repertory.

Chapter Seven

REFORMATION IN GERMANY AND
RENAISSANCE IN FRANCE

WITH Italy a battleground between France and Spain, the leadership in literary production, not surprisingly, passed from her to the two stronger powers, whose literatures were as yet but little affected by the new ideas. The immediate benefit fell to France, whose scholars and noblemen, travelling in the train of her invading armies, quickly made contact with the courtly culture of the Italian princes, and adapted it for themselves.

France's military triumphs on the field of Italy were more glorious than permanent. Her capture of the book trade from the Venetian printers, on the other hand, brought her permanent advantages far greater than the temporary possession of Milan, or an impermanent alliance with the Pope or the Venetian republic itself.

Printing, although a German invention, had not been developed to the full north of the Alps. For too long the craftsman's endeavour had been to produce by mechanical means the best imitation of manuscript that was possible. Books, therefore, remained expensive, editions were small, and even then collectors often rejected the machine-made substitute in favour of a hand-written copy. Printers made small profits and often found it difficult to remain in business, until in 1494 Aldus Manutius adopted entirely new methods of production.

Manutius had been a gentleman in the service of Pico de la Mirandola until the moment when he inherited a small press in Venice, which he immediately turned over to the production of cheap editions. Freeing himself from the tyranny of manuscript imitation, he used light italic types, replanned the printed page so that it appeared rather grey than black, and reduced the size of his volumes to a handy 8vo. The result was revolutionary, but its benefits were no longer confined to Italy after Manutius's death in 1515, when the lead passed to

Paris, with Lyons, an important *entrepôt* on the road to Italy, as the second centre of the trade.

Now the presses were turning out unprecedented quantities of Latin classics, works in Greek, books of chivalry, devotional books, and such masterpieces of the vernacular as the still popular *Roman de la Rose*. King Louis XII had issued an edict in favour of printing, exempting it from heavy duties. But important though this encouragement was to the growth of French culture, his successor, Francis I, and that king's enlightened sister, Queen Marguerite of Navarre, played an even greater part in the stimulation of literature. Hitherto the provincial nobility had kept their circles of poets and entertainers; the *Rhétoriqueurs*, the last generation of *ballade*-writers after the fashion of Machaut, depended on the Dukes of Britanny, Bourbon, and Burgundy. But with the eclipse of the grand nobility under the new centralized monarchy, an event parallel with the contemporary extinction of the great families in England during the Wars of the Roses, patronage had come to depend principally on the royal court, and Francis I, deeply committed to the Italian wars, also openly favoured the new Italian styles of writing.

While France in the beginning of the sixteenth century was beginning to take over and naturalize the triple inheritance of humanism, the Petrarchan style, and Platonic philosophy; Germany, without any proper national existence, without a literary language, and without a vigorous court life, either at its imperial centre or in its ducal capitals, was able to accept only the scholarly lessons of humanism, which produced for her no vernacular literature, but precipitated fundamental questionings in the field of theology and ecclesiastical organization.

The study of the Bible in Hebrew and Reuchlin's interest in the Jewish philosophy of the Kabbala led to conflicts in which the outstanding voice was that of DESIDERIUS ERASMUS (1469–1536), a Dutchman who wrote in Latin, and whose edition of the New Testament, translated from the original Greek, remained for centuries the basis of all New Testament scholarship. But when out of this new Bible reading, which called into question the authority of the Vulgate, or standard Latin version, and out of discontents with the Church's corruption, there arose a Protestant movement led by Martin Luther, a humanist only in so far as humanism would serve his theological ends, Erasmus declared himself reluctantly on the Catholic side, of which he had been an indignant critic, and a large number of humanists made the same decision.

Thereafter Reformation and Renaissance parted company. But Luther, though lacking any such purpose, strongly stimulated the growth of literary German. For his Bible translation, his hymns, and his polemical writings set a standard for the direct and homely use of language, and the Protestants' use of a church service in the vernacular prompted much poetry, some of which rose in the seventeenth century to a very high level.

German remained, however, up to the age of Goethe, a language with no international standing, and all scholarly writing which hoped to find a considerable audience had perforce to be in Latin. If books written in the vernacular did occasionally gain renown, it was in their Latin translations. Such a book was Sebastian Brant's *Narrenschiff* (*Ship of Fools*) of 1494, a verse satire in which a hundred fools set out for Narragonia, each representing one of the follies of the age. The *Narrenschiff* is medieval in tone, as are the tales of Till Eulenspiegel, which describe a series of pranks played by a roguish peasant on priest, craftsman, and respectable citizen. The book is typical of Low German humour, in both senses of that adjective. From Germany also emanated the original and equally medieval stories of Faust, who sold his soul to the devil, and of Fortunatus and his inexhaustible purse, both of which were first put into literary shape at the end of the sixteenth century.

Whereas Germany took only so much from the Renaissance as made for the Reformation, France, while offering a less fertile soil for theological revolution, accepted the new writing, and by the middle of the sixteenth century possessed a native group of writers more brilliant than any which Italy or any other country had known since the days of the *dolce stil nuovo*.

The initial Italian influence on the most interesting of the *Grands Rhétoriqueurs*, JEAN LEMAIRE DE BELGES (1473–*c.*1524), was somewhat like that of classical architecture on the building of Elizabethan England; it provided him with a number of additional decorations to apply to his already heavily decorated poems. Advocating a close alliance between Florentine poetry and French, he made some experiments in the writing of *terza rima*, which proved as incapable of striking root in French soil as in English. But by using the *alexandrine*, a neglected medieval metre, he prepared a far more valuable legacy for the poets of the Pléiade and for their successors. In his large prose work too, the *Illustration de Gaule et Singularités de Troie*, he reproduced the story that the Franks had first sprung from Trojan ancestors, a patriotic myth which was afterwards used by Ronsard for his unsuccessful epic, *La Franciade*.

Lemaire de Belges, for all his decorative Petrarchism, remained a poet of the late Middle Ages, as did CLÉMENT MAROT (1496–1544), the son of a leading *rhétoriqueur* and the chief poet of the transition who, but for the circulation of the new ideas, and but for the demands of the court to which he was attached, might well have been content to develop the techniques which his father had taught him in his apprentice days. It was fashion that made him the first French sonneteer. For the best of Marot is to be found in his occasional poetry: in such an Epistle as that addressed to the king in which he begs to be let out of prison, and in that other in which he pleads his empty purse, and tells how he has been robbed by his valet. Here we are in the world of Villon. For, like Villon, Marot drew no dividing line between his poetry and his life. He was a master of the *rondeau* too, and celebrated his love for a court lady in that measure with all the delicacy of Charles d'Orléans; and he originated the *blason*, a form of verse patently medieval in its inspiration, with his *Blason du beau tétin* (*Blazon of the Fair Breast*), which set all his fellow poets to work addressing the other members of the female body; the nose, the voice, the knee, the mouth, and other more hidden charms.

Only in his verse renderings of the Psalms was Marot in any real sense an innovator; and these cost him his exile from

France. Though indifferent to religious disputes, Marot was, nevertheless, reluctantly caught up in them. Thanks to his *Thirty Psalms*, he found himself identified with the Protestant cause, where his lukewarm sympathy no doubt really lay. In his youth he had been imprisoned for a piece of silly bravado, for publicly eating bacon during Lent; and in 1529 he had written in defence of a Lutheran burnt at the stake. Several times he had been imprisoned and several times pardoned, and each time had owed his release to his patroness, the king's sister Marguerite of Navarre, herself the author of *The Heptameron*, a set of tales in the style of Boccaccio. But now, towards the end of his life, he was compelled to take the side of the Reformation, though once established in its centre, at Geneva, he found Calvin's stronghold of piety unsympathetic. When he arrived, he offered to complete his version of the Psalms, but was refused a subsidy by the City Council. He was then suspected by the pious elders of being given to gambling, which he probably was; and so he departed for Savoy, whence he sent poems to France for every state occasion, in the hope of being pardoned yet again. But his hopes were vain, and he died at Turin, leaving a son to continue his craft.

Equally uncomfortable, as a liberal caught between the uncompromising extremes of totalitarian scholasticism and reform, was France's first great modern writer, FRANÇOIS RABELAIS (*c*.1483–1553). A humanist by conviction and early education, a worldly monk, a physician skilful in his art, and twice the secretary of one of the great political churchmen of the day, Cardinal du Bellay, Rabelais stood throughout his life for the inquiring mind. All dogmas were to him ridiculous, and there were few men to whom he could offer wholehearted allegiance: only Erasmus is referred to with unfailing respect throughout his great five-volume work. For the rest he mocked the ancient learning, while rejoicing in its minutiae, and hymned the new, invoking his readers to drink deep of its heady wine. But Rabelais was a master of mystification and ambiguity. In praising the bottle symbolically, he also praises it literally, for it is hard not to take the conversation of the boozers, in the fifth chapter of *Gargantua*, as a paean in counterpoint in praise of liquor, pure and unadulterated. Again, though he jibes at monks and friars as tipplers, lechers, and holy-pious frauds, one of the heroes of his book is a friar, stalwart Brother John of the Hashes. It is possible, too, to read into his love for his heroes, the good old king Gargantua and his adventurous son Pantagruel, an enthusiasm for the national monarchy, but at the same time one finds, in the chapter devoted to King Picrochole and his campaigns, some well-placed satire against such wars of aggression as the French monarchy was then waging in Italy. What François Rabelais unfailingly stands for throughout the *Gargantua* and the *Pantagruel* is freedom to criticize by satire, freedom of literary invention, and freedom of the imagination.

His large work is uneven, since it was sixteen years in the writing, years in which it and its author were under sporadic fire from the theologians of the University of Paris, stubborn and obscurantist defenders of the old scholasticism, whom he attacked at first openly, and then beneath the thinnest of disguises, throughout his five books.

These books, while united by their characters, differ considerably in their subjects. The *Pantagruel*, the first to be written, is transparently propagandist in its advocacy of a humanistic education, and in its attack on the Sorbonne. There is also a great deal of mockery in it at the expense of the romances and books of chivalry then in vogue, which were later to give Cervantes a butt for his satire. The *Gargantua* which, though it tells of Pantagruel's father, was written second in the series, develops the subject of humanistic education, and outlines a utopian scheme for a humanists' retreat, an abbey for both sexes, whose motto and watchword was 'Do as you will.' In this book there is more realistic detail than in the first. The setting of Gargantua's wars, for instance, is in the country where Rabelais had spent his own youth, each hamlet being referred to as a mighty city. Even the dispute between the good old king and the foolish Picrochole refers obliquely to a long ago feud between Rabelais' own father and a neighbour over some fishing rights. The third book, with its long account of Panurge's visits to a multitude of oracles to inquire whether, if he marries, his wife will be faithful, breaks entirely new ground and forms

Rabelais' contribution to the stock medieval debate on the nature of women; while the fourth book tells of a long voyage, in which Rabelais parodies the travellers' tales of Jacques Cartier and other contemporaries, who were even then exploring uncharted oceans. But it owes some debt also to such ancient travellers through imaginary worlds as the Greek Lucian, author of *The True History*. The fifth book, which was put together after its author's death and was perhaps completed by another hand, traces the voyage to its goal at the Oracle of the Bottle, whose only advice is 'Drink!'

Rabelais is a sheer and astounding master of technique, and of language, as capable as James Joyce after him of abrupt variations of style, of satire by parody, and of full-blooded comic invention. His coarseness is the coarseness of the *fabliaux*; his humour that of a man captivated by the endless variety of comical possibilities in every situation, of a scholar who suspects pedantry everywhere, of a man with a vast carnal appetite, which amuses rather than disgusts him. He shows few signs of suffering from a bad conscience like Swift's.

In his life, he was no happier than Marot. Violently critical of Church corruption, he showed sympathy with the Protestants, however, rather because they were persecuted than for their reformed theology. Like Marot also, he put his faith in the royal house and in patrons who were not always powerful enough to protect him. His attitude was that of a sceptic who did not doubt the fundamental tenets of the Catholic faith, of a humanist who had hopes that the growth of knowledge would one day lead to a better organization of society, at least for such an educated minority as he placed in his abbey at Thélème.

A speculative intellectual who ended as a complete unbeliever and only owed his immunity from punishment to the protection of the Queen of Navarre was BONAVENTURE DE PÉRIERS (*c.*1510–44). After collaborating in the Protestant translation of the Bible, and himself making a French version of Plato's *Lysis*, he wrote four allegedly mythological dialogues which were suspected of pouring scorn on the whole

Christian revelation. This *Cymbalum mundi* was, however, sufficiently cryptic for its author's purpose to be in doubt. Was the Philosopher's stone, brought to earth by the god Mercury, intended to stand for the Gospels? Was the god himself meant to represent Jesus? Were the three learned men who discussed its interpretation caricatures of Luther, Bucer, and Erasmus? The details of de Périers's prosecution have not survived, nor is his book itself much read. It is, however, a masterpiece of sly narrative, as are his *Nouvelles récréations et joyeux devis*, short stories with a broad, peasant tang. As a poet, he is not altogether independent of Marot. His poem on the rose takes many lines to offer to virgins the advice which Herrick was able to compress into four brief quatrains. He is more original in his contribution to the *Blasons du corps féminin*, an address to the navel, which leads him into strange and Platonic speculations concerning the origin of souls, the primitive Androgyne – who would of course be navelless – and the methods of contemplation practised by orthodox monks.

The second great French prose writer of the sixteenth century, MICHEL DE MONTAIGNE (1533–92) belonged entirely to the new world of sceptical humanism. He was a lawyer and country gentleman who let life teach him its lessons, and who wrote them down in the form of essays; the form itself is of his own invention. At first his subjects were chiefly drawn from his reading. Deeply under the influence of a fellow humanist and fellow lawyer, ÉTIENNE DE LA BOÉTIE, (1530–63), a man of considerably more passion than Montaigne and a fervent advocate of tolerance, Montaigne adopted a line of moderate Catholicism, which allowed him to preserve his neutrality during the wars of religion. From de la Boétie he learned the value of friendship, and of a steadfast spirit, and the necessity of translating one's knowledge into terms of everyday living. The early death of his friend was the most profound experience of his life; one which kept ever before his mind the insecurity of earthly honours and possessions. His legal career was but moderately successful, since he was neither eloquent nor active as a place-seeker. Twice mayor of Bordeaux, he acquitted himself satisfactorily in his office; but at the end of his life, when the offer of a good court appointment came, he refused it, preferring to spend the last years of his life quietly on his estates.

The earliest question which he strove to answer in his casual writings was the Stoic's; 'How can a man live and die with dignity?' His conclusions, in keeping with this new age of individualism, echoed Seneca's: man must cultivate will and reason. In pursuit of reason, he read voraciously in French and Latin, and was thus carried beyond the stoical position. From the new astronomy of Copernicus, he learned that man is not the centre of the universe; and Pliny taught him how little man differs from the animals. 'What do I know?' he asked. Accepting the doctrine of Pyrrhonism, he learnt to stomach the fact that reason taught him nothing. That all things were relative, that what was true in one land and age was untrue in another, that one must not judge: such is the practical wisdom to be extracted from his *Apology* for the Catalan theologian Raymond Sebond, whose work he had translated. Montaigne then turned to active affairs, left the estate which he had inherited from his father, and travelled in Germany, Switzerland, and Italy.

Now there was no subject left for him to study but himself. At the age of forty-seven, he had cut the ground of objective science from under his feet and, least introspective of men though he was, was driven to autobiography. But travel opened his mind to new impressions; the countryside, its inhabitants, the monuments of antiquity gave him practical and delightful illustrations of the relativism which he had hitherto accepted rather austerely. Journeying from spa to spa, in search of relief from his distressing disease of the stone, he found many things to note, to consider, and to refer to the arbitrament of his one constant, his own temperament. Recalled to France by his election as mayor of Bordeaux, he spent four years tactfully trying to reconcile enemies who were soon to be at one another's throats. When his second term was up, plague was raging, the wars of religion were inevitable, and what he felt most strongly was that his writing had been interrupted by his spell of practical affairs. Now he resumed his self-portrait, not out of any feeling that he was unique, but in order to draw a representative man. 'Everyone looks ahead, but I look within: my only concern is with myself. I never cease to reflect on myself; I observe myself and note the taste of myself': such a statement might seem to prelude the squirming frankness of Rousseau. Occasionally, Montaigne is over-intimate, in the revelation of sexual and clinical details. But for him 'Every man bears within him the complete pattern of the human condition'. Montaigne looked in himself for the features which united him with his fellow men. Now the supreme virtue in his eyes is moderation; there can be no stoical gestures in the face of approaching death, and the acceptance of beauty where he finds it is more important to him than the stubborn pursuit of truth: reason and faith must each be allowed their domains.

Montaigne outlined no philosophical system; what life taught him he noted in passing; and in so doing drew the portrait of a civilized individualist who has been a pattern to Frenchmen in each succeeding century, a man free from egoism, who paid no more than perfunctory respect to religion, and yet who, by his openness to life's lessons, attained a maturity beyond the reach of his more positive contemporaries. 'If I were a painter,' he wrote, 'I would make art natural, where so many others make nature artificial.' The secret of Montaigne's attraction is this naturalness; he allows himself to speculate and digress, apparently at his whim. But in fact he generally keeps himself under tight control, and his seemingly effortless style is far more classical and conscious than appears at first sight. For he successfully creates the illusion that the reader is listening to his author's mind at work; and this demands a far greater mastery of style than Rabelais' cruder ventriloquism.

Remarkable though the great prose writers were in this French Renaissance, it was primarily an age of poets. Here the influence of the Petrarchans first inspired a small circle in the half-way-house of Lyons before exercising its full impact on the circle of court poets known as the Pléiade. The Lyons school accepted the Italian influence in all its purity. MAURICE SCÈVE (c.1500–c.1560), indeed, was so ardent an admirer of

Petrarch that he laid a rather dubious claim to have discovered Laura's tomb at Avignon. Like the Petrarchans, though probably unlike Petrarch, he loved an unattainable mistress, the poetess Pernette du Guillet, for whom he wrote poetry of considerable complexity in *dizains*, a ten-line verse form which he packed as full as a sonnet. *Délie*, the name by which he addressed his lady, stands as an anagram of *l'Idée*, the Platonic *idea*, and his four hundred and forty-nine short poems are arranged according to a Pythagorean theory of numbers to represent the stages of the mystic way; and here Scève may have been thinking of the mathematical symmetry of the *Commedia*. As a further complexity, moreover he addresses Pernette under three aspects, as Diana, Hecate, and Selene, the moon.

Such is the very complicated structure of *Délie*, which in fact tells a simpler story than might appear. For its subject is the poet himself, his introspections, his jealousies, his enforced chastity, and his memories of previous loves. The astonishing thing is that this strange amalgam, which caused the poem's neglect between its own times and its quite recent return to favour, is fused into true poetry. Many of its *dizains* are obscure, almost all being capable of more than one interpretation. Moreover some of the poet's allusions are very difficult. Nevertheless Scève succeeds in conveying a kind of tortured passion comparable to that of Donne, though in a style closer to that of an equally curious English poet, Sir Philip Sidney's friend Fulke Greville. Scève's other principal work the *Microcosme* is a philosophical poem concerned with the theme of human progress.

Of the other poets of the Lyons school, PERNETTE DU GUILLET herself (*c*.1520–45) was little more than Scève's rather lighter and more melancholy disciple. LOUISE LABÉ (*c*.1524–65 or 66) on the other hand, like Gaspara Stampa among the Italians, made her poetry out of her own life. Using Italian models, she applies them to her personal tale of frustrated love. Her three elegies are intimate and discursive, while her twenty-three sonnets are direct and passionate. Married to a respectable and elderly Lyons citizen, she indulged in amours which drew on her the direct rebuke of

Jean Calvin, but which she was not ashamed to proclaim in verse. She copied little from Petrarch except his tricks of antithesis, which she used to illustrate her own contradictory moods. She knew nothing of metaphysical overtones, but used the sonnet as a direct vehicle for her confessions.

PONTUS DE TYARD (1521-1605), the link between the Lyons group and the Pléiade in Paris, is said to have addressed his *Erreurs amoureuses* to Louise herself. He was a Burgundian gentleman, a friend of Scève's, and at first a Petrarchan sonneteer, until he began under the influence of Ronsard to attempt less precious forms. His rhymed Odes, metrically much less ambitious than his greater contemporary's, have a modest charm, as of a more classical and less middle-class Marot.

Though Pontus de Tyard carried the Lyons influence to Paris, and though Ronsard greatly respected the work of Scève – which fell into almost immediate oblivion – the predominant influence with the Pléiade was not Italian but classical. The presiding influence at the birth of this new school of poetry was Jean Dorat, a Hellenist, who had been the master first of the young courtier PIERRE RONSARD (1524–85), and his friend JEAN-ANTOINE DE BAÏF (1532–89) and afterwards of the second great poet of the group, JOACHIM DU BELLAY (1522–60). Homer and Pindar, Horace and Virgil share these young men's interest with Plato and Petrarch; and true to French practice, then and now, before writing their poetry they issued a manifesto, du Bellay's *Deffence et illustration de la langue françoise,* in which they claimed that the vulgar tongue must now be made the equal of Latin, by imitation of the Ancients. Their idea was not new, but their poetry was. It blended the influences of Scève and Marot, and made of the sonnet sequence a personal vehicle which responded to them as intimately as it had done to Louise Labé.

Ronsard, the master spirit, was the first to free himself from subservience to Petrarchan models. His first book of *Amours,* addressed to Cassandre, contains much striking and sometimes condensed imagery – of which Scève had been sparing – mixed with some preciosity. This is true love-poetry, as du

Bellay's slightly earlier sequence to Olive – the first to be written in any language other than Italian – is not.

From the beginning momentary harshnesses came to interrupt du Bellay's Petrarchan confections. There was already an exasperation in the poet's tones; things did not go so smoothly with him as with his perhaps more talented friend. As a courtier, Ronsard was already the friend of kings, while du Bellay suffered, first from the lack of a patron, and then from an illness, which left him deaf. Ronsard also suffered from deafness; but to him it was almost an advantage, since but for this infirmity he might have climbed to yet higher positions at court, to the neglect of his poetry. It was under pressure of bitter experience that du Bellay abandoned the Petrarchan convention; his *XIII Sonnets à l'honneste amour* are a pure distillation of love unfulfilled. But Ronsard experimented with new styles out of an excess of energy: a form once perfected no longer satisfied him; by 1550 both poets, for different reasons, were attempting to find French equivalents for the classical ode.

Ronsard began with a grand flourish of mythology, but even his first book of Odes contains a charmingly turned piece or so of the kind that he was afterwards to call the *odelette*. His grand constructions, with contrasting strophe and antistrophe, although they were rich in variations of cadence, were little liked. The true Ronsard, with his belief in the Muses, and his love of his own countryside, appeared only sporadically in them. So soon he tired of experiment, and wrote his own poetry once again; in the second and third books of his *Amours,* which were addressed to Marie, passion shook itself free of preciosity.

Du Bellay also, after committing himself, though less deeply, to the grand architectural ode, began to write from the heart. His two sonnet sequences *Les Antiquitez de Rome* and *Les Regrets* speak out of a growing bitterness. At last provided with a post by his relative Jean du Bellay, who had also been Rabelais' patron, he was moved to disgust by the contrast between the magnificence of Rome's ruins and the corruption of its inhabitants; also by the triviality of his minor diplomatic mission. In his loneliness, he looked back to the Loire country where he had spent his youth, with exasperated longing. He survived his return to France by only three years.

Ronsard meanwhile was turning himself into a laureate, offering counsel to the king, celebrating great events with patriotic fervour and attempting to provide France with her missing epic *La Franciade,* in which he endeavoured to trace her people's descent from the heroes of Troy. The poem was a grandiose and unfinished failure, but with his other court poetry, it gained him three priorships and a canonry. Ronsard had not only raised the poet's status far above the level attained by Marot, he had also established a laureate's right to celebrate great themes. But he was never successful in his treatment of them. His best poems continue to be addressed to his loves, real and imaginary.

Ronsard and du Bellay, together, succeeded in their aim of writing a poetry worthy of the French language; and it was really they who established the diction and forms that were to last, despite Boileau's adverse pronouncèments, until the age of the Romantics. Had Scève's example prevailed over theirs there might have developed a French counterpart to our own Methaphysicals, for he wrote out of psychological complexity, whereas any complexities in the writing of the Pléiade and their successors were complexities of form or language only. Accepting the influences of Greece and Rome, of Plato and of Petrarch, the Pléiade found an eclectic solution, which allowed them to write personal poetry and poetry of generalized emotion, on the subjects of love, antiquity and, even, of religion; and which fixed the special relationship of the French myth to that of Rome. The other members of the Pléiade, of whom Rémy Belleau Jean-Antoine de Baïf, and Étienne Jodelle were the chief, were original only within the framework laid down by the leaders. Belleau writes charmingly and allusively of precious stones; Baïf attempts unrhymed verses for music, an interesting experiment repeated later in England by Campion, and Jodelle, in addition to some grandly rhetorical sonnets, wrote both tragedies and one of the first French comedies.

The French drama of the Renaissance followed the way of

the Italians, breaking completely with the old popular tradition, and starting afresh from classical models. It was a static and declamatory drama, appreciated by court circles, who compared it to the best that Greece and Rome had to show, and acted and enjoyed in the Universities, but almost entirely lacking in a sense of the theatre. The earliest plays of this new kind smelt most strongly of the study, and some indeed were both written and acted in Latin. Soon, however, strict Greek models, such as those followed by Lazare de Baïf in his adaptation of the *Electra* of Sophocles (1537) or in *Jephtha*, a Biblical tragedy in Latin, presented at the college of Bordeaux by the Scotsman, George Buchanan (1567), yielded to translations from the Italian itself and to Senecan tragedy.

Unlike the related plays of the 'university wits' in England, and of the pastoral satirists in Spain, this French drama learnt nothing from the popular theatre of the Middle Ages, but grimly pursued its own academic way. The old companies of amateur guildsmen, whose plays were now thought fit for no one but 'servants and common mimes' found their activities limited first by a decree of Francis I, forbidding them to indulge in satire, and then by an order of the High Court, issued during the religious disputes, which prohibited the performance of plays on sacred themes. By 1580 the chief companies had ceased to put on plays altogether.

Meanwhile, the Protestant faction had produced some theological drama, which bridged the gap between the mysteries and such later tragedies on religious themes as Corneille's *Polyeucte*. One of their chief propagandists, THÉODORE DE BÈZE (1519–1605), Calvin's biographer, who completed Marot's translations of the psalms, composed a single well-written Biblical tragedy *Abraham sacrifiant*, which keeps very close to the medieval models.

It is ÉTIENNE JODELLE (1532–73), however, who has the distinction of being the first French tragedian. His *Cléopatre captive*, a 'Senecan' work in five acts with choruses, is closely related to the artificial drama of Fulke Greville and Samuel Daniel in England. His story is taken, like Shakespeare's in *Antony and Cleopatra*, from Plutarch. But the play has something of the flavour of a post-mortem debate. When its action begins Antony is already dead, and the only point in doubt is the fate of the captive queen, who discusses her intended suicide through four acts and dies off stage between the fourth and the fifth. Other 'Senecan' plays were not so sparing in spectacles of blood and torture. But ROBERT GARNIER (1545-90) the author of one Biblical and six Roman tragedies, which contain some fine choruses, was also content that his massacres should take place off stage and that his actors should declaim rather than perform. Garnier was himself a lawyer, which may account for this preference for argument over action, so different from the practice of the contemporary English and Spanish theatres, but important for its influence over the mature French drama of Corneille and Racine.

Comedy was less of a favourite with the erudite theatre than tragedy or tragi-comedy. Beginning with translations from Plautus, Terence, Ariosto, and some other Italians, it produced its first original work in Jodelle's *Eugène*, a classical comedy crossed with medieval farce. Other adaptations from the Italian into a workmanlike French prose by PIERRE LARIVEY (*c.*1540-1619), a man of Italian birth, seem to come rather closer to the requirements of the theatre, but it is not known whether they were acted. The one public playhouse in Paris, the Hôtel de Bourgogne, which remained in the hands of the Confrérie that had staged the mystery plays, was let out to various troupes of comic actors, some from Italy or even from England and others who earned their livings for the rest of the year on the fair grounds of provincial France. But here there grew up towards the beginning of the seventeenth century a company which by 1629 had gained the monopoly of the theatre and a royal appointment, and which employed a 'paid poet', ALEXANDRE HARDY (*c.*1570-1632). This prolific hack was a stock purveyor of romantic melodrama of little literary value who lifted his plots sometimes from contemporary Spaniards or Italians, and sometimes from stories of Greek and Roman history. He rendered one important service to French drama, however, by seriously reducing the rôle of the chorus.

Two major attempts to write poetry on a large scale, the

Semaines of GUILLAUME DU BARTAS (1544–90) and *Les Tragiques* of AGRIPPA D'AUBIGNÉ (1551–1630) are both magnificent failures, which seem in retrospect to fit better into the English tradition than into the French. Du Bartas, indeed, with his curious medievalism and his quaintly virile language, when presented in a free translation by Joshua Sylvester very greatly influenced not only the English metaphysical poets, but Milton himself. Setting out to describe, one by one, the days of the Creation, he looked on the world with innocent eyes, at a moment when classical spectacles were becoming fashionable. The French tradition had broken much more violently with medievalism than the English, and recognized no grandeur that was not reminiscent of Virgil. Marot and Rabelais had not long been dead when du Bartas challenged Ronsard's hegemony, but his inventive style and the roughnesses of his form already seemed uncouth. His faults were patent. In his attempts to be arresting, he piled up detail upon detail; his Paradise is an urban pleasance, into which God has inadvertently introduced a couple of gawkish peasants. Goethe, nevertheless, said that du Bartas had written some of the best verse in French; and for one whose taste has been educated on Shakespeare and Milton, or upon Goethe himself, the *Semaines* will seem to contain a quality of greatness that is missing in the main tradition of French verse. An attempt to read the bulk of the work, however, will probably prove unsuccessful.

The same may be said of d'Aubigné's *Tragiques*, a savage defence of the Protestant cause which rises to passages of fine rhetoric. D'Aubigné also wrote Ronsardian love sonnets, an autobiography in the third person, and an *Histoire universelle*, recounting the whole progress of Protestantism in Europe. Without being a writer of the first rank, he has suffered from the neglect of Protestant writers which has obtained in France ever since the defeat of the Huguenot cause. During the rest of the sixteenth century and the first quarter of the seventeenth, much good poetry was written in France by Protestants and Catholics alike, a great deal of which has neither been read nor reprinted until recent years. PHILIPPE DESPORTES (1546–1606), a poet with a certain tenuous charm, reconciled the example of Ronsard with that of more recent and minor Italian Petrarchists. But now the Italian style had begun to look affected. Desportes's fireworks go up one by one, but never blaze forth in a set piece. A more intense light is cast by JEAN DE SPONDE (1557–95), a counterpart of Donne in his single-minded preoccupation with death, and also in his colloquial tone. His religious poems, few in number, form a pendant to his *Meditations sur les Pseaulmes*. For he was primarily a theologian, first on the Protestant side and then, synchronizing his conversion with that of his master Henry IV, on the Catholic. With his conversion, however, his writing of poetry came to an end.

Another and more curious religious poet, JEAN DE LA CEPPÈDE (1550–1622) published three centuries of sonnets towards the end of his life, the *Théorèmes sur les sacrés mystères de notre redemption (Themes on the Sacred mystery of our redemption)*, poems of a curious and sometimes hermetic symbolism which set out to relate the events of the Old Testament to the New. La Ceppède's passionate theology has affinities with our own Metaphysicals. But the problems which he treats are grounded not in his individual experience, but in his faith. La Ceppède is extravagant in his imagery; and in this, as in his use of colours, he seems to be related to the Spanish school whose work he may never have read. His syntactical boldness and his individual use of pagan mythology suggest a brooding and provincial Góngora rather than a tortured Donne.

A third religious poet whose work has only recently come to light is JEAN-BAPTISTE CHASSIGNET (*c.*1570–1635), a provincial gentleman and the local historian of Besançon, whose poetry was all written by his twenty-fourth year. His *Mespris de la vie et consolation contre la mort (Scorn of life and consolation against death)* contains 434 sonnets, as death-obsessed as Sponde's but somewhat more various and, like his, colloquial in language.

The tide of French poetry was however running against colloquialism, and towards a fixed style and a 'reformed' vocabulary. The poet whose example led to this codification of poetic practice was a conservative revolutionary, a master of formal verse with a somewhat dangerous sense of conviction.

Brushing aside the decorative Desportes, then in courtly favour, FRANÇOIS DE MALHERBE (1555–1628) set out to 'amend' Ronsard's faults of diction and scansion, only to give up, exhausted, when his work of rewriting was half done. It was not until he was fifty that he attained official recognition from Henry IV, and he then had to his credit only a small quantity of poetry, some of which contained the very 'baroque' excesses of imagery against which he protested. But Malherbe, in his splendid but shallow 'State' poetry, had achieved a grand style in keeping with the pretensions of the Bourbon court which, with the civil wars now over, was about to assert France's position as the dominant power in Europe.

Malherbe's sublime common sense, the dignity and mechanical subtlety of his line, really made a far less fundamental break with the tradition of Ronsard and Desportes than this self-appointed laureate alleged. Certainly some of the mythological references, even a little of the imagery in the old poetry, had been recondite. But difficulty of theme had never been a failing of the Pléiade; this they left to the minor religious poets, who had not been in the direct line of descent at all. Malherbe's victory, therefore, was not hard to win: like Waller in England, fifty years later, he met with no major opponents. The Malherbe code, with its list of permitted rhymes and its index of indelicate phraseology, triumphed at the expense of lyrical poetry in France, which hardly outlived the libertine generation – the counterpart of our cavalier poets – who put up a hopeless rearguard defence against him. Malherbe's real service was not to poetry, which he hamstrung, but to the drama, to which he passed on the legacy of a firm and clear diction.

On his side, his friend and junior, HONORAT DE BUEIL, SEIGNEUR DE RACAN (1589–1670) wrote a charming pastoral play, *Les Bergeries*, – to be considered in a later chapter – in verses delicately cadenced in a minor key; his odes and ceremonial poems, however, echo his master's style. But Malherbe's successor in the classical mode was FRANÇOIS DE MAYNARD (1582–1646) a lighterweight poet who handles his rather worn imagery with a delicate remoteness. His is the

poetry of art. For du Bartas' peasant couple have long ago retired, and now thoroughly urban nymphs and shepherds play
catch with the apples in a thoroughly urban paradise.

Among Malherbe's opponents, the satirist M A T H U R I N
RÉGNIER (1573–1613) forms a link between Marot and
Molière, independent both of the Pléiade's influence and of
Malherbe's. A nephew of Desportes, he enjoyed a Bohemian
life until the success of his satires turned him into a public
official. Régnier was a moralizer, a master of realistic detail,
with an eye for character and a tolerance of human foibles.
His tone was conversational and his images the sharp images
of the street, which he used naturally with no suggestion of
the burlesque. But against Malherbe he fought a losing
battle, with the result that the next considerably French satirist
Boileau inherited blunted darts.

Also on the losing side were two poets of great powers, who
wasted them in a sniping defence of free thought and free
language against the advancing might of the new and com-
placent conformity. In his command of a vocabulary which
united terms learned and scurrilous, M A R C - A N T O I N E D E
G I R A R D, S E I G N E U R D E S A I N T - A M A N T (1594–1661) recalls his Spanish contemporary Quevedo, whom he certainly
read. In an age of growing politeness, he aggressively struck
Bohemian poses, celebrating wine, cider and tobacco, melons
and cheese, attacking the Puritanical English and drawing his
self-portrait as *le poète crotté* who knew Paris from Villon's
angle. Saint-Amant, nevertheless, ended up as a member of the
Académie, and the author of a religious idyll, *Moïse sauvé*. His
friend THÉOPHILE DE VIAU (1590–1626) was more truly a
Bohemian, who depended on various patrons and was condemned to be burnt for blasphemies which he swore he had
never written. His sentence was, however, commuted to one of
banishment, which lasted for almost the remainder of his life.
His poetry is natural in language, and shows a romantic feeling
for nature. But his powers of imagination were far less bold
than Saint-Amant's.

These are by no means all the good minor poets who wrote
between the end of the Pléiade's reign and the final onset of
conformity which synchronized with Richelieu's rise to

power. The last of the independents was a solitary Huguenot, LAURENT DRELINCOURT (1626–81), who seems to echo La Ceppède from the defeated side. Freedom of lyrical invention did not arise again in France for more than 150 years.

Chapter Eight

THE GREAT AGE OF SPAIN
AND PORTUGAL

ON reaching Spain, the new fashions were far less destructive of the medieval tradition than in France. While the *Rhétoriqueurs* came at the end of a long line of poets, and were engaged in formalizing a manner which had been stiff enough from the first, the Spanish poets of the fifteenth century, Santillana and Manrique, were on an ascending scale, and left tradition richer than they had found it. Therefore while the new centralized monarchy in France, with its growing army of civil servants, diplomats, and courtiers, looked with admiration at foreign fashions, and demanded innovations that would put their poetry on a level with that of the Italians, the newly united kingdom of Ferdinand and Isabella, with less sense of its native inferiority, was content, after the first surprising impact of humanism and the new Petrarchan poetry, to reject the former, as inconsistent with its own rigid and narrow Catholicism, and to assimilate the latter into a style half Italianate, half Moorish and Andalusian. Spanish poets abandoned the writing of traditional *romances*, *letrillas* and *villancicos* only during the initial phase of Renaissance influence, while Spanish prose retained an ironic and not over-Latinized colloquialism until well on in the seventeenth century.

The most striking work of the new age, the fourteen-act play usually called *La Celestina*, written by the converted Jew, FERNANDO DE ROJAS (*c.*1465-1541) is roughly contemporary with the pastoral drama of Encina and the primitive sword and cloak theatre of Torres Naharro. In it, however, the old and the new age are successfully blended, as are the two media of drama and embryonic novel; like Rabelais' *Gargantua*, it stands on the threshold of a new world with its eyes turned back on the old. For its central character, to whom it owes its name, is the Archpriest's Trotaconventos, built up to Falstaffian stature: and its lovers, that Calisto and Melibea after whom the book was originally named, are a man and a girl in the grip of their passions, who bring a whole world – all the principal actors in the play, that is – down with them in their fall. *La Celestina* is one of the first works in literature in which events arise from character. Calisto's pride, which demands a conquest, and Melibea's infatuation with her own beauty are new motifs. The work pays not the slightest lip-service to the idea that we are part of a universe reaching, in Dante's sense, from heaven to hell. We are in the world, and the green-eyed, red-lipped Melibea is the incarnation of its beauty, as the bawd herself personifies its everyday vice, its common well-meaning comfortable a-morality. A seller of cosmetics and patcher of broken maidenheads, who talks in proverbs and keeps her finger on the erotic pulse of her town, the Celestina is greeted at every street corner by respectable citizens who call her Madam. She is cynical, wise, sentimental, and even generous, but at moments suddenly close and short-sighted. Calisto, grandiose, rhetorical and improvident, falls to his death while going to keep an assignation with his love; and she, absorbed entirely in her desire for him, kills herself; while the bawd who has brought them together loses her head, and quarrels with her accomplices over the money that Calisto has given her. Then when they have killed her, and are in their turn arrested by the police, the stage is left bare, as after a 'Senecan' tragedy. But the effect is altogether different. We have met recognizable characters, and their fate has arisen out of what they are. It is possible to imagine Romeo and Juliet united; it is only a trick of chance that prevents it. But the marriage of Calisto and Melibea is an impossibility; they are hollow creatures, bound for disillusion or disaster.

This tragicomedy was clearly written to be read. It is realistic, yet flamboyant in its language which, like so much of the best Spanish writing, rises to heights of Latinity, and falls to depths of ironic bawdry on a single page. It is, on the whole, pessimistic in tone, and pagan in outlook, the work of a man severed by the Inquisition from his own faith and un-touched by the Christianity to which he had made a formal adherence. He has seen the ugliness of the world and can find nothing stronger to contrast with it than a humanistic belief in the grandeur of human character. It is this that makes him one of the forerunners of the great novelists. For there are few characters as round, as boldly drawn and as convincing as his, before the age of Balzac and Dickens. The rest of Spain's humanistic writing was largely critical and experimental. JUAN LUIS VIVES (1492–1540), a friend of Erasmus and Thomas More, who held a fellowship at Corpus Christi, Oxford, until Henry VIII's divorce suit compelled him, as the unfortunate queen's compatriot, to leave for the Continent, wrote entirely in Latin. His treatise on the education of women had a large circulation and was much translated, while his commentary on St Augustine's *City of God* was put on the Papal index. A lesser but more extreme humanist, JUAN DE VALDÉS (*c.*1490–1541) translated some of the Epistles and Psalms, and in his commentaries drew on Eckhart and Tauler, thus preparing at least some intellectual influences for the coming generation of Spanish mystics. His brief *Diálogo de la Lengua* is a delightful treatise on the living language, which pleads for a natural and not over-Latinized or Italianized vocabulary, and takes its good and bad examples from popular speech. No critic has ever preached sound taste more appealingly. Valdés had a natural palate for fine writing; he spoke warmly of the *Celestina* and of Manrique, and was guardedly critical of Amadis and his brood. In religion Valdés came to adopt a Protestant standpoint, though without leaving the Catholic Church.

Bad taste, on the other hand, received a great impetus from the writings of ANTONIO DE GUEVARA (1480–1545), whose *Reloj de Príncipes* (*The Dial of Princes*), a fictional work containing some letters purporting to have been written by the Emperor Marcus Aurelius, was much translated and widely read. His 'high and sweete style' was founded on the sort of rhetoric which Rabelais mocked at and which led in England directly to Euphuism.

Two curious works of humanistic fiction, once both attributed to Cristóbal de Villalón, who flourished about the middle of the sixteenth century, have now been taken away from him on evidence scarcely stronger than that which first fathered them upon him. If *El Crótalon* (*The Timbrel*) and the

Viaje de Turquía (*The Turkey Voyage*), were by the same author, he would be the biggest figure in Spanish prose between *La Celestina* and *Don Quixote*. The first of these works takes the form of a series of conversations between a cock and a shoemaker, which run to philosophical fantasy, worthy of the Greek Lucian himself, who – with Ariosto perhaps – inspired them. They are adventurous, ironic, and anti-clerical. Student pranks alternate with a battle between the frogs and the rats; there is a voyage to the centre of the earth that foreshadows Don Quixote's descent into the Cave of Montesinos, and a flight up to Heaven to take a look at God's throne *in situ*. The *Viaje de Turquía* is a book of travel, in dialogue form, which gives a minute account of life in Constantinople. It is ironic also, Rabelaisian at times, and full of character and adventure. Both works give versions of the tale of the Wandering Jew, a detail which suggests some common factor, if not in authorship, at least in the milieu from which they originated. The writers of both – if they were two – had knowledge of Greek, a fine prose style, a nice irony and great powers of invention.

The beginning of Spain's Golden Age, however, dates not from any work in prose, but from the publication in 1543 of a single volume containing the poems of two poets, already dead: JUAN BOSCÁN (*c*.1490–1542) and GARCILASO DE LA VEGA (1503–36). Here, nine years before the appearance of Ronsard's first *Amours*, the Italian style was perfectly adapted to the Castilian tongue, which rejuvenated measures that in their native Italy were growing somewhat formal. Boscán, a stay-at-home Catalan gentleman, had been urged by the Venetian ambassador in Madrid to write some poems in the new style. He was, in fact, better fitted to write prose, and had made a good Spanish translation of Castiglione's *Courtier*. He succeeded, however, in adapting the forms of the sonnet, and even of *terza rima*, though his writing remained too flat for his purpose, since he lacked the passion of a poet. He was, as Gerald Brenan has written, the Ezra Pound rather than the Eliot of the new movement.

The more inspired rôle was played by Garcilaso, a man as unhappy in his life, love and temperament, as Boscán was fortunate. A gentleman soldier, reminiscent of our own Sir

Philip Sidney, he seemed the perfect model of a courtier. But his unhappy love for a Portuguese lady, Dona Isabel Freire, and his rash participation in a friend's love intrigue, drove him into exile, and caused him in the end, after a brief sojourn in Naples, to seek his death on an unimportant battlefield, at the age of thirty-three. It was only in his last three years that his writing reached absolute maturity, and by this time, like Ronsard and du Bellay, he had seen beyond the neo-Petrarchan models that he had begun by imitating, to the permanent values of Virgil and Horace. Therefore, while his forms remained Italian, his choice and his economy of language harked back to the great age of Rome.

His first Eclogue, probably his finest poem, takes the form of a long dialogue between two shepherds, who have lost their loves, and in each loss is reflected the poet's own sorrow for Dona Isabel, doubly lost to him by her marriage and by her subsequent death in childbirth. His lines follow the patterns of the voluptuous, musical post-Petrarchan poetry of the Neapolitan school. But if Sannazaro's *Arcadia* dictated his pastoral settings, and if Poliziano's *Orfeo* gave him the mythology of a Golden Age, his own strength of emotion, his love of Latin directness, and the fresh bite of his Spanish words saved him from the Italian failing of rhetorical mellifluousness. Garcilaso did not speak directly of his own experience, yet this is – as Sannazaro's was not – personal poetry. He possessed other qualities also which the Italians lacked, a strong architectural power, and a sense of contrast which enabled him to take the utmost advantage of the variations of pace and mood, made possible by the varied length of his lines. His music is as subtle as Spenser's in the *Epithalamium*: but at the same time he is so precise, flat, and almost colloquial in his choice of words that there is no danger of sound swamping sense. He writes of a golden age, but his shepherds carry wooden crooks, and are dressed in the homespun of the Spanish upland pastures.

Another less flowing Italian measure which Garcilaso used was a variant of the *canzone* called the *silva*, which combined eleven-syllable and seven-syllable lines; and this he made so much his own that it came to be known as the *lira*, from the first line of his fifth *canción*, *Si de mi baja lira* (*If from my humble lyre*). Garcilaso's lyre was, indeed, humble. His idylls were set in Spain, and they reflected the essentials of his own melancholy plight. His trees, indeed, are beeches and dwarf oaks; the rivers at which he pastures his flocks are the Tagus and its tributaries, and the distant Danube, on an island of which he passed his exile; and though there are nymphs and dryads and pagan gods in both elegies and eclogues, his shepherds speak the language of mortals, as had those of Theocritus and Virgil. Garcilaso perfected no literary vocabulary, but he raised pure Castilian to heights where it could compete with the now over-refined language of Florence and Naples, and where it could challenge comparison even with that of ancient Rome.

Garcilaso created the new Spanish poetry in a bare three years; and the effect of that 1543 volume on others was equally swift. Only one poet of the older generation protested against the importation of the new forms, and the old were swept out of sight, to remain among the people until they could be reincorporated into polite poetry by Lope, by Góngora, and by Quevedo.

The first poets in the Peninsula to use the new measures after Garcilaso, adapted them to an even graver music, and to more philosophical themes. Of these LUÍS DE CAMÕES (*c.*1524–80) wrote almost entirely in Portuguese, and although his international reputation rests predominantly on his epic *Os Lusíadas*, he would certainly rank among the best poets of the Renaissance for his lyrical poetry alone. This is more various and a little less finished than Garcilaso's, and the product of a similarly unhappy life, which, however, toughened him into stoicism. The best of his *canções* and sonnets take the Italian style back to the purity of Petrarch; his words have a hard, even a raw edge. Self-pity was not the chief lesson that he learned from his unhappy loves and his unsuccessful soldiering in the Portuguese dominions. In his epic – which will be considered with the two other epics of that age, Tasso's and Ercilla's, in the next chapter – he soared in the service of a national theme to Virgilian grandeur. His own unhappy experience of garrison life at Goa and

Macão was not denied, but subordinated to the glorification of his country's mission. In the same way in his lyrics, his own unhappy love was subordinated to the worship of transcendent beauty. There one sees, behind the figure of the unlucky lover and maimed soldier, Luïs de Camões, the shape of humanity pursuing and losing an ideal of womanhood that carries with it the image of the soul's fulfilment. That Camões would never give up this quest, which was as compelling to him as the quest for the Indies to his hero Vasco da Gama, is clear from the conclusion of several of his poems, among them the sonnet *Jacob e Raquel* in which Jacob says

> *Mais servira se não fora*
> *para tam longo amor tam curta a vida!*

(But I would serve longer if life were not so short for so long a love); and from the farewell to one of his *cançãos* in which he calls to new life that old *troubadour*'s paradox:

> *e se alguem te preguntasse,*
> *canção, porque nam moiro,*
> *poses-lhe responder que porque moiro.*

(and if anyone asks you, song, why I am not dying, you may answer him that it is because I am dying).

Camões did not confine himself to Garcilaso's media. He used a simple quatrain; he used the traditional *redondilha* for his magnificent poem of exile *Babel e Sião (Babylon and Zion)* – a piece with Biblical echoes, which Lope de Vega called 'the pearl of all poetry': and he turned Boccaccio's and Ariosto's *ottava rima* to solemn effect in his *Oitavas sobre o desconcerto do mundo (Octaves on the disorder of the world)* which are the Renaissance equivalent of Manrique's *Coplas*.

Camões, in his lyrical poetry alone, is a giant among Renaissance poets, the master of a line from which all superfluities have been cut away.

The sonnet and the eclogue were already acclimatized to Portugal when he started writing; he was not technically an innovator, as Garcilaso was. But it is difficult to say more of his older contemporary, FRANCISCO DE SÁ DE MIRANDA (*c.*1490–1558), or of Miranda's follower, ANTONIO FERREIRA (1528–69) or of DIOGO BERNARDEZ (*c.*1530–1600) than that they used the new medium freshly. Portugal's blossoming was short; for in 1578, her last king, Don Sebastião perished in a disastrous battle with the Moors, and after 1580, when she was joined to Spain, it seemed once more likely, as in Gil Vicente's time, that her language would sink to the level of a mere provincial dialect, like Galician.

Camões' almost exact Spanish contemporary, Luis de León (*c*.1527–91), a friar and a humanist, reinforced the Latin content of the new poetry and diluted its neo-Petrarchism. As a theologian, a Hebrew and classical scholar, he bestrode the humanistic University of Salamanca like an intolerant colossus, till some rival professors discovered that his great-grandmother had died at the stake as a relapsed Jewess. He had, moreover, laid himself open to ideological charges, having translated the *Song of Songs* into Spanish and called into question the literal accuracy of some passages in the Vulgate. After five years in prison, he was lucky enough to be acquitted of these charges; and, on returning to his lecture hall, he opened his first address with the words 'As I was saying the other day . . . '

Luis de León's first important poem, a piece dating from his youth, had been a Horatian ode in praise of the quiet life, written in Garcilaso's *lira* measure. The courtier's or scholar's longing for retirement, away from the rivalries and bustle of the town, was a stock Renaissance theme. It owed something to Horace, something to the pastoral convention, and something to the cut-throat nastiness of the contemporary struggle for place and survival. But Luis de León was repeating no poetic clichés. His longing was for a retirement from active life altogether, into a world of contemplation. The contrast between spiritual reality and earthly illusion is the constant burden of his writing. Of this he had an intellectual vision, achieved by persistent thought and study. He was a mystic, not of the emotional but of the intellectual way. A scholar, a Platonist and a Christian at once, he had learnt the lesson of self-discipline; and as a poet, the disciple of Virgil and Horace, whom he had translated, he had learnt to apply an equal discipline to his verse. Its beat is sober, compared with Garcilaso's. But though it has a less sensuous flow it too has a musical beauty, spare, classical, and intense. Luis de León's vocabulary is exalted, almost Miltonic; his images are bold and uncoloured. Sometimes, indeed, as in his ode to the musician Salinas, he seems to overhear and to convey the austere and secret music to which, according to his Platonic belief, the whole universe moved:

> *Ve como el gran maestro,*
> *a aquesta immensa cítara aplicado,*
> *con movimiento diestro*
> *produce el son sagrado*
> *con que esto eterno templo es sustentado,*

(It sees how the great master, playing on that immense cithern with skilled motions, produces the sacred sound by which this eternal temple is sustained.)

This verse is omitted from some editions of Luis de León's poetry owing to the fact that its theology is considered dubious.

Where Luis de León purified Garcilaso's measures, the other principal poet of the new style, FERNANDO DE HERRERA (1534–97) embellished them with Biblical echoes, over-emphatic, monotonous, crude, but also – in another way – Miltonic in their grandeur. Herrera was an Andalusian, a lover of colour, of the glint of metals and of high-sounding names. The self-appointed laureate of Philip II's triumphant empire, he celebrated the naval victory of Lepanto, and the death of Don Sebastião in battle with the Moors, clashing the cymbals and beating the funeral drums with equal accomplishment.

Herrera lived the whole of his life in his native Seville, where he formed a literary circle. Harassed by poverty, he took holy orders, indulged in a Platonic love affair, and as a 'state poet' performed for his nation the function that Malherbe was to perform twenty-five years later for France. But whereas Malherbe's influence made for sobriety and correctness, Herrera, although a theoretical advocate of clarity and strict classicism, gave licence by his example to most of the rhetorical excesses of Góngora and the silver age.

ST JOHN OF THE CROSS (1543–91) a poet of small output and of less technical originality than Herrera, left behind him, in addition to six lesser pieces, three major poems written in prison and celebrating, in the metaphor of the *Song of Songs,* the love of the soul for God. St John probably did not know Garcilaso's poetry at first hand. But he had almost certainly read it in a form translated *a lo divino,* for pious reading, according to the strange custom of the time, with a divine lover carefully substituted on all occasions for an earthly one. Certainly he used Garcilaso's *lira* measure, and drew his imagery, in part, from that first of Spain's new poets. In this form he described the high ecstasy that he had known, in which his soul had been lifted and, in a moment out of time, united with God. His extended prose works are no more than commentaries on the raptures so perfectly recorded in these three poems, which soar to a height where they seem to escape beyond the realm of poetry. St John's life was that of a strict ascetic; which brought him twice into conflict with his laxer brethren, and earned him imprisonment, torture and, finally, banishment to a 'desert house' in Andalusia.

Of Spain's four great poets of her golden age, three were unknown in their lifetimes. Only Herrera, the least of the four, was published in his own day, in a peculiar orthography of his own invention. His reputation at that time was considerable, though it has sunk since.

But far more important than those of the poets were the reputations of the prose writers of that time. The mystical treatises written by St John in explanation of his poems come as a culmination to some sixty years of devotional writing, which place sixteenth-century Spain almost on a level with the Rhineland of 200 years earlier. There is, however, about these Spanish mystics a more sectarian air than one finds in their great German predecessors, from whom they seem only to derive a thin line of parentage by way of Juan de Valdés. For the most part the spiritual revival in Spain was a phenomenon of the Counter-Reformation: a reply to the Protestant offensive, which in fact threatened the Peninsula less than any other country. Perhaps its only great effect was on the lax religious orders, which were all, more or less, compelled to reform themselves in order to compete with the new secular priesthood founded by Ignacio Loyola, whose *Spiritual*

Exercises were published in 1548, and with the Carmelite convents which were reformed by Santa Teresa, both as a result of the Reformation's challenge.

The new devotional writing was in no sense Platonic; Plato had now come to be associated with learned paganism and the cult of mere courtliness to which Europe's inheritance from the Florentine academy had sunk. Among the older mystical writers, Henry Suso had come to count for more than the pseudo-Dionysius; and emphasis on the physical details of the Passion entirely replaced the metaphorical treatment of the soul as a spark of the divine. St John himself, nevertheless, in his *Dark Night of the Soul* reached a position almost as lofty and untheological as Eckhart's. His prose, however, is far less interesting than that of Luis de León, whose profoundly intellectual religious approach made him more conscious of his task as a writer. What Garcilaso did for Spanish poetry, Luis de León did for Spanish prose, leaving it with a formal style moderately Latinized and firmly based on the language of Old Castile. His *Perfecta casada* (*The Perfect Bride*) continues the age-old argument on the nature of women, and shows a side of this ascetic scholar which is most human, most sensitive to the sorrows of worldly life, and most appealing. His second great prose work, written in prison, is a delicate dialogue on the names by which Jesus is called in the New Testament (*De los nombres de Cristo*). Here, particularly in his comments on the Good Shepherd, there are idyllic passages that proclaim him the contemporary of the pagan Garcilaso.

Luis de León, alone of these Spanish mystics, shows some compassion for the persecuted Jews. SANTA TERESA (1515–82), on the other hand, though she must often, in her journeys from city to city, have witnessed the hideous burnings of relapsed Hebrews, never mentions them once in her otherwise most human writings. Teresa was a woman of great energy, untouched by the speculative intellectuality of the Platonists. Her reading was the Bible and St Augustine, and her activities, once she had heard the call to devotion at the age of forty, were largely concerned with Church politics and administration. Nevertheless for the benefit of her somewhat obtuse confessors and for the nuns in the reformed convents which she founded, she wrote two principal treatises on the religious life and an autobiography, which is a masterpiece of intimate and salty self-revelation. Teresa was not concerned with style; she wrote as she talked, using a wealth of popular phrases, and describing her spiritual progress with a humorous objectivity, which makes her *Life* the most readable and the most entertaining of all religious revelations.

The same natural style and the same realism are present in an even higher degree in the master work of Spain's greatest writer MIGUEL DE CERVANTES (1547–1616). His first work was a novel in the pastoral convention, *La Galatea*, and he was still not absolutely disillusioned with these tales of shepherds and shepherdesses when he came to begin the first part of *Don Quixote*. For several of the interpolated incidents are in this vein, while the tediously long *Tale of Foolish Curiosity* reads like a stilted and protracted tale from the *Decameron*.

Cervantes' life had been as adventurous and as unsuccessful as that of Camões, though his greatest disasters had been rather of the purse than of the heart; and his attempts to make a living by the writing of plays and by filling minor government posts, did nothing to restore his fortunes. He was in prison, probably for failing to produce receipts for official disbursements, when he began to write his satirical attack on the ballads and *romances* then so much the fashion, which developed into the first part of *El ingenioso hidalgo Don Quixote de la Mancha*.

This work, the success of which was instantaneous, went far beyond its original purpose, as from the moment when Cervantes sent his knight out on his second expedition in the company of his squire and foil Sancho Panza. Now the book became a tale of adventure among ideas. Don Quixote's beliefs and Sancho's disbeliefs ranged over a whole field of possibilities. For not only were there physical encounters with windmills and country barbers, with galley-slaves and goatherds, but the whole theme of romantic love was treated all over again and from a new standpoint. What did it matter that the lady Dulcinea was only a brawny peasant girl, if Quixote believed in her and acted as if she were a princess? Even when – in the second part – the knight was confronted with his imagined mistress, the illusion held; and as the story went on his sober, doubting squire began to believe in her too. Cervantes was by education a man of the new, critical school: he had set out to mock the credulous romanticism of a generation addicted to ballads and tales of chivalry. But he created an even greater myth himself. His two characters and their adventures are, as one reads on, a great deal more convincing than the madness of Orlando or the deeds of Charlemagne and his knights. Cervantes had performed for Spain the miracle previously performed by de Rojas of creating real persons.

Literature, up to the beginning of the sixteenth century, had created very few living characters. The Middle Ages, with their belief in universal types and their refusal to consider a man alone, in isolation from his nation and Christian society as a whole, had militated against character drawing. When Cervantes gave life to his knight and squire, in the years in which Shakespeare was inventing Hamlet and Prince Hal, Falstaff and Lady Macbeth, there were perhaps only half a dozen figures from poetry or fiction whom we can now think of as drawn in the round: as capable, that is, of existing outside the story of which they form part. Spain had its bawds, Trotaconventos and La Celestina, to whom Cervantes was to add a third representative of the same sordid trade, 'the feigned aunt' of his *Exemplary Tale*. There was also the Wife of Bath, Montaigne as he appeared in his self-portrait, Villon as he emerges from his poems, and a very few others, among whom do not figure Pantagruel and Panurge, who are no more than great puppets manipulated by their author. But major characters, such as we meet at their greatest in the nineteenth-century novel, hardly existed.

After the success of the first part of *Quixote*, Cervantes turned to the short story, as it had been left by Boccaccio and his successors, and wrote his *Exemplary Novels,* the best of which – the satirical stories – are on a level with his masterpiece. *La Tia fingida* (*The Feigned Aunt*) and that tale of the thieves' kitchen, *Rinconete y Cortadillo*; the fantastic tale of the student who imagined himself to be made of glass, *El Licenciado Vidriera*; the lyrical tale of the gipsy girl with its interpolated poems, and the solider satire of *El Coloquio de los*

Perros (*The Colloquy of the Dogs*), are realistic and splendidly told: the Italianate stories, on the other hand, are much on the level of *The Tale of Foolish Curiosity*. But Cervantes had so fecund an imagination that in his tale about the deluded student he squandered on a few pages an idea every bit as promising as that of his ballad-crazed gentleman, Master Quexada or Lantern-Jaws, who grew into the Knight of the Dolorous Visage.

The second part of *Don Quixote*, which Cervantes felt compelled to write because a sequel by another hand had been put into circulation, is far more consistent and far more deeply imagined than the first. Here we see the knight affected by Sancho's doubts and finally disillusioned, and Sancho so convinced by his master's delusions that he imagines himself for a day on end the ruler of that 'isle' which the Don had promised him. Here we have the Don's descent into the underground world at the bottom of Montesinos' cave, the visit to the gentleman in green, in whose person Cervantes embodied his ideal of combined homeliness and learning; here we have the idyll of Camacho's wedding, a true version of pastoral, also the Don's confrontation with his mistress, and the grand Ariosto-like ride through the skies on the enchanted steed, Clavileño.

Here the flights of Cervantes' imagination are more sustained, and the reader's sympathy is more firmly enlisted for his knight than before. For Quixote's version of the world is more beautiful, and also more dramatic than reality; and his disillusionment is something that one comes to fear. His adventures are real in a sense that nothing in Ariosto is. For given free powers of imagination, the romantic writer need never stop. But Cervantes – no romantic – heightens the effect of his invention by contrasting it continuously with an uglier reality; which greatly enhances its power to convince.

Cervantes' style, like Santa Teresa's, is essentially colloquial; one seems to hear his intonations, telling the story as his innkeeper told stories in the midday heat, to a group, not of courtiers, but of common citizens. Sometimes, as in *The Tale of Foolish Curiosity*, or in the Captive's account of his adventures among the Moors, which was founded on Cervantes' own experience after his capture by pirates, his prose grows more conventional, and its rich earthiness is exchanged for something in the nature of smooth, featureless stone. But generally he is the master of a direct style which, however, found very few imitators in Spain, where prose soon began to take on all the artifices of an involved Latinity. His true descendants were the single French novelist René Lesage, and the great succession of English story-tellers from Fielding to Dickens.

Don Quixote, however, must not be thought of as a novel. It is a comic epic, the tale of a would-be hero on the level of fact who turns himself into a true hero on the level of ideas. The old legends of giants and dwarfs, of heroes and villains and courtly love were reduced to nonsense, and a new, Renaissance hero, a man who makes the world conform to his dreams, was created. Then tenderly, reasonably, inevitably, he too was shown to be a thing of illusion. Unhappily, the world did not accept Cervantes' lesson, and as the force of religion and of humanistic moderation declined, Quixote's arose in many spheres, building empires, making laws, and piling up fortunes, which were no more real than the barber's bowl was Mambrino's helmet or a flock of sheep the armies of Charlemagne, and which brought disaster not only to the dreamers, but to thousands who, perhaps half-shared, perhaps entirely rejected their dreams.

Chapter Nine

ITALIAN EPIC, SPANISH DRAMA, AND GERMAN POETRY

DESPITE their mentor Aristotle's preference for tragedy, the classicists of the Renaissance rated the epic above all other literary forms, and placed Virgil above all other epic writers. This, in an age of growing nationalism, is not surprising. Virgil had told the story of Aeneas, but he had also exalted the national theme, showing the Latins as a chosen people, derived from the heroes of Troy, and their destiny as beneath the special protection of the gods.

Hitherto the epic in modern Europe had been written in Latin, as befitted so solemn a purpose. Petrarch's *Africa* treated a national theme, that was only by reflexion contemporary, in that a parallel might be seen between the Roman war against Carthage, and the Christians' war against the unbeliever. The new epics, however, came closer to Virgil; for their authors lauded the destiny and achievements of their own countries, tracing the ancestry of their heroes back, as Virgil had done for Aeneas, to the classical past.

The first great Renaissance poem in epic form, Ariosto's *Orlando furioso*, was dismissed by the humanistic critics as no true epic. In fact its discursiveness, its humour, and its humanity prove it to be rather the sixteenth-century's equivalent to a prose *romance* than a poem in the class of the *Aeneid* or the *Chanson de Roland*. Its purpose was at best to entertain, while the writer of true, Virgilian epic considered it his business to instruct, to exhort, and to elevate its audience. Elevation and gravity of language should, in the opinion of the age, be matched by elevation and gravity of thought: qualities which were perhaps felt by Pope Leo X to be missing from the Gospel story. For three years before the publication of Ariosto's poem, he commissioned MARCO GIROLAMO VIDA (1480–1566), an Italian cleric who afterwards rose to be a bishop, to write a *Christiad* in Latin, which was to polish up the New Testament story, much as Virgil, according to an important Italian critic, had polished up the crudities of Homer.

Vida had a fair pictorial sense, and could sometimes achieve the grand style. But in his version the room in which the Last Supper was held became

> Flaming with gold, with pictur'd columns bright,
> A vasty Hall.*

and we seem to be in Tintoretto's Venice.

Vida's work had little effect on other poets, although traces of its influence may be found in the duller patches of *Paradise Regained*, and although Alexander Pope thought him an immortal, at least for his criticism. Vida's real importance is that he and his contemporaries evolved a theory of the epic to which later poets tried to conform.

Luís de Camões, the first of these, was the most Virgilian, and the greatest. Exiled from Portugal to the inhospitable shores of India or China, there to assist in the spreading and maintenance of Latin culture, in the face of Eastern civilizations, which he lumped together in his thoughts as Moorish or pagan, Camões drew a whole nation as a hero, and involved all the gods and goddesses in its destiny. *Os Lusíadas* (*The Sons of Lusus*) uses Vasco da Gama's voyage to the Indies as a framework in which to inset all the great scenes in Portugal's history; scenes which he selected from one standpoint only, for their relevance to the fight against the infidel.

Such a poem might have been as stiff and theoretical as Ronsard's ill-starred *Franciade*. But Camões was himself a son of Lusus who knew the hardships and had shared the adventures of the Eastward voyage. He was, moreover, a Latinist and a poet, which made him capable of manipulating the Virgilian machinery for his own purpose. The gods were to him the forces which had flung him like a tennis ball here and there, west and east, in the course of his restless life: the seas, the storms, the ports, and the enemies that da Gama had known he had known also. The tale he told was drawn from recent history that was far from dead. His, therefore, was a realistic epic, written in the Italian *ottava rima* and raised above

*Trans. C. S. Lewis.

the commonplace and discursive by Camões' powers of organic enrichment, and by his sense of history. His imagery – as living as Dante's – is founded on exact observation and memory, raised to sublimity by the greatness and the classical associations of the theme. All the machinery of the ancient epic is there; the rhetoric, the invocations, the gods, and their high debate; and all is turned to a Virgilian purpose, to the glorification of a national destiny. Portugal, the smallest of the nations was, as a representative of the great Latin past, conquering an empire comparable with that of Rome. The language, a new language used to great effect by no previous poet except the dramatist Gil Vicente, took on Roman echoes. Camões was indeed bold enough to challenge comparison with Virgil in his opening line.

The Empire which he celebrated broke up, however, in the years of Camões' death, on the defeat of Don Sebastião, a disaster which was celebrated not in Portuguese but in the Spanish of Seville by a poet of the nation which had received the lion's share of the little Atlantic kingdom's assets.

A less literary epic, describing events to which the author stood even closer than Camões to da Gama's voyage, is *La Araucana* by ALONSO DE ERCILLA (1533–94), who himself took a leading part in the Spanish conquest of Chile, which is his subject. As a work of art, *La Araucana* is less finished and less perfectly constructed than *Os Lusíadas*. Ercilla did not conceive it as a whole, but added scenes as they occurred. The real subject of the poem is the Araucanian Indians, in whom Ercilla found all the virtues that the eighteenth century was to find in the 'noble savage'. In contrast to them the Spanish leaders are sketched realistically; one is lazy and negligent, another brave and spirited. Their virtues and failings, however, are only life size, while the heroism of the Indians, fighting a long and hopeless battle in defence of their poor country, has a tragic grandeur. If the poem has a hero it is their chief Caupolicán, whose barbarous execution by the Spaniards after thirty years of dogged resistance draws from Ercilla the bare comment that if he had been in charge, it would never have occurred. The poet of *La Araucana*, however, was in no doubt about the justice of the Spanish and Christian cause, and glorified the name and mission of his master Philip II by including descriptions of the battle of Lepanto and the capture of Saint-Quentin in the second part of his poem, on the bare excuse that they were contemporary with the events he was describing.

The framework of *La Araucana* is, despite its realism, Virgilian, and even from its first line shows itself to be in reaction against the romanticism of Ariosto. 'I sing not of ladies, of love, and of the chivalrous deeds of love-lorn knights,' begins Ercilla. But from his Latin models, he takes on rhetorical habits that mar his otherwise straightforward poem. Debates, like those of Milton's fallen angels, are held among the Chilean tribal chiefs, with long and moralizing speeches assigned to each; and Ercilla himself only too often breaks into sententious moralizing. Sometimes too, he carelessly repeats the pastoral platitudes, assigning lilies and roses to landscapes in which they certainly never flourished. But many of his descriptions are at first hand, and many of his metaphors are drawn from the world he had seen; a body of Araucanians rush from their ambush on to a Spanish column like a hungry alligator on a school of fishes. His battle scenes too are carefully drawn, and the tribesmen's arms, tactics, fortresses, and way of life are presented in vivid detail, with a wealth of well accumulated adjectives. Ercilla writes as a man of action, to whom war seems inevitable, and for whom fear is natural in the bravest, whose bravery lies only in mastering it. His is the world of *El Cid*, squeezed into a conventional silver-gilt frame; and his poem, which was greatly admired, by Voltaire amongst others, right into the nineteenth century, testifies to a state of objectivity in its author which is rare to-day. For it would be impossible to imagine a high officer in the sordid colonial wars of this century homerically celebrating his enemy's bravery and deploring his execution; any account he might settle down to write after his retirement, would probably take the form not of a heroic poem, but of a self-justification against his political superiors.

It would have been vain to look to Italy for a poet of Ercilla's directness, candour, and balance. The author of the *Gerusalemme liberata*, that country's counterpart to the works of Camões and Ercilla, was a poet in the modern sense; one emotionally at odds with the society in which he lived, whose poetry derived its grandeur not from a simple vision of life, but from his own subjective complexities.

The first attempt at a national epic to be made in Italy had been a dull and didactic failure. GIANGIORGIO TRISSINO (1478–1550), the author of the first regular Italian tragedy, had laboured for twenty years at a work on the liberation of Italy from the Goths, twenty-seven books of which were devoted to the conquest of Italy by Justinian. This was not the way to wean readers from Ariosto's chivalries to worthier themes. It was TORQUATO TASSO (1544–95) the son of a poet and, like Ariosto, attached to the court of Ferrara, who struck the compromise between the discursive romance and the strictly unified epic demanded by Vida. His method was to compress the old material of chivalry into a classical poem, confining himself to a single hero and weaving his incidents into a single plot. In contrast to Camões he was primarily a love poet, and, though he took as his theme the Crusade against the Moslem, a purpose to which each of the new nations paid lip-service, even when profiting from a sound Levantine trade, his theme had not the immediacy for him that da Gama's voyage had for the Portuguese poet.

Tasso's first epic *Rinaldo*, written when he was eighteen, is a romantic medley, theoretically unified by a single hero. His *Aminta,* written for the Este family, is a verse pastoral in the tradition of the *Arcadia,* which was a favourite both in the original and in translations throughout the seventeenth century, and which displayed his great lyrical powers. But by the time that this was published he had largely completed his second epic, the *Gerusalemme liberata.* This romantic treatment of the first Crusade is lacking in the sense of history that infused the *Lusiads.* All kinds of wonders, hairbreadth escapes, choices between death and dishonour, martyrdoms, and heroic battles speak for a wayward fancy in the poet, which refused to be confined within the limits of his martial story. There are angels and there are magicians; but neither are as real as the classical gods used by Camões with a purely symbolic purpose. Camões draws a clear world in which we can see all the issues at stake. But Tasso seems to incorporate into his poem elements related not to his story but to his own conflicting passions. The poet in fact is at odds with his medium, but is forced by the strict climate of criticism to write heroically, where he would have preferred to write psychologically. It is as if Shelley, born into the seventeenth century, had been forced to make his Prometheus conform to a Miltonic theology.

Tasso's pastoral and his epic brought him a short spell of prosperity, which was interrupted by a complete breakdown. The conflicts that can be seen in the strongest passages of his poem were unresolved; two outbursts of frenzy, the second more severe than the first, cost him seven years of confinement. During his imprisonment he wrote continuously, and published a tragedy *Torrismondo* on his release. But his inspiration had died, and he spent the last six years of his life under Papal protection, labouring at a revision of his *Gerusalemme*, in a frantic endeavour to make it conform to the rules of Vida and the prejudices of the Inquisition.

His poem is the supreme achievement of sixteenth-century Italy. But in its subjectiveness lie the seeds of the exaggerative and cryptically romantic style of the succeeding age. The Counter-Reformation had closed down on freedom of thought. Italy's last two philosophers, Giordano Bruno and Campanella, perished, one at the stake, the other after spending thirty years in prison. Poets had learnt in the Renaissance to speak of the individual and to portray him as free. But now neither in Italy nor in Spain was any freedom of thought or expression possible. Poetry had therefore to confine itself to the elaboration of safe themes; and those poets who were impelled by the force of their own conflicts to draw another picture of the world, took refuge in madness or sickness. Tasso was the first great artist to be driven insane by the rigidity of post-Renaissance state Christianity; he had many successors.

Italian poetry of the sixteenth century was chiefly lyrical; and Tasso was most perfectly successful in his lyrical love poetry, which is, at times, closely related to that of GIAMBATTISTA MARINO (1569–1625) who gave his name to the new mannerism which infected Italian poetry.

Marinism is but one aspect of an international style, strongest in the Mediterranean countries, which exploited surprise, violence, and incongruity of detail, and which aimed rather at astonishing its readers than at affecting their emotions of awe and sympathy. The Baroque style was both a continuation and a reversal of that of the Renaissance. Classical mythology, the pastoral convention, Petrarchan sentiment, all were used, but shown in movement and contradiction, not as before in tranquillity. A sonnet may be built up on one sustained metaphor, a comparison of the sea to the sky, and of its fish to the stars. Marino seizes on a curious detail in a landscape, and embellishes it with far-fetched associations; but soon the embellishment has obliterated the simple outline; the hanging ivy disguises the firm trunk of the stifled tree. Where Garcilaso, Camões, or Philip Sidney reduced complexities to the unity of a single emotion and a single vision of a simpler existence, Marino suffused his landscapes with a subjective violence which could not be expressed, as in a Protestant country, in the form of metaphysical speculation, but must take the form of distorted vision. In this his true ancestor was Torquato Tasso. To compare his sonnet on sleep (*O del Silenzio figlio e de la notte*) with that of Sidney is to see at once the new age's preoccupations with Hell and the image of death; the motives of the fourteenth century have returned, even as the mystical preoccupations of Santa Teresa and John of the Cross repeat those of Suso and Tauler.

Marino's chief poem, the *Adone*, abounds in sensuous descriptions; it is digressive and catches echoes from a thousand sources; detail has obliterated its architectural form; and an example has been set, which will be followed in France, in Spain, and even in England, and which will lead to the decay of poetry in at least the first two countries.

Marino's chief contemporaries in Italy were the unfortunate friar TOMMASO CAMPANELLA, a belated son of Ficino's Academy, who spent nearly thirty years of his life in prison for holding heterodox views, which he incorporated in poems far less finished than Marino's but stamped with a stubborn sincerity; GABRIELLO CHIABRERA (1552–1638), a prolific and accomplished lyricist who tried many styles and made music out of each; and FULVIO TESTI (1593–1646), who followed first Marino, then Chiabrera, and ended as a writer of patriotic poetry, indignant and satirical by turns. Italy had now lost that lead over other nations which had set her literature in contemporaries' eyes on a level with those of Greece and Rome. The Baroque style was for her a catastrophic decadence.

For Spain on the other hand, the twin conventions of *cultismo* or the Latinate style, and of *conceptismo*, the practice of elaborate metaphor – the first appealing to the eye, the second to the ear – marked a short peak, which nevertheless tipped over into an abyss as profound as that into which Italian poetry fell after Marino. These exaggerative mannerisms, the first of which is exemplified in the later work of Góngora and the second in Quevedo's poems, were the product of tendencies already at work in Herrera, even in Garcilaso. It was no doubt the Arabic influence still active in Andalusia, even after the expulsion of its last unabsorbed Moorish inhabitants, that sent Spanish poets in search of colour, embroidery, and violent contrasts. Most of the poets of the Gongoristic school were southerners. The few poets from the North, LUPERCIO LEONARDO DE ARGENSOLA (1559–1613) and his brother BARTOLOMÉ (1561–1631), who belonged to Saragossa, both took Luis de León as their model, and wrote poetry of Roman restraint, or occasional pieces that were limpid and realistic. Both brothers were historians attached to noble families, and both sighed with a sharp Horatian fervour for the peace of a retired life, far from the bustle of the courts. Both also wrote sonnets testifying to a sober religious standpoint. Lope de Vega spoke of them as coming from Aragon to reform the Castilian tongue. If that was their purpose, they were not successful.

LOPE DE VEGA CARPIO (1562–1635), the most prolific of Spanish writers, was a man of humbler stock, and far closer in his tastes to the people than to the court. When he came on the scene, Spain was ready for a native theatre; troupes from Italy had been visiting Madrid in his boyhood. But all the drama that Spain had produced were those few classical and pastoral plays of a courtly type, written by Encina and

Torres Naharro, and the intermezzos or *entremeses,* short farces of the type of our own *Gammer Gurton's Needle,* which had been brought to a pitch of small-scale and colloquial perfection by the actor manager LOPE DE RUEDA (*c.*1505–1565). But though he, Cervantes and others had attempted to write full-length plays on Italian models, nothing of any great interest – with the possible exception of Cervantes' patriotic Roman play *Numancia* – had been produced until that 'portent of Nature', Lope de Vega, began to write; nor was there any place of performance except the inn courtyards until 1585, when three theatres were built in Madrid.

Two years older than Shakespeare, Lope lived to the age of seventy-three and left behind him, besides much prose and poetry and two or three epics, the vast total of 1,700 plays, of which 470 survive. His plays are written in a variety of verse measures, which change with the nature of the action. Spanish dramatists developed no single serviceable metre to match the blank verse of the Elizabethans. The subjects of his plays are also most various, including as they do historical drama, sentimental comedy, and plays on religious subjects. But throughout he is a dramatist more concerned with events than with character, with external action rather than with inner motive.

Though conscious that what he wrote was inferior to the ancient classics and blaming his audiences for their low tastes, Lope insisted on preserving his freedom from the so-called Aristotelian rules. Like his contemporaries in England, he relied on plot and sub-plot, the latter providing comic relief. For while the masters were involved in questions of love and loyalty, rivalry and honour, their servants parodied their actions, making their earthy fun of the lofty sentiments which they proclaimed. The *gracioso* or peasant clown, who sometimes spoke in dialect, was a character perfected, if not invented, by Lope who survived as an essential element not only in Spanish drama, but abroad also, in the shape of the immortal Figaro, and as the comic servant of a hundred English eighteenth-century plays.

Being himself a poor man's son, and moving among humble people, Lope was much taken up with the subject of class distinction, and wrote three of his best plays upon it. In these, *Peribañez*, *Fuenteovejuna* and *El mayor alcalde el Rey* (*The Fairest Judge is the King*) he showed peasant heroes in revolt against their noble landlords and justified in their resistance by special intervention of the king. Here, of course, Lope was not writing from a revolutionary point of view, but in the royal interest, since the Spanish kings were even then engaged in breaking the power of the provincial nobility. These plays have, strictly speaking, no hero; in *Fuenteovejuna*, in particular, the whole protesting village plays the heroic rôle. Indeed, in all Lope's plays there is a lack of central characters; several intrigues are set going and, without respect for the unities of time or action, are somehow resolved by the end of the third act. The best of them, indeed, remind one of the early Shakespeare from *Love's Labour's Lost* to *All's Well That Ends Well*. Tragic subjects he avoided, leaving only one principal play *El Caballero de Olmedo* (*The Knight of Olmedo*) to which he gave the name of tragedy: and this was only acted once.

Lope was a master of local colour; his village songs and village scenes are authentic, as is the waterfront at Seville in *El Arenal de Sevillla* (*The Arenal of Seville*). For plots he went sometimes to history, sometimes to the Italian story-tellers, including that same Bandello whom Shakespeare drew upon. His methods of construction were straightforward, and he recounted them quite baldly in his verse essay *Arte nuevo de hacer comedias en este tiempo* (*The new art of playwriting in these times*): 'in the first act outline the case, in the second connect the action in such a way that, half way through the third, scarcely anyone can guess how things will end.'

This prescription might have proved stultifying, if Lope had not had great lyrical powers. True, little of his verse – except his songs – is capable of being detached, as Shakespeare's is, from its place in the play. But his whole invention is poetic; the formalism of his verse, the stock nature of his 'cloak and sword' action, and the simplicity of his effects give his plays some of the qualities of a spoken opera. The actual lines count for less than the sequence and contrast of his scenes, each confined to a single mood. His is a world in which the sentiments, turning on points of honour, *love, and justice, are predictable; only the outcome of the events is not. But even here the chances of true love being parted or wrong being perpetuated are small. The pleasure of a Lope play, therefore, lies in the variety of its embellishment rather than in the depth of the issues at stake. Pity and terror are not aroused; only delight and curiosity.

Lope's most perfect work, however, lies in the field of lyrical poetry. A few of his love-sonnets, some of the *Rimas sacras (Sacred Poems)*, which were the product of a religious crisis in his life, together with the poetry of his sacred masque, *Los Pastores de Belén (The Bethlehem Shepherds)*, formed into a small anthology would show him to be the best Spanish poet in the Renaissance style after Luis de León.

Lope de Vega was not uninfluenced by the new fashion of Góngora and his circle, even though he combated it, at the cost of taking part in personal vendettas, which went against his nature. He was a simple, pleasure-seeking man, though afflicted with a conscience which drove him into taking minor orders, perhaps in an endeavour to break away from a life of amorous intrigue which brought him little but pain, loss, and sorrow. But simple though he was, there was some unsatisfied yearning within him that drove him to prodigies of labour; to write his vast numbers of plays, his pastoral novel the *Arcadia*, and his huge epics, the first of which was directed against Sir Francis Drake, and another composed during the Armada voyage itself, in which he took part. Only the third, *La Gatomaquia (The Battle of the Cats)* – a lively, rather prolix burlesque – is at all readable to-day.

His last work, the revision of one of his earliest, was at the same time his most personal. *La Dorotea*, a prose play modelled on *La Celestina*, tells the story of his own early love affair with a woman who was faithful neither to her husband nor to her lover. The prose dialogue is rapid, yet written with care; and since the action takes place in literary circles there is a good deal of conversation about the styles and schools of the day, in which one is reminded of the best prose writing of the early Renaissance. But in the charming interpolated verses one

* el pundonor

seems already to be much closer to the new mannerism of which Lope was, as has been said, the declared enemy.

Lope's first stage successes were the signal for a spate of dramatic writing, which was encouraged by the fact that few plays were allowed to run for more than three or four performances. Histories, Italian story books, and the *romances* were looted for plots. But among Lope's close contemporaries only one, GUILLÉN DE CASTRO (1569–1631) stands out for his two plays on the subject of the Cid, episodic in themselves but successful in transferring to the stage some of the glamour and immediacy of the *romances*, and striking enough to provide Corneille with his plot for a more unified piece on the same subject: his famous *Cid*.

Spain's next great dramatist, the friar GABRIEL TÉLLEZ (1571–1648), who wrote under the pen-name of TIRSO DE MOLINA, is chiefly known for his treatment of the Don Juan legend, the subject of many plays after his own *Burlador de Sevilla* (*The Practical Joker of Seville*). Tirso brought to the stage gifts quite the opposite of Lope's. He was primarily a prose writer and a historian. As a versifier therefore, he did no more than imitate the fashionable styles of his day. Where Lope dropped many an anthology piece into his dialogue, Tirso can be credited with but one, a reaping song from a piece whose subject is the story of Ruth.

Tirso's first subjects were religious. Indeed, one cannot think that his Order would have allowed him to set up immediately as a purveyor of secular comedies. He was much more interested, however, in character than in theology, or even in action; and his creations are much less standardized than Lope's. He particularly delighted in drawing women of spirit, and often indulged in the Shakespearian device of sending them out in masculine disguise; a trick much less justifiable on the Spanish stage than on the English, since there the women's parts were taken by women, not by boys. Among Tirso's gallery of masterful heroines is a queen, the heroine of *La Prudencia en la Mujer* (*Prudence in Women*), who gives her ministers lessons in statecraft; the delicious minx in *El vergonzoso en Palacio* (*The Shy Man at Court*), who adopts every device to force her bashful lover to propose: and

Mari-Hernandez, the Galician peasant lass in the play which takes her name, who succeeds by sheer persistence in marrying a nobleman, though only after she has herself been ennobled by the king. For the Spanish public would not have accepted such a solution as a marriage between persons unequal in rank.

Tirso has a rich sense of comedy, which readily spills over into satire. For he had a grudge against society, arising, it is said, from his having been born the bastard son of a great nobleman, a humiliation which he was unable to forget. His greatest play, which has given the world one of its legendary figures, Don Juan, the reckless amorist, was in part a satire against the young sprigs of the nobility, who were no doubt his half-brothers and half-cousins. But Don Juan stands for much more than this. He incarnates the Renaissance, as seen by the generations that followed it. He is Castiglione's courtier run to seed, a pursuer of delights, which he appears to feel are owed to him, but which never satisfy him, rather than a deliberate destroyer of honour; the woman's point of view never even occurs to him. Each seduction is for him a sort of military operation, wittily but apprehensively commented on by his valet Catalinón, a *gracioso*, who plays Sancho to his reckless Quixote. Don Juan's recklessness is not that of an immoralist, only of one who thinks that there will always be time to repent. When at last he is grasped by the stone statue of the nobleman he has murdered, he accepts his damnation. For behind the façade of his egoism lies a Spanish fatalism; he is possessed by an inner violence which drives him to desperate action; for him sensuality is a kind of ordeal. But he never supposes that he can defy the moral laws and finally get away with it. He is too Spanish for that.

Until recently Tirso had been credited with the invention of this plot. But latterly a prototype for Don Juan has been found in an Italian play concerning an atheistical nobleman who seduced a nun, changed places with his servant and disappeared in a clap of thunder. Other parallels occur in a minor French piece which was staged in the same year in which *El Burlador* was printed, also in a comedy by Calderón. If Tirso was not the absolute originator of the character or the situation, still less can he be said to have exhausted the possibilities.

For one thing, he never lets his audience see into his hero's mind. His is an objective and satirical portrait conceived in the blacks and whites of right and wrong. Don Juan never reflects; he is allowed no soliloquies. He is not, therefore, comparable with Hamlet nor yet with Faust. Nevertheless, he stands for much more than himself, because in this play moral and historical issues are firmly embodied. It is the Counter-Reformation's condemnation of the Renaissance gentleman; and it brings religious judgement into the secular play.

One other piece which raises fundamental issues, lacking the humour and realism of *El Burlador*, succeeds less well in driving its lesson home. *El Condenado por desconfiado* (*The Man Condemned for Lack of Faith*) contrasts an ascetic, who loses his beliefs and is therefore damned, with a brigand, who makes a deathbed repentance, and is therefore saved. This is a straightforward theological play, of a type that Tirso did not generally write; and it is possibly the production of a more devout friar who passed it off under his name. It has nevertheless power such as only a consummate dramatist could have given it.

There is no doubt that with his satire and realism, Tirso must many times have offended his religious superiors. He was finally reprimanded when only half way through his possible span as a dramatist for the frankness with which he depicted vice on the stage. Whereupon he ceased to write plays, at a moment when he had not yet brought his gifts to perfect fruition. With a far more restricted range than Lope's, he had written some plays as good as those of that 'prodigy of Nature', and drawn one figure whose legend has proved an inexhaustible subject for later writers. Beginning as an imitator of Lope's fast moving lyrical comedy, he had gone some way to developing a drama of characters. But such innovations required to be taken far further than he had gone at the moment when he 'abjured his rough magic'; characters, to be convincing, required to be shown from the inside. Lope had already gone as far as the Shakespeare of *As You Like It*; it was Tirso who might have given us the equivalent of *Hamlet*. Instead, the tragic phase was omitted from Spanish drama: and with Calderón, Lope's equal though in a still narrower field, metaphysical symbolism, corresponding rather with that of Shakespeare's final phase, concluded the life-cycle of Spain's classical theatre.

Half-way in development between Tirso and Calderón was the poet MIRA DE AMESCUA (*c*.1574–1644), a priest who was author of several religious plays, and of *El Esclavo del demonio* (*The Devil's Servant*), which tells of a sinner's pact with the devil and of his subsequent conversion. Another dramatist who continued in a more popular vein deriving from Lope was VÉLEZ DE GUEVARA (1579–1644), whose play on the subject of Inés de Castro, Portugal's national heroine, comes near to tragedy. Yet another contemporary, JUAN RUIZ DE ALARCÓN (*c*.1581–1639), a little hunchback from Mexico, produced well-turned comedies, not very elaborate in their poetry, which set an example to the French writers of the next age. His best piece *La Verdad sospechosa* (*The Suspicious Truth*) tells of a congenital liar, whose fictions reach a rare height of inventiveness. A much lampooned and bitter individual, Ruiz de Alarcón seems unconsciously to have sided with his enemy of society, who succeeds in escaping punishment until the fatal moment when he ventures to tell the truth and is disbelieved. Corneille took this play as a basis for his *Le Menteur*.

PEDRO CALDERÓN DE LA BARCA (1600–81) was the most finished dramatist, though not the greatest genius, to devote himself to the Spanish theatre. To compare him with Lope is to contrast highly-wrought silver with crude gold. Calderón viewed everything, if not theologically, at least dialectically. Plot construction, verse writing, the introduction of humour, the rules of the *pundonor*, the rights of jealousy, and the poetry of love: every detail of his plays was systematized. Not for nothing had he been educated in a Jesuit school. Yet, always and everywhere, there was an element of violence that would not fit in.

Though first intended for Holy Orders, and though theology was in his bones, Calderón decided on a stage career and, coming to the theatre a few years only before Lope's death, he succeeded to that 'prodigy of Nature's' popularity. At first he was content to write for a popular audience. Having learnt how to give them a cloak and sword comedy as ingenious as Lope's and far better unified, he passed on first to plays of honour and revenge, then to religious melodrama. The young Calderón, for all the formality of his plots, was a boisterous man who wrote his love scenes from experience, and knew jealousy at first hand. But always, whatever his subject, one finds a note of bewilderment in his lines; the world of appearances did not quite convince him. As a theologian, he saw in it a stage upon which the action passed according to logical rules, which he wished to accept, but against which something in him always rebelled. He always set his characters dancing to the tune of a well-built plot. Yet his rhetoric refused to confine itself to the neat task he had given it. The gestures of his characters became exaggerated, because something in himself had been left out of account. It is not surprising that Shelley and the German romantics valued Calderón so highly. They did not appreciate his strangely formal language, his hyperbole, or the exuberant chop-logic of his speeches. What they saw in him was the foiled romantic, whose Promethean heroes refused to be bound to the harsh rock of his Counter-Reformation theology.

Many of them indeed have a romantic look. The prince who gives his name to *El Príncipe constante* prefers to die a prisoner of the Moors rather than buy his freedom at the cost of surrendering a fortress. But this is not a play of simple heroism; the prince is a poet, and the action passes like a pageant of bright colours through a mist. The same is true of what seems at first reading a simple comedy of intrigue and secret doors, *La Dama duende* (*The Enchanted Lady*). But here the hero mistakes his mistress, when she pays him secret visits, for some kind of ghost or fairy, and again dream and reality are confused. Calderón's plays of jealousy and revenge may appear to be more realistic than these. But so astounding is the code whereby it is legitimate for a man to kill his wife on the barest possibility that she may one day betray him that in such pieces as *A secreto agravio secreta venganza* (*For a Secret Affront Secret Revenge*) or *El Mayor monstruo del mundo* (*The Greatest Monster in the World*), we seem to be in a world even stranger than the brave new world of the Constant Prince. In fact, Calderón uses these exaggerative treatments of the stock theme of the *pundonor* as a means of canalizing the violence that he cannot keep out of his writing. Had he written *Othello*, he would have justified the Moor's murder of Desdemona on the grounds that only thus could he save himself from the pangs of jealousy, to which no gentleman ought to submit. Here, in fact, we are moving through another dream, though one that was shared by the larger part of Calderón's audience, who subscribed to the decaying military illusion that a man's greatest treasure was his reputation, and that nothing mattered but appearances.

Calderón's greatest work, *La Vida es sueño* (*Life is a Dream*) attempts a solution of this problem of dream and reality. Yet it is impossible to find any deeply philosophical implications in it. It seems to be an allegory, but does not work out. When we see the prince Segismundo first in a dungeon, then in a palace, and then restored to his dungeon, we are merely confronted with a mystery. If life is like this, wherein lies his responsibility? Soliloquy follows soliloquy. He passes from lyrical reflexion to violence, and then in the third act to meditation. If the play had been written by a modern dramatist, there would have been but one character; all the rest would have been figures in the prince's dream. *La Vida es sueño* marks the highest point of the Baroque drama; all is fluid, but all is held together by a single poetic idea.

El Mágico prodigioso (*The Prodigious Magician*), Calderón's other masterpiece, is a play written on a variant of the Faust legend for the municipality of the small town of Yepes. In it a young pagan sells his soul to the devil, to obtain the love of a Christian maiden. But spells have no power over her freewill; he is converted, and the two perish on the scaffold. The poetry of this play is so outstanding that it tempted Shelley to make a partial translation, in which, despite his misunderstanding of Calderón's rhetorical style, he brings out that vein of romantic extravagance which is at its strongest in this play.

Calderón's career as a dramatist was interrupted by the long interval of the Catalan war and the Portuguese revolt during which time the theatres were closed. In these campaigns, which marked the first stage in the break-up of Spain's empire, he fought as a soldier, and in the only play that bears any marks of that experience Calderón ventures for the first time on social criticism. *El Alcalde de Zalamea* (*The Mayor of Zalamea*) is a fresh treatment of a plot on which Lope had already written a play. It is concerned with the old theme of honour, but with a peasant's honour, maintained against the vulgar pretensions of a blackguardly captain who has seduced his daughter. Here we almost seem to be back in Lope's world, where honest independence counts for more than blue blood. Calderón's *Alcalde* is far better constructed, however, than its model. The characters are reduced in number, and the plot is pulled together from duality into unity. But what counts most is the play's geniality. Pedro Crespo, the mayor, is the only peasant in all Calderón's plays who is not a clown; he is in fact, with his sparring partner, Don Lope de Figueroa, one of the few real personalities that Calderón ever drew.

The result of his war experience on his writing was, except in this one instance, deplorable. His romantic violence ebbed away, and his powers of formalization increased. Calderón's output for the next thirty years consisted of theological melodramas, commissioned by various municipalities, and mythological spectacles designed for the court, which had become more interested in stage machinery than in the drama itself. He also produced a number of plays for music, which took the name of *zarzuelas* from that of a princely hunting-box at which they were performed. Meanwhile he had taken priest's orders, and lived in half-retirement, surrounded by a huge collection of religious gew-gaws.

Now that he had somehow quelled his violence, Calderón wrote in an even more formalized rhetoric than before; moments of poetry are few in these late plays. He seems even to have invented a system of imagery which enabled him automatically to pick out the right adjective or metaphor. Everything was predictable in the half-allegorical style that he affected. If appearances were not real, at least they could now be prevented from springing any surprises. His sacred plays illustrated the Catholic dogmas with more than his original certitude, while his entertainments exploited a whole phantasmagoria of Greek legend, allegory, melodrama, contrast, and extravagant scenic effect. If he is at any moment in touch with anything more real it is when he is writing of human love, which still seems to him, in the Platonic sense, to reflect some other-worldly reality.

Spanish drama petered out. Calderón had attempted almost everything, leaving only satire and realism, which were exploited by FRANCISCO DE ROJAS ZORILLA (1607-48) who was also the author of one original play on the overworked theme of honour in which the characters behave rather more naturally than Calderón's. But for the rest, all veins were exhausted.

Spain's last epoch produced three outstanding writers of lyrical verse and of prose, who with talents equal to Calderón's, carried Spanish literature into similar blind-alleys. LUIS DE GÓNGORA (1561-1627) was born in the year before Lope de Vega, and shared with him the new partiality for popular themes and rhythms. The *romance*, the *villancico*, and the *letrilla* no longer seemed rustic and awkward. They were now written, however, in a sophisticated manner which turned them into a kind of witty half-pastiche. For the new poetry was a court poetry, highly Latinized in vocabulary and soon to imitate even the Latin syntax; and Góngora, its chief practitioner, turned from the sonnet to the *romance*, applying the same decorative style, with equal ease, to each. As an Andalusian, he was particularly drawn to the ballads of the Moorish frontier.

> *Lloraba la niña*
> *(y tenia razón)*
> *la prolija ausencia*
> *de su ingrato amor.*

(The girl was weeping – and she had reason – for the prolonged absence of her thankless lover.)

All is as of old but for the tell-tale word *prolija*, which belongs to the new age. In many of Góngora's *romances*, nevertheless, one seems to hear the music, to see the dancers. Ceasing to follow each word, one forgets the obscurities, does not note the baroque by-play of black and white, of castanets and fingers – a pure seventeenth-century conceit – as one watches the country maidens tread their measure beneath the pines of Júcar.

Góngora uses a palette of strong colours: scarlet and white

of cheeks, gold of the sun, transparency of water; and soon the colours come to replace the objects and 'snow clad in a thousand colours' connotes fair country-girls in their best clothes. This is an exaggeration of the style developed by Herrera, and it is the stuff of most of Góngora's sonnets. The working out of their metaphors, and the contrived music of their word-order is a matter of consummate ingenuity. The subject hardly matters: it may well be no more than a formal compliment to the king or a courtier, or praise of a building or a town. For his more sustained flights in this *culterano* style, Góngora turned to mythology and Arcadian pastoral, producing in his *Fábula de Polifemo y Galatea* (*Fable of Polyphemus and Galatea*) and in his two *Soledades* (*Solitudes*) miracles of complexity in which the legend is entirely overlaid by its elaborations. He seemed to be on the way towards founding a new poetic language made up of the Italian inheritance and so much as he could usefully draw from the *romance* tradition. But in doing so he dried up his own natural poetic talent. He had contrived a technique of such remarkable subtlety that it was hardly possible to use it except for its own sake. The instrument had destroyed its master.

Until poetry readers of the present century came to appreciate the complex styles of such writers as Mallarmé, most of Góngora's poetry was neglected; the eighteenth century paid him lip-service, the nineteenth century included in its anthologies only a few of his Herreran sonnets and simpler *romances*. The last thirty years have seen taste run to the other extreme, and for a brief moment in the twenties, Spanish poets even attempted to write their own poems in this style which their fathers had rejected for its contorted obscurity.

With Góngora's return to favour several other practitioners of this Latinate style have been re-edited and read again. Of these, two in different ways carry the Gongoristic style to fresh extremes. *Paraíso cerrado para muchos, jardines abiertos para pocos* (*Paradise closed to the many, Gardens open to the few*) by PEDRO SOTO DE ROJAS (1585–1658) describes the author's formal gardens in Granada so allusively that the poem can hardly be read without the introductory commentary by a fellow poet; while the fables and sonnets of GABRIEL

BOCÁNGEL (1608–58) strike remarkable images, as that in which a trumpet note heard over the sea is compared to a bronze bird, but too often bury them in conventional hyperbole. These writers show us nothing of themselves except their consummate craftsmanship.

Spanish poets did not move unanimously in the new *culterano* direction. But even Lope, who opposed Góngora, imitated many of his mannerisms, and JUAN DE JÁUREGUI (1583–1641), another resolute opponent, actually wrote his one fine poem, on the subject of Orpheus, in a manner palpably influenced by the tendencies he attacked. If one compares this *Orfeo*, however, with Góngora's fable of Polyphemus, one sees that the new style used sparingly heightened the lights and deepened the shadows, as in a Salvator Rosa picture, while used as Góngora used it, it seems to describe a landscape as artificial as a museum panorama. Jáuregui's entrance to the infernal regions is 'horrid' in an almost romantic sense, while Góngora's cave of the one-eyed giant is merely curious.

Other poets who used the Gongoristic style sparingly, or who developed their own elaborations of language and metaphor along roughly parallel lines were many. Among the most interesting were JOSÉ DE VALDIVIELSO (1560–1638), whose nativity poems and Christmas hymns combine charm and artifice, puns and piety in a most delightful way; PEDRO ESPINOSA (1578–1650), a poet who, in his fable addressed to the river Genil, blends music, mythology, and natural detail into a style elaborated rather from Garcilaso's than from Herrera's, but who produced little more after suffering a disappointment in love, JUAN DE TASIS, CONDE DE VILLAMEDIANA (1582–1622) Góngora's friend and patron, and a fine sonneteer, who was banished from court by Philip III and murdered on his return; and LUIS DE CARILLO Y SOTOMAYOR (1583–1610), who drew his own lessons from Herrera and wrote sonnets with a complexity similar to Góngora's, though on metaphysical subjects. Some of Góngora's enemies claimed that it was really Carrillo who had invented the *culterano* style, and that its chief practitioner had no more than imitated him. This accusation is palpably baseless, since Góngora's scope was far and away greater than Carrillo's.

The second great writer of the Spanish decadence, FRANCISCO DE QUEVEDO Y VILLEGAS (1580–1645), was primarily a satirist, whose early poems celebrating his loves have a bitter vein of realism which contrasts favourably with the artificialities of the *culterano* style. He was an enemy of Góngora's, but while criticizing his mannerisms, he himself elaborated mannerisms of equal complexity. His theory of *conceptismo* insisted on pure and colloquial Spanish, and aimed at vivid imagery, which came to be built up into sustained conceits. The difference between *cultismo* and *conceptismo* is, as Gerald Brenan points out, much like the contrast between Donne and Milton. But this fails to make the point that the two styles differ not so much in principle as in method. Góngora draws on Latin and imitates Latin syntax; Quevedo, sharing his desire to perfect a literary idiom, introduces popular speech and even thieves' slang for the same purpose. The true contrast is not between these two, but between the pair of them and such a poet as either of the Argensola brothers or Malherbe, who deliberately restricted their vocabulary and barred curious, local, and recondite turns of speech.

Quevedo's realism was paralleled in France by that of the lesser libertine poets, Saint-Amant and Théophile de Viau; but no Spanish Malherbe arose to restore the purity of style that he, Góngora, and Calderón had destroyed.

Quevedo was a man of great learning and enormous vigour, whose poetry though of great bulk was no more than occasional. His principal works are a picaresque novel *La vida del buscón* (*The Sharper's Life*) which will be noticed in a later chapter, and *Los Sueños* (*The Visions*), morbid and expressionistic hell-scenes in which lawyers, barbers, tailors, judges, poets, dramatists, bores, and fine ladies are subjected to obscene, Bosch-like tortures. Heartless and farcical, feverish and grotesque, it is the book of an exasperated and lonely man who saw his own country falling into decay, who pinned his faith on one politician, the Count of Olivares, to whom he addressed his most famous poem, his *Epístola satírica y censoria* (*Satirical and Admonitory Letter*). But Olivares, far from saving his country, precipitated it into further decline by renewing the war against Holland.

Quevedo was an impassioned humanist a century too late, a satirist in the Roman tradition, and a stoic, who watched the advance of old age and natural decline with a resignation not unblended with a certain spite against the world that so disappointed him.

> *Vencida de la edad sentí mi espada,*
> *y no hallé cosa en qué poner los ojos*
> *que no fuese recuerdo de la muerte.*

(I felt my sword subdued by age, and could find nothing to rest my eyes upon that was not a reminder of death.)

Quevedo's satirical vein was worked out by two later poets, ANTONIO ENRÍQUEZ GÓMEZ (1602–60) and MIGUEL DE BARRIOS (1625?–1701) with whom Spain's silver age ends. Both were of Jewish blood, the one a civil servant and the other a soldier, and both ended their lives in Holland, restored to their own religion. Thus did the Inquisition put the last touches to the work of destruction which it had begun with the imprisonment of Luis de León. Spain was reduced to a dead conformity of belief, in which even spiritual independence perished. MIGUEL DE MOLINOS (1627–96), a Jesuit mystic and an elegant writer, was compelled by the Holy Office to foreswear his quietist philosophy, and spent the last nine years of his life imprisoned in a monastery.

Another victim of the Church's censorship on thought was the Jesuit, BALTASAR GRACIÁN (1601–58), a college rector and military chaplain of wide reading, whose recipe for successful living and worldly success seems to bear little relationship to the faith he professed. Theoretically an enemy of Machiavellism, he in fact outlined a philosophy based on an up-to-date version of the Italian's power politics. The chief attribute of a successful man must, in his view, be prudence and freedom from illusions; he must welcome new fashions and turn them to his own purposes.

For a while Gracián encountered no difficulty with his

Order. His three short treaties on the Hero, the Politician, and the Man of Discretion, subtle, witty, and sententious, together made up a seventeenth-century equivalent of Castiglione's *Courtier*. His principal work, *El Criticón* (*The Criticaster*), however, although published pseudonymously, aroused his superiors, who imprisoned him on bread and water. He attempted to leave the Company, but in vain, and died in disgrace.

It is hardly surprising that an organization whose purpose was one of unquestioning obedience failed to appreciate this very individual writer, who seemed to reveal both its ruthlessly practical policy and its failings. *El Criticón,* the third volume of which got him into trouble, is an allegory, which tells of the adventures of two friends, a rational man and a savage who, after meeting on a desert island, make a tour of the world, travelling from misfortune to misfortune in pursuit of a purely human immortality, which, as they see it, is achieved only by heroes, poets, and painters. The book is acute and civilized, and was much admired in France and in England. It is now a respected but neglected classic.

Perhaps Gracián's most lively work, however, is his little manual of the conceptist writers' stock-in-trade, complete with a catalogue of all the different kinds of conceits. Gracián saw through all the contemporary artificialities. He remained, nevertheless, an extremely artificial writer.

While the seventeenth century saw the subordination of Renaissance exuberance to a mannered style and conformity of thought in the Catholic countries, in those lands where the two sects were still at odds, and where freedom of expression consequently prevailed, the late Baroque age was both positive and productive.

In Holland, where the medieval dramatic forms still enjoyed popular favour, the transition from old to new styles was slow and individual. The Dutch poets of the early seventeenth century, PIETER CORNELISZ HOOFT (1581–1647) and GERBRAND BREDERODE (1585–1618), wrote lyrics more or less influenced by Renaissance models, but spontaneous and realistic in the manner of the songs from the old moralities and of the interior and tavern painting of the day. Comedy also was developed on models partly native, partly based on Terence, while the contemporary Latin dramas written in the Jesuit schools influenced Holland's greatest poet and playwright, JOOST VAN DEN VONDEL (1587–1679), a satirist, deeply involved in the sectarian disputes of the time, who finally moved over from Protestantism to Catholicism. His earliest drama echoes the language of the Bible and of du Bartas. Then he turned to the Classics, first to reinforce his satirical style, and then for models on which he built his favourite tragedy *Jephta*. His masterpiece is the lyrical drama *Lucifer*, a Sophoclean play with magnificent choruses which together with his odes and laments, remain the peak of Dutch poetry.

The style of *Lucifer* is said to have influenced Milton. Certainly the Dutch school as a whole stimulated the poetical revival in Germany, which took place towards the end of the devastating Thirty Years War, in which the German cultural tradition almost perished. Dutch influences first took root among the Protestants of Silesia who, lacking a University of their own, were in the habit of travelling to Holland to study. The new tendencies sprang from a book on poetics by MARTIN OPITZ (1597–1639), which explained, with examples, how the chief Romance metres and stanzas could be adapted to the German language. But true impetus to the rebirth of literature in this distant province, outside the borders of the old Roman Empire and still heavily Slavonic in population, was the writing of the great Silesian mystic, JAKOB BOEHME (1575–1624), a Protestant shoemaker, with the deep experience of an Eckhart. Boehme restated the deepest truths sometimes in a difficult alchemical language, which went back to that of the Swiss physician PARACELSUS (1493–1541), and sometimes with the colloquial clarity of his *Dialogue between a scholar and his Master concerning the supersensual life*, which remains almost the perfect introduction to the mystical viewpoint.

Boehme's non-Catholic teaching, which spoke of God as the divine ground of all things, with good and evil as his manifestations at man's level, not only profoundly influenced the German poetic revival, but also affected such poets of the more distant future as Blake and Goethe. Here, for the first time in Western Europe, a spiritual message was pronounced which was addressed directly to each man, without reference to his dogmatic beliefs.

Germany was preconditioned by its Lutheran inheritance to the writing of religious poetry. But the most profound – though not the most accomplished – poet of the new school was a Catholic convert, who published under the name of ANGELUS SILESIUS (The Silesian Angel) (1624–77) little gnomic poems distantly suggestive of Blake's, which he collected in a volume called *Der cherubinischer Wandersmann* (*The Cherubic Wanderer*), and also some hymns which use the erotic metaphors of the *Song of Songs* in a rather pedestrian way.

A greater poet than this Silesian mystic is the dramatist ANDREAS GRYPHIUS (1616–64), also a convert to Catholicism, whose talents ran parallel with those of Vondel, who to some extent influenced him. Some of his plays are on Christian subjects, some are court pastorals, and sometimes his language seems to show some indirect influence from Shakespeare, of whom the Germans had learnt something from travelling theatrical companies, which paid their first visit in 1587.

Gryphius is best known, however, as a lyrical poet whose treatments of the *Vanitas vanitatum* theme seem, with their devout and four-square courage, to confront the worst that civil war could bring and to outstare it. Of all the poets of the Baroque age, none spoke so simply as Andreas Gryphius, and none showed as great affinities, in attitude if not in style, with our own Metaphysicals. He is certainly the best of an interesting group which includes PAUL FLEMING (1609–40), an individual love-poet, who also wrote poems of unclouded religious feeling based on a theosophical viewpoint, derived by way of Boehme from Paracelsus and HOFMANN VON HOFMANNSWALDAU (1617–79), a sensualist, who found his models in Ovid and Marino, and whose poems lie closer to the main European tradition than those of the other Silesians. He too, however, like all the German poets of this age, hears the thunderous voice of Eternity booming in his ears, and in chiding his coy mistress can think of no fitter rebuke for her coldness than to remind her that it will soon be death who will be stroking her breasts.

This group, who have lately been the subject of several anthologies, show that German poetry has at least a longer ancestry than nineteenth-century critics supposed. German writers, as a whole, however, continued to write largely in Latin, and it was not until the middle of the next century that Germany began to gain national confidence and to recover from the setbacks she had suffered in the Reformation and in her thirty years of religious war.

The end of the seventeenth century saw Italy and Spain in eclipse, and the adumbration of a new classical style in France based on a unity of construction, which had been violated by all the great writers of the first half of the century; by the dramatists of England and Spain, and by all the schools of Baroque poets who had put decoration and detail before directness of statement. But not only did the new classicism purify the language, insist on the unities and standardize the forms of literature; it also put an end to the incipient romantic individualism of those stoical poets who had made poetry out of their doubts, their beliefs, and their despairs. Henceforth the standard was that of social conformity, rather than of belief; and for the dissident were reserved not the penalties of the Inquisition, but imprisonment within the walls of a private neurosis by a society intolerant of eccentrics. In this new age, whose first exemplar had been Tasso, suicide and the madhouse were the last resorts of men of genius, who had lost the ready bond with their fellow men offered to them by an integrated society and even by the Renaissance ideal of the individual. Now the artist was a lone soul cast on his own resources; and secular mockery sometimes treated him with even greater cruelty than a religious tribunal. The enlightenment which had begun in the Florentine Academy had lost its virtue in extending its territory, and now the wisdom of the Ancients was presented as if it were no more than a recipe for national grandeur, worldly morals, and an art which glorified both.

Chapter Ten

THE GREAT AGE OF FRANCE

W HEN, some time before the middle of the seventeenth century, the lead in the Arts passed from Spain to France, the virtues of balance, order, proportion, and the unities, derived by Renaissance critics from their reading of the classics, became, in theory, universally obligatory. No work of art could obtain currency that did not at least claim to possess them. Yet no living work could in fact conform to theories that set intellectual organization so far above emotion as hardly to allow a poem or play any emotional inspiration at all. A truly classical age, which conformed to all the rules, would have had no place for Racine or for Pascal. Indeed, it would not have listened to its own prime theoretician RENÉ DESCARTES (1596–1650), whose theory of a rational universe depended on an emotional intuition, like the lightning flash that struck him on the night of 10 November 1619.

Hitherto Descartes had always been seeking for a key to the world's mystery; to find an entirely new system by which all questions alike could be solved. He read the Catalan mystic Ramón Lull, but it was not a mystical apprehension that he sought. To him mechanics and geometry seemed to offer models to which a new universal science must conform. Then on the night of his illumination, he reached the triple certainty that all knowledge was one, that it was the work of a single mind, and that it took the form of a poetic intuition. Descartes devoted himself to the pursuit of this universal science which would enable man to subdue nature, to lengthen his own life, and to know the relations and proportions that bound one object to another. He had found a rational God, had deified the rational quality in man and in nature, and now sought to demonstrate the truths of metaphysics in the same manner as a geometrical theorem. There was no room in his theory for the God of the Bible, no room for facts incapable of proof. Christianity bases itself on historical facts, but Descartes could see no certitude in history. Knowledge had come to him in a flash of intuition, and there were no contradictions in it. However, although Descartes was not himself a vulgar rationalist, Cartesianism soon came to fix its faith on human reason alone.

Descartes spent much of his life abroad, as a soldier, as a curious spectator of the passing scene, and finally as a scientist. Then, after a long residence in Holland, he died on a visit to the court of Christina of Sweden, leaving a single important book in French, his *Discours de la Méthode* (*Discourse upon Method*), and other writings and correspondence in Latin, all written with a clarity and logic greatly in advance of the more muddled theorizings of his Renaissance predecessors, or of his own contemporary PIERRE GASSENDI (1592–1655), who mildly defended the *libertinage* or Epicureanism of the Saint-Amant circle.

Religious controversy – all within the Catholic Church, for Protestantism had been finally defeated – ranged between the extreme right wing of the Jesuits, who taught that grace was a universal gift, and the Jansenists, who believed that the elect were strictly limited in number. These latter – a Catholic counterpart to the Calvinists – exercised a great influence on cultured circles, and from their centre at the Abbey of Port-Royal, which included a nunnery, a school, and a theological centre, waged a long war against the Jesuits, a war which did not end with the dispersal of the Port-Royal community and the destruction of their abbey.

Jansenism stood for a return to the Christianity of the Fathers and for a strong moral order, took a hostile view of the arts, and fixed on the Jesuits, whose pliant modernism had been so effective in rebuilding the Roman Church, the label of casuists, which they have never shaken off to this day. Its greatest apologist, BLAISE PASCAL (1623–62) was a sickly mathematician, who underwent two profound religious experiences, which brought him into close contact with Port-Royal, though he never entirely identified himself with its point of view. His first great work, the *Lettres provinciales* (*Provincial Letters*) took the form of eighteen pamphlets in defence of the Jansenist leader Antoine Arnauld, who was being accused of heresy by Rabelais' old enemies, the Sorbonne theologians. These took the form of a scathing attack on Jesuit laxity, and a lucid exposure of the contradictions in Jesuit theology.

Like Descartes, Pascal was a scientific thinker, always ready to clinch a theoretical point with a concrete illustration, and arrogant in his scorn of compromise and muddled thinking. His masterpiece, *Les Pensées* (*Thoughts*), exist only in the form of notes made in the last years of his life, for a book which he intended to write in defence of religion. Pascal accused Descartes of striving to erect a philosophical system in which God only acted as a first cause, and then retired from the scene. If he too had a thirst for order, he had, combined with it, an ever-present sense of the immeasurable. He saw man caught between the infinitely large and the infinitely small, in an aching despair of ever knowing their nature; and here he had arrived at the position of rational theology's most bitter critic, the heretical Giordano Bruno. Only in God, said Pascal, could all contradictions be reconciled. As for rationalism, 'What are our rational principles,' he asked, 'but our habits of thought? . . . and habit is our second nature, which overlies and destroys our primal nature.' Pascal did not despair; he accepted as certainties what Descartes dismissed as mere probabilities; the truths of historical fact. He claimed to be guided not by reason, but by an infallible feeling or spiritual apprehension. He made no defence of the common proof of God's existence based on the order of the Universe. On that side all was uncertainty. Only Christianity, with its affirmation of Man's divine origins, of his primal fall and his redemption, could offer him comfort or enlightenment in the ceaseless anxiety in which he lived. Here Pascal turned as resolutely to the Bible for confirmation as Descartes had turned away from it. He saw the drift towards a religion of reason, and counselled a gambler's throw on the card of unreason. His was the faith of a St Augustine, a Christianity of crisis, when true belief seemed mere foolishness: and as such it was far in advance even of the Jansenist faith which he had defended. Arnauld and his friends were, in most ways, no more than a political opposition to the Jesuit party, to the

Papacy's extreme claims and, sometimes, to Gallican counter-claims. But Pascal was a most violent critic of humanism itself, of natural law and of rationalistic optimism. He saw that Man had fallen, and gambled on the Love of God as the sole possible redemptive force.

To place beside Descartes and Pascal a master of fine, but rather grandiose prose, JACQUES-BÉNIGNE BOSSUET (1627–1704), a bishop and the champion of moderate Gallicanism, would appear absurd, but for the fact that he attempted to represent the mean between them, combining as he did all the trappings of emotion with a tightly organized argument. What seems to be missing is the urgent note of conviction, which was common to both Descartes and Pascal. In his *Oraisons funèbres* (*Funeral Orations*) we catch the bishop in a florid attitude of Baroque devotion, celebrating the triumph of death over such noble characters as Charles I's widow Henrietta Maria, and Maria Theresa of Austria, Louis XIV's queen; while his sermons, with their striking images and the masterly build-up of their rhetoric, are remarkable rather for their style than for their content. Bossuet was an ecclesiastical politician, and as such could not afford the luxury of an irrational faith.

It was not, however, either the philosophers or the preachers who exercised the greatest direct influence on the development of French literature. What was new came rather from the salons of distinguished ladies where the arts were a subject of frequent discussion, where artists were entertained, and where amateurs attempted to vie with them. Whereas in Spain literature had grown up around the court, the University of Salamanca and the cities of Granada and Seville, and in Italy a few princely families had played the leading rôles as patrons, in France the patronage of letters had first been in the hands of non-political nobles and their ladies, but was afterwards taken over by one all-powerful minister, who saw in it a possible weapon of propaganda.

The first great mistress of a salon was the Marquise de Rambouillet, whose *Blue Room* was a centre for those writers who owed most to Italian and Spanish fashions. Here a verse anthology was collected; here various old poetic forms were revived and practised. The forgotten *rondeau* was once more perfected by Vincent Voiture; the *vers marotique* was developed, and Marot's reputation as its originator inflated at the expense of Ronsard's. Here too even more artificial forms, such as riddles and enigmas, were elaborated; and here finally Malherbe, after being snubbed in his lifetime, was lauded and imitated after his death. Indeed, it was from this *précieux* or precious circle that the new classicism was preached in his name.

The Hôtel de Rambouillet led the fashion for almost forty years, only to yield in about 1650 to Madeleine de Scudéry's circle, where preciosity took a sentimental form and where the subtle steps of the love affair were meticulously worked out and codified, in the form of the *Carte du pays de tendre* (*Map of the Country of the Affections*), which the hostess incorporated as the engraved frontispiece of her novel *Clélie*.

Meanwhile, however, the rise to power of Richelieu had brought into being an official rival to the salon in the form of the Académie, whose rulings and judgements were to take on a semi-authoritative importance. No longer was patronage to rest with noble families who were for the most part in political opposition to the royal house and the minister. The arts must be brought under control, like every other branch of the national life. Richelieu was an enlightened dictator. He had a love of the stage, and had erected in his own garden a theatre which could compare with any in Paris. His natural bias was towards the new classical theories, which were in keeping with his ambitions for France's imperial greatness. Richelieu and Olivares, in their respective countries, both strove to centralize authority, and to bring all activities beneath their control. But while the Spanish minister, hymned by Quevedo as the honest man who would revive the sober age of old, succeeded only in losing Portugal, in driving the Catalans into revolt, and leaving Spanish literature to its decay, Richelieu began that expansion of his country that Louis XIV was to continue, and stimulated a literary revival which could never have sprung from the salons of the *Précieuses*.

The Académie Française originated in about 1626 as a private circle, to become an official body in 1635, whose duty it was to 'give definite rules to the language, to purify it, and to make it eloquent and capable of serving the arts and sciences.' To this end it was commissioned to compose a dictionary, a grammar, a treatise on poetics and one on rhetoric. Thus the first officially sponsored literature was provided for, and in 1637, with its observations on Corneille's controversial masterpiece *Le Cid*, the Académie's first official pronouncement was made.

It was not by chance that the Académie first concerned itself with the question of drama. For the French theatre, after lagging far behind those of Spain and England, was now perfecting its own forms, at a moment when the Elizabethan stage was in its Caroline decline, and when Calderón was approaching the end of his great productive period. The stage too was readier to be subjected to academic rules than the novel, which was developing simultaneously, or than poetry, which had lost its impetus.

French drama had reached its melodramatic nadir in the sanguinary tragedies of Alexandre Hardy. New inspiration came first from two poets, neither of whom was primarily a dramatic writer. The *libertin* Théophile de Viau's *Pyrame et Thisbé*, styled by him a tragedy, was primitive in its stagecraft. The scenes were unlinked, one set of characters entering after another to deliver its speeches and retire. But here for the first time there was no violence, and the language remained always on an elevated plane. 'Except for those who have no memory,' said Mlle de Scudéry's brother, Georges, fourteen years after its first presentation by a strolling company, 'there is no one who does not know it by heart.' Literature had once more taken over the stage: and a year later another poet, this time a close friend of Malherbe's, presented a pastoral play of great lyrical beauty. *Les Bergeries*, by Honorat de Bueil, Marquis de Racan, set out to continue the tradition of Tasso's *Aminta* but achieved an individual blending of poetry and social comedy which still maintains its charm. Both these plays were hailed by the *précieux* and given gala performances. Almost simultaneously, moreover, a professional dramatist, JEAN MAIRET (1604–86), began to write pastorals without the conventional choruses and with real peasants for characters. He too was moving towards the comedy of manners.

By 1631 the theatre, according to the minor dramatist André Mareschal, had become the country's favourite entertainment, and romantic tragi-comedies, which took plots either directly from Spanish plays or from incidents out of pastoral novels, were extremely popular with a young society that was bored by Hardy, and had never given a thought to the unities. Spain, viewed from Paris, was the country where girls were passionate and intrigues were the rule, and Spanish plays enjoyed a popularity which lasted for a good fifteen years.

Meanwhile theorists had once more brought forward the allegedly Aristotelian rule of the unities, which aroused great antagonism among the practising dramatists. In 1628, however, Mairet himself had come out in their favour, and in 1630 *Clitandre* the first tragi-comedy to conform to them was produced by the young dramatist Pierre Corneille. Three years later tragedy itself, which had almost dropped out of the repertory – as it had done in England – in favour of the bastard tragi-comedy, was revived by the presentation of *Hercule mourant* (*The Dying Hercules*), by another young dramatist, Jean Rotrou, closely followed by Mairet's own *Sophonisbe*.

The new French drama had by now an enthusiastic public, though as yet only one primitive theatre in Paris itself, the Hôtel de Bourgogne, which was always occupied by the same company. It was possible, however, for visiting troupes to hire disused tennis courts in the capital, though this involved the payment of 'the usual fees' to the old *Confrérie,* who held a monopoly. But the independent companies were free to stage their plays in a great number of provincial towns, and the provinces had consequently a lead over the Capital. Up till then, except when a performance was being put on at court or for some nobleman, theatrical resources were slight. The stage was no more than the rectangle of a tennis court, with seats and boxes on three sides and a number of rooms at the back of the fourth, in which interior scenes could be performed, and in front of which such elementary properties as pillars or an arch could be erected. Corneille, in his early comedies, used these as a number of adjacent houses or shops.

With the coming of the unity of place, however, this primitive method of signifying locality became no longer necessary. But if their resources in this respect were not so great as those of the Spanish theatre, the French had, with the adoption of Malherbe's poetic reforms, a conventional language and conventional verse forms much superior to the diluted lyrical forms, with their constant variations, that prevailed in Spain. If the French alexandrine couplet was less pliable than the English blank-verse line, interspersed with prose dialogue for the humorous or trivial passages, it had the advantage of keeping the action and sentiment always on an exalted plane, and of allowing a subtlety of reasoning, impossible in the Spanish metres, though practised by Shakespeare, in his greatest soliloquies, in England.

For while English drama is concerned with character displayed in action, and that of Spain moved towards the formalism of music, the French theatre of Corneille, Racine and many lesser tragedians was essentially a drama of motive, an internal drama in which a character's reflexions upon the action carried more weight than the action itself.

PIERRE CORNEILLE (1606–84) was a briefless lawyer from Rouen, who after scoring a quick success with his first comedy – a type of play which had disappeared almost as completely from the fashionable boards as the tragedy – wrote seven more pieces in quick succession, five of them comedies also. Corneille had quickly sized up the Capital's requirements, and he allied himself with one of the best actors of the day. Always an opportunist, when he found the theorists greatly concerned with the matter of the unities, he made his own compromise solution of the vexed question. It was not till his sixth play that he introduced any character or motif that suggested an individuality strongly contrasted with that of his fellow dramatists. In this play, *La Place Royale*, there appears the first Cornelian hero, a man resolved to remain free.

Living in the world of Descartes, Corneille was primarily concerned with questions of will and resolution. His heroes and heroines are always faced with decisions which require in the first place an intellectual solution and, after that, the emotional force to carry it through. What is more, the problems that he chose for his plays were, for the most part, the problems that confronted his contemporaries. His setting might ostensibly be Roman, but in reality his scene was Richelieu's France, in which for the first time a totalitarian statecraft was demanding obedience at the expense of class and family loyalties.

Corneille's first great play Le Cid brought him sharply up against the new totalitarianism. The play, based on de Castro's Spanish original, dealt with the rival claims of love and duty, and closed with an uncertain decision in favour of the former: Chimène was left at the end of the fifth act pledged at some distant date to marry Rodrigue, her lover and the killer of her father. But Le Cid's great originality lay in its characters, whom Corneille showed at moments of great moral stress. Rodrigue resolves to fight his bride's father: Chimène resolves to call for the death of this man whom she loves. Hitherto French dramatists, like the Spaniards from whom they took many of their plots, had been interested in love and intrigue, adventures, and unexpected happenings. The characters were mere types: the bombastic captain, the princess in disguise, the exiled prince turned pirate. But French drama now was existentialist – a drama of crisis.

Le Cid met with an unfortunate reception. Corneille had been taken up by Richelieu a year or two before but quickly dropped. For he was a difficult man, with the reputation for driving a very hard bargain, and he had his enemies. The play was attacked, therefore, for its failure entirely to observe the vexed unities, by some critics objectively, by others out of prejudice. Then the Académie, anxious to enhance its authority, asked the author's permission to pronounce on the matter; and, the majority of its members being cold theorists, the resulting report failed to point out anything but the weaknesses in this work of genius.

The play's author, in the meantime, had embarked on a scurrilous offensive against his critics, which was cut short by Richelieu himself. For three years Corneille was silent. Then, in 1640, he produced a Roman tragedy, dedicated to the great statesman himself, and pointing a moral that he would approve. *Horace* is concerned with the divided claims of love and patriotism, which it resolves in favour of the state. Its hero is a man brought up to serve totalitarianism, for whom personal emotions are a weakness to be conquered. Corneille's next play, *Cinna*, carries this argument a stage further, and shows natural humanity overborne by the exigencies of state-craft, while *Polyeucte*, the third of his Roman tragedies, in-troduces the theme of martyrdom in the service of religion. Corneille had passed over to the totalitarian side.

'Corneille painted men as they ought to be,' said La Bruyère. Certainly the characters in these four great plays are superior to the run of mankind in their clarity and resolution. What they lack in psychological subtlety they make up for in strength of mind. They are the creatures of an age in which a statesman as devout as Richelieu's assistant Père Joseph could deliberately prolong the Thirty Years War, which was destroying Germany; in which planned campaigns of ag-gression and extermination of minorities could be waged for the glory of a king or a minister.

The great power of Corneille's principal plays lies in the economy of their construction, the simplicity of the issues raised. Corneille cut away all secondary developments, and subordinated his own exuberant rhetoric to the purposes of his main plot. Even if he violated the Aristotelian rules by presenting scenes lacking in unity to the heinous extent of being played not in one room, but in two different rooms in the same house, he observed them in the essential sense of allowing nothing to intrude into his lines that did not bear directly on his single theme.

Corneille's later plays are romantic melodramas which con-tain many good characters and many good scenes. But from *La Mort de Pompée* (*Pompey's Death*), his fourth Roman tragedy, which referred to the death of Richelieu, his popular-ity waned. In 1652 he retired from the stage, only to return and, like Calderón in his old age, devise spectacles depending rather on stagecraft than on dramatic situation. But by now a new dramatist had come forward, whose concern was with problems not so much of action and motive as of conscience. For as Corneille declined so Racine stepped into his place.

Corneille was far from being the only popular dramatist of the 1630s and 40s to move from tragi-comedy to tragedy and thence back to melodrama and opera. This was the general line of evolution followed by his own brother THOMAS (1625–1709), by JEAN ROTROU (1609–50), author of a religious tragedy which foreshadows Racine's *Esther*, and by TRISTAN L'HERMITE (1601–55), a poet in the Marinist tradition, the heroine of whose *Mariane* is even more sublimely single-minded than any of Corneille's female characters.

Comedy in these years remained neglected but for an adaptation or two from the Latin of Plautus or from Lope, by Rotrou, and a few pieces by Corneille himself. His *Illusion comique*, a fantastic pantomime full of magic and violence, remarkable for a plea in the last act in favour of the theatre, predates *Le Cid*, while two neat and witty comedies adapted from the Spanish – *Le Menteur* (*The Liar*), a version of Ruiz de Alarcón's *La Verdad sospechosa* and its sequel, adapted from a comedy by Lope – follow the Roman tragedies.

At the moment of Richelieu's death the classical values had conquered throughout France. Indeed, there had been little real opposition to a movement in the arts that modelled itself on the attitudes of the Augustan world. Everyone conformed to the new demands for order, balance, and a language worthy of a nation that was soon to spread its influence in the wake of its armies, and even further than they penetrated, to Spain, to Italy, to Germany, and to the England of Dryden and Congreve. But if Roman heroism and the worship of power had in fact clamped down entirely on the worship of liberty, which one still finds in Corneille's early heroes, there would have been no room for such lyrical poets as Tristan l'Hermite and Racan, none for Pascal or Racine, and none for such independent satirists as La Fontaine and Molière. Classicism was a façade behind which there continued to exist much that was rare, original, individual, and fundamentally critical of the new social order.

JEAN DE LA FONTAINE (1621–95) was a critic rather of human nature in general than of the world of Versailles, which does not seem to have touched him very closely. On his contemporaries he left the impression of a melancholy and somewhat vague person who could not express himself in speech, and who never seemed to be quite present at any conversation. Some thought of him as a visionary; others that his apparent distance sprang from an ironic detachment, and that his gaucheness was a conscious tactic. Certainly he succeeded, at a time when everything depended on patronage, in securing himself patrons; at the fall of his chief supporter, Fouquet, he was quickly able to attach himself to a duke and the cultured wife of a financier, though without betraying the fallen chancellor. With Louis XIV, however, he never found favour. Beginning in the Marinist manner with a long poem on the subject of Adonis, he went on to develop the *vers marotique*, retelling a number of stories, many of them indelicate, in verse couplets. With these treatments of anecdotes drawn from Rabelais, Boccaccio, and lesser Italian sources, he went beyond Marot, to revive the old *fabliau* that had pleased the medieval burghers. These found favour also with the nobility of the salons, and La Fontaine then went on to revive another medieval form, whose roots went far back into the Classical past, the fable.

La Fontaine had made a wide study of these tales, and knew not only the well-known collections of Aesop and Phaedrus, but many lesser collections, some of them extremely rare. His first book of fables, dedicated to the seven-year-old Dauphin, for whose education they were intended, contains pieces that are as well known as any poems in the whole of European literature. Here La Fontaine freed himself from the rhymed couplet and from the archaism of the *fabliau*; he nevertheless preserved old turns of phrase that were out of favour with the new grammarians of the Académie. From the start, these most accomplished poems possessed wit, pithiness, and a fundamental humanity. He made no attempt to make his animals behave like animals; nor did he choose this medium out of any contempt for men. The form enabled him to make observations about mankind in general, in not too unkind a spirit. There are no political morals to be drawn from the early fables; the lion was not Louis XIV; he was any great man who pressed with too heavy a paw on the small and insignificant; and if occasionally a piece seemed to contain a private allusion, La Fontaine left it out of his printed collections, as he did with his tale of the Fox and the Squirrel, which latter beast figured in Fouquet's coat of arms.

La Fontaine published twelve collections of fables in all, in the last of which he seems to have turned somewhat away from general issues, and to be looking more closely at his own world. Now he is addressing not the childish Dauphin, but the adult public which loved his wit even as it neglected his lessons. Now his stories are devoted to the ambitious, to flatterers, and to toadies. '*Je définis la cour*' (I am drawing the court), he explained, and prelates, judges, ministers, all became his butts. He also showed a greater awareness of current philosophical controversies and championed a somewhat pessimistic epicureanism against Descartes' picture of a rational Universe. For La Fontaine the Universe was irrationally divided between the clever and strong few who eat, and the great majority of the weak, who are eaten. What is more, it would be foolish of the wolf to renounce his meal of mutton. Does he see the shepherds doing so? The moral he draws is not one of revolt, but of submission. Yet there are compensations in humble living, and among the greatest of these is friendship.

For these later fables, La Fontaine, having exhausted his Western sources, drew on collections from China, from India, and from the Near East, and as he progressed his treatments became more various, sometimes almost elegiac, sometimes epigrammatic. The last books, indeed, were certainly not addressed to simple children.

The rest of La Fontaine's work includes *Psyché*, a successor to his *Adonis* written in the same unpopular Marinist style, which had consigned his first poem with those of Saint-Amant and Tristan l'Hermite to oblivion, and a few attempts at dramatic composition, most of which were unfinished or have not survived.

The second great critic of the contemporary scene, JEAN-BAPTISTE POQUELIN, better known by his stage name of MOLIÈRE (1622–73), was a dramatist before everything. Unlike Corneille's, his interest in the theatre began from the actor's end. As a boy of the middle class, he joined a troupe of strolling comedians, who failed to establish a new theatre in Paris, and so gave performances for more than a dozen years in a variety of provincial towns chiefly in the south. French comedy had been much less influenced by the Classics and the Renaissance than tragedy, and the plays in which the young Molière acted derived to some extent from the old farces, to some extent also from the *commedia dell'arte,* with its improvisations, its gagging, and its stock characters; Pantaloon, the retired tradesman; the braggart Captain; the Doctor or pedant; Pulcinella, Harlequin, Columbine, and the rest. Touring companies had brought these plays, which had no literary merit, to all parts of Europe; and in France they were most popular. Molière's company attempted to rival the Italians, and put on their own farces. When they came to Paris in 1658, however, with Molière himself in control, they had not the courage to rely on their home-spun products, but put on a season of Corneille revivals, which met with no success. So they followed up his *Nicomède* with a little one-act farce, called *Le Docteur amoureux* (*The Doctor in Love*), which tickled the Parisians. Molière then staged a couple of his own comedies of intrigue, with himself in the chief comic parts. Their success was immediate, and the company were summoned to play before the King.

Molière's first two plays, *L'Étourdi* (*The Blunderer*) and *Le Dépit amoureux* (*Lovers' Spite*) differed very little from the ordinary Italian comedies in verse, with their intrigues, their disguises, and romantic impossibilities. Yet in each there was a character, and a scene or two, that promised something different. Mascarille, the comic servant of *L'Étourdi* – Molière's own part – is a real creation, and *Le Dépit amoureux,* though the poorer play of the two, is certainly well written. A third piece, *Les Précieuses ridicules* (*the Ridiculous Blue-stockings*) however, introduced a vein of satire that readily captured the public. The butts of this prose farce were the affected *précieuses* in small town society, but the audiences took it as an attack on the Paris salons themselves. The result was an intrigue to get the new troupe sent back to the provinces. Their theatre was pulled down, almost over their heads, but the King granted them the lease of the hall of the Palais-Royal, and here they stayed.

In his next short comedy Molière created for himself the title part of Sganarelle, the imaginary cuckold, the first of his comic heroes, and the forerunner of such greater creations as Tartuffe, and Alceste in *Le Misanthrope* (*The Misanthropist*). For Sganarelle is more than a pantomime clown: he is a poor absurd puppet, ill-adapted to life, ludicrous in his speeches and actions, yet pathetic in his helplessness.

After an unsuccessful romantic drama, Molière went on to write two three-act plays of a new kind, something between a comedy and a farce, in which the Sganarelle part was developed. *L'École des maris* (*The School for Husbands*) is a comedy with a comic-pathetic lover and a charming young heroine, who blushes at the tricks she must resort to in order to deceive him, but deceives him all the same. *L'École des femmes* (*The School for Wives*), its successor, is rather more substantial, and here Arnolphe – Molière's own part, developed from that of Sganarelle – attempts to educate for himself the perfect wife, but cannot prevent her falling in love with a younger man and marrying him.

Molière had now brought French comedy to the perfection of its previous peak in *Maître Pathelin*. What is more he seemed likely to drive the more serious drama from the Paris stage. He had, however, made a great number of enemies, and for a second time they attempted to ruin his reputation. They found obscenity – a fashionable new term of abuse – in *L'École des femmes,* and even claimed that the maxims which Arnolphe attempted to teach his simple bride were a parody of the Ten Commandments. Molière struck back with a *Critique*, a short farce ridiculing his critics, and carried on his counter-attack in an *Impromptu*, presented before the court at Versailles. Intrigue and polemic only strengthened the vein of satire in him, and his next play, *Tartuffe*, set out to ridicule a type very active among his enemies, the religious hypocrite.

Le Tartuffe, in the final form in which we have it, has lost the last traces of the *commedia dell'arte*. There are no more conventional characters: Molière is now interested in giving individuality to each. Nor is he playing for quick laughs. Up to *L'École des femmes*, he had been moving away from the stock farce towards a comedy of his own, with a bourgeois setting. His early plays can be performed without any setting at all; they take place anywhere and nowhere. But the action of *Le Tartuffe* can only pass in an over-furnished middle-class apartment: only there can the vacuous Orgon – another version of Sganarelle, played by the author himself – attempt to hand his whole family over to that sordid Machiavellian, that unctuous and lecherous mouther of religious platitudes, who gives the play its name.

Le Tartuffe met with great opposition, and Molière did not receive a licence to act it in public for three years. In the interval he had been compelled to alter it considerably, and perhaps to remove some identifying characteristics from the hypocrite himself. In its final form it was taken by the Jesuits as an attack on Port-Royal, by the Jansenists as a satire against the Company of Jesus. No party, however, had the strength to strike back: it was not until after Molière's death that his victims took their final revenge by once more blackening his reputation.

Molière's next play, *Don Juan*, is not quite substantial enough for its subject, which had suddenly become so popular in Paris that three different versions were being played simultaneously. Molière did not go back to Tirso's play for his plot, but compressed the tragi-comedies of his competitors into a quick-moving farce, which took place in the last twenty-four hours of Don Juan's life and almost obeyed the unities. There was no room, therefore, for the Don's many seductions, nor for the murder of the Commander. Nor did Molière attempt any examination of his hero's motives, as the French tragi-comedians had done. His Don is a libertine and an atheist, brave, charming, reckless, and aware of no profounder law than that 2 and 2 make 4. He may well have been modelled on one of the many free-thinking noblemen about the court. More original, perhaps, is the character of Sganarelle, which the author himself acted. He is far from being a mere clown, or the voice of peasant commonsense. He is rather his master's accomplice, half proud of the Don's villainies and half frightened; and when the final curtain falls, he comes off with no greater penalty than the loss of his wages.

After a side glance at the doctors, who were yet to feel the full weight of his satire, Molière next wrote a character play, whose central figure *Le Misanthrope* invites sympathy as well as laughter. In conception no doubt he was intended to stand beside *Tartuffe* in the gallery of contemporary aunt-sallies. He is the remorseless critic of society, exasperated by the mincing manners of his day. But his hatred for contemporary conventions is absurd; he is thin-skinned, peevish, and lacking in sense of proportion. Yet he is a large figure, surrounded by pygmies, and into his mouth his creator put many of his own exasperations. If Molière was not himself a misanthropist, he had at least many scores to settle with critics and intriguers. It was not easy to forgive the prohibition which was preventing the playing of *Le Tartuffe* during the two years that he spent on this next masterpiece – from which Wycherley stole his character of *The Plain Dealer*.

After several more trifles, including *Georges Dandin,* a rather savage comedy about a young lady who cuckolds her middle-class husband – a situation which Molière knew from his own experience – *L'Avare* (*The Miser*) presented a bourgeois interior as merciless as that of *Le Tartuffe*. Harpagon, the miser, is comical and absurd in his petty tyrannies and his thirst for flattery. But he is also pathetic. Everyone deceives him, yet his obsessive vice robs him of all sympathy. Like Alceste in *Le Misanthrope* and unlike Tartuffe, he is a figure designed for the author's own acting. It was his last great part, for he was by now a sick man, already suffering from the lung complaint that was to kill him. Moreover, *Le Misanthrope* had been only moderately successful; and this new play pleased the public even less, particularly because it was written in prose, and they no doubt had expected verse.

After three years filled with more trifles, Molière recaptured his popularity with a satirical entertainment, *Le Bourgeois gentilhomme,* with music by Lully. Other entertainments were followed by two more comedies: *Les Femmes savantes* (*The Learned Ladies*), a fuller development of the satire against female affectation begun in *Les Précieuses ridicules,* and a final attack upon the doctors in *Le Malade imaginaire* (*The Hypochrondriac*), a comedy-ballet whose central figure, the man obsessed with his own imaginary illnesses, is on the scale of Molière's portraits of the miser and the hypocrite. He is in fact a brother of Harpagon and a cousin of M. Jourdain of *Le Bourgeois gentilhomme*. But even as the playwright was attacking medicine's grosser pretensions, he was dying of an illness which no doctors could arrest.

Molière wrote as a Cartesian, who rejected all scholastic formulas that based their authority on the opinions of the ancients, and accepted the discoveries of his day. He was not a sceptic, but a shrewd middle-class critic of the contemporary scene with absolute mastery of the theatre, whom shrewd observation and personal exasperation sometimes led into satire, and who was at times tempted to draw characters too large, too detailed, and too many-sided to fit into a neat play. When he started to write, comedy was an ephemeral branch of the drama; tragedy and tragi-comedy alone seemed respectable. But by grafting the quick humour and clowning of the *commedia dell'arte* on to the drama of character and situation he gave Europe its first and greatest native comedy after Shakespeare and Ben Jonson.

Europe's first polite and polished satire, the satire of the rapier which replaced the bludgeon, was written by another plain member of the French middle class, NICOLAS BOILEAU, known as DESPRÉAUX (1636–1711), who has been credited with the codifying of Malherbe's rules of language, and who rather easily acquired the reputation of a seventeenth-century Horace, which was enhanced by his championship of the ancients against the moderns in the great literary controversy of the time.

The subjects of Boileau's satires and epistles were, for the most part, literary. He stood for a common sense much less imaginative than Molière's, attacked reputations that were already faded, and praised his great contemporaries when they were already generally accepted. His most amusing piece, however, is a description of the noises of Paris, which can be compared to Gay's and Swift's diatribes against the foulness of London; and his most ambitious work, *Le Lutrin*, a mock-heroic account of a quarrel about the placing of a lectern, though timid, is a burlesque of a new kind. For while such poetry had hitherto described great events in low language, Boileau expended all the resources of a classical style on an event of the utmost triviality. The poem is a forerunner of Pope's *Rape of the Lock*, but nowhere in Boileau does one find the polished malice of his English disciple. He took care to offend as few men as possible, though he had the courage to come out on the side of Port-Royal against the Jesuits.

Port-Royal's greatest son, JEAN RACINE (1639–99) openly quarrelled with the Jansenist hierarchy in middle life, but remained throughout deeply influenced by the point of view which Pascal represented. The cycle of development which had begun with Corneille's heroic style and Descartes' valuing of thought above emotion had run full circle. With Racine, as with Pascal, emotion now counted for everything, and the central point of all his plays was a psychological crisis in the protagonist. Using the same alexandrine couplet as Corneille, Racine softened its rhetorical music, making it speak the language of the confessional. Pessimistic and introspective, his is the drama of the individual conscience. Love, for him, was a madness, like that of Tristan and Iseult after they had drunk the potion.

Racine's first play, *La Thébiade* (*The Tale of Thebes*) was produced by Molière in 1664, the year after the controversy over *L'École des femmes*, when Molière was himself beginning to write *Le Tartuffe*. It was a blood-drenched play dealing with the final extinction of the house of Oedipus. His next, *Alexandre*, has a pastoral touch, and seems to owe something to the contemporary novel. Indeed, the ageing Corneille saw as much when the play was privately read to him, and – perhaps self-interestedly – advised its young author to apply himself to some other branch of poetry. But what Corneille took for a weakness was, in fact, Racine's great strength. For in *Andromaque*, his third play and his first great success, he brought to the stage a subtlety in the expression of mood and emotion that the novel itself had as yet hardly attained.

Rhetorical tragedy had been content to show its figures from the outside, to bring them to decisions as palpable as sign-posted cross-roads. Corneille had perfected a style as glittering as Marlowe's, and as incapable of translating a Hamlet's changes of thought and intention. Molière had injected the drama with new life drawn from the unscripted *commedia dell'arte*. But Racine, while ostensibly going back to the Greeks, in fact developed from the pastoral novel his methods of portraying the internally divided mind, first revealed by Pascal in his theology of crisis.

All Racine's plays are concerned with the passion of love; and his chief figures are almost all men and women in love with one person and pursued by another. His stock dramatic pattern, indeed, has been called 'the grand chain'. Racine recognized that in the seemingly Christian circles of the French court, as elsewhere, were men and women for whom honour and glory meant nothing, who recognized no moral or religious code, but only the iron law of desire and attainment. Even Louis himself grovelled to Louise de la Vallière when she rejected his advances and retired to a nunnery. Corneille had drawn his age in an ideal pose of its own choosing; Racine, less flatteringly but more accurately, gave it its real features, but for purposes of the most elementary disguise clad it in the Greek peplos, in Roman armour, or in the turban of the Ottoman.

Andromaque shows Racine's grand chain in all its perfection; Oreste loves Hermione, who loves Pyrrhus, who loves Andromaque, who in her turn is faithful to the memory of her dead Hector. The play was a success, but Corneille and his clique accused its author of lacking a sense of history. Certainly the scene of *Andromaque* might as easily have been Versailles as Buthrote, a city in Epirus, as the stage-directions read. Indeed, its heroine was said by some to have been modelled on the exiled Henrietta-Maria of England, faithful to the memory of her martyred Charles.

Always sensitive to criticism, Racine next attempted a Roman play with every detail true to the age of Nero, its hero. *Britannicus* presents the emperor long before he became a monstrous tyrant, at the moment when he revolts against the guidance of his mother and her counsellors, and against his own better nature. The plot is, in fact, a modern or a timeless one; and it repeats Racine's own experience when he revolted against the domination of Port-Royal. The framework is Cornelian, but the content is entirely different. For what dramatist before Racine would have had the courage to present such naked truth? Here was none of the old sententiousness of political history, with its neat morals. Here was psychological accuracy, truer than history itself, which – as Aristotle said – always conventionalizes.

Racine next turned to comedy, and gave to Molière's theatre *Les Plaideurs* (*The Pleaders*), a sparkling satire on the law, which he had at first intended as no more than a plot upon which the Italian players could improvise.

The unities, which had presented difficulties to every dramatist till now, did not trouble Racine, who moved steadily towards greater and greater concentration. Twenty-four hours were for him almost too generous a provision of time, since the crux of a play lay always in its moment of revelation, when the characters saw and accepted their situation. *Bérénice*, an unsuccessful play produced to the order of Henrietta-Maria, is even more spare of detail than its predecessors. Two lovers are brought to make the Cornelian choice between love and duty. But here Racine's analysis of their sentiments goes subtly wrong, for they always appear to have more than one eye on public opinion. Stung by the failure of *Bérénice*, Racine turned from smug and statuesque nobility to melodrama and passion, presented in *Bayazet*, whose setting was the harem of the Sultan's court. Uncharacteristic though the play was, it set him back on his true course, and in *Mithridate*, the Roman play which followed it, he gave his audiences all that they looked to him for, though nothing new. The plot was quarried out of Plutarch, and was only indirectly tragic. For on his death-bed the violent old king united the two young lovers, Xipharès and Monime, and the curtain fell with this pair together in their grief, seeking vengeance against the Romans, who one knows will finally triumph.

There is an idyllic beauty in Racine's portrayal of these two lovers, which informs the whole of his next play *Iphigénie*,

an adaptation from Euripides that recalls the atmosphere of
the pastoral novel rather than that of heroic Greece, with its
all-presiding deities. For, true to the Arcadian convention,
Racine could neither permit his heroine to die as a sacrifice,
nor allow a god to save her; and true to the modern faith that,
hard though it is to trace the workings of destiny, punishment
is indeed proportionate to crime, he put in Iphigénie's place
a woman deserving the fate from which he excused his
heroine. But it was impossible to keep the magical and irrational element entirely out of a play, which in most details
followed its Greek original. The sacrifice of Iphigénie's substitute causes the heavens to thunder and the winds to rise
even as they did for Euripides. Nor is Racine's Agamemnon
entirely a character of the modern world, when he resolves
that his son shall die for the furtherance of his own ambitions.
Iphigénie is, in fact, full of incongruities. But thanks to the perfection of Racine's verse and technique, they are not quick
to spring to the eye.

Phèdre, which was so bitterly attacked by Racine's enemies,
seems to-day to be without a blemish. Here, as in *Andromaque*,
there is but one theme, that of love; and here for the first time
the Greek and modern elements in Racine's tragedy are
welded into one. Hippolyte, pursued by the furious love of
Phèdre, his stepmother, is no charming young Frenchman;
he has no pity for her or her weakness; nor is Phèdre so much
a woman in love as one possessed by an inner fury. The god-
dess that broods over this tale of incestuous passion is no
Catholic deity either; she stands rather for the weight of
heredity that continues with us and governs our conduct,
struggle though we may. Only Pascal might have understood
the true emotional charge in this masterpiece, which is truly
Greek in its remorselessness, and looks forward to Ibsen in
its summoning up of ghosts that no Cartesian reason can
lay.

Racine's own generation admired *Phèdre* for its pathos; and
we are better able than they to recognize its power. It is in
every sense a final work, since it combines all the elements
that are to be found scattered through his earlier plays; the
economy and strict morality of *Bérénice*, the violence of

Bayazet, the classical dignity of *Britannicus*, the magic and the depth of *Iphigénie*.

The real cause of Racine's retirement from the stage at this point was not the hostile reception of his masterpiece by a clique, which supported a lesser play on the same subject by a minor poet. He had long felt uncomfortable about his connexion with a section of society that seemed so frivolous by Jansenist standards. Moreover his religious feelings were driving him towards a reconciliation with Port-Royal; and the king's offer of a post as historiographer royal gave him the opportunity that he needed. It is doubtful, anyhow, whether he could see his way forward from *Phèdre*, which had probably taken him three years to write. It was his perfect play, and he knew it.

For the next twelve years Racine devoted himself to his court duties and to family life. Then he wrote two more plays freer in form, that stand to his great tragedies as *Samson Agonistes* to *Paradise Lost*. *Esther* and its greater successor *Athalie* are choral pieces on Biblical subjects, written to be performed not by the Paris theatre but by a girls' school at Saint-Cyr which had the protection of the king's morganatic wife, Mme de Maintenon. *Athalie*, however, was far beyond the capacities of a schoolgirl's understanding; the wicked and haunted queen is a figure on the scale of Phèdre, and the play's hero is God himself, by whom justice is finally done. Thus Racine ended his career as a dramatist with a play of acceptance as positive as those of Shakespeare's last phase.

The comparison between Shakespeare and Racine, so often attempted, cannot be carried far. Organically, Racine's plays are so closely knit that it is impossible to think of his characters or his speeches as in any way detachable. Lady Macbeth seems to have an existence beginning before the rise of the curtain; Phèdre or Iphigénie live only in the concentrated twenty-four hours allowed to them; all their qualities are expressed in a single situation. In the same way the dramatic speech of Racine's characters is proper only to the drama. His plays contain no anthology pieces, only unforgettable lines that crystallize a situation, statements in which passion or revelation are compressed into a language highly conventional, yet absolutely fitting to Racine's purpose. It is the formality and compression of his language that makes him untranslatable. Corneille can be adequately rendered, as he was in Dryden's day, in heroic couplets. Racine, however, allows the translator no licence. The sound and subtlety of his line is inimitable. Even the method of speech traditional in the French theatre, the rhetorical delivery rather to the audience than to the other actors, is an inseparable part of a Racine performance. Corneille can be presented in new ways; there is room for a fresh interpretation even of *Le Cid*. But a performance of *Iphigénie* or *Phèdre* is a ritual for which no actor or actress can be entirely adequate; they are as much plays of the mind as they are plays of the stage.

French drama, in general, even in Racine's day, was beginning to decay, and as in Spain, the musical spectacle was already drawing the bigger audiences. PHILIPPE QUINAULT (1635–88), author of comedies and of pleasantly romantic historical dramas, turned his attentions to opera after 1671, and was Lulli's regular librettist until religious scruples drove him to renounce the theatre. Corneille's younger brother Thomas too, the author of several popular pieces in the Spanish style, of comedies written for Molière's theatre and of a drama on the subject of Queen Elizabeth I's relations with Essex, afterwards worked for Lulli, though he devoted his last years to the writing of learned works for the Académie.

Molière's successors in the comic field were a pleasant light satirist, FLORENT CARTON DANCOURT (1661–1725), like Molière a man with the theatre in his bones, and JEAN-FRANÇOIS REGNARD (1655–1709), who had a talent for inventing intrigue, but was no great creator of characters. The novelist Lesage came nearest to Molière himself in his one memorable play *Turcaret*, a satire on a shady financier.

With PIERRE MARIVAUX (1688–1763) French comedy returned to a charming preciosity, sentimental, witty, and constructed to a pattern in which disguises and revelations, love, and setting-to-partners were the principal ingredients. Marivaux's characters are courtiers in an ideal world where love is nothing but a sentimental titillation. In his sentimentality, indeed, he looks forward to the more lachrymose comedy of the new century. Fortunately, however, a Marivaux heroine requires no handkerchief more substantial than a gossamer web.

The pleasing gossip of MME DE SÉVIGNÉ (1626–96) poured out, by no means artlessly, in some 1,500 family letters, the highly-polished and disillusioned *Maximes* of FRANÇOIS, DUC DE LA ROCHEFOUCAULD (1613–80): and *Les Caractères* of JEAN DE LA BRUYÈRE (1645–96), together with Charles Perrault's retelling of such famous tales as those of Cinderella, Red Riding Hood, and Bluebeard, to which he attached his own little morals, are the highlights of a prose which was, however, gradually learning to put its most sustained efforts into the novel. All of these but Perrault are students of their own century, bent on recording its habits of thought and its values, and aware as no group of individuals had hitherto been that the society in which they were living was unique. La Rochefoucauld saw this new world through the eyes of an aristocrat the power of whose caste had been broken by the dictatorships first of Richelieu and then of Mazarin; Mme de Sévigné belonged to the new minor aristocracy, who pretended to no power, but prided themselves on leading a highly civilized life; while La Bruyère, a man of the middle class, with a clear vision of the decay that was already setting in, satirized the whole of society in his apophthegms *On the Manners of this Century*.

La Bruyère's method was that of a caricaturist, he attained at times a savage poetry of distortion, but he was also capable of rare psychological insight. His *Characters* are generalized portraits of gentlemen who frequented the households which he had served. LOUIS, DUC DE SAINT-SIMON (1675–1755) on the other hand, in his *Memoirs*, which cover the period from 1691 to 1723 makes no secret of his victims' names. Again, where La Bruyère writes a condensed and fast-moving style capable of compressing as much into a line even as Racine's, Saint-Simon lays his colour on more impressionistically, and often writes in a part for himself well in the foreground of the story.

Both La Bruyère and Saint-Simon in an emergent democracy, like that of England, would no doubt have gone into politics on the Whig side, though for different reasons. La Bruyère was already aware of the hardships suffered by peasant and townsman, which were the price France was paying for the glory of her court. But Saint-Simon was frustrated, restless, and malicious; and his zeal for reform was that of a man permanently in opposition rather than that of a clear-sighted critic.

The great age of France was passing in military defeat, in senseless luxury, and in a new preciosity, divorced from the Roman dream of greatness which had inspired the earlier preciosity of Richelieu's generation. But literature did not die in France as it had done fifty years earlier in Spain. For criticism, even under Louis XV, was freer than on the farther side of the Pyrenees, and rationalism, deriving from Descartes, together with sentimentality, whose later spokesman was Rousseau, were preparing, beneath the noses of the government, the intellectual weapons with which the Revolution was to overthrow it.

Chapter Eleven

THE EARLY NOVEL,
THE REIGN OF REASON, AND THE
BIRTH OF SENSIBILITY

THE novel proper begins when readers become interested in the life and fortunes of men of their own day, described with some measure of realistic detail, and with reasonable attention to the laws of probability. Neither Rabelais's great work, nor yet *Don Quixote* can therefore be placed in this new category, since in both the probabilities are vastly outnumbered by the fantastic impossibilities. *Pilgrim's Progress*, and *Gulliver's Travels*, in the same way, must be excluded for their lack of concern with individual character. Figures who stand for qualities or humours may be brought on the stage in a morality or in Jonsonian comedy, but they immediately break the framework of a novel, in which every character must act sufficiently like the common man, with his mixture of qualities and motives, to pass in a crowd. It is impossible also to think of the various Arcadias of the sixteenth century as conforming to this new medium. For although their pastoral backgrounds are not so fantastic as the uplands through which Pilgrim wandered in search of the Heavenly City, or as the islands visited by Mr Lemuel Gulliver, they are a fairy world in which the ordinary rules of conduct do not obtain, and in which magic is always round the corner.

Were it not for its ungainly dramatic form, de Rojas' *Celestina* might claim to be the first of Western novels – a novel of dialogue only, but greatly concerned with character and with the working out of character in the form of destiny. This medium did not die with its inventor, but was developed by the Portuguese, JORGE FERREIRA DE VASCONCELOS (1515–63) in his love-stories the *Comédia Eufrosina* and the *Comédia Ulysippo*, also in *La Lozana Andaluza* (*The Gay Andalusian*) by Francisco Delgado, a lively scenario with a Joycean richness of language, set in the brothels of Rome. It reached its final form in Lope de Vega's *La Dorotea* of 1632. But by this time it was abundantly clear that this was not the way in which prose narrative was to develop, and that the novel proper required, in addition to character and dialogue, some description, reflexion, and comment, and also a greater appearance of actuality.

The first true novel was a slight and unspectacular work, purporting to be the autobiography of a poor boy who had been servant successively to comical representatives of each of the three orders of society, a blind beggar, a priest, and an impoverished gentleman, and ended up as town-crier of Toledo. This anonymous *Vida de Lazarillo de Tormes* (*Life of Lazarillo de Tormes*) – (1554) is well tinged with anti-clerical satire, and obviously emanates from Erasmist circles. It has been attributed, though perhaps without much foundation, to the mysterious Cristóbal de Villalón, amongst others, and were he the author of this book as well as of the two others that bear his name, he would certainly count as one of the greatest figures in sixteenth-century literature. But in fact nothing satisfactory can be said about the authorship of *Lazarillo*, the prose of which is plain and vigorous, and the tale most economically told.

The next work of fiction to win wide popularity, *Guzmán de Alfarache* by MATEO ALEMÁN (1547–after 1613) is a more ambitious achievement, both in its length and its choice and variety of language. It is less direct too, in its narration, a moralizing element, derived from current works of devotion, being superimposed on the theme of low life and adventure derived from *Lazarillo*. The book's author was a man of Jewish blood, who had known prison and poverty, who had made a journey to Mexico, and was to some extent a professional writer. His attitude, like that of an earlier converted Jew, de Rojas, was pessimistic; and the sermons which he put into his character's mouth were no doubt genuine expressions of his own outlook.

Guzmán de Alfarache is the first work to be described as a picaresque novel: that is to say, one put into the mouth of a roving servant, who goes from master to master, seeing life always from the underside. The original *picaro* was thought of, however, not only as an engaging rogue, but as a representative of common sinning humanity, whose redemption might be expected at the end of the book. Soon, however, roguery crowded out morality; and neither Defoe, Lesage nor Fielding, who inherited and developed the picaresque form, placed their characters in any religious framework whatever. Their delight was simply in the varieties of human fortune.

The third Spanish novel to gain wide success was a fictitious book of memoirs, *La Vida del escudero Marcos de Obregón* (*Life of the Squire Marcos de Obregón*) by VICENTE ESPINEL (1550–1624). This imaginary squire is not, strictly speaking, a *picaro*, but rather a disillusioned adventurer, who meets plenty of people in the course of his rovings, most of whom are, unlike the characters in *Lazarillo* and *Guzmán*, quite pleasant. Nevertheless, the book was strongly influenced by Alemán's, even to the inclusion of some moralizing passages, which are, however, seldom tiresome.

Each of these novels, as is evident from their form, was confronted with an audience which wanted to be convinced of their authenticity. Every early novelist seems to have imagined a typical reader who would ask him, 'How do you come to know all this?' For that reason he either told his story in the first person, relating only such facts as would have been known to the narrator, or resorted to the device of an imaginary book of memoirs. This convention very much retarded the development of the realistic novel, which furthermore required a hero.

The picaresque novel was essentially unheroic; its general level of sentiment seldom rose above that of a certain *camaraderie* between rogues. More often, however, it was frankly tough and cynical, as in *La Vida del buscón* (*The Sharper's Life*) (1626) by the poet Quevedo. There had been some social caricature in *Guzmán de Alfarache*, and a certain amount of satirical comment, coming from the mouth of the author rather than of his hero. But Quevedo's is far more of an author's book, for it tells a story, similar in outline to that of *Lazarillo*, in most elaborate language, embellished with conceits far beyond the vocabulary of the poor boy who is supposed to be telling the story. Quevedo had little interest in humanity, which disgusted him as it disgusted Swift. His *Vida del buscón*, therefore, is a half-grotesque, half-tragic puppet show. The wretched priest, whose prototype was lightly satirized in *Lazarillo*, turns in Quevedo's hands into a complete and cruel caricature.

A more elaborate exercise in satirical double-meanings and perverted language, modelled on the style of Quevedo's *Sueños* is *El Diablo cojuelo* (*The Lame Devil*) by the dramatist Luis Vélez de Guevara. This tale, in which the devil removes the roofs of various houses in Madrid for the benefit of a student who has released him from a bottle, is racy despite the elaboration of its style. This idea was not allowed to rest in its original form, however, but was developed by René Lesage, more than sixty years later, and became his first success, *Le Diable boiteux*.

After this the novel progressed no further in Spain, but was grafted on to a type of prose narrative that had been elaborated separately in France. Before passing over to France, however, it is necessary to notice a single picaresque tale written in German, *Der abenteuerliche Simplicissimus* (*The Adventurous Simplicissimus*) by JOHANN VON GRIMMELSHAUSEN (1622–76). This is a development from the moralizing *Guzmán de Alfarache*, and leads its hero from the world of the flesh to retirement and a hermit's life. But on the way he meets with a multitude of diverting adventures, visits heaven and hell in a dream, interviews Jove, watches a band of witches set off for their Walpurgis night flight, and meets soldiers, tradesmen, and gentlemen of all conditions. *Simplicissimus*, in fact, unites all the principal themes of its age. It is a sort of Pilgrim's Progress through the aftermath of the Thirty Years' War, and leads to the same eventual goal as Bunyan's journey through the land of allegory. But while equally pious in outlook, it is considerably more various in incident. There are five books by Grimmelshausen himself, and several continuations by other hands.

Grimmelshausen, an old soldier, who had lost his Protestant parents in the war, became a convert to Catholicism, and agent to various landowners. He began writing, when still a soldier, tales about simple people, intended to challenge the popularity of the French courtly novels then in fashion; and after finding his true vein in the metaphysical picaresque, wrote yet one more tale of adventure with a worldly heroine called Mother Courasche.

The French novel of the seventeenth century makes no such fresh beginnings as that of Spain, and is seldom as free from artifice as Grimmelshausen's masterpiece. It is the product of the Arcadian pastoral, leisurely, digressive, and at its best redolent of meadow, pasture, and park: a safe setting for conversation and love-making now that the age of civil wars was over, at least in France. The first of these shapeless works to achieve a wide popularity was published in five parts, which appeared over a period of twenty years, between 1607 and 1627. *L'Astrée* purported to tell of events which had taken place in a little Arden, watered by a tributary of the Rhone, in the fifth century A.D., under the gentle moral guidance of the Druids. This convenient recession in time was intended to disguise the fact that the principal love-story related was actually the author's own. HONORÉ D'URFÉ (1567–1625), a minor nobleman at the court of Savoy, had been in love with his brother's wife, whom he had married after his brother had divorced her. Their marriage, however, had ended in separation. *L'Astrée* set the fashion for the novel of countless episodes, bound together by a common interest in the fine gradations between virtuous and frivolous love, and was no more than the most popular of some 600 of the kind which appeared between the opening of the century and the complete publication of *Clélie*, a Roman story by MADELEINE DE SCUDÉRY (1607–1701), written in collaboration with her brother Georges, the author of tragi-comedies in the Spanish manner.

Mlle de Scudéry had succeeded the Marquise de Rambouillet as the most influential woman in literary Paris. The Hôtel Rambouillet had enthused for the morals and sentiments of *L'Astrée*; Mlle de Scudéry's salon practised the refined science of the love affair, plotted out on the engraving, already referred to, which served as frontispiece for her *Clélie*. The settings of her three novels were various, but all alike presented in hardly disguised detail the portraits and the relationships of the contemporary great. *Ibrahim ou l'illustre Bassa* was an oriental tale of passion and jealousy; *Artamène ou le grand Cyrus* told of the loves of the Duc de Condé, masquerading in the fancy dress of the Persian conqueror, and Mandane, a Median princess in whom all informed readers recognized the Duchesse de Longueville.

The novels of Mlle de Scudéry represent the Cornelian aspect of the new popular medium. Heroism, reputation, conquest, and moral rectitude were the qualities that counted with her and her circle. There was, in her skilfully mapped country of the affections, no coast subject to the tempests that blow in from the sea of passion. The prevailing wind was that of sentiment and mild reason.

The writer who first allowed adult passion to play a part in her novels was herself a thwarted, analytical aristocrat, who had been a friend of Mme de Sévigné in her youth, and who shared a household with the aged, peevish, and gouty Duc de la Rochefoucauld in her maturity. MME DE LA FAYETTE (1634–93) may have invented little that was new. Analyses of feelings were common in the popular pastoral and its descendants. What she did was to compress the tale of a single relationship into no more than a long short-story, and to use her own experience rather than her friends' as her subject matter. Her first novel was a short adventure story set in ninth-century Spain, which was signed by her collaborator, Jean Regnault de Segrais. Her masterpiece, *La Princesse de Clèves*, appeared anonymously in 1678, and it is probable that La Rochefoucauld had a hand in it. The setting is conventionally historical, the characters being members of the court of Henri II. The Princess, its heroine, has married a man whom she can only respect, and falls in love with the Duc de Nemours, who is engaged to the King's daughter. Here we seem to be confronted with a Cornelian choice between love and duty. But in the passion of the Duke and the Princess there is an element of destructive violence, as there is in that of Phèdre for Hippolyte. The novel is not a work of the same scale as Racine's, but in the same way it lets in the forces of unreason. The Princess confesses her love to her husband, in the hope that he will allow her to leave the court. But he, though he realizes her plight, turns in on himself and tortures himself with jealousy, once he sees that his own love for her is hopeless. Ultimately he dies, but though the Princess is now free to marry Nemours, she retires into a convent. What she longs for is rest, and this craving she disguises as a phantom duty to her dead husband, which allows her to overcome the remains of her passion. Passion for her had become, as it was for Phèdre, an evil; though duty now no longer stood in the way, it was necessary for her to retreat. Pascal had said that there could be no love without 'excess'; the fatal love that Tristan and Iseult quaffed in the potion was now seen once more as an egoistic rebellion, the enemy not only of religion but of social conformity also, which Mme de la Fayette incarnated in her heroine's imaginary duty to deny herself. Passion leads to destruction; only in reasonable repose can safety for man or society be found.

While the aristocratic novel attained shape, formality, and a sober moralizing style, the middle-class story, though depending always on Spanish models, moved towards a realism more factual than psychological. The success of *L'Astrée* was quickly followed by a mock pastoral, which attempted to do for this popular form what *Don Quixote* had done for the tales of chivalry. CHARLES SOREL (1600–74) told the tale of a Paris merchant's son who turned shepherd and grazed his flock of skinny sheep on the banks of the Seine. He had already written a picaresque novel of Paris life, called *La Vraie Histoire comique de Francion* (*The True and Comic Story of Francion*), which takes its hero through every walk of society, and mingles the broadness of the *fabliaux* with strokes of realistic description, fantasy, and extravagance.

The most fantastic of seventeenth-century writers, whose imagination had most of the qualities necessary in a writer of science-fiction, was CYRANO DE BERGERAC (1619–55), who has nothing in common with the hero of Rostand's play except the name. His two *Histoires extraordinaires* tell of voyages to the moon and the sun, as gripping as Lucian's, and made more lifelike by the introduction of Copernican astronomy. Cyrano was a *libertin*, perhaps the actual *libertin* whom Pascal had had in mind when he began to collect his *Pensées* as an armoury to be used against him. Cyrano is flamboyant in style, and not without a certain preciosity. But he saw many of the implications of the new scientific knowledge, and was sufficiently productive as an inventor of theories to have quickly encountered the enmity of the Church. Of the many half-developed ideas which he left, some were afterwards turned to good use by Voltaire and the *Encyclopédistes*.

The French picaresque and French science-fiction were, however, eclipsed by the more Spanish variety of adventure story, lightly burlesqued to conform with French taste, and introduced by the dramatist, Paul Scarron, whose *Roman comique* tells of the adventures of a company of strolling actors. Scarron is all action and grotesque humour. ANTOINE FURETIÈRE (1619–88) on the other hand, a friend of Molière, Racine, and Boileau, returned to a realistic description of Paris life, particularly of its legal and literary underworld. These works are as episodic as *L'Astrée* and its brood, and show little interest in the development of character. Indeed, their effect would have been slight without the more thorough exploitation of all the Spanish elements by ALAIN RENÉ LESAGE (1668–1747). Lesage's reputation is at present low. *Le Diable boîteux* is no more than a free, but able adaptation of Vélez de Guevara's story, which is itself derivative from Quevedo; and *Gil Blas de Santillane*, though its incidents are independent of actual Spanish prototypes, contains no more than the Spanish ingredients, presented in a tone of light satire. Its hero studies at Salamanca, is captured by brigands, escapes, serves many masters, rises to fortune, loses his fortune, makes good again and finally retires to lead a life of peace and luxury. The story carries one with it, but never gives the impression of being told at first hand. Lesage indeed sees Spain through its books, thus setting a bad example to the writers of the Romantic age who, equally nourished on a literary knowledge of Spanish life, wrote as if colour and romance automatically began to prevail on the other side of the border.

Lesage wrote a number of other novels in the Spanish convention, and with Spanish names and settings. He was a professional author, and one of the first of his kind to support himself without patrons or sinecures, entirely on the output of his pen, from which flowed also, in addition to his one comedy in Molière's vein, *Turcaret*, a great number of little farces to be acted at fairs.

As a social observer, Lesage was shrewd, if not very original, but his types have, perhaps, a greater quality of life than those of Scarron. A more acute observation was shown by his contemporary fellow-dramatist Pierre Marivaux, whose characters are presented less invariably in action. Marivaux was the author of two long novels which display not only the realism of urban life but some of those qualities of sensibility which were to be more fully developed by his English contemporary Samuel Richardson. His characters are shopkeepers, and we are shown the insides of their shops, but without the careful detail of a Furetière or a Scarron. For what really interests Marivaux most is the workings of their minds, their attitudes to love, their self-deceptions. In describing all this, he reintroduces, though to a lesser extent than in his plays, an element of preciosity, one class lower than that of the Hôtel de Rambouillet. *Marianne*, the story of a coquette, is to a large extent a coquette's handbook, which keeps the reader always pleasantly titillated by the expectation that at any moment some young lady will lose her virtue. But very little happens, either in this book or in its successor, *Le Paysan parvenu* (*The Peasant who has Risen in the World*). Marivaux's great strength lies not in his plots, but in his delineation of character, especially of female character, which he does not flatter. His Marianne, nevertheless, is loveable as Mme de Lafayette's princess can never be, however much one feels for her in her predicament.

An attempt to force the reader's sympathies in a way that neither Mme de Lafayette nor Marivaux would have thought permissible, was made by the ABBÉ PRÉVOST (1697–1763), the translator of Richardson, and author of the famous short novel, *Manon Lescaut*, which was originally inset in a much longer work, now seldom read.

Prévost, an abbé in little but name, was a professional writer who, having fled his monastery, spent much of his

active life in Holland and in England, where he met the
literary great of his time, but also became involved in less
reputable company, and was more than suspected of having
committed forgery. Despite this, however, and despite a life
of dissipation, he finally succeeded in reconciling himself to
the Church, which accepted him as a secular priest, and in
attaching himself to a noble French family, in whose service
he spent his old age.

Manon Lescaut is a tale technically as economical as a Racine
play. In its cautionary aspect, it was intended to show the
tragedy of a weak man's infatuation for a worthless woman,
who betrayed him on every occasion, but whom he nevertheless followed to banishment in the American colonies, in the
hope that there she would have no opportunity of playing him
false again. But Prévost's narration is not objective. He takes
des Grieux's part and, identifying himself with his exemplary
weakling, allows him to wallow in mingled self-pity and
egoistic pride in his power of loving so fatally. Manon herself,
whom Prévost shows us only through her lover's eyes, and
whose betrayals are never made convincing, as they might
have been by Marivaux, has taken on, thanks to her adoption
as the heroine of nineteenth-century operas, the features of the
'noble whore', in whose service any man might worthily
sacrifice career and peace of mind. For the Romantics,
quaffing the potion of sexual love was a heroic act which
exalted the veriest nincompoops into Tristans and Iseults;
and in this way a technically excellent but emotionally warped
little story has falsely assumed the value of a classic.

Prévost's other writings include some stories with Irish
backgrounds, so full of ghosts and assassinations as to fore-
shadow the 'gothick' novels of 'Monk' Lewis and Mrs
Radcliffe. But, despite his professional proficiency, he is
famous for nothing except *Manon Lescaut*.

Another writer who exploited the theme of love, though
in a less exalted and more salacious sense, was CLAUDE-
PROSPER DE CRÉBILLON (1707–77), whose wittily written
revelations of vice in high circles delighted the aristocrats
whom he portrayed, ostensibly for the benefit of men of
sounder morals, who probably never read him. This is

Crébillon *fils*. Of his father, the dramatist, Boileau's 'drunken Racine', there is little to say.

On the whole, these developments of the novel, over-whelmingly bourgeois in their plots and in the standing of their authors, reveal a growing self-confidence in a middle class, for whom the loves of linen-drapers, adventurers, whores, and actors seemed more interesting than the courtly amours of the great.

The strongest criticisms of the luxury and corruption of the gentry came, however, not from the middle classes but from its own most intelligent members. La Rochefoucauld, a sur-vivor from earlier days before the royal power had been firmly established, cynically criticized the morals of his time, and survived to witness the onset of a new decay in the final decade of the seventeenth century: La Bruyère, with greater psychological breadth, used his *Caractères* (Characters) as a means of showing up a society which was plainly going down-hill; and FRANÇOIS DE FÉNELON (1651–1715), a liberal cleric, attached to the quietist wing of the Church, and under fire from Jansenist and Jesuit alike, raised his voice for tolera-tion. Having been appointed tutor to the ten-year-old Duc de Bourgogne, Louis XIV's heir, he wrote for him a didactic novel, *Télémaque*, which continued the story of the *Odyssey*. Fénelon intended to instil into the young pupil the idea that a benevolent despotism was preferable to absolutism, and that even kings were not above the law. The young prince, how-ever, in whom the enlightened opposition had placed their hopes, died young; and Fénelon, although rewarded with an Archbishopric, was to all intents and purposes exiled from court for his unorthodox views.

The Regency with which the eighteenth century opened acted in such a way as to increase the criticism of all en-lightened circles. The popularization of science, and the con-sequent spread of Cartesian rationalism, tended to weaken the general belief in the outstanding individual and his destiny. It bred no democrats, it is true, but this was an atmosphere in which democracy was likely to grow, stimulated particularly by the example of the successful compromise that had been worked out in England.

An intellectual opposition was growing up. PIERRE BAYLE (1647–1706), a scholar and critic who had moved from Protestantism to Catholicism and back, was in essence a liberal critic, though timid and conservative in politics. But even he was not afraid to protest against the stupidity of Louis XIV's treatment of the Huguenots, or to separate the ideas of morality and religion in his writings. Scientific tolerance was to him the highest ideal.

Thought which was hard to assimilate from Bayle's ascetic and dry philosophizing, was expressed with wit and crystal clarity by Corneille's nephew BERNARD DE FONTENELLE (1657–1757), who placed ideas very like those of the old *libertins* before far wider circles than had ever encountered them before. First noticed and pilloried as a conceited and empty man of letters by La Bruyère, Fontenelle nevertheless became one of the first of scientific popularizers, an essayist on astronomy, and an exposer of popular superstitions. In his *Entretiens sur la pluralité des mondes* (*Dialogues on the Plurality of Worlds*), he did more than any other writer to secure the general acceptance of the Copernican system.

Fontenelle, in a pleasant and witty style, cast doubts upon the validity of all dogmas. But it was a critic of lesser scope who was most instrumental in spreading the scientific spirit. 'I spend my life examining things,' wrote CHARLES-LOUIS, BARON DE MONTESQUIEU (1689–1755), in his *Pensées*; 'and each evening I note down what I have seen and noticed during the day. Everything interests me, and everything surprises me.' During his leisure this Bordeaux magistrate – a worthy successor to Montaigne – had written a number of papers on medical subjects, and a series of letters, ascribed to a fictitious Persian visitor, in which he anatomized the manners of Parisian society, not without malice. The Orient had lately become fashionable, the first translation of the *Arabian Nights* having been made only a short while before, and Montesquieu's Persian convention, of which he was more or less the inventor, gave him a chance to be both witty and penetrating. But this did not content him, and he set out travelling himself, spending two years in England from 1721 to 1723. This strengthened his Whiggery, and in his book on the decay of ancient Rome, he claimed that the cause lay in the loss of its original republican liberties. In his principal work, *L'Esprit des lois* (*The Spirit of the Laws*), he went further and, postulating the historical relativity of all legal codes, advocated the type of constitutional monarchy obtaining in England as the most suitable for the present age. In addition he attacked slavery, and delivered a devastating onslaught on the Inquisition, which had as lately as 1745 burnt a Portuguese Jewish playwright in Lisbon.

While Montesquieu's criticism of Bourbon absolutism was penetrating and incontrovertible, far more damage was done to the cause of absolute monarchy by the poisoned arrows of an enemy who was most often actuated by no more than malice, and who left behind him no work of greater importance than a well-shaped little novel or two.

FRANÇOIS MARIE AROUET (1694–1778), who took the name of VOLTAIRE, was the most complete representative of the eighteenth century, which he dominated from end to end, from the Regency almost to the Revolution. In his opinions he was clear-cut but shallow. The pupil of a Jesuit school who had turned to literature for a living, Voltaire was quickly in trouble. Twice he was put in the Bastille, and after his second imprisonment he left for England. With a successful tragedy and a satirical poem to his credit, he made good use of his exile, learning the language, meeting everyone of importance, including Pope, Swift, and Congreve, reading Shakespeare and coming to admire English political institutions. On his return to France he published a study of Charles XII of Sweden, and a series of *Lettres sur les Anglais* (*Letters on the English*), which by introducing the contemporary commonplaces of England to French readers founded his serious reputation. But Voltaire thought of himself as the heir to the great dramatists of Louis XIV's day, and persisted in the production of classical plays in verse which, while adhering to Racine's forms, re-admitted melodrama in settings which ranged from China to Peru. Lacking both psychological insight and all sense of poetry, however, he resorted to a high-flown rhetoric, which deceived contemporary audiences but rings hollow to-day. His one important service to the drama was to extend the range of its subject matter, which could now include political intrigue and even allow speeches in favour of liberty.

After a second period of exile in Lorraine, again occasioned by an unlucky satire, Voltaire returned to Paris under the protection of Mme de Pompadour, and was elected to the Académie. But in 1749 he accepted an invitation from Frederick II of Prussia, with whom he had long been in correspondence, and spent three years in Berlin. Here he published his *Siècle de Louis XIV* (*Age of Louis XIV*), a very objective piece of history which he based on his own researches and on many conversations with survivors from those great times.

Despite his pretence to philosophy, Voltaire is at his weakest in the field of general ideas, just as, though aiming to give France that national epic that Ronsard had failed to write, he was incapable of longer flights of poetry than a bright epigram. He seems consistently to have misjudged the nature of his own talents.

He owed his influence chiefly to his simple style and his directness. Despising metaphysics, Voltaire adhered to a Deistic standpoint for no better reason than because God was necessary as a first cause and a safeguard for popular morality; atheism he associated with the crimes of the Borgias. Like Shaw he threw off ideas which were mostly other men's irresponsibly but brilliantly; and since all difficult thoughts were alien to him he made philosophy appear a simple science.

Voltaire's reactions were always those of the common man. Impelled by the disaster of the Lisbon earthquake, which followed on the destruction of Lima by the same impersonal agency, he struck back with a satire on the idea of a benevolent god, and on the optimistic philosophy of Leibniz – or his travesty of it. This attack took the form of the most entertaining of novels, entitled *Candide ou l'Optimisme*, in which disaster after disaster strikes his innocent hero till, after failing to find happiness even in a smooth-running Utopia, he ends by cultivating his own garden, in despair of the world and its ideals.

Written when he was sixty-five, *Candide* seemed to Voltaire the least substantial of his works. Now it is almost the only prop of his faded popularity, though equally entertaining are two or three other short pieces in the same vein, chief among them *L'Ingénu* (*The Simpleton*), in which he demolished the still hardly emergent idea of the 'noble savage' by bringing his Man Friday into contact with polite society, and *Zadig*, an oriental allegory written a dozen years before *Candide*, in which a figure much resembling Voltaire himself in a turban is shown defying the worst the gods can do. 'Men blessed Zadig, and Zadig blessed Heaven,' it concludes; which shows that philosophical optimism came as easily as philosophical pessimism to this born writer.

Though Voltaire repeated the heresies of the *libertins* so charmingly, for all his malice, and so reasonably as to impress his age, the climate was turning against superficial rationalism. Montesquieu, and Voltaire himself, had seen the beginnings of the English compromise. Tolerance, the value of the individual, and an optimistic philosophy, were also preached by the MARQUIS DE VAUVENARGUES (1715–47), La Rochefoucauld's counterpart as a writer of maxims for the new age. Vauvenargues was an unsuccessful man, who had been crippled in the war of the Austrian Succession, and whom Voltaire vainly attempted to help into a diplomatic post. His essential work lies in a single small volume of perceptive judgements which, while not advancing far from a standard attitude of irreligion, show a warmth somewhat greater than La Bruyère's perfunctory gesture of sympathy for the underdog.

Vauvenargues, Prévost, and Montesquieu show in their different ways a new generosity and a belief in the validity of unintellectual human values. JEAN-JACQUES ROUSSEAU (1712–78) made the eighteenth century's first great plea for unreason, and for the simple man. A poor boy who had led a picaresque life of which he made the most in his single great work, his *Confessions*, Rousseau's first impact on Paris was that of an intellectual with new theories about the primal virtue, the primal liberties. Reviving the pastoral theory of a golden age, he placed it in the childhood of each man and in the childhood of mankind. If one is to believe his autobiography, his ideas were entirely the product of his own experience and intuitions. But there is no doubt that on coming to Paris he fell under the influence of the *Encyclopédistes*, a group of intellectuals far from uniform in their outlook who were engaged in the compilation of an encyclopedia, at first intended to be a mere adaptation of an English work, but which later developed along its own lines, sceptical, scientific, liberal and confident of the march of human progress. Rousseau at first collaborated in this work, writing articles on music, a subject on which he was no expert, but later quarrelled with his fellow *Encyclopédistes*. His mind and his heart, as he observed in his autobiography, contradicted one another at every step. But despite his lack of deep emotion he decided from then on to trust his heart. His first principal work, *La Nouvelle Héloïse* (*The New Heloise*), a novel in letter form, presents an idealistic picture of an unfortunate love affair of his own. Its charming Alpine setting, its repeated scenes of tenderness, and its lyrical appeal to the heart struck a public that was growing tired of Marivaux's petty themes, of Prévost's essential banality, and of Crébillon *fils*'s dubious wit. Society fell for Rousseau much as the 1920s fell for D. H. Lawrence. Here was a new version of pastoral, middle class, mildly sensual and elevating in its idealization of the dictates of the simple affections.

The hero of *La Nouvelle Héloïse* was a country schoolmaster. Education was the sole subject of the book's successor *Émile*, a didactic work which has inspired most of the modern theories of progressive education. Rousseau, whose own learning had been acquired imperfectly and sporadically during his early wandering life, exalted Nature's lessons above man's. If the initial wisdom of the child were not overlaid with ready-made instruction and morality, if the child were treated as a plant capable of growing according to its own laws, if teachers would be content merely to remove obstacles from the child's way, all would be well.

The *Contrat social*, published between his two novels, makes a similarly sentimental approach to history. Man was once free, but gave up his liberty at the end of the golden age in return for protection against enemies and criminals. But the people remain sovereign and, in Rousseau's view, are justified in breaking their contract with the State if it does not fulfil its side of the bargain. Such a theory proved an inspiration to the revolutionaries of the next decades, and has remained the basis of most democratic beliefs ever since. As history, however, it is obvious nonsense. But Rousseau made no attempt to look into the nature of primitive society. That was not his way.

Rousseau's *Confessions* were an attempt at self-justification written towards the end of his life when he was already accusing all his former friends of having conspired against him. The work is therefore not entirely reliable for facts. It was, however, the first attempt in modern literature at a self-portrait; and in this aim was overwhelmingly successful. Rousseau portrayed himself, warts and all, and owing to a rather embarrassing trait in his character, tended often to exaggerate his defects. Certainly his heart led him into a number of false situations from which his head was incapable of extracting him. But at the same time, he showed here, to an even greater extent than in *La Nouvelle Héloïse,* a power of natural description, a talent for the analysis of sentiment, and a pleasingly straightforward, though sometimes rhetorical style, which make the book consistently readable, even at such embarrassing moments as those when its author is indulging in obviously pathological accusations against the philosopher Hume, who was his host during part of his short sojourn in England, and against Denis Diderot, who had probably been responsible for launching him on his career as a writer.

DENIS DIDEROT (1713–84), the outstanding intellect among the *Encyclopédistes*, threw off ideas as freely as a tree grows blossom, but brought hardly any of them to fruition. It is likely, though Rousseau would deny it, that he set Jean-Jacques thinking about the causes of human inequality, an essay on which subject brought him his first public acknowledgement. Diderot himself, the product of a similar hard upbringing, had been intended for the Church, but refused to take orders, and drifted into a Bohemian life. Then for twenty years he worked, with small economic rewards, on the preparation of the *Encyclopédie*, which met with much official opposition owing to the objectiveness of its articles, but which was never suppressed for fear that it might be published abroad, thus profiting foreign booksellers instead of the French publishing trade.

Essentially the *Encyclopédie* set out to popularize and expand the ideas of Bayle. It absorbed what remained of the old rationalist and *libertin* spirit, and carried it to the extreme of implying that a human being is no more than a machine whose thinking and morality are conditioned by its physical circumstances. Such bold conclusions, which contributed to nineteenth-century thought even down to that of the Behaviourists, were in large part Diderot's own. Marxists have even proclaimed that he was a premature discoverer of their theory of historical materialism. Diderot and Rousseau, in fact, between them, contributed the majority of the ideas that obtained in the following century; mechanical progress, evolution, human perfectionism, and the substitution of a vaguely spiritual morality for clear-cut religious belief, as well as a considerable contribution to the theory of democracy, all spring from the *Encyclopédie* and from its dissident contributor Jean-Jacques Rousseau.

Diderot, moreover, was original also as a novelist and as a dramatic critic. His novel, *La Religieuse (The Nun)* is a didactic work directed against the consigning of unwanted daughters to a life of religion. Its description of a convent and its inhabitants, allegedly penned by a poor girl who is kept there against her will, is unflattering, but not altogether unjust. Nevertheless, such abuses could not be ventilated under the *Ancien Régime*, and this story was not published until after the Revolution. Nor did Diderot's little dialogue, *Le Neveu de Rameau (Rameau's Nephew)* appear in its complete form until well into the nineteenth century. It was, perhaps, the first 'imaginary conversation', an art form afterwards developed by Landor and recently adapted most successfully by a number of writers to the technique of broadcasting. Here Diderot confronted an old philosopher, the spokesman for the cultured rationalism of the old generation, with a young ex-musician, the nephew of Rameau, who denies the existence of morality and decency and believes only in the sensual pleasures. Diderot was far from having all the qualities of the novelist. Nevertheless his characters come to life as he makes them talk or write.

As a dramatic critic too, as in most of his thinking, Diderot was far-sighted, though himself incapable of developing his ideas. He saw that classical tragedy and comedy were exhausted, and advocated a new form of tragi-comedy with a realistic plot, and characters chosen less for their individuality than for their place in the social scale. The drama which he envisaged would, furthermore, be capable of treating moral issues. Diderot's own plays, however, were static, relying on moments of silent tableau for effects that, in true drama, could only be achieved by action or dialogue.

This prescription for a mixture of moral medicine and treacle contributed to the popularity of such plays as Michel-Jean Sedaine's *Le Philosophe sans le savoir* (*The Unconscious Philosopher*); a drama with a middle-class moral directed against duelling. Sentimentality and uplift invaded even the realm of comic opera. But no audience could repeatedly be moved to tears by a moral lesson. The only considerable dramatist to follow Diderot followed him only from a distance. Pierre-Augustin Caron, who took the name of BEAUMARCHAIS (1732–99), after attempting the bourgeois drama, returned to Molière's comedy, refreshed by some new touches from the *commedia dell'arte*, and pointing a sound middle-class moral or two as Diderot prescribed. *Le Barbier de Seville* and *Le Mariage de Figaro* are now chiefly known in their operatic settings by Rossini and Mozart. Figaro is the *gracioso* of Spanish comedy, the Harlequin of the Italians, turned liberal-democrat and almost edging the gentry off the stage. But Beaumarchais was less a moralist than entertainer; his arrows were not barbed; and so, despite a temporary ban, the *Barbier* was even acted at Versailles, where Marie-Antoinette herself played the part of the charmingly empty heroine, Rosine.

The final years of the French monarchy saw the publication of two single novels, each in its way outstanding; the emergence of a prolific novelist, whose work succumbed beneath his collector's zeal for detail, of a fashionable pornographer known rather by his name than his writings, and of France's first lyrical poet of stature since La Fontaine.

The two novels, *Paul et Virginie* by the amateur scientist BERNARDIN DE SAINT-PIERRE (1737–1814) and *Les Liaisons dangereuses* by the military expert CHODERLOS DE LACLOS (1741–1803) point the huge contrast between middle-class and aristocratic thought, on the eve of the Revolution.

Paul et Virginie, like *Manon Lescaut* a short novel interpolated in a large work which is no longer read, is the idyllic story of a pair of lovers set in the exotic landscape of Mauritius, and ending with the pathetic death of Virginie, drowned before the eyes of her Paul.

As sophisticated as Bernardin de Saint-Pierre's tale is naïve, *Les Liaisons dangereuses* (*Dangerous Relationships*) is a well-planned novel on the theme of seduction, in which the sex-war is conducted with full military rigour. It is an unpleasant little masterpiece, written like *La Nouvelle Héloïse*, twenty years before, in epistolary form, and showing the reverse side of Rousseau's idyllic medal. Laclos's characters can allow themselves any fault except a lapse into sentiment. That, in their amoral society, would be a withering disgrace.

Laclos's work was rejected by the very circles which he portrayed, and in which the sneaking sensuousness of Crébillon *fils* retained its popularity. RESTIF DE LA BRETONNE (1734–1806), the author of a whole *comédie humaine* of eighteenth-century Paris, sentimental, naturalistic, and over-detailed, has hardly proved readable at any time, though both he and the MARQUIS DE SADE (1740–1814), a tedious self-dramatizing pervert, enjoyed a brief hour of revival during the chaotic revaluations of the 1920s.

ANDRÉ CHÉNIER (1762–94), the son of a French diplomat and a Cypriot wife, and himself a diplomat, at first accepted the Revolution, then rejected it and was executed as an 'enemy of the people'. His poetry makes fresh use of the classical myths, without romanticism and without any feeling for their symbolic content. His is the world of Poussin reproduced in sensitive verse, which, like Racine's, seems a little too smooth to carry much charge. It is the world as Keats saw it motionless in the sculpture on his Grecian urn, or as Narcissus saw it reflected behind his head as he gazed into the pool. It is not till his last poems, which were written in prison, that some feeling – which is not entirely self-pity – informs his impersonally beautiful lines. *La Jeune Captive* (*The Girl Prisoner*), almost the last piece that he wrote, is also the most moving. Though muted, it is a real and humanitarian indictment of the Terror.

Chapter Twelve

ITALIAN REVIVAL AND THE
AGE OF GOETHE

THOUGH eighteenth-century France was less productive of great writers than England, which had Richardson, Fielding, Pope, Sterne, Johnson, Gibbon, Cowper, and so many more to its credit, yet in Rousseau and Diderot she could claim to have produced two men who were more influential than any others in fixing the shape of the future. For Rousseau, in placing himself in the foreground of all his work, finally broke with all that remained of the medieval ideal of artistic anonymity, and Diderot in his scientific theorizing went beyond such mere popularizers of the last generation as Fontenelle, and foreshadowed those writers at the end of the nineteenth century, such as H. G. Wells, who attempted to lead scientific thought, instead of merely interpreting it.

Over the rest of Europe, the chief advances in the first half of the eighteenth century lay in the field of drama and dramatic theory. Molière had built on the impermanent improvisations of the *commedia dell'arte* a literary comedy, far more influential beyond its frontiers than Ben Jonson's similar achievement half a century before. Comedy had been developed more slowly than tragedy, but it had now reached a stage much in advance of the Latin plays, which had hitherto been almost the only classical examples available to dramatists who did not want to follow the medieval farce. Terence and Plautus had enjoyed an influence in Renaissance Europe far in advance of their true worth. But Molière had now shown how comedy could be at the same time dramatic and satirical, and how it could hold up twin mirrors, to character and to manners.

The new comedy spread quickly, first to Denmark, a country which so far had little modern literature, and which relied largely on foreign companies for its drama. LUDWIG HOLBERG (1684–1754) gained his first fame with a satirical poem. When he turned to comedy he drew on many sources, but modelled himself most closely on Molière. Holberg had lived in England and visited France. He saw the extent of Denmark's cultural backwardness, and hoped to cure it by satire. He was not, however, certain where to begin, and attacked all alike: bourgeois, peasants, nobles, and the would-be enlightened. He was often inventive, but seldom capable of developing his original ideas. At one moment, in a play called *Hexerei* (*Witchcraft*), he anticipated Pirandello by bringing a group of characters from his early plays on to the stage, to protest against his treatment of them; and in other plays there are characters sketched straight from life, of whom one of the most original is the hero of *Den Stundelse* (*Not a Moment to Waste*), who attempts to do three things at once, cannot settle to anything, and consequently has not a single moment to spare. But Holberg's is not the achievement of a major dramatist, although he certainly counts as the founder of his country's literature.

While Denmark was broadening the territory of Western literature, which was to spread in the course of the century to Sweden also, a revival of Italian drama, again attributable in part to Molière's example, seemed about to bring that country back as a leader in the dramatic field. Italy's principal dramatist of this age, the Neapolitan PIETRO METASTASIO (1698–1782) devoted himself chiefly to the writing of libretti, some of them modelled on the classical formulas of Corneille and Racine, but with their tragedy resolved in tender arias, in which conflict melted into harmony. Metastasio's musical melodramas enjoyed a European success. But the theatrical revival in Venice, though more local, was in the long run also more productive. The *commedia dell'arte* was dying; the same characters had for too long been raising the same laughs by the same devices, though brought up to date with topical tricks and allusions. But gradually the influence of literary comedy increased and standard Tuscan speech came to be preferred to dialect. The comedy of manners was, in fact, having its effect on the popular farce, especially in the theatre of Milan. But it was in Venice that two dramatists, both deeply imbued with the popular comic tradition, actually transformed the old farce into the new comedy.

Count CARLO GOZZI (1720–1806) brought to the theatre a mind in love with fairy tales. *The Loves of the Three Oranges, Turandot, The Magic Bird* were some of the titles of the philosophical fables which he presented with some scenes in colloquial prose and verse, and some just indicated in outline for the actors' improvisations. Everything is fantastic, yet all Gozzi's effects depend on the contrast between his prose and his verse, between dialect and Tuscan, between satire and dream. Gozzi was at heart an ironist, with a deep antipathy to the sentiment which was brought to the stage in equally fantastic disguise by his rival, and perhaps superior, CARLO GOLDONI (1707–93), who also began by working for the *commedia dell' arte*, but soon migrated to Paris, to write for the Italian players there.

In contrast to Gozzi, who was an aristocrat out of sympathy with the intellectual tendencies of the eighteenth century, Goldoni was a bourgeois inclined to the sentimental realism which was becoming fashionable. Despite his good humour, he had come to despise the traditional buffooneries of the Italian stage. His master was Molière, whom he sometimes equalled in powers of invention, but never in observation or in the art of pointing a moral. Goldoni was a prolific dramatist with a genuine sense of comedy, who would have liked to be more serious than his temperament, and the players for whom he wrote, allowed. He believed that honest hearts dwelt chiefly beneath fustian coats, and so transformed the comic old merchant Pantaloon into a benevolent character, capable of harmonizing lovers' quarrels and presiding over a happy ending.

Goldoni, like Holberg, is an inventive dramatist. In one play a troupe of actors are found rehearsing another of Goldoni's pieces, which gives him an opportunity for satirizing the besetting evils of the theatre: personal rivalries, senseless gagging, vulgarity, and lack of moral purpose. In another play, *La Locandiera* (*The Hostess of the Inn*) the inn itself is more important than the characters, as is also the coffee house in *La Bottega del caffè*. Indeed, his sense of locality is so strong that many of his plays take Venice for their subject, picking out a group here, a group there, to build up a whole gay picture of Venetian society. The entire city is presented, from the gossip in her boudoir to the waiting gondolier, from the hardworking housekeeper to Anzoletto, the young husband run into debt by a foolish wife.

Both Gozzi and Goldoni are dramatists of genius, and the first to feel the limitations of the theatre for which they wrote. Gozzi played with philosophical meanings but could not be more serious than the players allowed: and Goldoni, for all his castigation of the comic stage as he found it, could not develop a serious comedy of character or of manners without actors and a public prepared for such a change.

A single rebellious, somewhat naïve figure, in his attitudes a forerunner of Romanticism, violently broke the dream-like spell of Metastasio, and introduced the French tragic formula on to the Italian stage. VITTORIO ALFIERI (1749–1803) wrote some twenty-two tragedies, many of them treatments of Greek mythology. But some, *Filippo* for example, interpret scenes of past history from a modern political point of view. In this piece, the unfortunate Don Carlos is made to voice liberal enthusiasms, certainly out of keeping with the reign of his father Philip II, who gives the play its name. The theatre, as Alfieri saw it, was a place in which men must be taught to battle against oppression, and a tragic hero was synonymous with an innocent victim. He was declamatory, melodramatic, and cold except when fired by political enthusiasm. His most entertaining work is his autobiography, which was not published until after his death. For in his life he travelled widely, to Russia and England among other places, and in his old age had an affair with the Young Pretender's wife, with whom he ended his days. His disciple VINCENZO MONTI (1754–1828) was no more successful with his tragedies and even more unreliable politically, praising first Napoleon and then the reactionary dynasty of Austria. Milton, Dante, Ossian, and Shakespeare swayed him by turns, for he was Romantic by temperament and anti-Romantic by conviction. In this he was perhaps the representative writer of the Napoleonic era.

A more pleasing poet who also held positions under Napoleon in his Cisalpine Republic, was the rather older GIUSEPPE PARINI (1729–99), a priest of country stock with an appreciation of classical literature, a Horatian felicity in his odes, and a satirical vein which he exercised against the profligacy and vanity of the nobility. With his younger contemporary Chénier, he is one of the very few eighteenth-century poets whose best verse can almost stand beside that of the Latin models which the whole age imitated. A more productive Collins, a less sententious Gray, a Dyer not confined by petty themes, Parini, though not a major poet, is one of the most gracious, the most austere and, within the tradition, the most original poets of his century.

Spanish literature of the eighteenth century contains little more than faint echoes of the French classical style which, with the establishment of a Bourbon dynasty, obtained an artistic hegemony fatal to the already dying mannerist style of the seventeenth century. Poets were few, and imitated either foreign models or the more sober school of Aragon. Luis de León and the Argensola brothers were greatly admired; Jáuregui was tolerated, and Góngora's reputation declined. A single poem on the bullfight by NICOLÁS FERNÁNDEZ DE MORATÍN (1737–80) has survived in most anthologies; the rest hardly even present a quarry for the most pedestrian scholars.

Two prose works alone stand out, both imbued with the picaresque tradition, which seems to have corresponded very closely to the life experience of any young man of the Spanish middle class bent on making his way in the world. The first is the autobiography of DIEGO DE TORRES VILLA-ROEL (1693–1770), a tough character who advanced from selling quack remedies and fighting the village bulls to a lectureship in mathematics – a subject still much confused with astrology – in the University of Salamanca. Villaroel was aggressive, class-conscious, and greatly taken up with himself; a Rousseau without ideals or theories who wrote in a seventeenh-century style, but lacked the pessimism of that age.

The second prose work which is still enjoyable is the

Historia del famoso predicador Fray Gerundio de Campazas (*History of the Famous Preacher, Brother Gerundio de Campazas*) by the Jesuit JOSÉ FRANCISCO DE ISLA (1703-81), a satire against rhetorical sermons intended to deal them the same lethal blow as Cervantes had dealt the romances of chivalry. The book contains some entertaining pictures of convent life; also the character of the perfect friar, whom a modern reader will find a perfect bore.

The one outstanding Spanish figure of the eighteenth century was the dramatist LEANDRO FERNÁNDEZ DE MORATÍN (1760-1828), son of the writer of the poem just mentioned, who was himself the author of some plays in the French manner. The younger Moratín translated *Hamlet* and Molière, and wrote comedies in Molière's style. He travelled widely and, like Vincenzo Monti, fell beneath the Napoleonic spell, retreating from Spain with the French armies, and dying in exile at Bordeaux. Moratín wrote his first plays in verse, but turned later to prose, an innovation in the Spanish theatre, which was still living on its glorious past. Always obsessed with the conflict between giddy youth and stubborn old age, he manages to get his audience's sympathy for the crabbed old husband bullied by his model retainer and deserted by his young wife in his early *El Viejo y la niña* (*The Old Man and the Girl*), and with the uncle who loses his silly bride to his equally silly young nephew in *El Sí de las niñas* (*The Young Girl's 'Yes'*), which was his last. His model for these ultimately appealing old monsters is no doubt Molière's Alceste, but Moratín has his own psychological penetration and his own sense of comedy. His impostor of a baron in *El Barón* and his victim, the dominating old widow Mónica, have each sufficient weight to carry a whole Molière play on their shoulders. Yet Moratín delights to throw them into collision. He is, in fact, a dramatist who can risk comparison with the best which his century can show; with the more farcical Goldsmith, the wittier Sheridan, the more formal Marivaux, and the endlessly inventive Goldoni. For he is not purely the disciple of Molière; he is also a premature Ibsen, who has caught a glimpse of the conflict of generations that tortured the Master Builder.

Moratín's drama, like that of all the early eighteenth century outside England, pays proper deference to the unities. It was to Germany that Europe was finally to owe her freedom from these not always harmful shackles, though the Germans might have remained enslaved but for Shakespeare's example, which gave Lessing and afterwards the *Sturm und Drang* generation a warrant to break with the formalism of the French style.

Despite the originality of the Silesian school, with its new amalgam of piety and the picaresque, of Marinism and echoes from the trump of doom, Germany was still heavily oppressed by French intellectual dominance at the beginning of the eighteenth century. The language itself had no standing, and had not yet evolved its equivalent of Tuscan. The first University lecture was not given in German until 1687, Latin being the standard tongue for all learned discourse.

The first writer to rebel against the reign of dialect opted for High German as the proper language for literature, and recommended the Saxon variety as the most suitable. JOHANN CHRISTOPH GOTTSCHED (1700–66), however, who dominated the literary field in the 1730s and founded the first German academy, did little service to his contemporaries beyond calling their attention to Germany's wealth of medieval writing. For the rest, from his chair of poetry at Leipzig, he tried to clamp the bonds of French taste even more firmly around his generation. Leipzig became a mere echo of Paris, producing nothing more original than the pleasing fables of CHRISTIAN FÜRCHTEGOTT GELLERT (1715–69) who also wrote a risky novel under the influence of Richardson, and some contributions to periodicals that echoed *The Spectator* and *The Tatler*.

This dictatorship of reason, which found its justification in the philosophy of GOTTFRIED WILHELM VON LEIBNIZ (1646–1716) – whose optimism Voltaire ridiculed in *Candide* – was speedily combated by JOHANN JAKOB BODMER (1698–1783), a Swiss scholar, who championed Milton as the representative of the imagination, and translated *Paradise Lost*. So the *Aufklärung* or 'Age of Enlightenment' was challenged, almost at its inception, by the admirers of England, who were ultimately to triumph with Herder and Goethe.

Germany's first considerable poet, FRIEDRICH GOTTLIEB KLOPSTOCK (1724–1803), owed everything to Bodmer's encouragement, to Milton's example, and to his own links with the traditional German pietism which derived from Jakob Boehme. His epic *Der Messias* in the classical hexameter is, in Lessing's words, 'so full of feeling that the reader feels nothing at all.' His odes, however, in free metres, owe something to Horace, but also contain a rough virility that looks forward to the odes of Hölderlin. Klopstock was an enthusiast, full of patriotic aspirations, and muddled admiration for *Ossian* – as presented by the unscrupulous MacPherson – and the Eddas. These dissimilar works he lumped together, believing them to have been the first great Germanic poetry, in this subscribing to the myth of ancestral greatness which has deluded German theorists even down to the inventors of the pure Aryan blond.

In contrast to Klopstock, GOTTFRIED EPHRAIM LESSING (1729–81) was a master of sanity, though lacking in that ultimate quality of imagination which might have made him a great dramatist. Educated at Leipzig University, he settled in Berlin as a journalist, where with Moses Mendelssohn and C. F. Nicolai he launched a series of letters on the subject of the 'new literature' which castigated Gottsched's party and Bodmer's alike, dismissed *Der Messias* as maudlin, and called attention to Germany's legacy of folk-song. In the famous seventeenth letter he went further, proclaiming that Shakespeare was the true model for any dramatist, and that even the old popular plays of the wandering players were more akin to the German genius than the theatre of Corneille. In his enthusiasm Lessing had turned first to Voltaire, then to Dryden. But soon he discovered Diderot, in his opinion the most philosophical spirit to interest himself in the theatre since Aristotle. Lessing had written and translated several light comedies. Now he wrote his first important play, a tragedy of common life, related to George Lillo's famous *London Merchant*, but influenced by Diderot's theories. *Miss Sara Sampson* tells of a pure girl ruined by a wicked libertine, and would raise more laughter than tears if presented to-day. It moved the German public, however, and was succeeded by *Minna von Barnhelm*, a serious comedy of contemporary Germany with a noble soldierly hero, a charming masterful heroine, and two servants, who provide the humour and without whom the play would count as a very serious drama of character. For Diderot did not encourage frivolous comedy, and Lessing's favourite English dramatist at the time was Farquhar, who lacks the sparkle of a Congreve, the wit and love of human oddity of Goldsmith. But *Minna von Barnhelm* was topical in its truth to the confused period that followed the end of the Seven Years' War.

Lessing's next and most influential work, the *Laokoon*, was an attempt to compare and contrast the arts, assigning its proper territory to each. As a document of the *Aufklärung*, it did that movement a great disservice, for with its plea for action rather than description as the true subject of poetry, it prepared the way for the violences of the *Sturm und Drang* writers and of the Romantics. 'All earlier criticism was flung away,' said Goethe, 'like a worn-out coat when it appeared.' But the book now seems more valuable as an example of clear reasoning than for the conclusions at which it arrived. All Lessing's principal discoveries were truths gathered by the wayside.

Lessing met with no official recognition from the Prussian king, who was heavily under the influence of Voltaire. He therefore left for Hamburg, where he wrote criticisms of the plays performed in the short-lived National Theatre. In these articles, with characteristic thoroughness, he went back to examine the theories of Aristotle. Tragic pleasure, he decided, lay not in the moral lesson received, as Corneille – his perpetual bugbear – supposed, but in the sympathy aroused. Its purpose is the stimulation of virtue. His conclusions sort well with his age. Having demolished the French theorists from Corneille to Voltaire, Lessing then went on to sweep away the unities, to which he had hitherto subscribed in practice. His next play *Emilia Galotti* portrayed a struggle between love and honour in the mind of a subtly conceived heroine, with a villain who was the grandfather of all stage villains. But the play remained Classical, at least in its externals.

The latter part of Lessing's life was devoted to a long controversy on the subject of miracles, in which he defended a purely rationalist standpoint of incredulity. But his polemics were silenced by the Duke of Brunswick, at whose court he was now living as librarian, and he turned once more to the stage, to write a play about the noble Jew, *Nathan der Weise* (*Nathan the Wise*), a philosophical piece with an oriental setting, extremely French in its construction, and written in blank verse – the first German drama in that metre. In it he summed up his enlightened and humanitarian message in terms quite uninfluenced by the free spirit of Shakespeare and of Diderot.

Shakespeare's plays were first put into German by a versatile writer with a fine prose style, unequalled in German until the time of Heine. CHRISTOPH MARTIN WIELAND (1733–1813) was the inventor of the *Bildungsroman*, the typically German novel of ideas, the ghost of which separates German fiction to this day from that of the rest of Western Europe. His *Agathon* tells the story of his hero's education in the lessons of life. Its setting is an imaginary Greece, and its sententiousness derives from Richardson's. Wieland then moved on, under the influence of Sterne, to attempt characterization and humour, only to resume the writing of his Greek stories. His *Oberon*, a fanciful epic with motifs drawn from Chaucer's *Merchant's Tale*, and the *Midsummer Night's Dream*, shows that Wieland understood something about English comedy. But he was baffled by *Lear* and *Macbeth*. His true merits lie rather in his activity as intermediary between Germany and the rest of Europe than in any work that he left in writing. In his journalism, he interpreted new thoughts and developments abroad, and by his mastery of the art of narrative found foreign translators and readers who had never had previous acquaintance with any work of German literature.

Another German writer to come under the influence of Sterne was the Göttingen professor GEORG CHRISTOPH LICHTENBERG (1742–99), who claimed to have gone to England in order to learn to write German. Lichtenberg, whose aphorisms are sharp, satirical, and beautifully balanced

in their choice of words, was an irrationalist, as directly inspired as Blake, who disguised himself to suit his age as the
very epitome of scientific rationalism. He was, as he himself
wrote, 'a very *Sonntagskind* for intuitions', and later romantics,
Jean Paul in particular, came to recognize this inspired
fritterer of his time and talents as their true ancestor. With
his Blake-like heart and his talent for Shandyisms, Lichtenberg
was a fierce enemy of sentimental hocus-pocus. '*Er trieb
einen kleinen Finsternis-Handel*' (He ran a little darkness-shop),
his epigram on some minor mystery-monger of his day, might
serve with equal justice for many a semi-charlatan who has
bounced himself into fame between Lichtenberg's day and
ours.

The *Aufklärung* was not of long duration. Soon the reputation of Jean-Jacques Rousseau swept across Europe, and
when in 1770 Goethe and Herder met in Strasbourg, and Kant
became professor in Königsberg, a movement which had been
in decline ever since Lessing had first praised Diderot began
to yield to something more German, more productive, and
also more destructive in its ultimate effects.

The first German to speak with a modern voice, JOHANN
GOTTFRIED HERDER (1744–1803), left no finished work of
importance, yet exercised the widest influence on his successors, particularly through the medium of Goethe, who
first revolved in his orbit and then eclipsed him. Herder was a
Protestant pastor, who had as a young man sat at the feet of
the crabbed old anti-rationalist professor JOHANN GEORG
HAMANN (1730–88), through whom he was linked to the
mystical school of Jakob Boehme. But Herder himself was no
mystic. He was rather the Diderot of his time and country,
who threw up a series of valuable ideas to be worked out by
other men. As Lessing had finally disposed of the theory of
the unities, so Herder solved the century-old dispute between
the advocates of the Ancients and the Moderns, by postulating
an evolutionary theory of literature in which everything had
its place. He was, however, passionately anti-French, saw no
virtues in Diderot and his circle, praised Shakespeare and
wrote discerningly about him, and collected ballads and folk-
songs of all nations after the example of our own Bishop

Percy, but more indiscriminately. For he included the faked *Ossian* of MacPherson, Homer, the 'Beauties' of Shakespeare and the best poems of the contemporary and homely Holstein poet Matthias Claudius among his specimens of the antique.

Championing Homer against the eighteenth-century's favourite, Virgil, Herder followed Rousseau in his advocacy of a return to nature. Nature to him meant not only Shakespeare and Homer, but obedience to the promptings of the heart – *Gefühl ist alles* (Feeling is everything) wrote the young Goethe, in this following Herder, under whose spell he had fallen in his later student days.

But though Herder called for attention to the voice of conscience and could think of Shakespeare as a natural phenomenon, above criticism, in his reviewing of modern books he was firm in his principles, looking always for the creative purpose behind the outward expression. The poet to him was a heaven-sent genius, and the Middle Ages a time of inspiration.

Whilst Herder thus prepared the way for Romanticism, complete with all its extravagances, the immediate results in Germany consisted of a little outbreak of lyrical poetry, some in classical stanzas, some in ballad metres, contributed to the *Musenalmanach* (*The Muses' Almanack*) a periodical published in the University town of Göttingen which, being on Hanoverian territory, acted as a centre for the spreading of English influence.

There had been only one lyrical poet of importance since the days of Gryphius and Hoffmann; the unhappy JOHANN CHRISTIAN GÜNTHER (1695–1723), a poet of great power, restricted in his themes by a disappointment in love and by his dissipated life. But Günther counts rather as a belated pietist than as the forerunner of Rousseau in his autobiographical honesty, and of Goethe and Hölderlin in the vigorous opening lines of several of his poems, which can seldom keep on their initial high level.

The *Musenalmanach* group were all lesser men than Günther. Chief among them were MATTHIAS CLAUDIUS (1740–1815), whose pious themes act as a link between these poets and the baroque generation, and whose *Der Tod und das Mädchen*

(*Death and the Maiden*) gave Schubert the words for his song and the theme for his quartet; LUDWIG HÖLTY (1748–76), technically the most accomplished of the group, who died young of consumption; and GOTTFRIED AUGUST BÜRGER (1747–94), the composer of dramatic ballads, among them *Lenore*, an anthology piece which was translated by Walter Scott at the beginning of his career, and again by D. G. Rossetti. This somewhat declamatory work was certainly one ancestor of Scott's own poetry, and no doubt a contributory cause of the outbreak of pseudo-medieval ballad writing that afflicted Robert Southey and many other men of his generation.

While *Lenore* has much to answer for, the drama of the *Sturm und Drang* group, a product of Rousseau's example and Herder's theories, plus an unacknowledged debt to Diderot for his advocacy of the bourgeois theatre, was responsible for a dangerous crisis in the new German literature, which seemed likely, in its revolt against the *Aufklärung*, to dissolve before ever it matured, in violence, shrillness, and eccentricity.

The play from which the *Sturm und Drang* movement took its name was written by a minor member of the group, F. M. VON KLINGER (1752–1831), a poor youth and a protégé of Goethe's, who later adopted a military career and ended his life as a lieutenant-general in the Russian army. Klinger's play, *Der Wirrwarr oder Sturm und Drang* (*The Shindy or Storm and Stress*) was extravagant, excitable, and loosely constructed, as were the principal plays of J. M. LENZ (1751–92), a more talented and more unbalanced member of the same circle, 'a shooting star over the literary horizon' as Goethe called him, who attempted to fuse comedy and tragedy and to break the drama down into a series of short scenes, which would bring it closer to the novel, in this seemingly anticipating the technique of the cinema. But the importance of *Sturm und Drang* lies not in the achievements of those dramatists who confined themselves to it, but as a stage first in the development of Goethe, and then in that of Schiller. In itself it represented a disorderly extreme from which German literature was rescued by Goethe himself, but into which it has several times been in danger of lapsing again.

JOHANN WOLFGANG VON GOETHE (1749–1832) went as a student of Leipzig, and there, in that 'little Paris', fell under the influence of the *Aufklärung*. But even in his earliest writings personal stresses mar the objective smoothness that the Age of Reason demanded. At twenty-one, after an illness and a violent love affair, he transferred himself to Strasbourg, where he suffered the sarcasms and fell under the spell of Herder, and where he met Klinger, Lenz, and other young men who were to fall just as strongly under his own spell. During the interval between his leaving Leipzig and his going to Strasbourg Goethe had encountered the old anti-rationalist tradition, emanating from Boehme, which proclaimed the possibilities of the soul's transformation in terms of alchemy. He had himself during those months dabbled in alchemical experiments; and this point of view certainly influenced his scientific attitudes throughout his life. At Strasbourg, however, he was introduced to Shakespeare, to the sentimentality of Goldsmith's *Vicar of Wakefield* and to Gothic art, which seemed to him the German style *par excellence*. From 1770 onwards Goethe was diametrically opposed, in religious outlook, in aesthetic tastes, and in his belief in the superiority of genius over reason, to the rational school of Leipzig. Wit yielded to inspiration.

As a lyrical poet he matured rapidly during this time, and as a dramatist he published the first play of a new kind, *Götz von Berlichingen*. The hero of this *Sturm und Drang* drama was a robber-knight, a figure in whom Goethe incarnated the poet's or man of genius's hostility to society. Here was Rousseau's spirit on the offensive, and allied with it an excitable nationalism, peculiar to the fissured nation into which Goethe had been born. His prime models for *Götz* were the historical plays of Shakespeare, in which he found a precedent for frequent changes of scene – he indulged in nineteen such shifts in his third act.

At the same time Goethe was working on the theme of the despairing scholar, Doctor Faust. The origins of the Faust legend lie very far back. Ever since the time of Marlowe's play they had been a stock theme for the German puppet-theatre, and Lessing had begun a play on the subject, but could do little with it, since to a rationalist Faust's damnation could be no more than a fantasy, knowledge being for him the supreme goal.

In Goethe's first version the betrayal of Gretchen was fully worked out, but the philosophical implications of Mephistopheles and the selling of Faust's soul were not. This theme of betrayal, which had already appeared in *Götz*, was for the moment more important to him than the conflict between the life of the senses and the life of the spirit which was to inform the main scenes of the completed *Faust*. Love was to Goethe inseparable from betrayal, the emotions aroused in him being always incommensurate with the promised union of souls, which Rousseau encouraged him to expect. Vamping up his own feelings, he swept one girl after another off her feet, only to find that he did not want her.

But such emotional self-intoxication could lead, as he saw, only to disaster for one party at least, for Gretchen or for the man himself, whom he drew in his cautionary novel *Werther*. Werther's case was his own, with the difference that he had broken away from a situation that could lead him nowhere: his love for Charlotte Buff, a simple girl who was betrothed to one of his friends. But another friend had just killed himself for hopeless love of a married woman. Goethe grafted this incident on to his own story. The novel, which is in the epistolary form of Richardson and Rousseau, actually incorporated some of the letters exchanged between himself, Charlotte, and his friend.

Götz von Berlichingen, with its patriotic theme, had started Goethe's popularity in his own country. *Werther* spread it abroad, and to all Europe he was now known as the author of this novel. But the world misread the book, weeping over its hero, and accepting his suicide as the noble and logical consequence of his passion. *Weltschmerz*, a restless self-pity which disguised itself as concern for the sufferings of humanity, became a fasionable emotion. Goethe, however, had sloughed it off.

The merits of *Werther* lie in its psychological accuracy. It portrays a state of mind not previously charted, and does so in the very language of the morbidity it anatomizes. Its failings were, as Goethe admitted, that it described Werther's weakness as if it were a passionate strength. Goethe's next important work, the play *Clavigo*, however, while still containing strands of self-revelation, returned to an almost French economy of construction. But its hero, another Werther with the same Hamlet-like irresolution, was not a figure to compare with the indisciplined and vigorous Götz. *Egmont*, the last work of his *Sturm und Drang* youth – for long unfinished – was a play which contained every weakness. Its hero is irresolute, but believes fervently in his genius, a power which drives him to fame and to destruction in defiance of all moral order and reason. The action is undramatic. But the one appealing character Clärchen, whose devotion to Egmont is like Gretchen's for Faust, has in despite of historical accuracy – for the real Egmont was a married man and the father of eleven children – made the play acceptable for its sentimental interest, even though it fails in every other way.

In 1775 Goethe ran away from one more abortive love-affair, abandoning the life of the literary amateur for that of a civil servant at the small princely court of Weimar. He was twenty-six, the world-famous author of a single novel, and a vigorous but uneven dramatist. Yet his supreme achievement was still a handful of lyrics, in which love, nature, and his inchoate belief in his own 'daimon' were fused into something new, which had sometimes all the inevitability of folk-song and at other times achieved a subtle perfection in those free verse forms of which Klopstock had been the inventor. But a few lyrical poems and the still fragmentary *Faust* bulked small in the luggage of a young man who had seemingly forsaken the unbalance of the poetic life for a career of hard and unrewarding work.

Goethe had lived through his own servitude to *Sturm und Drang*. The movement nevertheless persisted, and some four years later profoundly influenced a young man of lesser genius, who had, however, more to give to the German drama.

FRIEDRICH SCHILLER (1759–1805), a military doctor who had wished in youth to be a parson, expressed in his first important play *Die Räuber* (*The Robbers*) the same pent-up resentments and the same anti-social belief in the forces of nature that Goethe had put into *Götz*. Karl Moor, its hero, is a noble revolutionary, whose speeches have, in recent times, been known to raise a cheer from audiences who have lost all other freedom of comment. But his nobility lies not principally in his fight against oppression but in his final renunciation of his aims when he realizes that his means of attaining them are despicable. 'Two such men as I would destroy the whole moral edifice of the world,' he concludes: a realization still foreign to most statesmen, both revolutionary and otherwise. The play was an instant success, but the petty princeling whom Schiller served bade him write no more. So he left for Mannheim, and there took service as regular playwright to the local theatre. His next piece, *Fiesco*, failed because Schiller could not reconcile the historical knowledge which he had of its hero with the heroic rôle which he wished him to play. But his bourgeois tragedy, *Kabale und Liebe* (*Intrigue and Love*), a play founded on his own experience of hopeless love for a lady of rank at the court of Württemberg, was natural, unbombastic, and realistic in its portrayal of character. Rousseau-like in sentiment, and more concerned with love than with intrigue, it profited fully from Diderot's theorizing and from Lessing's practice.

Schiller too now seemed to have passed out of his *Sturm und Drang* period. His next play *Don Carlos*, however, which took him two years to write, is full of inconsistencies. It was begun as a love-tragedy in prose. But theorists, chief among them the weathercock Wieland, were demanding a return to the verse and the classical economy of French tragedy. Schiller changed his plan, therefore, and turned *Don Carlos* into a poetic and political play, at the same time abandoning the full revolutionary fervour of *Die Räuber* for the moderate idealism of Montesquieu. The play was saved, however, by its autobiographical content. Don Carlos's love for his stepmother, the queen, his sentimental friendship for Count Posa, and his longing to escape from Madrid, all reflected Schiller's own situation at Mannheim, whence he departed before *Don Carlos* was finished, going first to Leipzig, and from there, after visiting Goethe in Weimar, to Jena, where he had been offered a professorship of history.

Goethe meanwhile had been playing the petty official and master of entertainments at the court of Weimar, on intimate terms with the Duke, and sentimentally attached to Frau von Stein, a woman older than himself, who presided as his sacred Muse over his very small production. At most, he owed to her inspiration a further handful of fine lyrics, but his *Faust* had progressed no further. For some eight years his creative talent had been devoted to a novel of the theatre, *Wilhelm Meisters Theatralische Sendung* (*Wilhelm Meister's Theatrical Mission*), a work which bears the same relation to the later *Wilhelm Meister* that the incomplete *Faust* owes to *Faust, part one* in its published form. The *Theatralische Sendung* already contains the mysterious poetry of Mignon's songs, *Nur wer die Sehnsucht kennt, weiss, was ich leide* (*Only one who knows the sadness of longing can know what I suffer*) – which were to be an inspiration to the Romantics. But Wilhelm is not yet ready to learn the lessons of life off the stage. In the *Sendung*, Shakespeare and the theatre itself stand for a life of freedom in contrast to the middle-class routine which Wilhelm deserted to join the players, and in contrast too to the aristocratic narrowness of Weimar, where only his devotion to Frau von Stein caused Goethe to stay.

In several lyrical poems written at this time Goethe showed a growing acceptance of the limitations of human life as he found it. Man must recognize his place in the universe, he says, in the poem *Grenzen der Menschheit* (*Humanity's Limits*)

> *Denn mit Göttern*
> *Soll sich nicht messen*
> *Irgend ein Mensch.*
> *Hebt er sich aufwärts*
> *Und berührt*
> *Mit dem Scheitel die Sterne,*
> *Nirgends haften dann*
> *Die unsichern Sohlen . . .*

(For no man should measure himself against the gods. If he lifts himself up and touches the stars with his forehead, his unsteady feet have no hold . . .)

In his revulsion from the spirit of *Werther*, Goethe now paid more attention to his scientific investigations in which he sought a basis for the anti-rationalistic viewpoint of his youth. More interested in general principles than in small-scale experiment, he was moving towards his theory of the metamorphosis of plants, which postulated an evolution of forms very different from that which the Darwinians were to build up into an article of faith in the next century. For Goethe metamorphosis implied self-transcendence. A Werther could grow into the sane administrator of Weimar through an advance in self-knowledge, and the love for a noble woman.

But Goethe's evolution required a further experience, and in 1786 he abruptly left Weimar for Italy, there to have his first sight of the monuments of classical antiquity. He was away for almost two years, and during that time showed more interest in architecture and in drawing than in the making of poetry. He had taken some manuscripts with him, however; and when he returned, the unsatisfactory *Egmont* was actually completed, and two scenes were added to the *Faust*. But the essential achievement of this period in Goethe's life was his *Iphigenie auf Tauris*, a play in the French classical style on the theme of Euripides' drama; Shakespeare was forgotten. Schiller, nevertheless, found *Iphigenie* astonishingly modern and un-Greek; which it was. For here once more Goethe had written out of his own experience, incarnating in the figure of the Greek princess the 'eternal womanhood' of Frau von Stein, and in Orestes, himself rescued by her from the Furies of passion and conflict.

The verse of *Iphigenie* is as subtle and as rare as that of Racine. When applied to a modern subject, however – that of *Tasso* – it appears cold and stagey. The poet of *Gerusalemme liberata*, as Goethe saw him, was another Werther, in love with a woman beyond his reach, but saved from destruction by devotion to his art. *Iphigenie* is a quiet play, but its lack of action is atoned for by poetry. *Tasso*, on the other hand, is irremediably static and lacking in background. Goethe took no trouble to plot in the Renaissance world of his hero, and as a result the play, though formally most perfect, hangs somewhat rhetorically in a vacuum.

Goethe returned to Weimar where his new works were not admired. In some isolation, which was increased by his publicly taking a mistress of no great refinement, he pursued his scientific researches. His *Römische Elegien* (*Roman Elegies*) poems of retrospect, written in classical metres, were coloured by his new enthusiasm for antiquity. In their open eroticism too, they follow Latin models. For in his relations with Christiane Vulpius, his new mistress whom he was eventually to marry, Goethe abandoned the high ideals of spiritual love of *La Nouvelle Héloïse* for a compromise very close to Rousseau's own. For Rousseau's wife had been no Héloïse, but an illiterate serving-girl.

On his return from Italy, despite his dislike of *Die Räuber*, Goethe helped Schiller to get his chair of history; and once at Jena, Schiller produced two highly dramatic historical works, the first on the revolt of the Netherlands, and the second on the Thirty Years' War. As a historian he was a man of the Enlightenment, with a sense of character; but he brought no science to his historical writing.

From history, however, Schiller moved on, under the influence of the philosopher IMMANUEL KANT (1724–1804) to the study of aesthetics. Kant, whose position as a philosopher was similar to Goethe's as a poet and Beethoven's as a composer, seemed to have reconciled the idealistic and materialistic standpoints by postulating a true world the entrance to which was in the moral sphere, behind the shifting veils of the sensuous world, which was in itself unknowable. Kant's was in fact a Platonism divorced from its associations with religion. But even so it had, like Goethe's poetry and Beethoven's music, an emotional charge which contributed to the subsequent forces of Romanticism.

In 1794, after long years of mutual distrust, Goethe and Schiller became close friends, and each began to exercise great influence on the other's work. In that year Goethe published a fast moving poem on the theme of Reynard the Fox, his first important work since the publication of his fragmentary *Faust* four years before. In the interval he had been airing his dislike of the French Revolution in a number of minor plays and sketches, which failed through his inability to understand what the Revolution was about. Too old to enthuse with Wordsworth and Coleridge over this great release of natural forces, he took the aristocratic side from the start.

Schiller and Goethe, as poets, were complementary: Schiller, the more reflective, seldom looked at Nature; Goethe, the more objective, seldom looked within, and failed to apprehend the subjective nature of much that he wrote. During the course of ten years' collaboration in conducting a journal, of correspondence and of occasional conversation, each made the other more aware of his own strengths; and both were united in a common enthusiasm for Greek civilization, which they understood as a Rousseau-like era in which art and nature were one.

Goethe's first great work during this flowering of their friendship was *Wilhelm Meisters Lehrjahre* (*Wilhelm Meister's Apprenticeship*), an expansion of the 'Theatrical Mission', in which the hero was finally brought into touch with certain Masonic circles whose understanding of life's secrets lay along the lines of Goethe's own mystical scientific beliefs. All that is most entertaining in the book comes from the original, *Theatralische Sendung*, but there is much that is philosophically interesting in the material which Goethe added.

In 1797 both poets became interested in the writing of ballads, models for which had long ago been worked out by G. A. Bürger, and the resulting compositions, which in Schiller's case pointed morals and in Goethe's used myths to represent the mysteries of human nature, remained favourite anthology pieces throughout the nineteenth century. The most famous of all, Schiller's *Lied von der Glocke* (*Song of the Bell*), plots the stages of man's life with great lyrical accomplishment from the cradle to the grave. Like Gray's *Elegy*, it is a poem so hackneyed that it is difficult to read it with a fresh eye. Certain of Schiller's reflective poems, on the other hand, have a measured dignity and metaphysical subtlety that, surprisingly, seem to look forward to the Rilke of the *Duineser Elegien*.

There is considerable freshness also in Goethe's chief poem of this period, *Hermann und Dorothea*, an idyll in hexameters in the bourgeois tradition of Diderot, set in a small

Rhineland town menaced by the French revolutionary armies.

Schiller had by now turned back to Shakespeare. For though he steeped himself in the Greeks before writing his double play *Wallenstein*, the tragedy of a soldier in the grip of an adverse destiny, his destinies were not Greek and his dramatic pageantry was based on that of the two *Henry IV*'s. But he was wasteful in his methods. He had, as Coleridge said, 'the material sublime'. But 'to produce an effect he sets you a whole town on fire ... Shakespeare drops a handkerchief.' Schiller next went on to adapt *Macbeth* for the Weimar stage, showing the limits of his understanding, however, by substituting for the porter's scene a pious aubade, and making the play point a moral.

Wallenstein, with its military subject, aroused popular enthusiasm. All Germany was fired with a longing to expel Napoleon. But Schiller turned away from patriotic and Shakespearian scenes, and in *Maria Stuart*, his next play, considered moral problems arising from the career of the unhappy Queen of Scots. In its successor *Die Jungfrau von Orleans* (*The Maid of Orleans*), the former professor of history turned history upside down in the interests of shapely playwriting and caused the Maid to die on the battlefield.

For all its factual waywardness *Die Jungfrau* is classical in construction; and Schiller's next play, *Die Braut von Messina* (*The Bride of Messina*), might almost have been translated from Corneille. With *Wilhelm Tell*, his last play, Schiller returned to heroism, nobility, scruples, patriotic rhetoric, and spiritual regeneration. These last works are all on too high a plane of idealism to be convincing to-day, especially as their poetry is on an equally abstract level. It is to his early prose dramas with their greater realism that one is best able to return, and to some of those lyrical poems where Greek austerity keeps the moral in its place, or where – as in *Das Mädchen aus der Fremde* (*The Girl from Far Away*) – tradition seems to have assumed a firm control.

Schiller was not a great original genius; intellectually he stood much in debt to Shakespeare, Rousseau, Goethe, and Kant. But when he died Goethe missed his clear-sighted criticism. Seldom, indeed, in the twenty-seven years still remaining to him did he equal his best work of the past. The second *Faust*, the second *Wilhelm Meister*, his remarkable novel *Die Wahlverwandtschaften* (*The Elective Affinities*), a tale of four characters which works out a psychological theory with the abstruseness of Henry James in his last phase, the partial autobiography *Dichtung und Wahrheit* (*Poetry and Truth*), his lyrical poetry in the Eastern convention, and the final poetic monuments to his late love; works in which classical strictness alternates with romantic extravagance and the perpetual search for hidden significances: all this great output of Goethe's last years is like some huge natural eruption that marks the passage through life of a rare personage, who was not as other men. With the exception of a few poems, however, one turns to none of them as shapely works of art – which they are not. Most of them were too long in the making. Nevertheless his letters, his scientific writings, his later writings, all reveal him as a man of such all-round stature, of such an all-embracing curiosity, and of such insights that only the greatest, Dante, Shakespeare, or Cervantes, can be compared to him.

Goethe found Germany a land without literature. He left it a country in which, while writing flourished, it was dominated by a movement which he had always bitterly opposed, and which he had overcome in himself, in the person of Werther. For Romanticism, Classicism, and the drama of psychological conflict – all the great movements that were to absorb the energies of the nineteenth century – had been experienced and partly explored by that universal genius, Johann Wolfgang von Goethe, before he died, at the age of eighty-two, on 22 March, 1832.

Chapter Thirteen

THE ROMANTICS

THE reaction against rationalism which grew stronger as the eighteenth century progressed, contained many strands of thought, united into a single though multicoloured skein by a common belief that the way to ultimate truth lay through the emotions – and perhaps through higher emotions than man was commonly possessed of – and not through the intellect. But in thus denying the vision of God as mind, postulated by Descartes, the Romantics were not so much going against the originator of rationalism as returning to his sources. Knowledge, Descartes had said, came in a flash of intuition, and there were no contradictions in it. His followers had seen a great contradiction between matter and spirit, and had pushed back the domain of the latter till it embraced only the territory of cold morality. Intuition was for them, at best, a kind of hasty insight into the world of fact. For the Romantics, and for Rousseau as the first man of letters to proclaim the new doctrine, inspiration was everything; and inspiration came to man from his contact with nature and from sexual love. Its fruit was poetry.

Though Rousseau stands as the prime originator of the doctrine of inspiration, his own somewhat muddled theorizing would have had little influence without the less spectacular existence of a far stronger enemy to rationalism than this one heretical contributor to the *Encyclopédie*. The philosopher BARUCH SPINOZA (1632–77), had attempted to bring spirit and matter together, to show God as immanent throughout nature, and to point to a way of salvation not by religious belief or ritual but by self-knowledge. But this theory was too abstruse to gather round it the emotional resistance that was growing against the expulsion of everything miraculous from man's world. There remained, however, especially in Germany, treasured by small groups, the Protestant theosophy of Jakob Boehme, often diluted and distorted by accretions of crude astrology and even by cruder experiments in the magic art of alchemy, understood not as a metaphor for the soul's transformation but as a simple form of gold-making.

A great reinforcement for this persistent faith in the perpetual possibility of miracle, and in the existence of a hidden key to life's secrets, to be sought for by bands of adepts, came from the life and writings of EMANUEL SWEDENBORG (1688–1772), before whose vision the spiritual world assumed a concrete and earthly reality. A generation for whom material wealth, or the lack of it, and material exploitation were assuming greater and greater importance was readier to accept another world with which contact could be established by clairvoyance than one expounded in dogmas long worn thin, by priests who had for the most part long ago made their compromise with rationalism. The enthusiasm of a Wesley could rouse the uneducated, but only a scientific approach to religion could seriously impress those aristocrats and intellectuals who were not taken in by the limited and worldly knowledge paraded in the *Encyclopédie*.

While Swedenborg had, undoubtedly, himself genuine intuitions and true experiences, the manifold carriers of theosophical knowledge and founders of short-lived Masonic or Rosicrucian lodges contained many self-deluded theorists and even some charlatans. So much as is known of Martines de Pasqually suggests that a powerful influence in this direction was at work in France around 1770. But two later figures, far more clearly defined, CLAUDE DE SAINT-MARTIN (1743–1803) and FABRE D'OLIVET (1768–1825) conclusively demonstrate the power of a movement in thought the direct opposite of Diderot's in the very years when the themes of the *Encyclopédie* were enjoying a political triumph.

Saint-Martin was a minor nobleman and a copious writer who made no attempts to gather disciples. His attitude to the Revolution and to Rousseau was sympathetic, though he regretted Rousseau's lack of education. He saw that the Revolution took the well-being of the body for the well-being of the whole man, but rejoiced nevertheless at the death of the *ci-devant* Church. For his was a religion as vital as deism or the eighteenth-century Church was dead. 'Man is the tree, God is the sap,' said he ... 'and when the live sap flows in him, it transforms each of his branches into new trees.' Like Rousseau, he judges a man by the quality of his heart, and deplores the strange infections that have turned it into 'a light of abomination and a sign-post to error.' Claude de Saint-Martin devoted much of his life to the translation of Boehme.

Fabre d'Olivet, a younger man, the son of an old and resistant Huguenot family, explored one subject after another for its esoteric content. He re-examined the poetry of the *troubadours*, translated and commented on the Golden Verses of Pythagoras, attempted to plot out a philosophy of history, wrote a life of Paracelsus, and translated Byron's *Cain*. Much of Fabre d'Olivet's speculation would seem rash to-day when so much more information is available on such subjects as early philology, to which he devoted a whole book. But in his general endeavour to explain the material in terms of the spiritual, in his search for the essentials of ancient knowledge, which drove him to learn both Hebrew and Arabic, he remains a very modern figure.

Fabre d'Olivet, with scholarly caution, was less ready than Saint-Martin to preach in favour of 'what the vulgar call inspiration'. Nevertheless he too states that when he 'examines physical nature, he sees that no substance, no organized material, can exist and fulfil its own laws without receiving something like a breath of life ... Why then should spiritual man not also need the force of a propellent with affinity to him, to bring forth from him all the strength of his radical qualities ...?'

Here, once more, is the doctrine of inspiration, and with it in Fabre d'Olivet and his circle, the interest in the civilizations of the East, which formed another strand of the Romantic skein.

The first Romantic literature, however, was born in Germany, the fruit of the union between the old theosophy which emanated from Boehme and owed its modern strength to Swedenborg, and the new worship of nature and inspiration which derived from Rousseau. In its first incarnation, in the drama of the *Sturm und Drang* group, it quickly broke up in formlessness and hysteria, leaving its marks in the shape of

Werther and in Faust's longing to find that hidden key to nature's workings that had been the goal of the alchemists and Rosicrucians.

In later life Goethe proclaimed that Classicism stood for sanity, Romanticism for madness. He refused, indeed, to make more than the most distant acquaintance with the Romantic writers who were trying to claim his attention, with FRIEDRICH HÖLDERLIN (1770–1843) who, at his rare best, could equal him as a lyrical poet, or with LUDWIG TIECK (1773–1853) and E. T. A. HOFFMANN (1776–1822), the acclaimed leaders of the Romantic school.

Hölderlin stood a little aside from the main line of development, his aim being to return to a Greek directness, to recapture the lost Golden Age of Pindar, which he saw in terms of natural inspiration, an idea that he derived from Rousseau. Hölderlin's poetry was deliberately exalted. The few images that he takes from nature stand out boldly from a vast classical cloudscape in which men speak with gods, and Christ and St John seem at home upon Mount Olympus. The best of his odes are breath-taking, the worst hurry remorselessly on, their short lines conveying an imagined primitiveness which is not always convincing. His philosophical novel, *Hyperion*, written in Rousseau's epistolary manner, soars to heights at which the foundation of an entirely new society is discussed. Hölderlin died mad, and the finest of his odes were certainly written at a time when his contact with reality was strained. Except for *Hyperion* and two translations from Sophocles, none of his work was published in his lifetime. His reputation, indeed, did not grow until the period between the two world wars when it swelled to a point at which it threatened to eclipse the more human Goethe's. 'The gods have enough of their own immortality,' he wrote, 'and need Things.' Hölderlin's poetry fails by the ultimate test because it is always concerned with immortality, never with things, or even with men.

The chief German Romantics were story-tellers rather than poets. The influence of Swedenborg, reinforced by a growing popular interest in hypnotism, occultism, and allied phenomena, acting on an unbalanced imagination and a crude gift

for narrative, made of E. T. A. Hoffmann the first writer of
supernatural fiction, and the forerunner of Poe. Starting with
the common belief in inspiration, he went on to invent, on the
basis of contemporary philosophical theories, a world of
hidden influences and significances underlying our own.
Hoffmann's characters are haunted and controlled by disin-
carnate spirits, which are capable at times of assuming the
forms of travelling clock-makers or faithful family butlers. All
is mysterious, yet everything is firmly anchored down in a
reality which Hoffmann described in grotesque and convincing
detail. The supernatural is with him the more credible because
he has already made his reader at home in the house where the
ghost walks. His best stories are all short, and are set in a
framework after the manner of the *Decameron*, being discussed
before and after their narration by a group of students of the
occult, in whom his fellow Romantics of the Berlin school can
be recognized, thinly disguised.

Ludwig Tieck, the chief of them and a man of multiple
activities, was at his best as a writer of symbolic fairy-tales, of
which Goethe had produced a single example, and which
Hoffmann too had attempted with *Der goldne Topf* (*The Golden
Pot*). The brothers Grimm had recently collected and rewritten the best of the traditional German folk-tales, and these
Romantic writers felt impelled to produce an art form corresponding to them. They were, on the whole, less successful in this than Hoffmann with his tales of the supernatural.
They did, however, establish a Romantic prose style which
was, in effect, Germany's first prose style since Luther's
Bible.

Tieck also wrote Romantic plays, which contained good
scenes, but betrayed his sad lack of a dramatic sense, as well as
contributing to scholarship and criticism, and completing the
Shakespeare translation of A. W. VON SCHLEGEL (1767–
1845), who with his brother FRIEDRICH (1772–1829) elaborated a philosophical justification of Romanticism. The Shakespeare translations, which have remained the standard text for
the German theatre, convey the plays' dramatic mastery, but
completely blunt the fine edge of their poetry. The brothers
Schlegel performed a similar service and disservice for

Calderón, who was accepted for a while, thanks to *La Vida es sueño* and *El Mágico prodigioso*, as a Romantic forerunner.

CLEMENS VON BRENTANO (1778–1842), a man with more poetry in his nature than Tieck or Hoffmann, also attempted the Romantic theatre, but was happiest in his unfinished tale of the Middle Ages, *Aus der Chronika eines fahrenden Schülers* (*From the Diary of a Wandering Student*). Brentano's stories are idiosyncratic; when we imagine ourselves in a land of make-believe, suddenly we find ourselves on the edge of the French Revolution. But he had a homespun quality, which gives the best of his lyrics an anonymity like that of those folk-songs which he collected in collaboration with his brother-in-law, Ludwig von Arnim (1781–1831) and published under the title of *Des Knaben Wunderhorn* (*The Boy's Magic Horn*). Indeed he is chiefly remembered for this collection which had an enormous influence on German poetry, since it pointed out to the Romantic generation, much as Percy's *Reliques* had done in England, the wealth of Germany's popular heritage. A side of Romanticism very far from the popular tradition was developed by JEAN PAUL (Richter) (1763–1825), a master of complicated prose and the author of some long shapeless novels, aimless, whimsical, and much influenced by Sterne. He is interesting chiefly for his boldness in attempting to make the unwieldy many-tailed dragon of German prose turn eccentric cartwheels. But Englishmen may owe him some grudge, as the model upon whom Carlyle based his more than Teutonic version of English. Doctor Teufelsdröckh and his clan all originate with Jean Paul.

The most popular Romantic writer, whose imagination dwelt on the age of chivalry and who left behind one immortal tale *Undine*, the story of the water-pixie who married a mortal, was FRIEDRICH DE LA MOTTE FOUQUÉ (1777–1843), a writer now largely forgotten. Better remembered, though for a single story, is ADALBERT VON CHAMISSO (1781–1838) a botanist, who gave to the world the figure of Peter Schlemihl, the man who sold his shadow, in whom, perhaps unconsciously, he symbolized his own misfortunes; being half French, half Prussian, a man without a country, and a forerunner of many such in the next century.

A more difficult writer, who was without doubt the best poet in the Romantic movement proper, was FRIEDRICH VON HARDENBERG (1772–1801), who published his work under the name of NOVALIS. His few poems use mystical language, but betray a most unmystical infatuation with the thought of death. As a young man, he had become engaged to a thirteen-year-old girl who had died shortly afterwards; and in his cult of her, he elaborated a private symbolism. So though he thought of his *Hymnen an die Nacht* (*Hymns to the Night*) as spiritual, they contain autobiographical elements full of self-pity, which made them the favourite reading of our own suicidal poet, James Thomson. Novalis's prose consists of two unfinished novels, chiefly remarkable for his symbol of the blue flower of romantic yearning, a development perhaps of Rousseau's wayside periwinkle, which stood for him as the symbol of memory.

A more balanced member of the Romantic group was the Prussian civil servant JOSEPH VON EICHENDORFF (1788–1857), whose poetry, though on a small scale, suggests a connexion with that of the age of Gryphius, and whose prose narrative *Aus den Leben eines Taugenichts* (*From the Life of a Cheerful Idler*) has a light charm, rare in the Romantic age. Unlike Novalis, Brentano, and Hölderlin, Eichendorff was a well-balanced man, a Catholic by upbringing, who delighted in the small joys of life. His poetry, therefore, despite its overtones of Eternity, is well anchored in his native Silesia. With half Brentano's talent, he scores more than double Brentano's successes. In the Romantic drama, however, for which, like Brentano, he chose Spanish models, he was no more successful than the rest of his generation.

The outstanding dramatist of the Romantic group was HEINRICH VON KLEIST (1777–1811), a young man who stood somewhat apart from the group and whose plays were first collected by Tieck, after their author's early suicide. Goethe had speedily detected a morbid strain in his writing and had not encouraged him. But Kleist had an intense belief in his own destiny, and polished and repolished his idiosyncratic plays, for which he could find no producer. They are highly compressed, full of tension, violence, and fundamental despair. His dramatic climax is most often the moment in which a character breaks down. In this respect *Prinz Friedrich von Homburg* is his most striking play, though his *Der zerbrochene Krug* (*The Broken Jug*), was the only one that seemed presentable until the expressionists and existentialists, after our two world wars, found his violence congenial. In perspective, he appears as a belated member of the *Sturm und Drang* group, though with greater psychological penetration. His prose stories, related with admirable economy, quickly suggest a situation which they cannot always develop.

The principal link between the German Romantics and the French school that succeeded them was MME DE STAËL (1766–1817), the daughter of Louis XVI's finance minister Necker. An eighteenth-century figure, though affected by the prevailing cult of Rousseau, she went into exile after the Revolution and during a visit to Germany made contact with both the occultist and literary circles, coming strongly under the influence of the Schlegel brothers. Her account of German thought in *De l'Allemagne* (*On Germany*) (1810) found France in a state of literary stagnation, the Revolution and the Empire having stimulated nothing but journalism, oratory, and stage melodrama. Her advocacy of German profundity, therefore, as an alternative to the Latin clarity of the French eighteenth century had immediate results. Goethe, Schiller, and Hoffmann were translated, and the English Romantics, Scott and Byron in particular, were greatly read.

The first French Romantic, FRANÇOIS-RENÉ, VICOMTE DE CHATEAUBRIAND (1768–1848), like Mme de Staël left France during the Revolution and returned under the Empire. Like Rousseau, though writing in a far grander style, he tended to introduce his own figure into the forefront of his works: a custom which had taken partial root in Germany, and which was to be a predominant feature of Romanticism in other countries. Chateaubriand had visited America, and had spent the years of his exile in England, earning his living by translation. After losing his faith, he regained it, and in his great *Génie du Christianisme* (*Genius of Christianity*), defended Christianity, not for its truth but for its achievements in the field of art and learning. In his naïvety Chateaubriand recalls not only Rousseau but Bernardin de Saint-Pierre. For his two famous stories, *Atala* and *René*, which he intended to illustrate the argument of his major philosophical work, have something of the false simplicity of *Paul et Virginie*. The first of them tells of the loves of a noble savage and a French maiden, and the second of the Wertherish melancholy that drove a young Frenchman into exile. Chateaubriand found Europe decadent, and saw his golden age in the still uncivilized world of the contemporary American Indian.

Like Rousseau in his illusions, he was, however, considerably more exotic and considerably more polished as a writer. Despite his sentiment for the redskins, he gave an objective account of his travels in America, also of a journey from Paris to Jerusalem. Resettled in France, he devoted the last years of his life to the composition of his memoirs, which contain his best writing, and which he intended for posthumous publication. These *Mémoires d'Outretombe* (*Memoirs from Beyond the Tomb*) give a partially fictionalized account of his life, with vignettes of his lonely childhood in the Château of Combourg which have an almost Proustian intimacy, and with all the grand pageantry of the Empire in which he had taken part. Chateaubriand had a great sense of colour, a true feeling for nature, and a love of ruins, wild seas, and stormy scenes. He was not moved by the theosophical speculations of the Germans, to which he responded ironically. His interest was in the surface of things, which he called to life in his grand descriptive style.

From Chateaubriand descends the great stream of French Romantic historians, chief among them JULES MICHELET (1798–1874) with his *History of France* and his strongly republican account of the Revolution.

Close to Chateaubriand in spirit also was the first of the French Romantic poets, ALPHONSE DE LAMARTINE (1790–1869), whose poetry was founded on a concordance between mood and natural surroundings. His religion was the vague Christianity of Chateaubriand, his feeling for nature was Rousseau's, and his lyrical gift, a little sweet at times, a little Wertherish, has nevertheless a strength that makes such a poem as *Le Lac*, for all its self-pity, universal. For Lamartine, the first French poet since Villon to write in the first person, described in very simple language experiences common to many, writing of memories of lost love, of a return to childhood's surroundings, of the loss of an early innocence and of early intuitions. He is vague in his details, and unsuccessful when he attempts a social theme. But there are moments when he touches the heights inhabited by his contemporary Shelley:

> *La lune est dans le ciel, et le ciel est sans voiles:*
> *Comme un phare avancé sur un rivage obscur,*
> *Elle éclaire de loin la route des étoiles*
> *Et leur sillage blanc dans l'océan d'azur . . .*

(The moon is in the sky, and the sky has no veils; like a lighthouse placed out on a dark shore, she lights from afar the track of the stars and their white wake in the ocean of blue.)

Lamartine intended a great Christian epic, of which two unrelated sections only came to be written. Of these *Jocelyn*, a tender story of love and renunciation, has the domestic qualities of *Hermann und Dorothea*. Yet its virtues lie not in its epic qualities, but in its detachable lyrical passages; while *La Chute d'un Ange* (*The Fall of an Angel*) almost achieves a style worthy of its subject, the love of an angel for a mortal woman. Lamartine, however, had not the poetic imagination to create a superhuman being like Milton's Satan; his angel lacks wings and his mortal has too much soul.

There is a little too much soul also in the plaintively resigned verses of the unhappy MARCELINE DESBORDES-VALMORE (1786–1859), a disciple of Lamartine, who suffered from an unhappy marriage and an unfulfilled passion for another man. Many of her poems evoke childhood memories with a charming simplicity, but there are few of them that are not marred by lapses into Romantic cliché.

While Lamartine has long been out of favour with critics, a poet of equal power, but with an outlook more stoical and less emotional, has remained in favour. ALFRED DE VIGNY (1797–1863) despairs, but refuses himself the luxury of overt self-pity. He loves and considers himself betrayed, and wherever he looks he finds man the victim of an unjust God. But de Vigny makes no Satanic gestures. The wolf dies, and does not complain. In this man must imitate the animals. He is, perhaps, the first poet deliberately to choose his subjects for their symbolic bearing on his own state. Eloa, his fallen angel, was condemned for the exercise of pity; Jesus on the Cross was perhaps indeed abandoned by his Father, who had, in *Moïse* already weighed down an earlier prophet beneath a burden too great for him.

De Vigny's style is far less plastic than Lamartine's. Often, although he uses the rhymed couplet, he attains some of the dignity of blank verse. There are moments, indeed, when if not Miltonic, he achieves at least the grand style of Matthew Arnold, with whom he has something in common, especially in his power of evoking, as Arnold did in *Sohrab and Rustum*, another age and landscape. At moments too he captures the essentials of another kind of Romanticism, with suggestions of magic which recall such Germans as Eichendorff, or Tennyson's 'The splendour falls on castle walls':

> *J'aime le son du Cor, le soir, au fond des bois,*
> *Soit qu'il chante les pleurs de la biche aux abois,*
> *Ou l'adieu du chasseur que l'écho faible accueille.*
> *Et que le vent du nord porte de feuille en feuille ...*

(I love the cry of the horn, at evening, in the depths of the woods, celebrating the lament of the doe at bay, or the hunter's farewell which a weak echo catches and which the north wind carries from leaf to leaf.)

De Vigny's output of poetry was small, and his prose *Journal d'un poète* is no more than a pendant to it. But *La Servitude et les Grandeurs militaires* (*The Slavery and Greatness of Military Life*), a book founded on his peacetime experiences in the Royal Guards, is one of the first accurate and modern descriptions of military life, its boredom and irresponsibility, its demand for abnegation and devotion. In this last he sees special possibilities of greatness open to a soldier, even while he dislikes the separation of army life from that of the rest of the community. 'The army is a nation within a nation,' is the conclusion of these exemplary tales. 'It is the vice of our times.' Nevertheless in war, and even in the impersonal peace-time service of this Moloch of inactivity, lies a man's opportunity of transcending his common and selfish desires. Vigny's other volume of exemplary tales, *Stello*, is devoted to three young poets, Chatterton, Chénier, and N. J. L. Gilbert – a minor pre-Romantic – all of whom are described as ill-fated guests at life's banquet. In everything that he wrote de Vigny saw the poet, and consequently himself, as an outcast from society who was nevertheless necessary to it. For he was the carrier of the essential knowledge, and the real God, the god of ideas, would eventually guide the ship of his creation into port.

If Vigny's claim for the poet was, for all his pessimism, a great one, that of VICTOR HUGO (1802–85) was greater still. For him the poet was not only a prophet and seer, but the very voice of God. As a young man of uncertain opinions, he availed himself of all the Romantic properties within his reach. His poetry was coloured, vigorous, and coarsely tuneful, drawing on Walter Scott and the Spanish *romances* for its subjects. But the best of his early work was more personal and more tender than Vigny's. Hugo wrote of his loves and his family, his faith and his dawning political belief. His thoughts were simple; he lacked Lamartine's exalted sentiments, de Vigny's bitter restraint. He saw a cow in a farmyard, described her, and compared her to Nature, 'the universal mother'; he looked up at the multiform clouds at evening hanging like God's glistening armour from the roof of His hall, and thought of the time when he would see them no more. These poems are Romantic commonplaces boldly and flamboyantly expressed; *Oceano nox*, his masterpiece in this *genre*, in its celebration of all the brave captains who have gone to sea and never returned, is the Romantic equivalent of Gray's *Elegy*.

Hugo had stormed the stage, established the Romantic theatre and seen it decline; he had created the Romantic lyric, and by 1840 had carried it as far as he knew how. The loss of a young daughter and a mental crisis which followed opened in the poet both greater depths and greater shallownesses. The poem written at Villequier – one of his greatest – refers directly to his loss and recommends an acceptance as strict as

Vigny's, of a fate about which he now felt capable of speaking. Hugo the prophet was born.

Politically a stout democrat, Hugo attacked Louis Napoleon and was forced to exile himself to Guernsey when the pinchbeck Bonaparte seized power. Here he began to write what he intended to be the epic of human history, *La Légende des Siècles* (*The Legend of the Centuries*), a series of pictures which began in Biblical times and continued into the distant future. Lacking any philosophical framework, the *Légende* hardly exists as a whole. Some of its parts, however, *Booz endormi* (*Boaz Asleep*), and *Le Mariage de Roland* have the colours of fine stained glass; the past for Hugo was a Romantic pageant. The present, however, was ugly, and tempted him to what he considered satire; which was in fact wordy vituperation. Hugo had made himself master of a high-sounding line in which he commented on international events or related small incidents from his family life, indifferently. But he was not dead as a poet; he continued to add to *La Légende*, endeavouring to pull his amorphous work together. Then, surprisingly, in *Le Fin de Satan*, which postulated an ultimate reconciliation between good and evil, and in such an occasional poem as that on the death of Théophile Gautier, he showed all the mastery of the lyric that he had possessed in early life.

Hugo's feeling for nature, his ready sympathy and pity, and his equally ready indignation, make him an attractive poet even when he is being extravagant. There is, nevertheless an element of tastelessness in his writing which spoils many poems that, without it, might have appealed. Yet, reduced to the bulk of de Vigny, with only his best preserved, he would seem more various than his restrained rival, more masculine and more inventive than Lamartine. It is only when he insists on being judged as the great poet that he believed himself to be that Hugo so catastrophically fails. For he had no deeper philosophy or understanding than that of a liberal and optimistic politician.

The poetry of ALFRED DE MUSSET (1810–57) has latterly suffered an eclipse even greater than that of Hugo and Lamartine. A young man of Byronic poses, he matured under the influence of a love-affair with the voracious novelist George

Sand, which left him first with a melodramatically wounded heart and latterly resigned. Musset's poems of feeling are few, and these are marred by a certain obviousness of expression. Too many rejected lovers have seen themselves through Musset's eyes for his language still to retain its freshness. He is moreover, like his early master Byron, valued more highly abroad than at home, a fate that befalls writers too free with cliché. His four *Nuits*, nevertheless, which take the form of conversations with his Muse about the loss of his mistress, and his letter to Lamartine are more honest revelations than the plangency of their language may suggest. One sees Musset whipping himself up into a passion of regret only to lapse into an honest and ironic resignation; and one feels that beneath the pose is a genuine and unhappy man stretching out for some ideal happiness of which he finds suggestions in childhood memories and in nature. In this he is the typical spokesman of the *mal du siècle*, already anatomized in *Werther*; the tendency, that is, to seek in worldly love the satisfactions which previous ages had hoped to find in the love of God. The Petrarchan metaphor had broken down, and sexual love now appeared as an end in itself. It is significant that Musset, the most extreme exponent of Romantic love, valued Petrarch as the equal of Shakespeare and Michelangelo.

The outstanding critic of the Romantic generation, C. A. Sainte-Beuve (1804–69), was the founder of literary criticism in the broad modern sense. 'I can savour a work,' he wrote in explanation of his method, 'but it is difficult for me to judge it independently of my knowledge of the man himself ... By their fruits ye shall know them.' Technical or historical criticism were by him subordinated to portraiture, and though sometimes at fault over his contemporaries, he made acute judgements over many major and minor figures of the seventeenth and eighteenth centuries, restoring the reputation of Ronsard, for example, though remaining blind to the generation of Sponde. 'What was his attitude to religion? How did he respond to nature? To women? To money?': such were the questions which he asked before making his portrait, which was of the whole man in the context of his writings.

The minor figures of the Romantic movement are more picturesque than their writing. One only deserves mention, ALOYSIUS BERTRAND (1807-41) author of a series of prose poems, 'fantasies in the manner of Rembrandt and Callot' entitled *Gaspard de la Nuit*, an evocation of his native town of Dijon at the end of the Middle Ages. Bertrand's talent was no great one, but he knew how to suggest an atmosphere with very few brush-strokes, and must count as the inventor of the bastard form which he practised.

For the rest, PETRUS BOREL, the Werewolf or Lycanthrope (1809-59), was one of the first poets to consider himself an enemy of society, and GÉRARD DE NERVAL (1808-55) hovered always on the edge of lunacy. *Les Chimères*, his collection of sonnets, draw on a personal mythology in which the gods of Greece and Egypt play idiosyncratic parts. It is possible to interpret every line of them in the light of his experience, his reading of the occultists, his knowledge of German literature. But these poems were written under the impact of madness, and can best be relished simply for their surface mystery and colour. Nerval did not, as the later Symbolists did, deliberately choose imagery to convey his secret meanings. He has had a spell of popularity of late. But one can hardly suppose that a reputation based on insanity will endure. His prose stories too are at their most haunting at the point when he could no longer distinguish between dream and reality. They are a series of fantasies concerning a lost love, the biographical details of which are not clear.

Though the most permanent achievement of the Romantics was in the lyrical field, their most immediate success was in the conquest of the stage. As in Germany, the new dramatists advanced under the banner of Shakespeare, the supreme example of a playwright who had ignored the constricting unities.

In the season of 1827-8 an English company visited Paris, and played the four great Shakespearian tragedies. Shakespeare, concluded Alexandre Dumas, 'was the greatest creator after God himself'. Victor Hugo, then a young man of twenty-five, issued his amorphous historical play *Cromwell* with a provocative preface, in which he claimed that the drama, far from holding the mirror up to life, should concentrate all the coloured variety of life into a single flame. His next play *Hernani*, a roaring melodrama, dripping with poison and bristling with knives, ran for a hundred tempestuous nights in the revolutionary year 1830, and aroused almost as much passion as the Revolution itself. Unlike Schiller, Hugo made no attempt to point morals: his historical plays were mere pageantry and violence, with occasional touches of a middle-class realism deriving from Diderot. In verse they swept all before them, but when he took to writing them in prose they were less moving to his large audiences. His lieutenant, ALEXANDRE DUMAS (1802–70), was not content to write historical pageantry, and attempted at least one realistic melodrama, his *Antony* of 1831.

Less successful, though more fruitful of new ideas, were de Vigny's attempts at the stage, beginning with his version of *Othello*, and continuing with a play on the subject of the young Chatterton, which is little more than a Byronic melodrama. But Vigny in his preface called for a 'drama of thought', in which the action should take place in the minds of the characters, and in which motive should count for more than event. He did not himself go far towards developing these ideals, which are nevertheless those which have pervaded the whole living theatre from Ibsen to at least Pirandello.

The most effective dramatist among the French Romantics was, in the long run, Musset, whose eighteenth-century poses, prior to his infatuation with George Sand, brought him close to the spirit of Marivaux. His hall-mark is a delicate sentimentality, and a charming melancholy that is thrown into higher relief by his affectation of concealing it beneath a mask of laughter. His first plays were historical pageants, but after *Les Caprices de Marianne (Marianne's Whims)*, he developed his own disillusioned fantasies, which captured the stage, particularly after the publicity of his disastrous liaison with George Sand, and brought him great consolation. His plots are ingenious, and his language witty. Essentially he is playing Romantic variations on historical themes, practising a kind of glorified charade which is at its most perfect in his comedy-proverb *On ne badine pas avec l'Amour* (*No Trifling with Love*), and in his very slight *Il faut qu' une porte soit ouverte ou fermée* (*A Door must be either Open or Closed*), which shows us a gentleman paying a social call upon a lady and ending up by making her a proposal of marriage. One could not be farther from the violence and colour of Hugo. The underlying mood, however, of the two poets is not so dissimilar as their manners: both are seeking an ideal world in another historical epoch.

The Romantic drama swept Europe, calling up from Spain the *Don Juan Tenorio* of José Zorrilla, in which the noble rake falls in love with one of his intended victims and is redeemed by her prayers. The *Hernani*, around which the battles of the Madrid stage were fought, however, was a play by the Duque de Rivas on the subject of honour; *Don Alvaro*, which was subtitled 'The Power of Destiny', was sonorous but ill constructed, and gave Verdi the libretto for an opera. More sober and traditional was *Los Amantes de Teruel* (*The Lovers of Teruel*) by Juan Eugenio Hartzenbusch, a medieval drama of passion, which is still actable as Hugo's melodramas are not.

Italy too followed in the Romantic wake, though with no outstanding play that deserves mention; and the movement spread farther yet as the nineteenth century progressed to affect the poet Alexey Tolstoy in Russia, and dramatists in Hungary, Poland, and the Balkans: countries whose first modern literature was Romantic and patriotic in tone. One country alone was comparatively unaffected by this highly-coloured drama, and this was England, where the few attempts by poets such as Tennyson and Browning to write for the stage were unsuccessful, and where the successes of Edward Bulwer Lytton and one or two others were short-lived. For there could be no great field for Romantic drama where Shakespeare continued to be acted and read.

The Romantic style affected the poetry of every European country, however, though in some its vogue was short-lived. The one considerable Spanish poet, JOSÉ DE ESPRONCEDA (1808–42), possessed a great power of language and melody but little thought. In youth, an impassioned believer in freedom, he became despairing in later years: and out of his despair composed his *Canto a Teresa*, a splendid but rather monotonous address to his dead mistress. He is more attractive, but cuts a slighter figure in his *Canción del Pirata* (*Pirate's song*) in which, standing on the poop of his ship in adolescent disguise, he hurls defiance at the world.

The first important poet of the Romantic movement in Italy, UGO FOSCOLO (1778–1827), adopted neo-classical forms, but was deeply influenced by Rousseau, and affected by *Werther*. At first, like other Italian poets, an admirer of Napoleon, he later became a fervent Italian nationalist and, on the return of the Austrians to Northern Italy, fled to Switzerland, and thence to England, where he made many friends but died in poverty. His great ode *Dei sepolcri* (*From the Tombs*) has an un-Romantic dignity that goes back in its philosophy to Lucretius. But its fundamental message is that of hope and endurance, in contrast to that of his closely related Wertherish novel, *Le Ultime Lettere di Jacopo Ortis* (*The Last Letters of Jacopo Ortis*) which ends in despair and suicide.

Also classical in his form, though working inside the Romantic movement, was ALESSANDRO MANZONI (1785–1873), the author of a single novel, *I Promessi Sposi* (*The Betrothed*), a historical story deriving from Walter Scott, but more various and reflective, more ironical and even comical than its model. At the same time, though concerned with violence it has none of Scott's black-and-white heroism, and makes up for it by a vein of seriousness that almost preaches, so strongly does Manzoni seem to advocate a kind of Catholicism shorn of its priestcraft. In its uncertainties and its contrasts, *I Promessi Sposi* is far more modern than the novels of Balzac, which it predates by a few years.

Manzoni's poetry too, though in part patriotic, lacks single-minded Romantic violence. Indeed, the best of it, apart from his ode to Napoleon, is to be found in the choruses of his two somewhat academic tragedies. The first of these, *Adelchi*, concerns the clash between Christianity and paganism in eighth-century Lombardy: and the second, *Il Conte de Carmagnola*, draws the portrait of a noble general brought down by political intriguers and condemned by the city he has served. Both are classical in structure, though the former deliberately violates the unities; but both are Romantic in tone.

Classicism and Romanticism, though differing less in essentials than in any other country, assumed in Italy political connotations. Romanticism, with its glimpse of a great historic past, was necessarily allied with the new forces of nationalism working for Italy's liberation. There were attempts, therefore, to pillory the surviving neo-classicists as friends of Austria and enemies of Christianity, to which the Classicists retorted by accusing their enemies of an obscurantist desire to return to the Middle Ages. In fact, both groups contributed to the renovation of poetic diction, which had been enervated by the persistance of Metastasio's Arcadianism. What is more, neither tendency was extreme, and both were, on the whole, universal in their themes.

Italy's greatest poet of the nineteenth century was firmly attached to neither side. GIACOMO LEOPARDI (1798-1837) was a despairing individualist, who looked back on childhood as the only Golden Age. Real happiness for him did not exist, and the prospects of human progress were illusory. His melancholy, deriving in part from ill-health, coloured all his poetry, which was the greatest lyrical poetry that had been written in Italy since the death of Petrarch. The language does not lend itself to the rhetorical flamboyance of a Hugo; it is more solemn and more economical. Leopardi's *Canti,* therefore, approach more closely to the rhythms of English poetry. He is near to Shelley in his *Canto notturno di un pastore errante dell'Asia* (*Night-song of a Wandering Asiatic Shepherd*), but recalls Wordsworth at times in his natural description, and the Keats of the Nightingale Ode in such a poem of pure regret as that written on a Saturday evening (*La Sera del dì di festa*). Leopardi's poetry is the essential distillation of sadness, which makes no Byronic gestures, which recognizes beauty even as it deplores its passing, and makes of the Italian language a new instrument which has never again been used with like effect.

Russian poetry, which joined that of the Western family at this point, bears more resemblance to that of Italy, or perhaps of England, than to that of France. The Russian language, hitherto almost unused for anything but popular balladry and historical chronicles, abounded in concrete words and lacked the vocabulary of poetic cliché. Church Slavonic, the literary language of theology, had not been firmly relegated to ecclesiastical writing until the middle of the eighteenth century, when the first grammar of colloquial Russian was composed. The dramatist D. I. FONVIZIN (1745–92) had written comedies for Catherine II's court, which were adaptations of Molière and Holberg to Russian themes. The neo-classic G. R. DERZHAVIN (1743–1816) had composed sonorous odes encrusted with bold baroque imagery. The more sentimental V. A. ZHUKOVSKY had made copious translations of the German Romantics and of Byron, of Homer, and of Gray's Elegy. The fabulist I. A. KRYLOV (1768–1844) had started by translating La Fontaine, but gone on to write his own fables, which are as pithy and proverbial as Sancho Panza's conversation. Krylov had in fact brought the fable back to its peasant origins, making it an instrument of realistic satire against bureaucrats, rich men and petty tyrants.

The Russian language was ready for a major genius, and A. S. PUSHKIN (1799–1837), when he came, was one of the stature of Goethe, who could not be fitted into the straitjacket either of Classicism or of Romanticism. In a short life, during which he endured the Tsar's displeasure and was exiled, only to be pardoned and to endure the Tsar's even more embarrassing favours, Pushkin worked at a feverish rate amidst the distractions of a court life that he loathed, to provide for a vain wife the luxuries which she demanded but which did not prevent her from sacrificing his life by involving him in a duel with her French lover. Forced into an over-production, from which, however, the quality of his work seldom suffered, Pushkin attempted as many styles of writing as Goethe, and was successful in each. He read and was influenced by Byron, Shakespeare, and Walter Scott, but though he learnt from each he wrote pastiche of none.

Pushkin's first important poem, *Ruslan and Ludmila*, is a decorative and Romantic fairy story, remarkable rather for its introduction and its satirical asides than for its narrative. Its

successor, *The Prisoner of the Caucasus*, shows signs of his
acquaintance with Byron, and displays also his clear eye for
the natural scene; indeed Pushkin was perhaps more interested
in his Caucasian landscape than in his creation of a Russian
Childe Harold.

Byronic also, in influence, was Pushkin's unfinished novel
in verse *Evgeny Onegin*. Yet, in its sentimental detail and its careful social setting, it almost suggests Jane Austen, while in its
description of streets and snow and winter it has qualities that
one finds rather in Cowper and Crabbe. Pushkin was already
a far more careful, far less histrionic artist than the poet of his
ostensible model *Don Juan*. As a lyrical poet too he was most
various; in his *Conversation Between a Bookseller and a Poet* he
scores his points by deliberate flatness, though in others,
particularly those with a Caucasian setting, he makes use of
copious Romantic colour; and at moments too, as in *The
Prophet (Prorok)*, *Exegi monumentum*, and *The Crucifix*, he
attains a hieratic solemnity, superior both to his classicism and
his romanticism.

Pushkin disposes, in fact, of all the resources of an untouched and highly poetic language, which make even such
a piece of sententious generalization as *The Coach of Life*
attractive. His longer poems tell stories of the past; and his
dramatic fragments, even when adapted from so second-rate a
writer as Barry Cornwall, come closer to Shakespeare than
the drama of any other poet. But Pushkin had not the qualities
of a dramatist; he worked in too concentrated a way, throwing
away scene after scene and speech after speech in his blank
verse drama, *Boris Godunov*, before he had exhausted their
dramatic possibilities. His four little tragedies, each no more
than a few pages long, contain material which a lesser genius
would have expanded into a whole play.

Primarily a poet, Pushkin also wrote a novel, *The Captain's
Daughter*, which derives, as Manzoni's *I Promessi Sposi* does,
from Walter Scott. But here, as in his Hoffmannesque short
story *The Queen of Spades*, he refined on his models, eliminating
inessentials and concentrating his dialogue. Pushkin, in fact,
after his Byronic beginnings, came to work hard for economy
of expression. Turning from one to another of the media

that had been developed in the West, he added something of his own to each. He was, in brief, Russia's one-man Golden Age.

There were, however, a number of lesser poets among the Liberal noblemen at Nicholas I's court whose poets would be more noteworthy were it not, on the whole, related to Pushkin's as the verses of the lesser members of the *Pléiade* were to Ronsard's. These minor figures were first reprinted in the Soviet Union in the thirties, and at least three of them seem to have merits of their own; E. A. BARATYNSKY (1800–44) for his economy and for his tender feeling, clothed in classical forms; DMITRI VENEVITINOV (1805–27) for a precocious power of combining the metaphysical speculativeness of a German with Pushkin's sound Russian realism; and ANTON, BARON DELVIG (1798–1831), who wrote stylized folk-songs, and poems in a classical manner, keeping himself free from the new Romanticism.

Romanticism took a firmer hold of Pushkin's junior and contemporary, M. Y. LERMONTOV (1814–41). Like Pushkin he knew the pains of exile and the threats of censorship that made a Russian writer's life uncertain. A man of Byronic gestures, he was lionized as the new hope for Russian poetry, but, consumed by the melancholy of a Werther, he restlessly courted duels, in the last of which he was killed. Developing Pushkin's Caucasian themes, he saw himself as the defiant brigand, at odds with society. In his novel *A Hero of our Time*, he drew himself as the 'superfluous man', the frustrated product of his age, a 'Childe Harold' for whom even the mountains offered no retreat. Lermontov, however, inherited from Pushkin an economy of phrase which makes his histrionics more bearable than those of Hugo or Musset. Many of his best lyrics crystallize a mood with unforgettable beauty; his brief *Sailing Ship* is pure magic, his address to the *Clouds of Heaven, Perpetual Wanderers* compresses the feeling of Shelley's *Ode to the West Wind* into a few lines, and even on the patriotic themes of *Borodino* or *My Country* he attains a greater dignity than such English practitioners as Southey. In his Caucasian tales too, *The Demon* and *Mtsyri*, there is a proportion rare in poems which invite such abandoned self-dramatization.

Lermontov was, in fact, a man of far profounder self-knowledge than the French Romantics, and with self-knowledge came a discipline of style which, unfortunately, he did not exercise in his life.

A similar Romantic flowering took place in Poland, a country which had been more nearly touched by the Western influences of the seventeenth and eighteenth centuries, by the Baroque, by the Jesuit drama, by Molière, and by the age of enlightenment. A Romantic drama, influenced by Shakespeare and Calderón, was developed by JULIUSZ SLOWACKI (1809–49), a lyrical poet who underwent Byronic influences and ended in Messianic mysticism. The same perturbations of thought afflicted ZYGMUNT, COUNT KRASINSKI (1812–59), poet, historical novelist, and visionary of his country's future. The greatest work, however, of this short Polish Renaissance was a novel *Pan Tadeusz*, written from exile by ADAM MICKIEWICZ (1798–1855), and telling, with some humour, of the country gentleman's life at the beginning of the century. Mickiewicz was also a translator of Byron, and a writer of historical tales in the manner of Scott. He composed Romantic drama, religious lyrics, love poems, and exotic Nature poetry. He was, in fact, the Polish equivalent of Pushkin or Goethe. But he too was afflicted by the inflated nationalism of Slowacki and Krasinski, the product, it might seem, of exile and of Poland's thwarted destinies. For that country's romantic movement, beginning in about 1822, was speedily extinguished by the failure of the 1830 rebellion.

In general, the Romantic movement, which had never been uniform, began to yield at the middle of the century to more objective, though often just as highly coloured styles of writing, in which the flaunting of the poetic personality was less Byronic, and in which new elements, sometimes exotic and sometimes rural, were admitted. But the superfluous man, the artist misunderstood, the unhappy lover, the Hamlet figure paralysed by his own sensitiveness, continued to be the forms in which the artist saw himself. Romanticism died hard: perhaps it has never died at all.

Chapter Fourteen

THE NOVEL IN ITS PRIME

By the opening years of the nineteenth century, it had grown far beyond the capacities of the theatre – hitherto the most popular art form – to amuse the literate public. Comedy, essay, sermon, history, and popular philosophy had satisfied at least the male reader in the eighteenth century. But now, with the spread of education, the woman reader had also to be provided for in the long winter evenings, when candle, and later gaslight, made the reading of print a possibility; and now, for the first time in the history of European literature, it was England with its new and prosperous middle class that led the changing fashion.

Richardson had moved whole households of the middle class, whose womenfolk in the seventeenth century had lacked the leisure and education to read. Marivaux and Rousseau, Scott and Mrs Radcliffe had put prose narrative above verse in popularity. Byron was the only poet to enjoy a European reputation; and this he owed partly to the flat rhythms of his verse and partly to the flamboyant gestures of his life.

The novel, which had at first disguised itself as a faithful narrative of facts known to the author, still continued in Scott's hands to insist on its authenticity. His opening chapters too often bore the reader with a fictitious account of the way in which the story about to be told came to the writer's knowledge. But authenticity, which had seemed essential to Defoe, and which had been the cause of the epistolary style's popularity, no longer seemed a desideratum. The ladies who patronized the circulating libraries did not demand to be assured that the events they were about to read of had actually happened. The middle-class novelist was on his way to take over the abandoned scaffolding of the epic poet, and to build whole worlds of the imagination, while the more aristocratic, following the tradition of *La Princesse de Clèves* and *Les Liaisons dangereuses*, contented themselves with the treatment of a single case, a neat setting to partners, or even a fragment of ill-disguised autobiography.

First among the aristocratic writers of the French Restoration was BENJAMIN CONSTANT (1767–1830), a liberal politician and the lover of Mme de Staël, whose single analytical novel *Adolphe* is doubled by *Le Cahier rouge*, a treatment in diary form of the same problem. At the root of all Constant's experiences was the modern conflict between heart and head. One woman pleased him intellectually, another physically; and rising one stage above the agonies of a Werther, he dissected this situation, brooded over it and deplored it, but knew no way in which it would be remedied. He saw himself as a case, and what he wrote became an exquisitely analysed case-history. Ellénore, the imaginary mistress of Adolphe, is a woman older than himself whom he has taken up out of boredom, and out of the need to fill some void in himself which he only imperfectly understands. Unlike the characters in *Les Liaisons dangereuses*, he takes no pleasure in her seduction: and when he longs to be rid of her, moral obligation enters in. He can only escape by deserting her for another woman, and so driving her to her death. *Adolphe* shows the plight of sensitive people in an insensitive society. Its hero is the child of his age, in which the rebel has begun to lose faith in himself and society remains unchanged.

A far greater novelist than Constant, whose masterpieces are as economically constructed, though many times the length of his brief and single tale, is HENRI BEYLE (1783–1842), who wrote under the pseudonym of STENDHAL. He too used his own life as his subject, and from it built plots to reveal the gradations between love and self-love. A non-combatant officer in Napoleon's armies, a non-participating sympathizer with the Italian patriots, a lover whose first advances generally led straight to disaster, Stendhal spent the last years of his life in a backwater, as French consul at Civitavecchia. His was a character divided between the eighteenth-century enlightenment of his brain, and the passionate promptings of what he thought of as his Spanish blood. His first book *De l'Amour* (*On Love*) was an unsentimental analysis of love in all its variations. With his second, *Racine et Shakespeare*, he plunged into the current literary controversy on the Romantic side, only to draw back quickly when the new school seemed too catholic and too mystical for his anti-clerical prejudices. His first great novel *Le Rouge et le noir* (*Red and Black*) shows his sympathies to be firmly on the side of the Reds and against the Church. But Stendhal's ideas of revolution are strongly bound up with his vision of himself, a middle-class man of culture who appeared an outsider to the newly entrenched aristocrats with whom he might naturally have consorted; and with his worship of passion, the element in himself to which his brain would never allow him to give free play. Julien Sorel, the book's hero, is an outsider too, a clever young man without a background who is resolved to storm the citadels of privilege. Employed as a tutor, he seduces his employer's wife for the purely cold-blooded gratification of his own uneasy pride. Then, moving on, he engages himself to an aristocratic girl, who is herself an outsider, and to whom he is bound by a love-and-hate relationship, and by an offensive alliance against the rest of the world. The lovers expect to be swept away by passion, but remain embarrassingly lucid and self-conscious. Only one thing can rouse Julien Sorel's feelings, and that is his fear of humiliation. Under the threat of exposure, he shoots his first mistress, and suffers death by the guillotine.

The plot of *Le Rouge et le noir* is perhaps over-melodramatic, but the psychological observation, the devastatingly flat scenes in which matter-of-fact conversation reveals the conflicts and contradictions in his characters' minds, the ironic anti-Romanticism, which sometimes veers towards tenderness, make this novel infinitely greater than its plot. Stendhal was in fact the first novelist, as Henry Green is the latest, whose characters are too subtle and multiform ever to act of themselves. He consequently set them dancing to stock tunes, as his only way of displaying them from every angle.

Stendhal's second great novel, *La Chartreuse de Parme* (*The Charterhouse of Parma*) takes a plot from an Italian short-story, and works it out in terms of a small imaginary Italian police-state at an uncertain but recent moment in history. The hero, Fabrice, is a more generous, less calculating young man than

Julien, and his unjust imprisonment in the Citadel symbolizes the trapping of the inoffensive, non-political man in the webs of politics. The political implications of the book, indeed, are much clearer than those of *Le Rouge et le noir*, and the melodrama of intrigue is here more satirically portrayed, as to the pompous accompaniment of grand airs from the Italian opera. The end is ironical and inconclusive. The hero is released by means of intrigues as sordid as those which led to his incarceration. His love for his gaoler's daughter becomes a high-class intrigue, and he himself succeeds to an archepiscopal see, where 'his piety, his exemplary morals, and his eloquence' soon won him a devoted following. Liberalism does not triumph: rather it seems to fade out, leaving the dictator the more benevolent for now having no more hidden enemies. Again, the characters, their moods, conflicts, and motives, are more important than the plot. Stendhal was a Liberal without respect for his fellow-Liberals, an analyst without a Utopia with which to compare the half-lighted world which he observed.

Lacking a conscious literary style, Stendhal deliberately modelled his plain prose on that of the Legal Code. 'To have a good epistolary style,' he wrote, 'one must write exactly what one would say to the person if one saw him.' This bald anti-Romanticism earned him few readers in his lifetime; and to this he was resigned, looking forward to appreciation a hundred years after his death, when the 'red' of an aesthetic revolution should finally have triumphed over the 'black' of prejudice and obscurantism. He did not have to wait so long, for after fifty years not only did he count as one of the first of French novelists, but his waste-paper basket was raided and his unfinished works – the abandoned political novel, *Lucien Leuwen*, and his fictional autobiography, *La Vie de Henri Brulard* – were published, to be followed in the present century by his journals, letters, and every scrap that can contribute to our knowledge of a man so many-faceted as to be inexhaustible.

A novelist of Shakespearian proportions, whom twentieth-century opinion has accepted with greater reservations than it accords to Constant or to Stendhal, was HONORÉ DE BALZAC (1799–1850), who created a whole world and called it the France of the Restoration. Though a royalist and authoritarian where Stendhal was an independent Liberal, Balzac's affiliations were all to the bourgeois novel of Restif de la Bretonne. The eighteenth century had little significance for him, indeed, except for the current which led from Swedenborg to Saint-Martin, and which offered a visionary or transcendental vision of human destiny. Balzac piled up realistic detail, but his attitude to life was essentially magical. Behind the cut-throat but never disillusioning struggle for wealth and fame, for mistresses, houses, and position, which was for him the stuff of contemporary life, he saw always the possibilities of quite other experiences and achievements, on which he dwelt in that part of his great *Comédie humaine* which he called his *Études philosophiques* (*Philosophical Studies*).

La Comédie humaine (*The Human Comedy*) was deliberately planned to challenge comparison with Dante's *Commedia*. It presents a vast panorama, made up of interlocking novels and stories, and intended to portray the whole of humanity classified according to a theory of the humours, and compared to the varieties of the animal world. All Balzac's characters move at the prompting of a single passion; all are the creatures of their environment. There are misers, intriguers, old soldiers, old maids, aspiring journalists, all motivated by crude loves, hatreds, and ambitions. There is no Stendhalian division of mind about his people, and consequently he is more successful than Stendhal in fitting character to action. The reader is held by the pattern of events, watching the progressive neglect of old Goriot by his three daughters, the sapping of the Hulot family's fortunes by their mean-minded poor relation, the financial disasters that overcome the feebly optimistic perfumer, César Birotteau, and the successful scheming of his virtuous apprentice, the future Baron Popinot.

Balzac was a great collector of knowledge, as of other bric-à-brac: and everything that came his way he incorporated into his novels. As a young man he had been articled to a lawyer, and the details of criminal and bankruptcy law which he acquired there enriched the texture of *César Birotteau*. As a slightly older man, he set up in business as printer and publisher, and his acquaintance with this trade supplied him with material for *Les Illusions perdues* (*Lost Illusions*). He drew little directly from his own biography. Yet his vision of the great world of kept-women and wealthy rakes which he described in *Splendeurs et misères des courtisanes* (*The Courtesans' Glories and Hardships*) is essentially the poor apprentice's view of distinguished society. His most glamorous figures are so often magnificent gate-crashers into a closed circle, bankers like Nucingen who rise from nothing, splendid rakes like Rastignac, mysterious criminals like Vautrin. His heroines too are, like those of Dickens, the over-virtuous figments of a fundamentally inexperienced mind.

There is no perfect novel in *La Comédie humaine*, though the small-scale *Curé de Tours* succeeds more perfectly than anything by Trollope, and in far fewer pages, in revealing the back-biting rivalries of a small Cathedral town. But none of his scenes from Parisian or from provincial life are dull; and there are in the *Études philosophiques* a number of tales that equal or surpass Hoffmann in their strange historical colour, eeriness, and hints of hidden knowledge. Balzac's earliest writing had been marked by the influence of Walter Scott and Mrs Radcliffe; and throughout the Romantic period the great public demand was for historical fiction, set for preference in the Middle Ages, which were for the Romantics a golden age, full of pageantry and violence, passion and mystery, such as existed for few except Balzac in the contemporary world of trade and uncertain prosperity.

Vigny attempted one historical novel, *Cinq-Mars*; Hugo, a year after the success of *Hernani*, launched his one great medieval novel, *Notre-Dame de Paris*, and ALEXANDRE DUMAS (1802–70), his ally in the theatrical war, poured out innumerable tales of seventeenth-century France, which proved so popular that he assembled collaborators to increase his rate of production. The most original, though far from the most popular purveyor of exotic histories, however, was PROSPER MÉRIMÉE (1803–70), a linguist and archaeologist with a careful and contrived style. As a historical writer Mérimée is flatter and more truthful than Dumas. His picture of the Massacre of Saint Bartholomew in his *Chronique du règne de Charles IX* is convincing in a way that Dumas's description of the same events is not. Mérimée was a repressed Romantic, with a detachment akin to that of Stendhal, who was his friend. His little melodramas of exotic life therefore, which seem so crude when used for the librettos of operas – his tales of passion in Spain, such as *Carmen*, and *Colomba*, his short novel concerning a Corsican vendetta – are in fact little masterpieces of ironic narrative.

The most popular novelist of the epoch, who wrote under the name of GEORGE SAND (1804–76) owed much of her fame, like Byron, to the legend of her life. Her tempestuous love-affairs, with de Musset, with Chopin and with many more, and her passionate feminism and humanitarianism brought her thousands of readers for tales of forbidden passion and social protest, distilled from her own life-experiences. But those of her books which are readable to-day are the pastoral stories which she wrote in the second half of her life. *La Mare au Diable* (*The Devil's Pool*) and *La petite Fadette* (*Little Fadette*) are true evocations of her native province of Berry. Also in her final phase, when she had no longer either private or public grudges to ventilate, George Sand showed an unexpected power of creating subtle characters, such as those in *Le Marquis de Villemer*.

Two novels with a melodramatic impact greater even than that of George Sand were Victor Hugo's *Les Misérables*, a vast melodrama with a convict for its hero, and his *Travailleurs de la mer* (*Toilers of the Sea*), a powerful story of the Channel Island fisheries. EUGÈNE SUE (1804–57), also with his stories of the Paris underworld and ÉMILE GABORIAU (1835–73) with his first detective Lecocq, made an amalgam of realism, melodrama, and social comment, which remained the stuff of the middle-brow novel till the end of the century.

A single work of far higher quality was the short novel *Dominique*, by the art critic EUGÈNE FROMENTIN (1820–75), a piece of half-disguised autobiography in the manner of *Adolphe*, which tells with admirable restraint the story of a hopeless love.

In her old age George Sand received the confidences of GUSTAVE FLAUBERT (1821–80), a man almost twenty years her junior, who had laboriously composed two novels and had another, the re-writing of his early *L'Éducation sentimentale*, (*Sentimental Education*), almost ready for the press. Lacking the spontaneity of a Stendhal, a Balzac, or a George Sand, Flaubert claimed as a virtue a verbal scrupulousness which was little more than a psychological tic. His devotion to his art, stressed in all his letters, was but the obverse of the utter barrenness of his life, his cult of friendships which had long since decayed, his coldness towards his mistresses, and his protracted dependence on his aged mother. *Madame Bovary*, his masterpiece, took Flaubert four and a half years to write. It is the careful story of a worthless woman in revolt against her grim Norman surroundings, which were also the background of Flaubert's exasperated life. Here was no obvious autobiography. Yet so fervently did Flaubert identify himself with his heroine that when he had at last made her end her life by taking a dose of arsenic, he was himself sick for days. The book was prosecuted for obscenity, which added to Flaubert's habitual disgust with the world but started it on the way to popularity.

Heavily documented in every respect as *Madame Bovary* was, Flaubert went to greater extremes in the writing of *Salammbô*, his historical romance of ancient Carthage, a story congested with highly-coloured detail. *L'Éducation sentimentale*, in which he told the tale of his own generation, of its revolutionary hopes, is spoilt too, though to a lesser extent, not by excess of detail but by its underlying rancour. 'Oh, how tired I am,' he wrote to George Sand, 'of the sordid worker, the inept bourgeois, the stupid peasant, and the odious churchman.' He cannot convey therefore the bliss that it was to be alive in that revolutionary dawn. At best he draws a picture of Romantic love, without the irony that he heaped on Emma Bovary for dwelling in a similar paradise of adolescent dreams. Such a subject demanded a broad social treatment. But Flaubert had not the breadth of vision to supply it.

Flaubert's *Trois Contes* (*Three Tales*) are all stylisticly perfect; and his final unfinished *Bouvard et Pécuchet* extracts the quintessence of absurdity from each ridiculous situation to which he subjects his two absurdly fatuous clerks. But he had grown exasperated even with his own exasperation, and abandoned the book half written.

Flaubert's reputation has rested for sixty years on the perfection of his craftsmanship. As a publicly devoted artist, he has, however, earned plaudits beyond his merits. For great though his technical perfections may be, though he may scrupulously have contrived the cadence of each sentence, there is missing from all his work the breadth of view of a Stendhal, the vast creative power of a Balzac, the depth of understanding of Dostoyevsky, or the calm sympathy that Tolstoy lavished on Anna Karenina, a woman who had many features in common with Emma Bovary.

With Flaubert the French novel entered into its decline. His pupil GUY DE MAUPASSANT (1850–93), a young man of infinite talent, devoted himself almost entirely to the short story, and at his best succeeded in creating in a few pages a reality as compelling as Flaubert had taken a whole novel to evoke. But Maupassant was essentially a light-weight writer, happiest when drawing Norman peasants with ironic sympathy, and in rounding off a little incident on a note of sexual failure or success. Retiring from the civil service, he made his living by his pen, and was consequently far too productive. Declining health too made him rely on mechanical formulas, and so turned him into the model for slick short-story writers even to our own day. His attitude was pessimistic, since he credited none of his characters with any virtue higher than that of a simple warm-heartedness. He indulged in no social comment, and introduced the supernatural only in a sensational way. *Le Horla*, however, a tale seemingly based on some hallucinations he had himself experienced, is as compelling as anything by Poe, while the best of his Norman tales, *Boule de Suif (Dumpling)*, *La Maison Tellier (At Mme Tellier's)*, and *Le Rosier de Mme Husson (Mme Husson's May-king)* are unforgettable both for the anecdote and the divine, earthy simplicity of the characters. The best of Maupassant's six short novels is probably *Bel-Ami*, a tale of that journalist's life which he knew so well.

Far more serious as writers, and far less successful in their creations, were the brothers EDMOND (1822–96) and JULES

DE GONCOURT (1830-70) whose novels of contemporary life were as highly documented as *Salammbô*. Their method was conscientiously to select the milieu which they wished to describe – proletarian life, the circus, or the fringes of the artistic world – and to collect all relevant detail down to the current slang expressions, which they introduced, to Flaubert's disgust, with all the relish of a Quevedo. Their reputation survives, however, not for their novels but for the journal, which comments on the whole world of the arts in which they moved. Their influence on taste also was considerable. For it was they who first studied and popularized the Japanese print, and they who first enthused for the rococo fashions of the eighteenth century. In the literary field too, they perhaps played a larger rôle than they are credited with, since they were among the first of novelists to invent for themselves neurotic heroines.

ÉMILE ZOLA (1840-1902), by far the biggest figure in this group of realistic writers, carried the theory forward from the plane of pure objectivity, at which Flaubert and Maupassant had aimed, to the stage of naturalism, which had been reached by the Goncourts in their proletarian novel, *Germinie Lacerteux*, but which was first defined by Zola in his preface to *Thérèse Raquin*, a novel which he described as a literary surgical autopsy. Zola took a purely physiological view of man, and described himself as a scientist. In fact he was as wildly melodramatic as Hugo. 'A work of art,' he said, 'is a corner of nature seen through a temperament.' His own temperament was enthusiastic, indignant, and wildly creative. Inspired by contemporary theorizing and experiment on the subject of heredity, Zola embarked on a cycle of twenty novels about various members of two connected families, the Rougons and the Macquarts, and thought of his work as a serious contribution to science. In fact, however, he described the world of the Second Empire with something of the thoroughness which Balzac had applied to that of the Restoration, though within narrower limits. The theory of naturalism demanded – or excused – a preoccupation with the lives of prostitutes, drunkards, and thieves. The Rougon-Macquart series has, therefore, few of the attractions of the *Comédie humaine* or of Pérez Galdós's cycle of Madrid novels. There is all the same a rough-hewn greatness that makes his *Germinal*, a tale of miners and the mines, the nearest thing to an epic in an age hostile to that form. The insistent stressing of hardship, of endurance, of darkness, of mass action and mass suffering give the book the raw poetic quality that one finds in Whitman; and the same crude majesty also pervades *L'Assommoir*, the story of a drink-shop.

Zola was, like Maupassant, always on the edge of journalistic life. But, unlike him, he involved himself in all the political issues of the day, generously defending the unjustly imprisoned Captain Dreyfus, and preaching a humanitarian and anti-clerical socialism. The theories of naturalism drove another and lesser member of this circle, J. K. HUYSMANS (1848–1907), out of disgust for the reality which he found under his nose, to extremes of decadence, aestheticism, and romantic Catholicism. A writer with something of Flaubert's neurotic devotion, he evolved a style of even greater complexity, which makes his search for artificial paradises rather wearisome reading.

ALPHONSE DAUDET (1840–97) was attached to the naturalist circle by ties of friendship, but never accepted their extremer theories, though he was persuaded of the virtues of documentation. Beginning with the picturesque fancy and Provençal settings of his celebrated *Lettres de mon Moulin*, he went on to produce a loving caricature of the bragging southerner in his *Tartarin* series. When he advanced to the fuller naturalism of *Jack* and of *Sapho*, he tempered it with his own lazy sentimentality. Flaubert considered Daudet to have charm, while Zola impressed him by his strength. But both, in his opinion, failed in the ultimate test, since neither of them was primarily concerned with 'Beauty'; and this, though modern views of beauty will not coincide with Flaubert's, is probably a fair judgement on the naturalistic movement as a whole. For if beauty is to-day to be identified with a deeper vision of truth, with a glimpsing by the artist of hidden relationships and significances, not only do Zola and Daudet fail, but Flaubert himself reveals his shallowness.

The naturalistic movement, though short-lived in France,

had considerable effects everywhere. To most novelists of the late nineteenth century, whatever their temperaments, it seemed important to reflect some rather sordid corner of nature in them. George Moore and Arnold Bennett, George Gissing, Hauptmann, Strindberg, and even Tolstoy, felt at some moments called upon to act as photographers to some unfamiliar and ugly corner of the contemporary scene. It would not be unfair to say, however, that no considerable talent, Zola's least of all, became bogged down by this theory, which required the novelist to blind himself to everything about his characters that was not purely physiological.

Italy's single important novelist, but for Manzoni, was a realist, who turned, however, in middle life from writing about elegance and adultery to his native Sicily, to describe the humble fight of its fishermen and vinegrowers against economic circumstances too powerful for them to resist. GIOVANNI VERGA (1840–1922) wrote many short stories. But his two chief novels, *I Malavoglia (The House by the Medlar Tree)* and *Maestro Don Gesualdo*, the latter of which was translated by D. H. Lawrence, swarm with vociferating characters, all indulging in their private lusts and feuds. Verga's preoccupation with the peasant's violence is akin to Merimée's. But he is a less 'literary' writer.

Verga's strengths are those of what the Spaniards call a *costumbrista* or local writer; and Spain's principal novelists of the nineteenth century stand outside the main European currents, devoting themselves to descriptions of life in a single locality. The best of these was JOSÉ MARÍA DE PEREDA (1833–1906), a retiring gentleman who described the villages of his corner of Northern Spain with a feeling for nature that is reminiscent of Wordsworth.

There is about Pereda's novels a certain amateurish clumsiness, however, that is not present in the work of JUAN VALERA (1824–1905), a writer with a sense of form, concerned with the eternal topics of love and religion, who fails, nevertheless, to come close enough to his characters to make them quite real or to involve them in vital conflicts. Valera's style has the grace of a Mérimée's; his psychological insight is often acute and his irony attractive. But lacking the element of feeling, even in *Pepita Jiménez*, his tale of a young seminarist, whose religious promptings melt away at his first contact with profane love, Valera fails to achieve a real immediacy.

BENITO PÉREZ GALDÓS (1843–1920), on the other hand, possessed all the immediacy of a Balzac, and was the creator first of a huge cycle of historical stories, then of some twenty-one novels of contemporary Madrid life which rival the *Comédie humaine* both in the variety of their characters and in the perfect but effortless rightness of their social setting. Galdós was a liberal with a very clear knowledge of the defects of Spanish society, which he expressed not by overt comment but by his choice of themes. In his ironic masterpiece, *La de Bringas* (*The Spendthrifts*) he shows the whole impoverished world of the court, everyone keeping up appearances but all living as pensioners of a Queen whose tenure of her throne is insecure. Señora Bringas herself, with all her pretensions, her spendthrift friend, the Marquesa de Tellería, and her nincompoop of a husband: all are figures of comedy, and all are symptoms of a nation in decay.

Here the central figure of the novel is the Señora, and the central theme the sufferings which the weakness of her character brings upon her: in *Tormento* too, the principal interest is in a woman and her weakness. But in Pérez Galdós's greatest novel, *Fortunata y Jacinta*, the central position is occupied by a weak young man, worshipped by the wife and the mistress, who share the honour of the book's title. Here the contrast between the barren and upper middle-class wife Jacinta, and the violent daughter of the people Fortunata, who has borne him a son, is reinforced by the contrasts of their two worlds, by the details of the prosperous silk-business to which the wife's family owe their fortune, and of the provision shop where Juanito, the husband, first finds Fortunata. The streets and squares of Madrid also play their part in the story, which is one of the nineteenth-century's great but neglected novels.

Among the characters in *Fortunata y Jacinta* are at least two unbalanced creatures, of whom one, Maxi Rubén, is shown crazily in love with Fortunata. The crazy, the unbalanced, the religious fanatics, had attracted Galdós from the beginning. But in his later phase he began to place them in the forefront of his books, devoting to the miser Torquemada, the strange Christ-like priest Nazarín, and the down-and-outs of his last novel *Misericordia* the attention he had formerly given to his middle-class society. In this way his tales gain a strange emotional force that sometimes suggests Dostoyevsky. But the best of Galdós is his social comedy, and here he challenges comparison with the highest.

A Portuguese contemporary of Galdós, whose work has been, like his, long in gaining acceptance outside his own country, was EÇA DE QUEIRÓS (1845-1900), a social satirist and an anti-clerical with a deep love for his native landscape, who drew witty pictures of provincial life, and who has been the only considerable novelist produced by Portugal.

While it is possible to see first realism and then naturalism sweeping Western Europe and influencing not only the serious novelists but the myriad purveyors of entertaining fiction who catered for the new literate classes, there is no doubt that after 1860 the greatest works of fiction were being written in Russian. The Russian novelists can be classified neither as entirely realist nor as naturalists. Yet they had from the beginning a certain social purpose which might have made them the unconscious forerunners of Zola and his school. Life under the Tsarist dictatorship was difficult for imaginative writers, harassed always by a petty-minded and obtuse censorship. Some social changes, therefore, were necessary, if only in their own interests. So, with the criticism of V. G. BELINSKY (1811-48), there begins the rejection of literature for entertainment's sake and an insistence on the necessary alliance between Liberalism and the creative arts.

The novel was the natural form of expression of the Russian writer. His interest from the beginning was with detail, with character, with landscape. Pushkin had himself attempted the historical novel, and his masterpiece, *Evgeny Onegin*, was an unfinished novel in verse. The first of the great Russians to devote himself more or less whole-heartedly to fiction, was no pure novelist. NIKOLAI GOGOL (1809–52) was an un-balanced genius who never succeeded in reconciling his grotesquely humorous view of the world with his moral, almost evangelical sense of purpose. It would be wrong to consider him the first of the Russian realists, for though his unfinished masterpiece *Dead Souls* is incidentally an attack on the corruption of landowners, Gogol is, like Dickens, only incidentally a social writer. For the inspiration of the magnificent plot to swindle the government by the purchase of *dead souls,* or serfs whose names should have been removed from the register, lies far closer to the spirit of Swift or of Sterne than to the objectivity of Balzac with his exhaustive knowledge of the ways of petty – and great – fraud. Gogol's short story *The Overcoat* is certainly realistic, but his comedy, *The Government Inspector* is wild and boisterous satire. His place lies in fact rather on the line of development which lead from the curious fantasy of Hoffmann to the nightmare super-realism of Dostoyevsky than on the plain road that led from Pushkin's stories to *War and Peace.*

The prime problem in Russia throughout the nineteenth century was that of East versus West, of Slavophil versus Westernizer. Was her literature, and her national life, tamely to follow the lead of her more advanced European neighbours, or had Russia something of her own to contribute, something peculiarly Slavonic which would make her the leader of the Balkan countries and the Austrian minorities as France was the leader of the West? Gogol must count as a Slavophil, especially in his shorter stories which reproduce the beliefs and atmosphere of his native Ukraine. S. T. AKSAKOV (1791–1859), however, was a more wholehearted representative of this reactionary yet idealistic viewpoint, whose autobiographical writings exhale a deep breath of the old way of life.

A greater writer than he, I. A. GONCHAROV (1812–91), remained divided between the two ideals, and from the material of this conflict which he could not resolve, composed his masterpiece, *Oblomov.* Oblomov is, like Lermontov's hero, a superfluous man, for whom there is no place in contemporary society. He is also a grotesque, a futile mediocrity existing on the small rents sent up to him from his badly administered estate, and depending at moments of crisis on the advice and support of his forward-looking friend Stolz. The future is clearly with Stolz and his kind. Oblomov is pathetically left behind by the march of events, sitting in his dressing-gown listening to his bustling landlady's salting and bottling of the winter stores, and willing to marry her rather than lose his lodgings. One's sympathy, however, is with this grotesque muddler, this spoilt child of an old order which had had its beauties. Goncharov's first novel, *A Common Story*, had treated the same theme, contrasting a worldly uncle and his callow nephew, and weighing the smart but hollow attractions of Petersburg life against the boredom of the country; and again in his third and last novel, *The Ravine,* Goncharov returned to the idea of the superfluous man, who longed to be everything by turns, but had not the resolution to be anything.

Goncharov's rival in popularity, whom he grew to think of as his persecutor and secret enemy, was the chief of the Westernizers, IVAN TURGENEV (1818–83), whose first successful book, *A Sportsman's Sketches*, was, nevertheless, an evocation of the old Russia. Turgenev was no propagandist. He showed the world of serfs and landlords objectively, against an impressionistic background, to such effect that the future Tsar Alexander II is said to have decided to abolish serfdom immediately after reading it. Turgenev's standards of writing were purely aesthetic. Yet social problems were in the air, and it was only in relation to them that he could set his characters moving. Most of them are members of the doomed landowning class, who live civilized lives in a mood of autumn melancholy. Life for them is very beautiful, but it has only a passing beauty. Fate, in the person of Bazarov, the liberal hero of *Fathers and Children*, is knocking insistently upon their wooden doors. But Turgenev was no more of a wholehearted liberal than Goncharov. In the novel *Smoke* he satirized both sides: in *On the Eve*, he wrote a novel in which the political interest was really subordinate to an unhappy love-story. Among his best characters are the superfluous men, Rudin, in the novel of that name, and Lavretzky in *The House of Gentlefolk*. For the artist and intellectual, in the Russian revolution which was brewing, was indeed a superfluous man.

Living much of his life abroad, and closely connected by sympathy with Flaubert, with George Sand, and with the young Henry James, Turgenev formed a link between Western literature and the new writing in Russia, which was being popularized in France by Mérimée in particular, but by other translators too who soon produced French versions of the Russian novels, many years ahead of the first satisfactory English translations. Turgenev's great merit, however, lies not in his liberalism, and not in his international importance, but in the sheer beauty of his writing, in his tender rendering of the Russian countryside, in his poetic treatment of changes of mood and fine shades of affection between his characters. Moral problems, too, are displayed by him in their personal implications; and his people, though often simplified, are true to nature in a way that even Balzac's are not. For Turgenev's was a broad vision where that of the greater nineteenth-century novelists was myopic.

A radical, far more partisan than Turgenev, who exhausted much of his talent on political journalism, was M. E. SALTYKOV-SHCHEDRIN (1826–92), whose single important novel, *The Golovlyov Family*, shows a bunch of aristocrats running downhill after the freeing of the serfs in 1861. On the other side, deeply rooted in the old Russia, was N. S. LESKOV (1831–95), whose homespun novels introduced all types and classes, and who reproduced the idioms and turns of phrase characteristic of each. Called by Gorki the most Russian of all Russian writers, he has never become a European figure.

Famous beyond the frontiers almost from the first, LEO TOLSTOY (1828–1910) was not only the greatest European novelist of his century, but also one of its most important figures. Tolstoy is remarkable for his enormous vigour, and for his persistence, even to the last, in developing his viewpoint far beyond the time when he was capable of embodying it in purely literary creation. The son of aristocrats, he left the University to join a regiment in that part of the Caucasus that had inspired both Pushkin and Lermontov. But military life disgusted him; gambling and drink attracted and repelled him.

Everything he did was violent, but already some element in him was seeking for a religious faith. His first writings were autobiographical. In the trilogy *Childhood*, *Boyhood*, and *Youth*, he recalled the feelings of his early life with a remarkable clarity. It was no doubt his early passion for Rousseau that had sent him in quest of his own past. But his favourite authors were Sterne and Dickens, and it was they who influenced his style. His autobiography became less true to fact as it progressed, and in addition he wrote a number of stories with Caucasian and military backgrounds, which would have been outspokenly pacifist but for the censorship.

Six years went to the writing of that greatest of novels *War and Peace*, which Tolstoy at first intended to be the first of a trilogy, the second and third parts of which were to deal with the events of two other critical moments in Russian history, the liberal Decembrist revolt of 1825, and the Crimean defeat of 1856. It was the first, perhaps the only novel to deal with events on two planes, and so to interrelate them that it is possible to see personal and national histories at the same time. For the Napoleonic invasions are not a background to *War and Peace*; they provide an additional dimension to the family chronicle as the events of the Trojan War give Agamemnon, Hector, and Achilles a stature that they would lack were they not playing a part in World events, and if the gods themselves had not been concerned in the fate of their nations. Not since *Os Lusíadas* had the national theme been so welded to the personal, nor were the destinies of gods, nations, and men so to be brought together again except perhaps by Thomas Hardy in his *Dynasts*.

On the personal scale the characters of *War and Peace* embodied the whole of Tolstoy's experience. 'The observations and experiences of army life; the pagan exuberance of his youthful bachelor revels; the glitter of fashionable balls; the physical intoxication of the hunt; his tenderness for his family; the philosophy painfully achieved through turbulent experience and profound reflexion; the whole of his rich and contradictory being, in fact,' wrote Derrick Leon in his masterly study of Tolstoy, 'is to be found in this monument erected to the memory of a previous epoch.' Nearly all his remarkable characters were drawn from the life, from his own family or his wife's, and, once drawn, they acted not as their creator dictated, but in conformity with their own natures. For after the initial act of creation, Tolstoy allowed his people to develop according to their own internal law; no one in *War and Peace* does anything that is false to what he or she is. The book contains no heroes or heroines, but just people living out their lives on the margin of great events, and among them two who incarnate two contradictory strands in Tolstoy's own make-up, the proud, reserved, and ambitious Prince Andrei, and the simple, good-hearted, ever questing Pierre Bezhukov.

Many of the latter's characteristics reappear in Levin, the restless doubter of *Anna Karenina*, who in the end learns from an illiterate peasant the truth that his mental over-activity has prevented him from seeing till then. The loves of Anna and Vronsky alone would have made the book the greatest psychological novel of the century. Here, with less strain than Flaubert in *Madame Bovary*, Tolstoy has created a woman who was all passion and jealousy, by dint, almost, of isolating those qualities in himself and calling them to life in another. In her lover there are facets of the young Tolstoy of the smart uniforms and the gambling debts. But, having created these characters, the author appears once again to stand back from them, and leave them to act according to their own natures. One cannot be quite sure that Flaubert practised a similar degree of detachment over Mme Bovary. His own revolt from the bourgeois life that she incarnated may well have been one of the factors that contributed to the scene of the suicide.

After *Anna Karenina*, Tolstoy drew aside from literature to seek for himself the truths that he had permitted his creature Levin to discover. His married life ran into a crisis from which it never recovered, and his religious and political activities dictated a form of writing, naïve, didactic, and somewhat flat. Out of this, however, came eventually a number of short stories and fables, chief among them *The Kreutzer Sonata* and *The Death of Ivan Ilyitch*, in which Tolstoy's powers of creating character appeared unimpaired, though he was no longer able to let his people act according to their own natures. His sexual asceticism and fervid belief in peasant virtue dictated the pattern of events. But in the tale of the dying judge *Ivan Ilyitch* there is a depth of perception that Tolstoy had not attained before, even in his great novels. A man is shown dying in all his spiritual nakedness, with the knowledge that all that he has been is as nothing, and that he has nothing to carry past the annihilating moment of death. That this discovery can be incorporated in artistic form implies a mastery as great as that of *War and Peace*, though on a different scale of creation. It is as if Tolstoy had passed the border of literary activity into the field beyond art, where stand the Gospels, the *Bhagavadgita*, the sermons of Eckhart, the poems of Angelus Silesius, and much of Blake.

Tolstoy's three plays of this period, though they have considerable dramatic power, were written for the People's Theatre which he patronized, and lack ultimate depth. His last novel, *Resurrection*, written when he was seventy-one, is a melodramatic story, with a moral both anti-governmental and anti-clerical. The early parts of the novel, in which the student Nekhlyudov meets and seduces Katerina Maslov has the beauty of remembered events in Tolstoy's earlier life. But her later conviction for murder, Nekhlyudov's change of heart, and her refusal to accept his sacrifice are factitious. Tolstoy was incapable of writing a long and sustained work at the level of spiritual insight which he had then reached.

FĒDOR DOSTOYEVSKY (1821–81) worked always at the level of *Resurrection*, drawing abnormal characters where Tolstoy endeavoured to show the normal transcending their limitations, and rejoicing in violence as the catalyst by which the change of heart could come. Dostoyevsky's own youth was violent and unhappy. Unjustly convicted of sedition, he was sentenced to death and only pardoned when he was already facing the firing squad. He spent eight years in Siberia – where Tolstoy too might have been sent but for his influential relatives and his European reputation – four of them in a penal camp and four as a conscript in a line regiment. Indeed, he came to literature with an experience that few writers knew until our own epoch of the concentration camp.

Dostoyevsky's early influences were Gogol, Hoffmann, and

Dickens, all masters of the grotesque, and he had not transcended them in the two short novels that he had written before his arrest. Yet already in *Poor Folk*, the motif of pity had been stressed. On his return from Siberia, Dostoyevsky published another short novel *The Insulted and the Injured* and his description of his Siberian experiences in *Memoirs from the House of the Dead*. He was already forty-four and up to his neck in debts when he began to write the first of his four great novels, *Crime and Punishment*, in a hotel room at Wiesbaden, where he could hardly pay for his meals. The theme had already been in his mind for a long time, that crime brings its own repentance, because by sinning a man has destroyed all that which is most valuable in himself. The student Raskolnikov commits a murder of which he is not even suspected. But his own psychological need to atone drives him into giving himself up, and joining his lot with a woman who has known every humiliation, with whom eventually, when the term of his imprisonment is up, he will build a new life. There is much in this novel that might seem to place it on the sensational plane of *Les Misérables*. There is the same obsession with crime, the same crudely worked up suspense. Will Raskolnikov confess to the police officer? The characters, unlike Tolstoy's, are above life size, and in Hoffmann's fashion extreme significance is attached to dreams and symbols. But Dostoyevsky's novels triumph over their limitations, as Graham Greene's – to quote a minor example from the school of Dostoyevsky – do not, because the change of heart postulated by Dostoyevsky has a universal application as Greene's Roman Catholic theology has not. Everyone is, in a sense, with Raskolnikov, pursued by his own sins and anxious for the release of emotion that Dostoyevsky recognized as man's highest possibility.

Dostoyevsky's next novel *The Idiot* presents a hero who has passed beyond the stage of atonement to a strange beatitude, but is unable to avoid a violent event to which he, Natasha, and Rogozhin are all driven forward, the murder which they foresee but which they cannot escape. After this, *The Devils* (first translated as *The Possessed*) is an unshapely book, having undergone severe structural changes during its writing. Its purpose was to attack the liberal politics of the Westernizers, but in fact it went farther and prophetically exposed the psychopathic motives that were to impel all the violent politicians of whatever colour, in Russia and abroad, from his day until ours. Stavrogin, the central figure, is a monomaniac, and the rest of the conspirators, 'flotsam and jetsam all of them', work out their ill-considered ideals in terms of argument and murder. But all the time Dostoyevsky was writing *The Devils*, he was considering the theme of his last novel and masterpiece, *The Brothers Karamazov*, which was to present a reconciliation of good and evil. In the cantankerous old man and his three sons he created characters who bridged the whole gap between Heaven and Hell, between the glimpse of Heaven revealed by Father Zossima, the elder, to Alyosha and the hell in which the old man himself lived, and where Mitya sojourned in his moral though not actual responsibility for his father's death.

Dostoyevsky's plots are the merest police court anecdotes; his characters are all larger than life, yet revealed with the greatest psychological insight, which makes them credible. But the culmination of his novels, the moment of sudden emotional enlightenment, is something that only he could achieve. His experience in Siberia, and the flashes of vision which, for physiological causes, preceded the attacks of epilepsy from which he suffered, gave him the greatest depth of any novelist. Tolstoy's panoramic view of the world, with the levels of god and man superimposed, and Dostoyevsky's lightning plunges into the depths and up to the heights mark the novel's supreme achievement.

The next Russian genius to emerge was an autumn figure, closer in feeling to Turgenev than to either of his country's giants. ANTON CHEHOV (1860-1904) was a brilliant impressionist who, though he was temporarily attracted by Tolstoy's religious and social theories, had on the whole a resigned and humorous attitude to life, which he saw as a pageant of multiform beauty and pathos, built up of random entrances and exits, unplanned and purposeless, yet with a certain ill-defined significance that makes his writing not altogether gloomy. Beginning as a retailer of comic stories for the cheap press, he remained always an anecdotal writer, yet in some of his best stories the point of the anecdote is that nothing really happened at all. Chehov's ambition, as he stated when criticizing *Anna Karenina*, was not to solve problems, but to state them correctly. Hence the exact rendering of mood in his stories, the precise analysis of a situation.

In a story like *The Lady with the little Dog*, a bored Moscow citizen starts up a flirtation in a seaside hotel, knowing well that such adventures with married women always end in boredom, yet unable to resist just one more. The pair enjoy one another's company, but when it is time to part the elderly man cannot throw off his chance mistress's memory. He visits her in her home town. They resort to various dodges to deceive her husband. 'At any moment it seemed to them,' ended Chehov, 'that they would find some miraculous solution round the next corner. But they knew, in fact, that the end was still far off, and that the most complicated part was just about to begin.' Chehov states a problem, where the later Tolstoy would have preached a moral, where Dostoyevsky would have driven the pair to violent resources, to murder, suicide, and repentance.

Chehov's is not the novelist's method; it is the accurate observer's; and from him we rise with a feeling that life, viewed in purely earthly terms, *is* like this. Chehov's range of characters is considerable, but none are above life size, and the standard he sets for them, when offering his sympathy, is only that of honesty. His people exist in their moments of honest feeling and resignation rather than in the long duration of their lives. Even his own life he seems to have viewed with this resigned detachment, suffering himself from thwarted love and from a long history of tuberculosis, and ironically, resignedly, watching himself suffer, with no more and no less compassion than he would have offered to any other man.

After Chehov, the Russian novel entered into a decline; great though its influence was on the rest of Europe, its powers of growth in its own country had ceased. Nevertheless the two main streams, the first deriving from Gogol and Dostoyevsky, the second from Pushkin and Tolstoy, continued to run parallel though less boisterously, until the Revolution cut short the grotesque and psychological school, and encouraged the realists to develop a tendentious and sentimental line in photography.

The one European country which produced hardly any novels of importance in the nineteenth century was Germany, where the poetic long short story or *Novelle*, and the philosophical novel or *Bildungsroman* absorbed all the talent that might have gone to the novel proper as well as much that might have been devoted to poetry. Among the regionalists who dwelt lovingly on natural beauty and who endowed their characters with all the simplicity of flowers walking was the Austrian ADALBERT STIFTER (1805–68), a quietist whose melancholy has lately become somewhat fashionable. A long autobiographical novel by the Swiss GOTTFRIED KELLER (1819–90) called *Der Grüne Heinrich* (*Green Henry*) has little more than provincial interest. His short stories, however, come nearer to the true folk-tale than most attempts to imitate an inimitable medium. His rough humour, and his rich fantasy, make of such stories as *Spiegel das Kätchen* (*Mirror the Cat*), the equals of the brothers Grimm's *Märchen*, while his elegiac *Romeo und Julia auf dem Dorfe* (*The Village Romeo and Juliet*), besides giving Delius the theme for an opera, has a melancholy beauty slightly reminiscent of a short story by Thomas Hardy.

Another Swiss writer, CONRAD FERDINAND MEYER (1825–98) wrote long *Novellen* of the historical past, in a limpid style, influenced by that of French, his second language. To a reader used to the movement and colour of the nineteenth-century historical novel, Meyer may seem cold, distant, and unduly reflective. To one, on the other hand, who can accept Stifter's quiet narrative, Meyer may convey a satisfying vision of the past. A single *Novelle* also, by the poetess ANNETTE VON DROSTE-HÜLSHOFF (1797–1848) called *Die Judenbuche* (*The Jew's Beech*) has strength, beauty, and a strange, cruel inevitability, while THEODOR STORM (1817–88) calls the romantic past of his native Schleswig to life in stories that achieve both a Wordsworthian beauty and a genuine eeriness.

But with the rise of Prussia, these old-fashioned forms

yielded to the historical novel glorifying Germany's past, and to middle-class fiction written under the influence of Dickens, the outstanding example of which is that classic of the business world *Soll und Haben* (*Debit and Credit*) by GUSTAV FREYTAG (1816–95).

One considerable novelist alone emerged from this confused literary scene, the elderly Prussian aristocrat THEODOR FONTANE (1819–98). Fontane had been dramatic critic, foreign correspondent, and war correspondent, in France, in England and in Scotland. He was nearly sixty before he began his first historical novel in the style of Walter Scott, and seventy before he began to write his series of novels of Berlin and of the East Prussian landscape. Fontane was a conservative by conviction, yet a liberal by temperament. As a critic he had championed the new drama of Ibsen, and as a novelist he followed the French realists, though all the time preserving his characteristic German background. Three short works, *Irrungen, Wirrungen* (*Trials and Tribulations*), *Frau Jenny Treibel*, and *Effi Briest* rise in an ascending scale of excellence. The last, the story of a girl condemned to a loveless marriage, whose brief affair with another man brings disaster on all, is in its ironical and detached way a stinging condemnation of the stuffy social code of the Junkers from whom Fontane sprang. He was surprised nevertheless to find himself fêted by the Jewish intelligentsia of Berlin, but cold-shouldered by his own people. *Effi Briest* is local in its subject matter, but Fontane's portrait of Effi herself, as of his other women characters, is tender, charming, and unsentimental. His last novel *Der Stechlin* (*Lake Stechlin*) displays his powers of catching the subtleties of conversation at their best, but is less shapely in its plot than his earlier successes.

An individual chronicler of German provincial life, WILHELM RAABE (1831–1910), is humorous and melancholy by turns. Beginning as a leisurely disciple of Jean Paul, influenced through him by Sterne and independently by Dickens, he developed a darker style in his *Abu Telfan*, only to return at the end of his life to his old humorous detachment.

Another writer of originality, whose work has been acknowledged in Germany, though not in England, is JENS

PETER JACOBSEN (1847–85), a Danish naturalist whose very careful language and deliberate impressionism convey poetic overtones which delighted Rilke, who was much influenced by him. He left only two completed novels, and a volume of stories, which are most individual, and which reflect his own divided personality, half Darwinian atheist, half Romantic dreamer.

With the growth in knowledge of psychology and history, and with the development of social theory, the novel began to decay in all countries. No longer did it seem possible to display a group of characters in a water-tight compartment, reacting solely in relation to one another. Time and space, which had seemed capable of division into satisfactory sections, now became confused. A novel could not confine itself to one generation; heredity demanded the inclusion of ancestors, whose actions might account for those of the story's central figures. Social complications again required a fuller documentation of background and circumstances. Realism, naturalism, satire, fantasy, the family chronicle, the description of genius and of madness, the growing self-consciousness of the novelist himself, all took the novel into byways where to equal the universality of *Le Rouge et le Noir*, *La Cousine Bette*, *War and Peace*, *The Brothers Karamazov*, and *Fortunata y Jacinta* became an impossibility.

Chapter Fifteen

POETRY AFTER THE ROMANTICS

REACHING its peak around the year of Revolution 1830, Romanticism began to decline almost immediately, giving place to no new classicism, however, but to a variety of literary fashions, each of which aimed at some departure from the egoism and the rhetoric of Hugo and de Musset. The first post-Romantic, nevertheless, HEINRICH HEINE(1797–1856), had something of Musset's flamboyant temperament, though united with a sardonic self-consciousness which was the mark of the Jewish intellectual. Like Musset, Heine struck attitudes. But unlike Musset he mocked himself. His early poems, *Das Buch der Lieder*, have a fancy-dress quality. They derive from the Romantic lyric; yet the gestures are a little too histrionic, the music a trifle too sweet. The metaphors of stage, carnival, dance, recur. The ironical twist, the clown's grimace are never far away.

Heine could, however, write poems of pure feeling; two cycles of *Die Nordsee* (*The North Sea*) have a majesty that links them with Goethe and foreshadows Matthew Arnold. But it is his ironic poetry that has best withstood the changes of fashion. Heine as a democratic liberal was unable to remain in Germany after 1831. He set up as a journalist in Paris, explaining the German Romantic movement to his French public and writing about France, which he dearly loved, for the benefit of the Germans. But his attitude to his own country was that of a bitter exile, and such light ironic verse as that of *Atta Troll* and *Deutschland* pilloried the conventionality and hypocrisy of his native land in Byronic fashion. In his prose too, always full of the liveliest comment, Heine developed a personal vein of fantasy, inventing such delicious characters as Gumpelino of the famous nose in *Die Bäder von Lucca* (*The Spa of Lucca*), and the Polish count Schnabelewopski.

Heine's prose is among the most delicate German written

in the nineteenth century. He could make the German sentence, heavy even in Goethe's hands, dance to almost French tunes; and in his final poems, those which refer to his own slow death from paralysis upon his mattress grave, he succeeds in transcending his romantic self-pity.

German poetry of the middle of the century developed, however, at its best, rather along Wordsworthian lines than towards lightness and irony. Though his popularity remained on a level at which he was referred to in one breath with Goethe and Schiller, Heine was fundamentally too European for the German taste.

ANNETTE VON DROSTE-HÜLSHOFF (1797–1848) and EDUARD MÖRIKE (1804–75) represent far better the strength of the German imagination, and its closeness to the old slow-moving life of field and forest, which was shortly to yield before a rapid and rootless industrialization. Annette von Droste-Hülshoff, a retiring aristocrat whose brief production of fine poetry sprang from an unhappy love for a man many years her junior, is crisply objective both psychologically and in her recording of landscape. Hers was an agonized sensibility that fought its own Romantic unbalance. She looked at the world with careful near-sighted eyes, and rejected the pantheism that seemed to come so naturally to her. But many moments brought her their revelations. In *Im Grase* (*In the Grass*) she felt the nearness of the dead beneath the ground; in *Im Moose* (*On the Moor*) she speaks of the momentary vision of her whole life as one, past, present, and future. Loosely, it would be possible to compare her to Emily Brontë, though her Catholic notion of sin adds an un-Brontëan dimension to her thought, superimposing upon the sustained vision of her fine poem on the moonrise the overtone of horror, arising from fear of the Judgement.

A more pagan vein of imagination was worked by the Swabian pastor Eduard Mörike, a scholar and metrical innovator comparable to his Dorset contemporary William Barnes. Defeated in youth in his search for love, Mörike found compensation, not in his religion, but in the creation out of earthy stuff of a private world founded on his native Swabian scene yet rich with unexpected possibilities of escape

from the here-and-now. His best-known short lyrics are full
of yearning, loss, and country joys. His lesser known and more
sustained poems tell of genial clumsy monsters, akin to those
invented by Robert Graves, who score off the gods and get
away with it. His verse is never more vigorous than when he is
celebrating *Suckelborst der Urweltsgöttersohn* (*Suckelborst the Son
of the Primeval Gods*). But his longer works are seldom unified.
His *Bildungsroman, Maler Nolten,* is a disorderly *Wilhelm Meister*
in which his counterpart of the fey Mignon plays the chief
rôle; while his idyll in the manner of *Hermann und Dorothea* is
full of interpolations and asides. But though Mörike does not
succeed on a large scale, there is no German poet of the century except Annette von Droste-Hülshoff, who can achieve the
mysterious intensity of such a poem as *Der Gesang Weylas*
(*Weyla's Song*), the purest distillation of longing for a lost
paradise.

The Austrian NIKOLAUS LENAU (1802–50), potentially
a lyrical poet of great power, failing to transcend a narrow
subjectivity, produced perhaps only a dozen perfect poems.
Deeply responsive to nature, he yet could not avoid painting
it in the colour of his own moods. 'Merely to have had poetic
emotion', he wrote, 'is to have taken a step towards immortality.' But his emotion was not sufficiently pure for his
delicate rhythms, his restrained language, and his original use
of symbols to make their maximum effect. Always the unhappy Lenau lingers in the foreground, on the edge of that
madness which finally swept him away. Hölderlin and Nerval
expressed their insanity spontaneously, without thought for
their own plight. Lenau, less in love with his dreams, hoped
always for a way out, yet decided that ultimately all comfort is
an illusion. Several other distinguished lyrical poets were
writing in German at this time, among them AUGUST
VON PLATEN (1796–1835), the victim of one of Heine's most
devastating attacks, and a conscious aesthete whose mastery of
form was remarkable in an age when form was neglected. His
sonnets, indeed, are among the best in German, and his
anti-Romantic satire still preserves its sting.

There was also Theodor Storm, whose poetry, coming
from the same rural source as his *Novellen*, is comparable at its

best with Eichendorff's and, being as deeply rooted in his Northern scene as Eichendorff's in Silesia, carries the same overtones of folk-song. At the same time, in Switzerland, C. F. Meyer, another writer of *Novellen*, was feeling out towards the more objective attitude of his French contemporaries, with a success that makes even his historical ballads readable. Meyer was not a great poet, but a miniaturist who, whether interpreting a moment of history or an experience of nature, always added to it something of his own reflective nature.

The German Romantic school had small influence abroad in its second phase. One poet alone, the Russian FËDOR TYUTCHEV (1803–73), stands out as a greater counterpart to Lenau, with a pantheism and despair similar to that of the unhappy Austrian but endowed with a philosophical power that enabled him to face his dark vision, and to find – as Lenau never satisfactorily did – his own symbols with which to express it. Tyutchev, a diplomat more at home in French and German than in his native Russian, was nevertheless a Slavophil with strong political opinions. He was quickly acknowledged as the outstanding poet of his generation by Tolstoy, and also by Turgenev, who was accounted the arbiter of polite taste. But Tyutchev himself took so little interest in his writing that he never even read his proofs, and allowed Turgenev to smooth away what he considered Tyutchev's metrical irregularities. For Tyutchev day was a golden cloak of order and light thrown over the black abyss of chaos and darkness, which faced the homeless orphan Man. His poems, which were accepted by the Symbolists as well as by his contemporaries, have a haunting beauty, which comes over even in indifferent translations. He is the poet that James Thomson might have been if he had faced his vision of the City of Dreadful Night, and glimpsed a mysterious meaning behind its gaunt façades.

Among Tyutchev's contemporaries who also fell under Turgenev's spell were Y. P. POLONSKY (1819–98), an uneven Romantic, with a homely touch that now seems a little tame, A. N. MAYKOV (1821–97), an aesthete with Classical leanings, and A. A. FET (1820–92), a poet of far greater range, capable both of music and precision, and in his final poems of a philosophical courage comparable to Tyutchev's, but more optimistic.

This generation of Russian poets suffered from the patronage of a growing reading public which first demanded sentimentalities, and then, about 1880, turned ungratefully from poetry to the novel.

A figure comparable to Tyutchev's, though, unlike him, many-sided, was Count ALEXEY TOLSTOY (1817–75), a distant relative of the novelist, and the author of a trilogy of Shakespearian plays on historical themes written in blank verse, of a historical novel, and of some delightful nonsense poetry, including a *History of the Russian Empire* in doggerel half Russian, half German, which anticipates *1066 and All That*. His best poems, however, echo the majesty of the Byzantine church service, or record sudden strange moments of insight, such as that in which, visiting an old mill, he was struck with the mysterious certainty that he had been there before: a haunting lyric unlike any other in European literature.

Some of Count Tolstoy's best poems, however, seem to capture the music of folk-song, and so to relate him to that second current of Russian nineteenth-century poetry, the would-be popular, whose first exponent, A. V. KOLTSOV (1808–42), sings delightfully of harvest and the young reaper, but falls into banality when he attempts urban sophistication.

N. A. NEKRASOV (1821–77), a gentleman, a radical, and a poet of far greater calibre than Koltsov, wrote political and satirical poetry enlivened by the breath of real popular vigour comparable with Whitman's but traditional in form. His *Red-nosed Frost*, a long poem about a peasant woman, is in the true tradition of peasant mythology, and his unfinished epic *How to live happily in Russia* is the most important single poem between *Evgeny Onegin* and the revolutionary *Twelve* of Alexander Blok.

Although Russia was the only European country to develop a new national literature in the nineteenth century, in Hungary, in Sweden, in Flanders, and in Provence there sprang up poets with fresh languages at their disposal, who wrote lyrically, with a new feeling of nationalism, and a closeness to whatever remained of the popular tradition. In Hungary SANDOR PETÖFI (1823–49) wrote love-poems, brief lyrics of a true intensity, as well as poetry of the 1848 revolution, in the suppression of which he perished. In Sweden, whose literature had hitherto followed the French lead, there had been one important poet in the eighteenth century, the light satirist C. M. BELLMAN (1740–95), whose Stockholm poems and famous epistles were sung to old folk-melodies. But now BISHOP E. TEGNÉR (1782–1846), by incorporating Icelandic themes in a Romantic poetry, swung his nation's new literature strongly under German influences. In Flanders, later in the century, GUIDO GEZELLE (1830–99), a Catholic priest and reactionary journalist, wrote unforced Romantic poetry, in every way original and close to the rhythms of popular speech. The poetry of nature and the poetry of mystical knowledge were equally at his command, and were it not for the restricted range of the language in which he wrote, he would count as one of the most original nineteenth-century poets.

With Gezelle, the revival of Flemish became a reality. But a similar attempt to bring to new life the old literary language of Southern France failed despite the devotion of a very considerable poet, FRÉDÉRIC MISTRAL (1830–1914), who composed rustic epics in it. Returning to the use of myth, which meant little to his sophisticated compatriots in Northern France, and studying the verse of the *troubadours*, Mistral, despite the grandeur of his faith and his vision of nature, struck no roots. The language in which he wrote was artificial, and no amount of cultural propaganda could call into being a national spirit in Southern France such as Petöfi had roused in Hungary and Gezelle in Flanders.

Fashions in France were moving in the direction of Parnassianism, in essence a Romantic protest against Romanticism, which originated with a poet of the Romantic generation itself, THÉOPHILE GAUTIER (1811–72). Starting as a macabre comrade of Nerval and the other eccentric hangers-on of the Romantic school, Gautier soon revolted against their

disregard of form, and promulgated a theory that the more re-
calcitrant the medium the greater the beauty of a work of art.
Partially trained as a painter, and earning his living as an art
critic, Gautier rejected all moral, social, and political implications in literature, demanding that a poem should be purely
formal, and that art should be practised for its own sake. This
challenge to Hugo, whose supporter Gautier had been in the
battle of the theatres, had entirely changed the direction of
French poetry by the mid-century. Henceforth Hugo's polemics were imitated by few, and Hugo himself had now his
occasional Parnassian moments.

Gautier attempted *terza rima*, and drew Spanish landscapes
with bright or subdued colours, using a palette as sensitive
as Góngora's, though less surprising. His outstanding innovation, however, was his attempt to blend the arts, to suggest
indeed that their media were interchangeable. This is not
surprising in an art-critic, but it had far-reaching effects on the
next generation, which in its search for 'correspondences' between one art and another was really seeking private and rare
sensations, such as it believed to be within reach of the artist
alone.

Gautier was trying in such poems as his *Symphonie en blanc
majeur (Symphony in White Major)* to co-ordinate the evidence of
all the senses into a single impression. He had a fine eye, and
an ear sensitive to cadences which Hugo, Vigny, and Musset
failed to catch. His lack, however, of any sustained standpoint
more valid than one of art for art's sake, prevents his *Émaux et
Camées (Enamels and Cameos)* from rising out of the category of
exquisite minor poetry, the best of its class and time. His
novels, of which *Mademoiselle de Maupin* is the best known, are
pictorially exciting, though emotionally naïve. For Gautier
was among the founders of the doctrine that art had a right to
be concerned not only with formal beauty but with sexual
eccentricity.

The aesthetic objectivity of *Émaux et Camées* was imitated by
LECONTE DE LISLE (1818–94), whose primitive visions of
the dawn of civilization, of the tropics and of the ancient gods,
were as carefully executed as Gautier's more sophisticated
evocations. A disillusioned pessimist, who had spent much of

his youth in the tropical island of Réunion, Leconte de Lisle used stronger colours than Gautier, and permitted – though unconsciously – his own pessimism to pervade even his most exciting evocations, such as that of 'Upsala, where the Jarls drink their good beer, clashing their golden cups and singing in chorus' or of a herd of elephants crossing a desert of red sand.

Leconte de Lisle was the chief contributor to a three-volume anthology, *Le Parnasse contemporain*, which gave the new movement towards form and objectivity its name. The most perfect practitioner of the Parnassian aesthetic, however, was J. M. DE HÉRÉDIA (1842–1905), a Cuban who managed to compress into a sonnet visions that Leconte de Lisle elaborated over two or three pages. He too had a deep though somewhat over-picturesque feeling for past civilizations, combined with a far finer gift of phrase than the rather monotonous Leconte de Lisle. But among the contributors to *Le Parnasse contemporain* were a number of poets who shared little with the actual Parnassians except their greater concern for formal perfection. It would certainly be impossible to think of the best of them, Charles Baudelaire, as an objective poet.

Parnassianism, despite the narrow limits of its achievement in France, had some effects on minor poetry abroad, where its accent on form and its fresh interest in the classical, as well as the medieval past, attracted and influenced poets as different as the Swiss novelist C. F. Meyer, the tamely impressionistic German DETLEV VON LILIENCRON (1844–1909), RUBÉN DARÍO (1867–1916), a Nicaraguan who rejuvenated the poetry of Spain and Spanish America, and, many years later, our own poet J. E. Flecker.

CHARLES BAUDELAIRE (1821–67), on the other hand, though Parnassian in form, not only destroyed Parnassianism in France and elsewhere, by his reintroduction of the Romantic egocentricity, but founded what we must still regard as the school of modern poetry. The part played by theology in the Middle Ages, by experimental science in the nationalist era, by metaphysics in the first epoch of German Romanticism, now came to be played by psychology, which has been for the past century the science – or semi-science – to which all the activities of civilization have to be related. Baudelaire was the first poet to offer his heart with some degree of analytical honesty to his reader. Byron, Hugo, Leopardi, Heine: all had attitudinized, but all had posed as whole men. Baudelaire, with greater insight, revealed the split in his own nature. Posing as a victim of the contemporary malaise, he displayed the melancholy, the perversity, the striving for genuine emotion of a man naturally religious, but lacking religious belief. Love offered him nothing but sensual excitement, ending – if not beginning – in disgust. The loved one had long since ceased to stand for the poet as an intermediary between the common and the divine vision: rather she represented the chief torturess of a hell from which there was no escape. Sex was for Baudelaire evil in itself.

What Baudelaire knew about his own nature and predicament – which was the nature and predicament of the generations that followed him – he had discovered for himself. In his technique, however, he was less original, for his line is essentially the Racinean line, used with less licence than a Romantic would have granted himself. In his imagery too, Baudelaire's originality was limited to the introduction of his *poésie des départs*, with its ships and trains and foreign ports, and to his horrified picture of great towns as greedy destroyers, for which he learnt something from de Quincey's *Opium Eater*, as he learnt from Poe to draw certain other aspects of nightmare and horror.

Baudelaire followed Gautier to the extent that to him all that was not art was hideous; and in his aristocratic pose, his dandyism, he cut a figure that appealed to the 'Decadents' of the century's end, who praise him for his 'Satanism' oblivious of the fact that it was only the obverse of his desperate search for good.

Chief among those successors who misinterpreted Baudelaire while pronouncing themselves his followers, was PAUL VERLAINE (1844–96), at his best an impressionist of delicate moments, and master of a pleasantly minor key, and at his worst a morbidly contrite convert to a milk-and-water Catholicism. Verlaine's charm is really a development of Gautier's. He too plays with colours and stresses the artist's essential independence of morality. If there are similarities between Manet and Baudelaire, Verlaine comes nearer to the Impressionists. But for him the closest sister art was music rather than painting, and fine tones meant more to him than any sharp-edged statement.

Far more important as a long-range influence, though seldom perfect as a poet, was STÉPHANE MALLARMÉ (1842–98) who, like Verlaine, began under Baudelaire's influence and contributed to *Le Parnasse contemporain*. Mallarmé, while taking over the doctrine of art for art's sake, went further than Gautier, and denied that a poem must present any logical statement. It need be no more, as he saw it, than a succession of images, linked together musically and conveying a mood or a myth to the subconscious mind of the reader rather than to his reasoning faculty. Mallarmé was an anti-scientist. He was also the opponent of the straightforward simile: 'this is like that.' Instead he substituted the first term for the second, thus producing a symbol the significance of which would be clear only to the reader psychologically attuned to the poet's way of thought.

From this substitution arose the great obscurity of much symbolist poetry, the poet's mind being hard to penetrate, and no explanations being offered. The resulting poetry was close in texture, and ambiguous. For while its manner of omitting links was no more than a new Góngorism with some real affinities to the Spanish seventeenth century, the range of images used was much larger, and there was no stock mythology.

Mallarmé's condensation of imagery has been even more influential than Baudelaire's new psychology in changing the direction of European poetry. Where Baudelaire sees the poet as a rebel, a superfluous man bent on showing the philistine that in reality it is he that is superfluous, Mallarmé feels himself a prisoner in the world of the senses, who yet by tireless devotion to his hermetic art may earn his moments of release. Most of his poems, especially his last, are so difficult as still to offer uncertain meanings. At his most sparkling, however, in *L'Après-midi d'un Faune* (*A Faun's Afternoon*), he conveys a mood, a music, and a sultriness which are the impressionistic equivalent of the Parnassian weariness of Tennyson's *Tithonus*.

J. A. RIMBAUD (1854–91) a strangely precocious youth who had written all his poetry before he was nineteen, and who then abandoned writing for ever, viewed the poet as a seer, who after deliberately confusing all the organs of sense, would be granted a direct vision of the universe. His early poem *Bâteau ivre* (*Drunken Ship*) is symbolist in that the ship and the poet are one. Other early poems, however, are objective in the manner of Baudelaire, drawing ugly little pictures of war and slums. But when Rimbaud had advanced to the stage of the disorderly mystic, he deliberately disturbed his vision, and in a series of prose and lyrical poems, *Les Illuminations* (*The Illuminations*) invented a phantasmagoria comparable to Hölderlin's in the poems of his madness. But whereas Hölderlin used a recognizable mythology, Rimbaud invented his own symbols, which were sometimes clear, but at other times reproduced the features of some trackless fairyland, where clarity and confusion were blended. His last collection, *Une Saison en Enfer* (*A Season in Hell*), shows Rimbaud's inability to find a way out through poetry.

'*Pleurant, je voyais de l'or – et ne pus boire,*' he says ('Weeping I saw gold – but could not drink'). Rimbaud then left France, and after earning his living by trading of various sorts, which took him to the Dutch East Indies and to Abyssinia, returned eighteen years later, with a fatal illness, to die at Marseilles.

The combined effect of Baudelaire, Mallarmé, and Rimbaud on European literature was slow to reach its maximum intensity, and has not yet worn itself out. Private imagery, the claim to visionary penetration, density of texture, subtlety of psychological revelation; all were the fruit of the revolution which they worked in nineteenth-century poetry. On the technical side, however, their influence was less than that of two lesser poets, TRISTAN CORBIÈRE (1845–75), and JULES LAFORGUE (1860–87). Metrically and linguistically, as has been said, Baudelaire did not advance far beyond the subtly varied alexandrine of Racine; his innovations were largely in the field of imagery; nor did Mallarmé require an idiom more developed than that of the seventeenth century. Rimbaud's prose-poems, following on Baudelaire's – which he had modelled on those of Aloysius Bertrand, the inventor of the form – satisfied his need for novelty. Corbière and Laforgue, on the other hand, set out to recapture the cadences of the spoken word and the rhythms of the music-hall song – the only folk-music of the day. Never since Saint-Amant had French poetry attempted to catch the tone of everyday speech. What Wordsworth had demanded and Browning to some extent achieved in England had remained unthought-of on the French side of the Channel. Corbière, a rebellious young Breton, with a poor constitution and a certain easy Satanism which he took from Baudelaire, was eager to suit the language of his verse to his own violences and to the rough coast of his native Brittany. His verse is deliberately angular, slangy, and broken, his poses romantically anti-Romantic. With a contempt for literature that was itself literary, Corbière set out to make even scenes in a sailor's brothel poetic.

Jules Laforgue, on the other hand, a more serious poet, self-mocking, ironic, yet seeking a truth behind the tinsel illusions that he anatomized in his *Complaintes,* did not live long enough to perfect his style, which had advanced from the stage of music-hall parody to that of a free verse with irregular rhymes in his last poems. Laforgue not only used the language of everyday speech, but introduced a new and shabby corner of the everyday world in which piano-scales were practised behind closed windows on melancholy Sunday afternoons in lost provincial towns, and where the poet disguised as a pale clown gazed with mute longing at the moon: a motif borrowed from Verlaine, and derived by him from Watteau's paintings, which circulated everywhere throughout Europe and America in the nineties.

Laforgue, though of French blood, was born in Montevideo, a town strongly under French cultural influence, which also sent home the writer of an obscure prose epic, *Les Chants de Maldoror (The Songs of Maldoror)*, which the poet described as more terrible than Byron's *Manfred,* and which the surrealists considered a forerunner of their own form of automatic writing. About its author, who called himself COMTE

DE LAUTRÉAMONT (1847–70), not very much is known. His poem is an exercise in adolescent Satanism, original in its imagery, but extremely literary in its language and theatricality.

The minor Symbolists who followed wrote pleasantly, developing various forms of *vers libre,* a medium of which several poets claimed to be the inventor. The general tendency of these writers, of whom ALBERT SAMAIN (1858–1900) and FRANCIS VIELÉ-GRIFFIN (1864–1937) were the best, was towards a musical impressionism much more conventional in language than that of Corbière or Laforgue. The movement had lost impetus, but gained in intimacy. Its one original poet of the second generation, the Belgian ÉMILE VERHAEREN (1855–1916), wrote powerfully of the horrors of the town, a theme borrowed from Baudelaire but treated with a Whitmanesque freedom. Verhaeren was a powerful but untidy poet, an experimenter in both subject and style, who does not fit at all readily into the French tradition, yet whose fervent dislike of industrialism comes very close to Zola's.

From the symbolist group emerged the *École romane,* whose leader JEAN MORÉAS (1856–1910), a Greek by birth, attempted to found a new classicism, which was really closer in feeling to the Parnassians, though less eclectic, since it looked only to the Greeks and Romans for models. The achievement of this group was small; but one short-lived poet, EMMANUEL SIGNORET (1872–1900), had a Mediterranean warmth and directness, which might well rescue him from his present oblivion.

The revival of classicism in Italy, on the other hand, where classicism, patriotism, and anti-clericalism formed a single consistent point of view, pagan in inspiration, followed naturally on the eclipse of Leopardi. Here GIOSUÈ CARDUCCI (1835–1907) wrote political odes of great power, celebrating the history and landscape of his country. His defiant *Odi barbari (Barbaric Odes)* though they are more restrained in form and language, have some of the rhetorical power of Victor Hugo. Romantic in his feeling for nature, Carducci was essentially classical in his attitude to mankind, to him the measure of all things. He was, moreover, like Hugo, and unlike most of his contemporaries, a public figure, as was GIOVANNI PASCOLI (1855–1912), a poet who emerged from a youthful melancholy into an optimistic socialism and patriotism. Pascoli was not as strong a poet as Carducci, but in a way parallel to that of the French symbolists, he extended the vocabulary of the Italian poet drawing not on urban colloquialism but on obscure rustic turns of phrase, which formed, however, a less permanent addition to Italian poetic resources than the innovations of Corbière and Laforgue to the French poetic capital of the twentieth century.

An extreme Romantic, GABRIELE D'ANNUNZIO (1863–1938), quickly eclipsed Pascoli in the rôle of public figure. Drawing both on Giovanni Verga and on Carducci, he proclaimed himself an adherent to *verismo*, the Italian school of realism. However, *verismo* to him meant not objective recording, but a carefully exaggerated transcript of sensual experience. Eroticism, pathological detail, and a preoccupation with death, sickness, and brutality made d'Annunzio's plays and poems deliberately shocking. For the classical rhetoric of Carducci he substituted a new rhetoric, barbarous, decadent, and inhuman. The close relationship between beauty and decay, which roused Baudelaire to a sense of sin, drove d'Annunzio to a 'carnality of thought'. He felt impelled to give every word 'the weight of blood'.

Decadence, the pathological worship of depravity, sexual abnormality, and vice, which had so far collected only a few minor artists among its adherents, had its origins in the crazy writings of the Marquis de Sade. Now it found precedents in the Satanism of Baudelaire, and in the novels of Huysmans, and emerged as the creed of a poet with first-class resources. D'Annunzio was primitive, crude, vigorous, and brave on the one hand, violent and luxurious on the other. He understood nothing of the fine shades of Mallarmé; he was a Victor Hugo with a strength of language that burst the tight classical bands in which Italian poets, Romantic as well as Classical, had for so long been content to be confined. D'Annunzio's drama *Francesca da Rimini* is a Senecan play of blood and horror, though its alleged theme is love. His lyrical poetry is the counterpart of Swinburne's, and shimmers with the same highly coloured imagery.

D'Annunzio left Italian poetry enriched with resources that she had never known before. Not however, till the collapse of Fascism, with which the spectacular d'Annunzio was an early sympathizer, did any new school of Italian poets emerge; and they owed little to d'Annunzio, more to the subtler influence of Mallarmé transmitted to them by Valéry and other French poets. DINO CAMPANA (1885–1932), while sharing some of d'Annunzio's linguistic excesses, is more genuinely appealing in his melancholy, and more various in his moods. His one important volume of poems and poetic prose came out just before Italy's entry into the First World War. He died in an asylum, and has gained his reputation only in the last ten years.

Nineteenth-century classicism found a pure exponent in Portugal, where the Romantic movement had produced only one outstanding figure, J. B. ALMEIDA GARRETT (1799–1854), the poet, dramatist, and restorer, by dubious processes, of the traditional ballads. Portugal's champion of a new classicism had not the vigour of Carducci, nor a sense of the grand style like Matthew Arnold. ANTERO DE QUENTAL (1842–91) was a philosophical poet, perhaps more philosopher than poet in his *Odes modernas*, but very much a poet in the 150 sonnets in which he describes the stages of his quest for a faith. Quental's sonnets, the most beautiful in Portuguese since Camões, possess the intimacy and exactness that we have come to expect from modern confessional poetry, and combined with it an exalted language that relates them to the sonnets of Dante and Cavalcanti.

By the beginning of the twentieth century, little major poetry was being written in France, in Italy, or yet in England. But the seeds of symbolism, almost pure of the tares of decadence, were springing up in the form of new poetry in Germany, in Holland, in Spain, and in Spanish America. The nineties, which were an age of decline in those countries with the oldest literatures, were times of fresh birth in those where tradition was weakest.

The only important German poet of the generation after the Parnassians was the urban RICHARD DEHMEL (1863–1920), whose verse romance *Zwei Menschen* (*Two People*) attempted unsuccessfully to express naturalism in poetry, but whose occasional lyrics continue the Romantic tradition pleasantly with original, though occasionally sentimental, novelties of phrase. The German lyric still remained, with few exceptions, a simple, rather provincial poem of feeling suitable to be set to music by Schubert or Schumann, Brahms or Hugo Wolf. It was not until French symbolist influences began to play on the Rhineland aesthete STEFAN GEORGE (1868–1933), on the poor Austrian gentleman RAINER MARIA RILKE (1875–1926), and on the Viennese Jew HUGO VON HOFMANNSTHAL (1874–1929), that German poetry came close once more to the European tradition.

There are aspects of Stefan George's poetry that are closely related to that of d'Annunzio. There is the same preoccupation with the artist's exceptional function and privileges. To George poetry was at first a religion, then a prophetic function. The poet was for him the privileged myth-maker of the age. George took from history symbolic personages through whom to announce his aesthetic theories, and put forward a new Beatrice or redeemer-figure, one Maximin, a personal friend who had died young. In his insistence on his right to dictate faith and beliefs to his admirers, George alienated many creative minds who had been attracted, if not by the man, at least by his fanatical belief in his mission. Von Hofmannsthal and the Dutch poet Albert Verwey refused to be swallowed up by the George circle, which remained closed and had very little influence on Wilhelmian Germany. George published privately, printed and spelt after his own fashion, and looked forward to the establishment of *Das Neue Reich*, in which his ideas would triumph. This bore no relation to that of the Nazis, who attempted to honour him. He refused their advances, and retired to Switzerland, where he died.

The best of George's poetry can be divorced from his myth and related to that of the French symbolists which he began by translating. 'A poem is not the reproduction of a thought,' he wrote, 'but of a mood,' and George's moods of melancholy, of wonder, and of expectancy are to be found most purely rendered in the books of his middle years, after he had ceased to echo Verlaine, and before he had become absorbed in his prophetic rôle. Here he wrote a precious but intensely musical line, which enriched a poetry that in the hands of Dehmel and his contemporaries had become flat, or else wildly experimental.

Whereas George's innovations were on the side of formal elegance, Rilke succeeded rather in extending the range of the German language, in making it capable of expressing the fine nuances of a Mallarmé, the impressionistic subtleties of Yeats. As he found it, the German language was muscle-bound; and as he left it, it was more agile than it had ever been, even in the age of Goethe. Like George, Rilke was a myth-maker, and his too was a private myth, though much more closely related to the other myths of his age. At first it contained two elements, brought to perfection respectively in the objective vignettes of his *Neue Gedichte* (*New Poems*) and the other-wordly reflexions of his *Stundenbuch* (*Book of Hours*). Although in the latter he introduced the theme of the wandering monks, whom he had seen on a brief visit to Russia, Rilke was not a religious poet. His myth, brought to perfection in his *Duineser Elegien* (*Elegies from Duino*), is an aesthetic one, with the poet at its centre, as he was for Stefan George. Rilke saw it as his task to immortalize the common things of the earth, to filter them through the fine mesh of his temperament till they stood in all their purity, like Platonic *ideas*, transmuted and capable of surviving both their own destruction and the poet's.

The detachment of the elegies is akin to Hölderlin's; in them angels and discarnate beings perform the same functions. But Rilke's poetry admits far more elements from the warm, contemporary world. The elements that he chooses to raise into immortality include the animals, the trees, the flowers, and the works of art, though seldom the people, of earth.

Rilke wrote with great difficulty, crowding his greatest production into a bare month for which he had anxiously waited for years. In that fruitful moment he not only put his

elegies into their final form, but also wrote two lyrical sequences, *Die Sonette an Orpheus* (*Sonnets to Orpheus*), with
whom he identified himself in his function as poet. Rilke's
prose *Aufzeichungen des Malte Laurids Brigge*, the notebooks of
an imaginary Danish poet, presents a delicate, rather morbid
picture of the artist as a haunted figure in a world of secret
portents and hidden significances. Though arresting, it is
less individual than his poetry, which remains among the
most significant of the century.

Von Hofmannsthal, like Rilke an Austrian, was however
more closely identified than he with the destinies of the decaying Habsburg Empire, of whom, with Schnitzler, he was the
outstanding writer. His early poems and poetic dramas placed
him midway between George and Rilke, partaking of some of
George's verbal richness and of Rilke's greater subtleties of
expression. In his middle years he adapted ancient plays,
among them, and most successfully, the Anglo-Dutch
'morality' *Everyman*, and wrote librettos for Richard Strauss's
operas which were works of art in their own right. Finally,
however, he developed symbolisms of his own in plays
written after the collapse of Austria in the First World War.
During these years he turned also to the writing of critical
essays.

The poets of the generation following Rilke and George
are disappointing, the two best being short-lived. GEORG
HEYM (1887–1912) echoes Verhaeren's horror of the great
city in language more economical than the Belgian's and, like
his, reminiscent of Baudelaire. GEORG TRAKL (1887–1914)
on the other hand, a purer symbolist, though at times echoing
Hölderlin, wrote invariably of an autumn landscape of
horror and suffering. An unbalanced youth, he quickly
resorted to drink and to drugs, and fell into a total despair,
which ended in his death from an overdose of opium in
the opening months of the First War. Largely forgotten
until Germany's collapse after the Second War, he pro-
vides a significant link between the Decadents and the
Existentialists.

German poetry in the last forty years has achieved little.
Perhaps it is only in the field of irony that any real originality

has been displayed. Here the Austrian CHRISTIAN MOR-GENSTERN (1871–1914) had already led the way with his whimsical characters, Palmström and Korf, and the wry fun of his *Galgenlieder* (*Gallows-songs*). He is a genius of the calibre of Edward Lear in his mastery of subtle word-play, that makes nonsense of all the philosophies. ERICH KÄSTNER (b. 1899), the author also of some very popular children's books, is a more bitter Ogden Nash, who mocks the modish-ness and amorality of Berlin society between the wars.

The serious poetry of this time, expressionistic in its fer-vour, has little to recommend it. FRANZ WERFEL (1890–1945), an Austrian with a religious sense which saw him through his expressionistic beginnings, allowed himself too great a display of inchoate emotion, while OSKAR LOERKE (1884–1941), a poet conventional in form and somewhat rhetorical, attempted to convey a hermetic message porten-tous but hard to decipher, and JOSEF WEINHEBER (1892–1945), another Austrian and the only considerable poet to attempt an unsuccessful compromise with Nazism, developed a splendid technique, but despite his Hölderlin-like attitudes, possessed no real vision. Since the war the influences of Rilke and T. S. Eliot have been strong; and the poetry of H. E. HOLTHUSEN (b. 1913) appears to be making new beginnings.

Symbolism and the influence of Stefan George in particular, have stimulated the writing of some very fine poetry in Holland. Here P. C. BOUTENS (1870–1943), a poet of great formal achievement with a mystical approach to beauty, dis-played a remarkable mastery of variation. Alone of the great symbolists Boutens was a classical scholar and translator and, like Rilke, sensitive to the necessary relationship between the symbol, chosen by the poet, and the underlying *idea* contem-plated by Plato. For only when the one approximates to the other can communication be made beyond a small and private circle.

ALBERT VERWEY (1865–1937), also a poet of intellectual strength, combined with a lyrical spontaneity and a genius for evocative description, stands between Stefan George, who admired and translated him, and the stricter examples of Dante and Goethe. Whether affected by symbolism like

Boutens, or broadly idealist like Verwey, or despairing like the deaf and isolated J. H. LEOPOLD (1865–1925), the Dutch poets of this very real renaissance held more firmly to traditional ways of thought and to classical forms than their contemporaries in other countries.

In Russia, where the symbolist era also brought a revival of poetry, links with Western Europe were more tenuous than in Pushkin's day. Here the motive force was provided by what remained of Slavophilism, and by a revival of spirituality partly theosophical and partly based on Orthodox Church mysticism. The first generation of symbolists, K. BALMONT (1867–1943), V. BRYUSOV (1873–1924) and F. SOLOGUB (1863–1927) were impressionistic, decadent, erotic, or perverse, but stretched the resources of Russian poetry in the manner of d'Annunzio. INNOKENTY ANNENSKY (1856-1909), who devoted much of his energy to poetic dramas and translations, has only recently emerged as a symbolist untouched by decadence, remarkable not only for sharp observation and an original choice of images, but also for the strictness and variety of his forms. Annensky's influence on the early Pasternak was considerable. The second generation, on the other hand, were profoundly Russian and fell under the spell of the mystical philosopher V. J. SOLOVYËV (1853-1900) who was himself a poet. Of these ANDREY BELY (1880-1934) devoted himself to fantastic novels rather than to poetry, and in a messianic frame of mind accepted the revolution, while ALEXANDER BLOK (1880-1921) who likewise accepted the events of 1918, was an apocalyptic poet, in whom dwelt a strange and haunting awareness of a reality behind appearances, akin to the vision of Tyutchev and Alexey Tolstoy. Choosing his imagery from life and history rather than from art, he sees the embodiment of truth in the figure of a strange woman who comes into a restaurant where he is drinking, and hears the clash of battle still ringing on the field of Kulikovo, where long ago the Russians fought the Tartars, and where God's voice sounds for him in the cry of the swans flying over. Blok's poetry is often a *danse macabre* in slushy city streets like those of Baudelaire's Paris. But always, like Bely, and unlike that disillusioned French aesthete, he believed in his country's mission. When the Revolution came he thought that now was Russia's chance to save the world, and in the last lines of *The Twelve*, a staccato sequence concerning the street fighting in Petrograd, he portrayed Christ leading the ragged Bolsheviks. Finally, in *The Scythians*, written at the time of the Brest-Litovsk treaty, he called on the rest of humanity to join Russia and create a new world. Blok had several times found refuge in drink but returned to his writing. The Revolution, however, drove him to a final despair, and these poems were his last.

Equally violent, but no visionary, was the futurist poet, V. MAYAKOVSKY (1894–1930), a convinced anti-symbolist who used coarse and deliberately shocking imagery, first as a pioneer futurist bent on 'throwing Pushkin overboard', and then as a propagandist for the Revolution. He remained unhappy in his own life, however, and committed suicide.

While the genuine poet in Mayakovsky died some years before the man, the peasant decadent S. A. ESENIN (1895–1925) remained true to his poetry despite his total unsuitability for the new society. His ideal was the 'old wooden Russia' of the peasant hut and ox-plough. Lacking education, and even reading, he dramatized himself as the 'Hooligan' – a peasant version of the superfluous man – and haunted the Moscow taverns, repeating his few poetic motifs in verses which never lacked the charm of unforced lyricism. One journey to Persia somewhat increased his resources. But like Mayakovsky he took his own life.

BORIS PASTERNAK (1890-1960), a poet of great originality who derived from the symbolists but absorbed many European influences, wrote lyrical poetry of great allusiveness with imagery that testifies to the working of all the poet's senses at once. There is intellectual construction behind Pasternak's poetry, with a surprising freshness that gives everything he describes a new look. But after a few years the Revolution ceased to encourage this very European figure, who then turned to translation, and made interesting though crude versions of the chief Shakespearian plays. For thirty years, he allowed only a small trickle of original poetry to appear, and these later poems were not radically different from his earlier work. But after Stalin's death he began to write and publish once more, and to show that his genius was not only alive but had undergone a great purification. The imagery of his poems was less extravagant, their unorthodox Christian subjects testified to the poet's suffering and to a deepening of his feelings. His novel *Doctor Zhivago*, published in all countries except his own, made him the centre of a political controversy, in which the book's merits were exaggerated. It is a poet's reading of the history of his time, rich in vision and description, but feebly constructed. It is not an autobiography. Zhivago lacks the central strength of his creator, the power that made him continue as a poet in the face of discouragement and abuse. This power is, however, fully expressed in the last poems.

The Revolution put an end to the writing of Western poetry in Russia. Some futurists struggled on; a charming poetess of intimate moments, ANNA AKHMATOVA (b. 1888), has long been silent. Her husband N. GUMILËV (1886–1921), a neo-Parnassian, was executed as a counter-revolutionary. E. BAGRITSKY (1897–1934), a Romantic who used language as boldly as Pasternak, also died young. The new poets are lesser figures.

A remarkable new book of poems entitled *Stolby (Columns)* by NIKOLAI ZABOLOTSKY (1903-1958), which appeared in 1929, presented a Swiftian picture, with violent imagery, of small-town life, with draymen, footballers, small clerks and fish on the slab alike unflatteringly portrayed. Zabolotsky seems to prefer the old peasant life of 'wooden Russia'. He was taken to task as a reactionary, and *Stolby* has not been reprinted. Typewritten copies, however, circulate clandestinely. Zabolotsky's later poetry was accomplished but no more. He hardly stands out among the many whose talents have been hampered by directives, which have limited their subjects and prescribed their strictly non-transcendental treatments. The best poetry of contemporary Russia is not lyrical but narrative and popular-heroic, and the outstanding poet in this genre is ALEXANDER TVARDOVSKY (b. 1910).

Among a group of young lyrical poets who have emerged in the last years, EVGENY EVTUSHENKO (b. 1933) is outstanding. His poetry is direct and simple in its evocation of his youth and in its assertion of the poet's individuality in a strict society to the ideals of which he subscribes. Though no rebel, Evtushenko has boldly attacked anti-Semitism in the poem *Baby Yar*, and commented freshly and vigourously on things and persons seen during his visits to the West.

The contemporary revival in Spanish poetry, on the other hand, has gone forward with an impetus which, in America at least, has not yet died down. Spanish poetry of the Romantic age was, as has been noted, provincial. The revival began with the posthumous publication in 1871 of some seventy-nine short lyrics by an ill-fated journalist and translator G. A. BÉCQUER (1836-70). This straightforward sequence, which tells of an unhappy love, broke with the Romantic convention of full rhyme, and adopted a very Spanish pattern of assonance, which made for far greater subtlety of music. His attitudes are akin to those of Heine in his later, despairing phase, but less theatrical. Bécquer wrote flatly, monotonously even, without rhetoric; but for the first time since Garcilaso here was a Spanish poet who spoke honestly on the subject of love, and who established new connexions, in some of his varied stanza patterns, with the traditional peasant measures of the *copla* – of which collections were beginning to be published. Spain, in fact, was reforming a link with her own past, as she had not done since the age of Góngora.

Another poet whose verse was the product of unhappy experiences was ROSALÍA CASTRO (1837-85), who wrote delicately in her native Galician, which had not been used since the time of the *cantigos d'amigo*, then long ago forgotten. Many of her Galician poems echo folk-songs. But others seem to reach out as if through a veil of mystery, to grasp some firmer reality behind the backcloth of Galicia's rivers, estuaries, and bare hills. This is the poetry of nostalgia and of suffering; and even more painful is her last volume, written in Castilian. Rosalía Castro's poetry is not as powerful as that of the nineteenth century's other great poetess Annette von Droste-Hülshoff. But it speaks directly of the life of everyday, of the starving peasant in a country as poor as Ireland, and of the emigrant on more prosperous shores longing for his native Galicia.

Neither Bécquer nor Rosalía Castro wrote powerfully enough to set going a revival of Spanish poetry; which actually began in Spanish America, under the impact of French parnassianism and symbolism. The new poets of Spanish America were many – JOSÉ MARTÍ (1853–95) in Cuba, JOSÉ ASUNCIÓN SILVA (1865–96) in Colombia, MANUEL GUTIÉRREZ NÁJERA (1859–95) in Mexico, and JULIO HERRERA Y REISSIG (1875–1901) in Uruguay. But all these were confined by poverty and provincial conditions to their own lands. One poet only made contacts with Europe, and this was RUBÉN DARÍO (1867–1916), whose native Nicaragua was too small to contain a writer of such vigour and originality. In his first book *Azul* (*Blue*) he mastered the Parnassian idiom; in his second *Prosas profanas*, he broke the dull moulds of Spanish Romantic poetry. A Swinburne in his vigour, his metrical innovations, and sometimes in his monotony, Darío was nevertheless a poet of greater variety than that late Victorian. Like him a pagan, he was excited by the beauty and luxury of the world: and though often moved by other poets rather than by direct observation, he saw many things that writers in Spanish had not seen before. His *Sinfonía en gris mayor* is Gautier's symphony in white transferred to another shore; and sometimes too, he seems to echo Whitman. But the effect of his poetry on Spain was almost that of a new Garcilaso. It was musical, and rhythmically buoyant; and it made the highest claims for the poet himself, not as a seer and prophet, but as nature's aristocrat, worthy to be listened to and fêted in all the capitals of the world.

Much of Darío's poetry to-day appears conventionally decadent in its imagery, and somewhat noisy in its affirmations. A few poems nevertheless remain. His first Spanish disciple, on the other hand, a modest craftsman, far more subtle in his effects, appears to-day one of the most important and delightful poets of that time. ANTONIO MACHADO (1875–1939) was a Castilian, a reflective man and a student of philosophy, who unlike the globe-trotter Darío seldom left his own country till the moment when he was driven out by Franco's armies, to die at almost the first village on the French side of the Pyrenees. Darío had occasionally written poems that owed something to the Spanish past as well as to the French present. Machado, however, anchored the new movement back into the Spanish tradition by the use of rhythms and imagery which were native to it. His is a local poetry which became national; a poetry which relates mood and landscape. It is bare, with a few images, yet each one compelling. Machado writes of the glory of Spain's past, of her miserable present, and of the future which he believed to be in store for her. One of his greatest poems is an elegy on the teacher Francisco Giner de los Ríos, whom he saw as one of the architects of that future. As Machado grew older his poetry became more metaphysical; influences of Verlaine, Bécquer and of Darío became welded in a style which was to be a model to the generations to come. But towards the end of his life he found himself short of emotion and out of sympathy with the new Gongorism of Lorca's generation.

Another intellectual poet, MIGUEL DE UNAMUNO (1864–1936), allowed metaphysical distresses to stifle his poetry except in a few pieces which, like Machado's, though with a more solemn, less certain and less musical beat, relate his bleak northern landscape with the moods of doubt and despair which threatened to overwhelm him. Whatever his subject or medium, poem, novel, essay or critical disquisition, Unamuno is always speaking of man's need to be assured of his immortality. He was not a professional philosopher but a sceptic in search of a faith, which he did not find; and the essence of his humanist dilemma is movingly embodied in his long essay on the tragic sense (*Del sentimiento trágico de la vida*).

A third poet in this group which brought to Spanish culture and literature a rebirth after the loss of the American war and of the last vestiges of Spain's overseas empire, was JUAN

Ramón Jiménez (1881-1958), an Andalusian, who continued Darío's work of incorporating French influences, drawing on Mallarmé in particular, whose subtlety and impressionism suited the brilliant landscape in which the poet
lived. His earlier poems shimmer with sunlight, or sparkle
beneath a southern moon. But later his imagery became
firmer, and his states of mind more consistently autumnal
and melancholy. Then in about 1916, Jiménez began to
move in the direction of pure poetry, to abandon rhyme
and assonance, and to write in a subtly cadenced *vers-libre*.
What he now had to express was the landscape of his own
mind reflected outwardly in the trees and stars, the clouds,
the sky, and the bare rocks of Andalusia. These poems
were slight and fragmentary, hanging on a single image,
and leaving a scent rather than a message in the reader's
mind. In the last years and during his exile in America,
where he went after the Civil War, his poetry took on a
somewhat firmer outline, and many of his best poems are
to be found in his later volumes. Like Yeats and Rilke, he
was perhaps slow in arriving at a mature style. In contrast
to Rilke he stretches out after things, but catches only his
own states of mind. But in his subtle and highly organized
poetry he reflects a soul steeped in the past of his own
Andalusia, and echoing its predominant moods at every
stage from its Arabic beginnings. Unlike Darío, he brings
the French style home to a country with traditions strong
enough to modify it.

The poetry of Portugal followed a parallel course to that of
Spain, with Eugénio de Castro (1869-1944) introducing
the symbolist style in the place of Darío, with Camilo Pessanha (1867-1926) as a leading symbolist, and with the somewhat mystifying figure of Fernando Pessoa (1888-1935)
as the counterpart of Juan Ramón Jiménez, who was in some
respects his master. Pessoa, who had spent his childhood in
South Africa, wrote at first in English, contributing his
Portuguese poems, which were not collected until after his
death, to a number of periodicals under three pseudonyms,
which he believed to represent three distinct facets of his
personality, one pastoral, one emotional, and one pagan and

intellectual. In his emotional incarnation Pessoa is at times over-rhetorical, but in pastoral or paganly reflective vein he has a great sense of form, which links him with both the medieval and the classical traditions.

The period between the two wars saw a succession of intellectual programmes formulated in France, and adapted to some extent abroad. What was lacking was genuine poetry. The leading French figure of this time, PAUL VALÉRY (1871–1945) reduced the violences of symbolism to a classical music in which body and spirit, object and thought, became reconciled. His small body of early verse derives from Mallarmé. Then after a long silence during which he occupied an important secretarial post, he emerged once more as a poet for a few years after 1917. Valéry's poetry is traditional in form, close in texture, and abstract in its preoccupation with love and death. It appears to come from a deeper philosophical level than Unamuno's, but is perhaps essentially concerned with the same questions. It is lucid, and yet refuses to become quite plain; pure, yet narcissistic in its constant reference back to the creative act. Valéry, like Rilke who translated him, and like Gide, finds no subject sufficiently moving to deflect his thought from his own processes of creation:

> Mais moi, Narcisse aimé, je ne suis curieux
>   Que de ma seule essence;
> Tout autre n'a pour moi qu'un cœur mystérieux,
>   Tout autre n'est qu'absence.

(But I, the loved Narcissus, am curious about nothing but my own essence; everything else is for me mysterious at heart; nothing else is anything but an absence.)

While Valéry failed to make concrete any objects outside his own mind, except perhaps in his one poem of Mediterranean sultriness, Le Cimetière Marin (The Cemetery by the Sea), the Catholic school of CHARLES PÉGUY (1873–1914) and PAUL CLAUDEL (1868–1955) wrote tendentiously to stimulate a revival of Catholicism and patriotism, which did not survive the slaughter of the First World War, in which Péguy was killed. Péguy's rhetorical style makes him seem a Hugo in vers libre, a man of the people and a simplifier of difficult ideas. Claudel on the other hand, writes in the style of the psalmodist poems rich in imagery ranging from the sublime to the naïve, which fail to coalesce into any tight shape.

The French poet who best represented the fashion-ridden decades between the wars was GUILLAUME APOLLINAIRE (1880-1918), an eclectic of foreign birth, who looted Rimbaud and Mallarmé of their originalities, and served them up saucily and attractively, with his own boldness of music and imagery, and with his own derangements of printing and punctuation. Apollinaire died of wounds at the end of the first war, leaving the Parisian field open to the frivolous talent of JEAN COCTEAU (b. 1889), and to the intellectual experiments of Dadaists, surrealists and others, who attempted to reduce poetry to a form of automatic writing, dictated by the unconscious mind which, thanks to the general circulation of Freud's theories, was supposed to have access to greater wisdom than the intellect. These new theories led to the writing of much private poetry, and petered out in the Itma-like absurdities of HENRI MICHAUX (b. 1899) and JACQUES PRÉVERT (b. 1900). They also influenced in passing, however, the three serious poets of France's older generation, JULES SUPERVIELLE (1884-1961), P. J. JOUVE (b. 1887) and PAUL ÉLUARD (1895-1952).

Supervielle, a Uruguayan by birth, writes a poetry of hints and nuances, of wide open landscapes, South American rather than French, of absences and of journeys. At a first reading he may seem as abstract a poet as Valéry, but on re-reading he offers intimate glimpses of familiar objects, of family life, and a warmth of feeling for children, for animals, and for simple things, hinted at with a whimsical but childlike simplicity.

Jouve, a more tortured poet, is a mystic caught up in the dark night of the soul. His imagery is often psychoanalytical; his cry for redemption Christian.

Éluard, for long a consistent surrealist, was at his finest when he expressed fundamentally simple things in mysterious language. When he threw off his surrealism in the interests of his Communist beliefs, his poetry, even when it retained its music, became coarse and over-positive. His early themes had all been those of sensual love; his later poems about universal fraternity, though contributing to the morale of the Resistance, were the work of a lesser poet. Éluard's imagery was throughout wayward and obscure. But the music of his words, and the gleams that he threw at intervals on a reality of emotion beneath his playful embellishments, made him a true poet, where the rest of the surrealists were untidy amateurs.

Since the war there has been a revival in the declamatory *vers-libre* style of Claudel, which is practised by SAINT JOHN PERSE (b. 1887) whose poem *Anabase* was translated by T. S. Eliot in 1926. He is a diplomat who has published occasional poems over many years and who has now collected a following. His poetry, individual in imagery, gives a wide view of the world, nostalgic in its evocation of places and of the past, of migrations, disasters, and of the working of the elements: all of which the poet sees from a tower of almost complete isolation. A similar isolation in the service of a grandiose myth, Catholic and Arthurian in its details, keeps PATRICE DE LA TOUR DU PIN (b. 1911) deliberately apart from the modern movement. His early poetry has moments of a Pre-Raphaelite charm; his more recent work seems distant and, though clear, uncoordinated. PIERRE EMMANUEL (b. 1916) is a religious poet of great power but with a defective sense of form. His long poems on Biblical subjects suggest that his weaknesses are those of a Hugo; his occasional short poems promise better things.

On the formal side RENÉ CHAR (b. 1907) writes prose poems which seem often on the point of coming clear, but which remain persistently clouded by the legacy of Rimbaud and of surrealism.

Italian poetry in the generation that followed d'Annunzio was at first wildly experimental, Italy being the cradle of the staccato futurist movement, whose glorification of war and hostility to the past made it a ready ally of Fascism. F. T. MARINETTI (1876–1944), the leader of this propagandist group, which issued its manifesto in 1909, produced no writing of value, and such influence as futurism maintained became difficult to distinguish from that of those other 'slaps in the face of public taste', Dadaism and surrealism.

A truer poet, GIUSEPPE UNGARETTI (b. 1888) accepted some of futurism's innovations, but rejected its rhetorical tricks. His is a small-scale poetry, careful of every sound and word, and technically much akin to that of Apollinaire and his group. French also in affinities is EUGENIO MONTALE (b. 1896), like Ungaretti a hermetic poet, whose writing echoes the defeat and discouragement of the Fascist years, but who emerged after the final defeat as the representative figure of the 1940s, the poet of the private experience. His imagery and symbolism are as wayward as Apollinaire's, but he speaks without rhetoric and with greater authority.

Montale is a poet of small production, as is also SALVA-TORE QUASIMODO (b. 1901), whose early personal poetry aroused no great interest, but whose war-poems, with their splendid humanity, broke the hermetic spell under which the Italian poets of the Fascist era laboured. His *vers libre* has affinities with Leopardi's, but his imagery is as modern as Montale's. Several other interesting poets began to write during and immediately after the war. But Italian poetry, unlike Spanish, still remains a derivative of the Paris school rather than the fruit of a national tradition.

More independent, though not of European stature, is the Portuguese poet and short-story writer MIGUEL TORGA (b. 1907), a doctor of peasant origins and deep religious pre-occupations, whose relationship to tradition is as independent as Lorca's, to whom he bears no resemblance in any other way, being a reflective poet of country moods.

Spanish poetry in the years between the wars was far less experimental and private than French, and far bolder than Italian or Portuguese. JORGE GUILLÉN (b. 1893) developed the techniques of Jiménez, giving sharp visual glimpses of landscapes at isolated moments. Guillén is the poet of light, and the translator of Valéry, clear, rapid, and brilliant, with no wish to convey anything but an impression. PEDRO SALINAS (1891–1951) was a love poet who practised the hints and evasions of a Supervielle, and revealed, beneath an imagery full of mists and absences, glimpses of real but modest emotion. Another poet of the same generation, VICENTE ALEIXANDRE (b. 1900), tended at first to reinforce his emotion with violent and psycho-analytical imagery, which stressed the elements that unite man's body to the material of the soil. Latterly his poetry has become more elegiac and more metaphysical. It reflects the isolation of a poet who has remained behind, when most of his contemporaries have emigrated. A more consistently independent poet, who nevertheless owes some of his greater fame to his personal charm and to his murder by Franco sympathizers, was FEDERIGO GARCÍA LORCA (1899–1936), a man fundamentally untouched by the modern movement in poetry, which he allowed to influence him only in a few poems written in New York. For the rest, Lorca was an independent traditionalist, who drew the whole resources of Spanish poetry into the service of his own vision. The sharp compression of his images, the off-beat music of his rhythms, the crude colour of his language, goes back to the poem of the Cid, to the *romances* and to the Baroque poets of the seventeenth century. Lorca's temptation was to use his material decoratively. His most popular *Romancero gitano* (*Book of Gypsy Romances*) calls to life a gypsy world that would be in danger of becoming a little too picturesque, if Lorca did not step back and, ironically, put his little tales of feuds and punishments, of martyrdoms and miracles, into the mouths of gypsy narrators, who speak his metaphors with relish. His attitude to these primitive Andalusians is like Synge's to the men of Aran. Theirs is for him the untrammelled life of poetry; they are savages noble in their adherence to their own morality, which is clearly indicated in such a poem as *La Casada infiel* (*The Faithless Bride*). Lorca was on their side against the advance of civilization, which appalled him during his stay in New York. But they stood for him also, as did his friends the bullfighters, for the forces of life and passion, defiantly facing ubiquitous death. Death was to Lorca the fascinating enemy, with which he was half in love, and his greatest poem is the celebration of that death in the shape of the bull that carried off his friend Ignacio Sánchez Mejías on the point of its horn, 'at five o'clock, at five o'clock exactly in the afternoon.'

Lorca seems at first sight no European poet. To understand him, it is necessary to know his native country, on the edge of Africa, and to be at home in the Spanish poetic tradition.

Images and colours appear arbitrary unless you know the tawdry church images, the uniform of the Civil Guards, the taverns and smithies of Lorca's corner of Spain. The same is true of Esenin's wooden Russia at the other end of Europe. Rilke, Valéry, and Pasternak use all the resources of our common European inheritance; Lorca and Esenin are local poets, but poets who speak of emotions far more clear-cut than the shades and indecisions of the more international voices. They are universal not in their backgrounds, but in the universality of their experience.

RAFAEL ALBERTI (b. 1902), a contemporary and friend of Lorca's, has accepted all the current influences, one after the other, and made fine poetry out of them all. His early masterpiece, *Sobre los ángeles* (*About Angels*) translates the seaboard of Cádiz into a surrealist landscape populated by angels that symbolize the natural forces and qualities of which man is a plaything. Yet Alberti's angels have strange little human quiddities; they are not of an entirely different flesh from the sailors and vintagers of the Cádiz shore. Many of these early poems speak of an unspecified disaster, a crisis in the poet and in the world around him. In the world around him there broke out the civil war of which the Spanish conflict was but a part; and Alberti took the Government side. His war poetry has a warmth and simplicity that had hitherto been lacking, both in his early traditional verses and in the Angel poems themselves; and this warmth persisted in the poetry written after his exile, in which he looked back with sorrow on his defeated country, tied down like a bull across the sea.

Another poet of that time was LUIS CERNUDA (b. 1904) a more classical figure, who in his residence abroad has learnt something of the marmoreal quality of Hölderlin, of the myth-making power of Rilke, and of Eliot's colloquial line. He is consequently the least Spanish of these poets, prone at moments to clothe impure emotion in a grand style.

The last of the poets of the Spanish republic, MIGUEL HERNÁNDEZ (1910–42), a peasant who wrote simply and with great economy of the war, and with emotion of a rare purity of his long imprisonment that followed, died in captivity. Like Lorca, he seems to have absorbed the whole tradition of Spanish poetry, and to have come through with a power of simple expression and a courage that persisted to the end.

> *Soy una abierta ventana que escucha,*
> *por donde va tenebrosa la vida,*
> *Pero hay un rayo de sol en la lucha*
> *que siempre deja la sombra vencida.*

(I am an open window listening, through which life goes out in darkness. But there is a ray of sun in the struggle that always leaves the shadows conquered.)

With the Spanish defeat and the coming of the Second War, the influences which had begun with the mocking Romanticism of Heine, the nightmare vision of Baudelaire and the shifting symbolisms of Mallarmé, were exhausted, and with them the poetry of most Western countries.

Chapter Sixteen

THE GREAT SCANDINAVIANS AND
THE MODERN THEATRE

THE Romantic theatre declined into common melodrama, which held the boards in most European countries throughout the nineteenth century. Few writers of calibre were tempted to provide the crude plots and resounding rhetoric which alone pleased middle-class theatre-goers everywhere. On the one side some poets experimented with historical and poetic plays which found no public; on the other, dramatic hacks turned out the repetitive and ready-made article to the theatre managers' timid requirements.

The Viennese theatre alone supported one not quite provincial talent who failed by far, however, to attain European stature. FRANZ GRILLPARZER (1791–1872), a poet rather than a dramatist, attempted to impose classical restraint upon Romantic material, taking such stories as those of Hero and Leander, Jason and the Fleece, and Sappho, and translating them into terms of love and destiny. His verse is smooth and reflective. But true to his own attitude to life, Grillparzer always remained fundamentally uninvolved, preferring to treat tales of long ago rather than matters of immediate interest. Both his work and his success were uneven; and though it is possible to say that he was one of the most important dramatists between Schiller and Ibsen it is largely in default of better claimants to the title.

If Grillparzer, despite his neurotic history, kept himself free of the violences of *Sturm und Drang*, the same can be said too of the revolutionary dramatist KARL GUTZKOW (1811–78), whose naturalism and philosophical sentiments exercised the same moderating influence as Grillparzer's classical restraint. Gutzkow, though primarily a political journalist, wrote a number of dramas of ideas, chief among them *Uriel Acosta*, whose hero was a free-thinking Jew. Here the drama seemed to have returned to the purpose set for it by Lessing and

Diderot. But yet one more disorderly genius came to twist it back once more in the direction of violence. GEORG BÜCHNER (1813–37), made his own individual use of the new naturalism, incorporating translations of the actual speeches of the French Revolutionary leaders in his pessimistic drama *Danton's Tod* (*The Death of Danton*). In a short life which ended in his twenty-fourth year, he translated Hugo, wrote a satirical fairy-tale theme, *Leonce und Lena* and a collection of fragmentary scenes for a tragedy of a poor soldier's love and jealousy, which form the libretto of Alban Berg's opera *Wozzeck*. Büchner won no reputation in his lifetime, but has been somewhat heavily overpraised in the last forty years. For there is something peculiarly German about his hectic genius, a quality that was present in the *Sturm und Drang* movement, and again among the Expressionists after the First World War.

Another dramatist who, although not Austrian by birth, was, like Grillparzer, conditioned by the demands of the Viennese theatre, was FRIEDRICH HEBBEL (1813–63). Hebbel wrote only a single play of modern life, *Maria Magdalena*. But in the historical dramas which his audience demanded he succeeded in developing modern ideas of motive. His characters, particularly his women, are psychologically less fantastic than the fancy dress they wear. Hebbel was essentially a Hegelian and a Prussian. He saw the conflict between the state and the individual, and insisted that the individual must yield, since 'in the state humanity lives as a whole, while in the individual only a single phase of it is developed'. Tragedy, therefore, was inevitable, and 'proved nothing but the emptiness of existence'. He did not succeed either in freeing himself from the trammels of verse, which called out a certain rhetoric from which a prose writer might have been free.

Herodes und Mariamne, a Biblical play and perhaps Hebbel's best, is both subtle and violent, while *Gyges und sein Ring* (*Gyges and his Ring*) carries subtlety to extremes by investing with philosophical significance a tale of pride, humiliation, and revenge which a Spanish dramatist would have seen as a drama involving only honour. But Hebbel's failure to discover the possibilities of symbolism explored by Ibsen leave him, for all his psychological insights, on the wrong side of the great divide that separates the modern from the melodramatic theatre.

The plays of RICHARD WAGNER (1813–83) can hardly be considered apart from the music which he wrote for them. In feeling a Romantic, he elaborated a music-drama which was intended to be a combination of the arts. In moving away from naturalism, in returning to the great myths for his subject matter, in widening the cleft between audience and stage (and, incidentally by lowering the lights at the beginning of each act, a practice which he originated) Wagner lent the art a new solemnity of great importance for the future. The spectators had come to take part in a ceremony, before which all critical power must abdicate. The roughness of the words must be counted as nothing beside the grandeur of the ideas and the action of the drama.

There was little in the dramas of the Danish Romantic ADAM OEHLENSCHLÄGER (1779–1850) to suggest that it would be in the joint kingdom of Denmark and Norway that the new drama would be born. Oehlenschläger went back for the subject matter of his poetic cycles, his long epics, his prose tales and his dramas to the old Norse legends. His Northern tragedies follow the line set out by the pre-Romantic lyrical poet JOHANNES EWALD (1743–81). But Oehlenschläger was a follower of Schiller, and Danish literature of the Romantic generation, despite its national subject-matter, was tributary to German, as in Holberg's time it had been tributary to French.

The new elements which were to transform the drama, changing its medium from poetry to prose, but reintroducing poetry in the form of symbolism to replace the outworn metrical forms, came from two sources: from the naturalistic theories of Diderot, which brought the stage back to problems of contemporary life and to the treatment of contemporary character, and from the rebirth of fairy-tale.

Perrault, in the seventeenth century, had collected the well-known tales of Mother Goose and put them into polished French; the brothers JAKOB (1778–1865) and WILHELM GRIMM (1787–1859) had retold the traditional German folk-tales to the Romantic generation, which had imitated them, producing a sophisticated counterpart to these *Kinder und Hausmärchen* (*Children's and Domestic Stories*), which continued to be written by Tieck, Hoffmann, Hauff, and many other writers in German down to Gottfried Keller.

Among those most influenced by this new style of fiction was the Dane, HANS CHRISTIAN ANDERSEN (1805–75), who experimented in almost every type of literature, but succeeded only in his charming autobiographies and in his fairy-tales. Andersen's fairy-tales are only to a minor extent either traditional or intended for children. On the technical side it is easy to see the influence on him not only of Hoffmann and Tieck, but of some earlier form of story-telling. His famous delightful *Big Claus and Little Claus* is a simple enough tale of greed outwitted. But Andersen attempts much more than that; to see life from new angles, as the Moon or a broken bottle has known it. Here he snaps old connexions and links things up anew. Then in *The Emperor's New Clothes*, he explains in a new way what it is to see with a child's eyes.

Andersen's finest stories date from a long visit to Italy, and sojourn at Rome when he was in his late twenties. The influence of Rome, and in particular of a circle of German painters working there, who called themselves Pre-Raphaelites, was considerable. A visit to Italy and sojourn in Rome had reorientated Goethe at the end of his residence at Weimar. Goethe's theory of colours and light linked on to those of a member of the Rome group, Charles Sebastian Cornelius; and Manet's resolve to paint light by means of contrasted pure colours after his return from Rome in the fifties testify to the continued existence of new thought, comparable perhaps to that of the Florentine Academy, but less public in its appearances; perhaps not even anxious to call attention to itself.

From Rome seem to have come many of the root ideas of the new age. To Rome went the nineteenth century's greatest dramatist, HENRIK IBSEN (1828–1906). Ibsen was the author only of two historical dramas when he obtained the post of stage manager at Bergen, which led him to the directorship of a theatre in Christiania (now Oslo), and these early plays were treatments of the traditional Norse material in the Romantic manner of Oehlenschläger. It was not till he visited Rome on a travelling scholarship that he began to work out his own ideas in two somewhat shapeless poetic dramas, *Brand* and *Peer Gynt*, which were not primarily intended for the stage.

Ibsen's early ambition had been to write historical drama as poetic as Schiller's, and as slick theatrically as the four hundred odd successes of the French Romantic realist EUGÈNE SCRIBE (1791–1861), whose works were performed up and down Europe. The Norwegian's first important play *The Pretenders* contrasts two men, the limited man of action who wins a crown, and the inspired visionary who hesitates. Then in *Love's Comedy* he shows how marriage suits the limited, but pulls the visionary down. By the time that he wrote *Brand* Ibsen had taken the opposite side in the social battle to that of Hebbel with his Hegelian Prussianism. He was for the individual at all costs, against the pettiness and spiritual degradation of society. But in *Brand* he took the next step forward and showed in the figure of the clergyman ready to sacrifice anything, even his own child, to his ideal, that idealism was not enough. 'Deus caritatis' thunders a voice louder than the roar of the avalanche at the end of the last act. 'God of Love.'

Peer Gynt is a play of deeper meanings, firmer in its symbolism, serious yet at moments naïvely funny. Peer is a nineteenth-century Everyman in search of his true self, the rebel, adventurer and commercial tycoon who is master of everything but his own soul. The play is episodic, the scenes being no more closely knit together than Peer's own character. Wherever he goes, he attempts to assert himself; refusing to sell himself to the trolls, he yet cannot find his way out of the mists that the monstrous Boyg casts around him. 'Go round about,' booms that supernatural creature's voice, but Peer cannot take his advice: he follows his nose, and finds in the end that the only reality in his mediocre life has been the love of a woman whom he has deserted. At first he is a graceless young rascal with an innocence about him that arouses one's sympathy, and this fundamental innocence somehow counterpoints even the later scenes, so that when the Button Moulder comes to melt him down at the end of his days, one hopes to the last that something will save him. In the end he learns that to be oneself – which has been his aim – is to slay oneself.

Peer Gynt contains far greater depths and resources of meaning than could be put on the contemporary stage. As a poem, it compares with Goethe's second *Faust*. Closer still to Goethe is the double play *Emperor and Galilean*, with its contrast between Christianity and Paganism, and its vision of a Third Empire that shall arise and subsume them both. The Emperor Julian fails to re-establish the old order, but in his failure triumphs, for he has been the instrument of a power greater than either.

Before Ibsen had finished *Emperor and Galilean*, he had begun to write plays of a new sort, more suitable for stage presentation, the principal purpose of which appeared to his contemporaries to be that of social comment. *The League of Youth* and *Pillars of the Community*, *A Doll's House*, *Ghosts*, and *An Enemy of the People* are – superficially – concerned with marriage, venereal disease, local government, and public honours; just as the superficial subject of *Bleak House* is the law's delays. Thus it was that the nineteenth-century public interpreted Ibsen, rejecting him as a rebel who called attention to subjects better left undiscussed. On a deeper level, however, Ibsen is talking about truth and lies, about the falsity of any life that does not acknowledge the truth about itself and does not accept all the implications of the past. In his poetic plays the principal characters had been male, and each had carried some part of its author in his make-up. Now, the guardians of the truth were women, and the imprisoning lie was personified by the male, the husband. Mrs Alving, in *Ghosts*, has accepted the double social morality of her husband, and so allowed the family curse of disease to be transmitted to her son. Nora, in *The Doll's House* adores her ideal husband, only to leave him, when she finds that their domestic happiness is founded on a series of fictions. Only if both husband and wife can change, she realizes, can anything new be built to replace the broken marriage, and as the door bangs behind Nora and the final curtain drops, he is inspired with a new hope that 'the miracle of miracles' may happen.

The miracle of miracles is shown in *The Wild Duck* to be,

not a flashing revelation of the truth, but a tender compassion for those who tend their illusions like the crippled duck in the attic, happier in their poverty and affection than in possession of a truth that they cannot face. 'Life would be tolerable enough,' they say, 'if we could only be rid of these infernal duns who come to us poor people's doors with their claim of the ideal.'

The symbolism of *The Wild Duck* is developed further in *Rosmersholm*, where the house, and all that it stands for, dwarfs the characters. Again in *The Lady from the Sea* it is the sea as a symbol of the truth in the thwarted Ellida that plays the hero's rôle. With *Hedda Gabler*, however, Ibsen returned to realism, with a study of a woman in whom the vital force has turned sour. Hedda recognizes and scorns the ugly provincial life around her; she calls her little society's cosy bluff, but though she is an enemy of the trolls, she has no glimpse of the truth herself, and so acts only as a force of destruction.

Symbolism returns in *The Master Builder*, where a man spiritually dead is aroused to follow an ideal that is not his, and falls to his death, from a tower which he knows he has not the head to climb.

Ibsen's last three plays occupy the position in his canon of Shakespeare's final comedies. They are concerned with death and resurrection, with escape from imprisonment in the bonds of sexual love in *Little Eyolf*, of an obsessive situation in *John Gabriel Borkman*, and of artistic creation itself in *When we Dead awaken*.

If all Ibsen's prose plays were to be put together and acted in sequence, they might seem to form the stages of a second *Peer Gynt*, in which the quest of man's true nature was steadily pursued through situation after situation until it was shown to lie in no active endeavour but in the power of what Keats called 'negative capability', or the art of not acting falsely out of an illusory ideal or an illusory picture of self.

The impact of Ibsen on the drama is probably still unexhausted. His first effects were to encourage a school of realists, who rejected the well-made plots of Scribe and Sardou, and, in the teeth of their reluctant audiences, insisted on discussing social questions. In Norway itself BJÖRNSTERNE BJÖRNSON (1832–1910) turned, under Ibsen's influence, from the writing of historical plays to the discussion of commercial and journalistic dishonesty, and to the question whether a man should come to marriage without sexual experience. In his greatest play, *Beyond Human Might* he drew the portrait of a clergyman capable of working miracles of healing, but unable to touch his own loving wife; and in a related play to which he gave the same name, he entered Ibsen's realm of symbolism, while at the same time touching upon capital and labour, and the conflict between planned rationalism and superstition.

Björnson's humanitarianism was matched by the social melodrama of HERMANN SUDERMANN (1857–1928) in Germany, and by the serious ventilation of social evils of EUGÈNE BRIEUX (1858–1932) in France, where Zola also applied his theories of naturalism to the theatre. Naturalism influenced the second great Scandinavian dramatist of the nineteenth century also, though AUGUST STRINDBERG (1849–1912) could not be imprisoned, any more than could Ibsen, in so narrow a theory. In fact it is doubtful whether Strindberg ever rightly found his medium. An early historical play, *Mäster Olof* seems to be a study in his own split personality, part idealist, part realist, part crazy visionary. His realistic plays *The Father* and *Miss Julie* are hammer-blows struck against the 'monstrous regiment of women'. All superfluities are cut away; scenery, subsidiary characters, any attempt to suggest a past or a background for his personages Strindberg scorned. In *The Pariah* the characters lose even their names, and become Mr X and Mr Y; the one-act play *The Stronger* is reduced to a monologue, the second woman being no more than a person addressed.

Strindberg's unhappy fate had by the end of the century linked him to two wives, from both of whom he had broken away; and each crisis had been dramatized in autobiographical and semi-autobiographical prose writing of great power. Now, however, religious interests become strong with him, and from admiration of Nietzsche and Poe he turned to his compatriot Swedenborg, and to Theosophy. The historical dramas which he then wrote revert to the themes of *Mäster Olof*, but now he peopled the past with madmen, with hatred, and with wild ambitions.

Strindberg's subsequent return to realism in *There are Crimes and Crimes* was unbalanced and short-lived. His later plays took the shape of dreams, symbolical in part, at times fanciful, but always weighted with a charge of autobiographical meaning, which carried them into the realm of universals. In *Easter* the dark and cold of winter, with its burden of inherited guilt, is dispelled by the spring sun, and the man Elis rises again. In the terrible *Dance of Death*, the hero Edgar gains a new vision, but is nevertheless driven to destruction by his remorseless wife.

In *The Dream Play* and *The Spook Sonata* Strindberg achieved the subjective drama after which expressionists, surrealists, and many others in the half century that has followed have tried in vain. Spectral characters make their unexpected entrances and exits, mouthing their habitual phrases, and differentiated only as an officer, a bill-poster, a cook, a milkmaid, a mummy, or the ghost of a consul. One recognizes, at least so long as one is in the theatre, that one's own mind, like Strindberg's, is peopled by such figments, and that the truth may somehow emerge from this medley all the same. The effect is not on the intellect, but on the emotions. Many things are suggested, though nothing more definite is conveyed than the picture of a crazy and poetic world, in which the truth has left its clues.

It would be foolish to suggest that Strindberg, for all the power of his imagination, was the equal of Ibsen, who clearly saw – as Strindberg did not – the nature of the problems he was dramatizing. Nor can one compare the successful Belgian dramatist, MAURICE MAETERLINCK (1862–1949), to Strindberg, although he was able to reduce the material of dream to more logical patterns. His static little plays *Les Aveugles* (*The Blind*) and *Intérieur* make a dream-like distance between audience and actors, which is more poetic than the rather sentimental and pretentious *L'Oiseau Bleu* (*The Blue Bird*).

Symbolism and the atmosphere of dream allowed a good deal of pretentiousness and false poetry to enter the theatre at the turn of the century. GERHART HAUPTMANN (1862–1946), a German poet, novelist and playwright, after the success of his realistic *Vor Sonnenaufgang* (*Before Sunrise*) and his social drama, *Die Weber* (*The Weavers*), drifted off into the semi-poetic symbolism of *Die Versunkene Glocke* (*The Sunken Bell*) to end up as a conscious and puny imitator of Goethe. FRANK WEDEKIND (1864–1918), on the other hand, remained stationary, repeating with more and more lurid detail his first *succès de scandale*, *Frühlings Erwachen* (*Spring's Awakening*) which treats of sexual precocity in children, and ends in suicide and heavy symbolism. ARTHUR SCHNITZLER (1862-1931) on the other hand, while strongly influenced by the prevailing sex-obsessions, wrote with a Viennese lightness, mingling sentiment and sensuality, objectivity and cynicism. Schnitzler was a typical artist of the decadence, whose talents did not survive the fall of Habsburg Empire. The symbolic plays of his last years were conventional and dull.

A new and refreshing influence came to the theatre, however, in the shape of Russian drama, which had been slow in making its effect on Western Europe.

After Gogol's boisterous comedy. *The Government Inspector*, comes the satiric though often kindly realism of A. N. OSTROVSKY (1823–86), whose comedies, chiefly of middle-class life, mingle laughter and tears in a way that was afterwards to be Chehov's. Ostrovsky drew many types: merchants, actors, rogues, and civil servants. But though a masterly portraitist, he was no constructor of plots, and many of his plays are merely episodic. Turgenev's plays also, particularly *A Month in the Country*, contributed towards Chehov's final achievement. This is typically the play of a novelist who feels at leisure to invent inessential scenes and allow his characters unnecessary speeches in order to build up an atmosphere. Turgenev underplays the melodrama, which a French dramatist would have translated into strong action. Natalia Petrovna is in love with her son's tutor, and so is her seventeen-year-old ward, but the youth is no Julien Sorel; nothing violent can possibly happen. A discontented wife can succumb to a passion which she knows is ridiculous, and a schoolgirl can mature into a young woman under the stimulus of an emotional experience. That is all.

Tolstoy's contributions to the theatre were secondary, taking the form sometimes of tracts written for his followers, like *The Powers of Darkness*, a peasant drama of murder and seduction, in which conscience is nevertheless allowed to work and a moral outlook to triumph, and *The Fruits of Enlightenment*, a moral satire which shows a group of aristocrats toying with spiritualism, and a peasant girl shrewd enough to take advantage of them.

None of these first Russian playwrights was predominantly a man of the theatre as Anton Chehov was, though he did not come to it until the majority of his short stories were written. He began, in fact, with the writing of mere episodes, and comic little farces, the counterpart of his humorous tales for the periodical press. Such a piece as *The Wedding* can best be acted in the style of vaudeville, with each character allowed to air his own little idiosyncrasies. This vein of humorous exaggeration runs right through Chehov's dramas, which are never intended to be taken tragically. Their author himself, indeed, though always hard-pressed by illness, dependent and ne'er-do-well relatives, and deep-seated tuberculosis, never consented to take things tragically, and seldom for long was willing to accept any of the current idealisms. What delighted him was life's absurd and boundless variety; what he valued most in people of any sort, and in his own characters, were those rare moments when they were true to the law of their own being. In this way, like Ibsen, he was always on the side of the truth.

Chehov's first play *Ivanov* was a social melodrama. Not till his second, *The Seagull*, did he find his own genre. Though he despised Ibsen, whom he described as no dramatist, whom he accused of not knowing life, and of not being simple enough, Chehov's poetic symbolism comes very close to the Norwegian's; his use of the seagull in this play, indeed, is very similar to Ibsen's of his wild duck. But, unlike Ibsen, Chehov is not interested in single characters and their fate. His plays have no heroes; they are concerned with groups of people and their relationships. The action is inconsequent, leading from nowhere to nowhere, and ending, as in *The Seagull*, in a suicide which is not to be taken tragically. Life is like that, says Chehov, and it is life that matters, not death. His third play, *Uncle Vanya*, is more shapely and as inconsequent. 'We shall go on living,' says the unattractive Sofia, left alone with her uncle, when all their little passion is spent, 'and when our time comes we shall die submissively.'

The Three Sisters and *The Cherry Orchard* are looser in plot, and the keynote of both is that of vague hope mingled with nostalgia for the passing of beauty. The sisters live in a dull little town and pin their hopes on escaping to Moscow, an event which will clearly never happen: yet somehow, in some distant and unpredictable future, 'in two hundred years, three hundred, perhaps a thousand years ... a new, happy life will come to be.' When the cherry orchard is to be felled, and all must leave the ancestral house for an uncertain future, the moral still seems to be that the present must pay for the evils of the past and that happiness is somewhere round the corner.

Chehov's plays, but for their symbolism, are completely realistic. People talk aloud, but are really addressing no one but themselves; all voice vague hopes and personal despairs; all are faintly ridiculous, and all are fundamentally lovable. Every sort of event takes place, yet nothing happens; there is no real change. Somewhere, he seems to suggest, there is a key to the secret of real change. In the world that he draws it is missing, but it is not altogether lost. For the mood of his work is always one of inchoate hope and true compassion. His autumn contains in it the promise of spring.

Maxim Gorki's most successful play *The Lower Depths*, which was presented in the year before *The Cherry Orchard*, is typically Russian in its episodic character. A group of down-and-outs are shown huddled in a cellar, each with his own story; and into this assembly of waifs comes the pilgrim Luka, who has learnt in his wandering a secret that he can transmit for a moment to this helpless cross-section of humanity, whose misery nevertheless will stretch on into the limitless future.

The last important dramatist in Russia before the Revolution, L. N. ANDREYEV (1871–1919) attempted satire, realism, and nihilistic symbolism, and gained great popularity without ever making systematic use of his talents. Alexander Blok too attempted a poetic drama, which did not, however, achieve the authenticity of his poetry. Clearly Russian dramatists were trying to get beyond realism, but their attempts were coloured by the strained condition of their society, incapable of reforming itself, or reaching the future that Chehov glimpsed for it except through violence and war.

Spanish drama, on the other hand, adapted all the novelties to be seen on the farther side of the Pyrenees to a mild tradition, unlikely to produce masterpieces but always calculated to entertain. JACINTO BENAVENTE (b. 1866), a gentle satirist, devised his own variations of themes drawn from the *commedia dell'arte* in *Los Intereses creados* (*Bonds of Interest*), and wrote at least one strong play of peasant life in *La Malquerida* (*The Passion Flower*). His output has been very great, almost as great as Lope's. MARTÍNEZ SIERRA (1881–1947) also and the brothers SERAFÍN (1871–1938) and JOAQUÍN (1873–1944) ÁLVAREZ QUINTERO have written charmingly, though their plays have been, on the whole, a little too frail for export. The only outstanding figure in the Spanish theatre, the poet García Lorca, clothed crude passion in his own characteristic poetry in *Bodas de Sangre* (*The Blood Wedding*) and *Yerma*, which are almost the only authentic tragedies that the present age has produced. There is a parallel, which has frequently been pointed out, between these plays and Synge's. Both writers distil a poetry from local speech which is rare in contemporary literature, and both were more dependent on the innovations of their contemporaries than a first sight of their work might suggest.

Entirely of his age were the plays of LUIGI PIRANDELLO (1867–1936), who as short-story writer and novelist was a naturalist of the school of Verga, but whose dramas, written in his later life, were inspired by the metaphysical arguments current among contemporary philosophers. His most celebrated piece *Enrico IV* (*Henry IV*) concerns a man who having suffered from a lapse of memory prefers to behave as if he persisted in his belief that he is, in fact, the emperor whom he had been representing in a pageant at the time of his accident. Pirandello is not here concerned with the nature of reality, but with the struggle between one person's beliefs and another's. Most of his plays in fact revolve around the clash between different versions of the truth. Whose is right? Again, each person believes himself to be a unity, and is in fact a group of different personalities who emerge and retire in turn. A character is 'naked', in the play of that name, and so attempts to clothe herself with a romantic personality. When she fails she takes poison. Some of his plots seem impossibly complicated, yet in the acting they work out clearly. For Pirandello was no more bound by his philosophy than was Shaw by the social opinions that he was ostensibly discussing. Both were primarily writers for the theatre, and both succeeded in making the ideas they played with live. Pirandello wrote a considerable number of plays, which have been unduly neglected outside Italy.

A French dramatist who played with other ideas current at the time, was H. R. LENORMAND (1882–1951), who made melodramatic use of Freud's theories in several powerful but episodic plays. GABRIEL MARCEL (b. 1889) likewise adapts the existentialists' theory of perpetual crisis to the service of his psychological dramas.

The chief tendencies in the French drama of the last forty years, however, have been ironical, and there have been a succession of Greek plays in modern dress, which began with the very accomplished drama of JEAN GIRAUDOUX (1882–1944), and have been continued by JEAN ANOUILH (b. 1910). Symbolism in a diluted form has now become a box office draw. The level of technical production in the Paris theatre has become so high that the dramatist is asked for little more than a libretto to be scored by actor and producer. The drama of the uncompromising Paul Claudel has consequently been eclipsed, since his masterpiece *Le Soulier de satin* (*The Satin Slipper*), a play with a double action and much serious argument of a Shavian kind, has too rare an appeal, while his *L'Annonce faite à Marie* (*The Tidings Brought to Mary*), despite the slow-moving, tapestry-like beauty of its scenes, is too quiet and simple in its unquestioning faith, to suit a theatre in which sophistication counts for everything, sincerity for nothing. Claudel's remoteness contrasts strongly with the passionate *engagement* of JEAN-PAUL SARTRE (b. 1905), a first-class man of the theatre whose ambition it is to be taken for a philosopher. His retreatment of the Orestes theme in *Les Mouches* (*The Flies*), and his evocation of a private hell in *Huis-clos* (*Vicious Circle*) are true reflexions of the horrors of the German occupation, while his less succesful *Le Diable et le bon Dieu* (*Lucifer and the Lord*) is as full of good argument as the best of Shaw.

If French drama has developed along slick lines that divorce it from the main literary tradition, German expressionism of the years immediately following the defeat of 1918 also explored, though more amateurishly, similar blind alleys of rhetoric and subservience to stagecraft. The revulsion that followed the Kaiser's overthrow was reflected in the theatre by the Expressionism of GEORG KAISER (1878–1945), of ERNST TOLLER (1893–1939), of FRITZ VON UNRUH (b. 1885), and of FRANZ WERFEL (1890–1945). With a violence that showed their kinship with the *Sturm und Drang* generation, they wrote plays in which characterization was entirely sacrificed, and the actors were no more than voices urging the needs, the sorrows, and the desires of generalized man. Reacting too quickly to the lost war and the disorder that followed it, these dramatists confused shrill rhetoric with poetry, and crude sentiment with argument. Their plays, though purporting to be of no time or place, were by their manner firmly anchored down to the year 1919. Expressionist technique was used with greater mastery by the Czech dramatist KAREL ČAPEK (1890–1938) in his fantasies of the machine world, which in due course influenced both the commercial theatre and the cinema. In its origins a poetic protest against mechanization and the decline in freedom that preluded the First War, Expressionism became politically involved with socialism and pacifism and, in its last stages, with Nazism, to which some of its less distinguished followers subscribed.

The German drama of the brief Weimar prosperity that followed was for the most part conventional, with a leaning towards historical pageantry. Werfel's intelligent *Paulus unter den Juden* (*Paul among the Jews*), with its examination of the first impact of Christianity, and Carl Zuckmayer's entertaining satire *Der Hauptmann von Koepenick* (*The Captain of Koepenick*) suggest the lines to which German drama was returning at the time of the Nazis' seizure of power.

BERT BRECHT (1898-1956), beginning as an expressionist, remained consistently experimental throughout his exile in Russia and his post-war residence in Eastern Germany. A universal adaptor, he produced little of great originality.

The history of the drama in the last thirty years has been one of an increasingly proficient commercial theatre, exploiting such *avant-garde* ideas as seemed fruitful, and either driving out the man of letters or teaching him, as broadcasting has also done, to write the plays that the public will accept. There is at the present moment no literary drama that is in advance of the common stage productions in London, Paris, Rome and New York. On the other hand the commercial theatre is employing finer talents and calling for greater ingenuity than in the years that followed the first War.

Chapter Seventeen

THE NOVEL LOSES FOCUS, AND
A HOPE FOR POETRY

ALREADY when the novel was still in its prime, in the seventies and eighties of the last century, the philosophical basis on which it rested as an art form was beginning to shift. Poetry was already beginning to choose its imagery not from natural observation, but from symbols belonging rather to the world of dream than to waking life. Drama too was coming to concern itself rather with hidden motives and significances than with the clash of character and the case of conscience. Man was beginning to lose belief in himself as a single unified character whose life was a battle-ground between the forces of good and evil, and whose destiny was to be decided by his actions alone. The stresses of society, the mechanical struggle to survive, the unconscious life with its profound influence on man's thoughts and actions; all began to demand a greater part of the novelist's attention, to deflect him from the drama of persons and their relationship, and to drive him towards speculation or impressionism, towards the construction of social theories, or towards an illogical and semi-poetical pre-occupation with the character's quite arbitrary 'stream of thoughts'. The novelist could no longer tell a plain tale; and the didactic German influence of *Wilhelm Meister* on the one side and the lyrical *Novelle* on the other began to predominate over the sound example of the French and the Russians.

The first major thinker to shake the West's belief in individual destiny was the philosopher ARTHUR SCHOPEN-HAUER (1788–1860), whose philosophy was strongly influenced by Eastern thought, and began to exert its influence about the middle of the century. Schopenhauer was a pessimist, who saw will as the motive force of the whole Universe, and who, following the Hindu point of view, proclaimed it wicked. His impact came at a moment when the advance guard of Western thought had begun to see that material progress and Rousseau-ish freedom were leading forward to no golden age. The artists in particular, whose hopes had until the failure of the 1848 Revolution been on the side of the progressives, had now retreated into opposition to bourgeois and aristocrat alike, proclaiming with increasing conviction through mouths such as Baudelaire's and Rimbaud's that they alone were the seers or mages, capable of changing the Universe – momentarily and for an aesthetic élite – by a deliberate confusion of the auditory, the visual, and the tactile, which would lead to a new quasi-mystical vision, also by dandyism, satanism, and other forms of radical detachment from the aims and interests of society in general. From 1880 onwards, indeed, the artist became a self-appointed outlaw, and his art a more and more hermetic practice, performed as a ritual for the few.

But not all artists were content thus to renounce responsibility and range like bandits on the frontiers of society. FRIEDRICH NIETZSCHE (1844–1900), in the first place a lyrical poet of great power, attempted by a philosophy which derived primarily from Schopenhauer's to offer the West a new vision. Reacting violently against the vulgarity of the new Prussia that had emerged from the war of 1870–1 – which was only a more blatant version of the materialistic vulgarity which was mastering all Europe and North America – Nietzsche called for an entirely new form of civilization, to be based on the emergence of the Superman. He rejected Christianity, and the limited Western view of History. He saw the events of man's life endlessly repeating themselves according to a recurrent pattern, and that there was no way out except by the creation of new men who would transcend the old even as modern man has transcended the apes. But Nietzsche's new theory of evolution swept aside the idea of automatic or even of planned change; this was no survival of the fittest, but self-creation by the ablest.

To the Darwinian nineteenth century, Nietzsche appeared not so much revolutionary as violent and insane. As they were able to ignore Ibsen's message by treating him as a mere social reformer, so it was possible for them to resist the impact of Nietzsche's thought by treating him as yet another poet in rebellion. In fact, however, Nietzsche was not so much a rebel as one who had seen through the facile belief in progress and preached a return to older ways of thought. To those familiar – as the nineteenth century, as a whole, was not – with the pre-Socratic philosophers, with the Platonic myths, the *Vedas* and the *Upanishads*, the ideas expressed in Nietzsche's master-piece *Also sprach Zarathustra* (*Thus spake Zarathustra*), though uncoordinated, would not have seemed strange. His philo-sophy, based on poetic insight rather than on any logical system, hints at much but expresses little in concrete form.

From 1890 onwards Nietzsche's influence was great, not so much on account of his cosmological ideas as for the im-portance which he attributed to intuition rather than intellect. The idea of man's transformation into Superman, parallel as it is to that of repentance or *metanoia* in the New Testament, was misunderstood. But his picture, incarnated in his own person, of the artist and philosopher in one, set a new ideal over and against that of the artist as outlaw, even if the artists of the next decades approximated rather to the model of Rimbaud than to Nietzsche's Zarathustra. Nietzsche's detractors how-ever – and his very difficult character earned him many – presented him as the advocate of violence and the remorseless enemy of the bourgeois world and its morals; which was but half the picture, though one very welcome to the *fin de siècle* artist, who adopted Nietzsche, in consequence, as one of his heroes. This misrepresentation caused Nietzsche also to be accused of helping to create the Prussian mentality which launched the 1914 war, although nothing could have been farther from Nietzsche's conception of the Superman than the wooden-headed Junkers of Potsdam.

Nietzsche's disruptive influence on the nineteenth century's picture of intellectual man, the purposive master of his own fate, was reinforced by that of the philosopher HENRI BERG-SON (1859–1941), whose belief in the intuitions and whose anti-mechanism set a number of novelists the task of attempt-ing something bigger than the tracing of a handful of human destinies. They felt challenged either to show the vital energy of man (Bergson's *élan vital*) at work in an outstanding genius, incarnating forces which underlie the flux of contemporary society, or to display that society as a whole, with all its tendencies and stresses, by the analysis of a small or test group; a task which Tolstoy had performed, though without conscious intention, in *War and Peace*. Tolstoy, in fact, was the outstanding literary influence behind the *roman fleuve* – in its English form the novel of generations – with its broad picture of the family or social unit confronting history.

But at the same time as the new philosophy, with its Eastern influences and reinforced by the openly Eastern Theosophy of Madame Blavatsky, was destroying the conventional picture of purposive man, various forms of psychological investigation, which reached their peak in the work of William James, but were most influential in the extreme and anti-religious forms set out by SIGMUND FREUD (1856–1939), were destroying the picture of man as a co-ordinated character, responding intelligently and predictably to the events of life. Complete acceptance of the extreme Freudian picture would have made the novelist's task preposterous. Who could be interested in the fate of a creature so devoid of possibilities as the Freudian man, for ever pursuing the non-existent hare of all-pleasure-and-no-pain? The growth of psychological knowledge provided, in the diluted form in which it was accepted, at least one more obstacle to the telling of a plain story.

The nineteenth-century novelist had considered it his task to show his unified characters in relation to a series of happenings, conceived as beginning with their birth and ending with the selection of life-partners by at least the younger of them. This neat framework was never entirely suitable except to the minor talents of a Jane Austen or a Trollope. Social criticism in Dickens and Zola, the social and historical setting in Balzac and Galdós, the interaction of history and personal destiny in Tolstoy, a concentration on characters at their breaking-point, where they become susceptible to new influences, in Dostoyevsky: all united to strain the classical formula, and to present future novelists with a wider field to survey; to increase the difficulties of their task of imposing shape on the shapeless. And now the new philosophy and the new psychology came to make the twentieth-century novelist's task still harder – to make it so hard indeed that perhaps only Marcel Proust entirely succeeded both in drawing a new picture and in constructing for it a new frame.

The first reaction of the *fin de siècle* novelist to the new challenge was to retreat, to consider only a firmly outlined *case,* taken in isolation from society at large as Henry James took it in his last novels, and as George Moore, practising a factitious realism, and claiming absolute and scientific objectivity, did in *Esther Waters.* A writer who chose another solution, but who worked nevertheless within the *fin de siècle* limits, was ANATOLE FRANCE (1844–1924), an ironic analyst of his time in his four-volume *Histoire contemporaine* (*Contemporary History*), and the constructor of neat and stylized little mirrors held up to history at such moments as that in which the Procurator of Judaea, in old age, actually fails to remember who the man Jesus Christ was. Anatole France was a Voltairean, a scholar and a humanitarian, blind to much, as his study of Joan of Arc shows, yet with a sense of history that makes his allegory *L'Île des Pingouins* (*Penguin Island*) a neat forerunner of David Garnett and Orwell, and his *Les Dieux ont soif* (*The Gods are Athirst*) a still valid and satirical picture of the French revolution, as seen by a progressive who cannot condone violence from either party. Anatole France, in his irony, in his stylistic perfection, and in his power of evoking a highly developed or decadent past, as in *La Rôtisserie de la Reine Pédauque* (*At the Sign of the Reine Pédauque*), or *Thaïs*, the tale of an Alexandrian harlot, exerted as much influence on such conservative *fin de siècle* writers as Norman Douglas, as by his satires on a younger generation to whom the moral of *Les Dieux ont Soif* was an urgent one. He is a writer at present unduly underrated.

The two outstanding achievements in the early twentieth-century novel which had taken cognizance of the new influences, were Thomas Mann's family saga *Die Buddenbrooks,* and Romain Rolland's long story of a musical genius, *Jean Christophe.* THOMAS MANN (1875–1955) was, except for Fontane, the first important German novelist to apprentice himself to the Western school, though at the same time he was also the interpreter of the pessimistic outlook of Schopenhauer. *Die Buddenbrooks* is a study in the decay of an upper middle-class merchant family in the patrician city of Lübeck; and, as its secondary theme, it is at the same time the story of the emergence from this same family of a creative artist. For Mann, art is the end-product of decay; and decay has for him, even for its own sake, a curious fascination. One of the most telling passages of the book indeed is a description of the slow odour of corruption seeping through the perfume of the flowers that have been placed beside a corpse in order to drown it.

Thomas Mann reverts to this theme of decay in one of the most powerful of his short stories, *Der Tod in Venedig,* in which love – perverted love, it is true – decay and death result from a breakdown in the traditional morals of a middle-aged artist, who has hitherto driven himself forward under the spur of his production, but who pauses for a moment on a visit to Italy, only to let in the forces of emotion and disintegration. Mann's nose for corruption also led him to expose the sordid boastfulness of Italian fascism in *Mario und der Zauberer* (*Mario and the Magician*) at a time when the infection was about to spread to Germany. But his biggest study in decay is his *Bildungsroman, Der Zauberberg* (*The Magic Mountain*), the scene of which is a Swiss sanatorium above 'the plain' of Europe. Here, in this retreat for the sick, where life did not exert its common claims, Mann draws in little all the forces then at work on the eve of the First World War. Among the hundred or so inmates of the Berghof are voices echoing all the predominant beliefs and passions that swayed the distant inhabitants down below, and fighting for the blank soul of Hans Castorp, the book's hero, who in some sense represents Germany, pulled in all directions by conflicting claims. *Der Zauberberg* is remarkable in its creation of a society in which a pneumo-thorax operation or a fit of coughing assume the importance of a marriage or a financial success or failure at a lower altitude. Here ideas matter, even though the convinced and the unconvinced alike face the prospect of an early death by tuberculosis. It is a world in little, in which corruption extends to every part.

Der Zauberberg took Mann some long distance from the main stream of European fiction, and his later novels have diverged yet farther. In the last years he has given his own versions, at great length, of the story of Joseph, of Goethe's life at Weimar, and of the Faust legend, brought up to date, and treated from an ironical and liberal standpoint, with references, veiled or open, to the contemporary state of the world, whose fever-line he has come to follow with all the attention that Hans Castorp once gave to his. Mann is, like the inhabitants of his Berghof, an analyst of disease without standards of comparison which are independent of that disease.

ROMAIN ROLLAND (1866–1944), on the other hand, though at first primarily concerned with the artist also, was anxious to show him as the symptom rather of a potentially healthy society than of a diseased one. The disease he saw in plainly political terms as the product of national rivalry and the greed for wealth. His Jean-Christophe, therefore, for whom he took Beethoven as a model, was shown as the joint product of German and French culture, who stood above the commonplace national antipathies and pecuniary sordidnesses. But the book, though it starts off as a work of genius, deteriorates long before it reaches its tenth volume.

Rolland did not value himself as an artist, but rather as a creator of opinion. Taking a strong pacifist attitude in the First World War, he moved to Switzerland; and seeing the world's salvation in a humanitarian socialism he fought bravely for it. His biographies of great men – of Michelangelo, of Tolstoy, of Gandhi – show the generosity of his enthusiasms. But as a creator he suffers from a divided attention. As a political thinker too he was unable to concentrate on a single object, but attempted to pay a combined worship to Lenin and Gandhi. Yet in the first volumes of *Jean Christophe* he created at least one work of permanent value.

The same cannot be said of his contemporary ANDRÉ GIDE (1869–1951). A prolific writer, with a talent for striking masterly attitudes, he was consistent in nothing but his habit of semi-poetic self-dramatization. In this he followed Rousseau, though with a more consistent idea of his audience than the author of the *Confessions,* and with a vein of satanism, which he justified by reference to Nietzsche, whose authority he invokes when boasting that he was often on the devil's side. Gide's confessions, written sometimes in the guise of autobiography, sometimes as prose-poetry, sometimes in the shape of unorthodox novels, and sometimes as a journal, return repeatedly to his two main themes; the rejection of his moral Protestant upbringing, and the vaunting of homosexuality. Gide likes to play with philosophical ideas. His most moving novel, *La Porte étroite* (*Strait is the Gate*) tells of a girl who sacrifices her love to principles, and his most entertaining book, *Les Caves du Vatican* (*The Vatican Cellars*), revolves around the performance of '*l'acte gratuite*' (the unmotivated act), which is in this case the pushing of an innocent imbecile out of a moving train. This book is entertaining in the same amoral way as *South Wind*. But Gide's more serious novel, *Les Faux-monnayeurs* (*The Coiners*), is marred by tricks which pass unnoticed in his works of lighter weight. The author spoilt this book, which might have been his masterpiece, by pushing himself continually into the foreground, as an author writing a novel: and not content with this, he followed *Les Faux-monnayeurs* up with a *Journal*, which was a commentary on its writing. But worse than Gide's perpetual throwing of the limelight on himself, is his rejoicing in petty nastiness. His characters are almost all unpleasant, and the author's prizes seem to be offered only for bad conduct. *Immorals* are rated above decent behaviour, and this without any breath of satire, but with semi-philosophical self-justification, based on the rejection of old conventions in favour of something worse.

MARCEL PROUST (1871–1922) anatomizes an ugly society from which he does not stand any more detached than Gide. Yet there is sufficient satire in his drawing of the unpleasant Baron de Charlus to show that the author, though sharing the Baron's vices, is far from identifying himself with his creature. Proust was the author of a single novel, which is both a study of an aristocratic society in decay and an analysis of subjectivity. The principal character of *A la recherche du temps perdu* (*In Search of Lost Time*) – that Marcel who both is and is not the author himself – goes through a vast cycle of memory, wafted back by a chance smell to a moment in his boyhood,

and returning at the end of the thirteenth volume to the point
where he had begun.

Time, love, jealousy, memory; all are shown as constituents
of a mind closed in on itself, but capable of breaking through
to momentary freedom in the act of creation. Proust gives
back the whole of his vast departed world – seen across the
gulf of more than twenty years which have culminated in the
War – complete with its ambitions and snobberies, its pathos
and buffoonery, in the same way as Rilke in the same years
was transforming the common objects of this world for the
benefit of his angelic spectators. Both wished to perpetuate,
by a single act of memory, patterns and relationships which
dissolved even as they were thought of. The vision to which
each aspired was one that, like the scene on Keats' Grecian
urn, would remain in arrested movement.

Proust's principle theme is love; and since his own loves
were perverted and unhappy, the theme of doubt and jealousy
is indissolubly united with it. For him love is a kind of disease, kept alive by self-torture. His characters in love are,
consequently, shown as self-absorbed: and, like Thomas
Mann, Proust is for ever attracted by the odour of decay. The
same pattern seems endlessly to repeat itself in his vast novel,
Swann's love for Odette adumbrating a theme that is afterwards recapitulated and expanded into 'Marcel's' obsession
with Albertine. The loved one has, particularly in the second
case, little objective reality; she is no more than an enigmatic
irritant.

But love is not the sole theme of the novel. Almost as
large, and particularly in the central volumes, bulks the social
comedy, with its panorama of aristocrats and climbers, each
carefully assigned to his or her exact place in the hierarchy of
precedence, also the artists and hangers-on shown in their
relationship to the princely Guermantes family. This aspect
of Proust's work is, however, no more than a subtler repetition of something already achieved by Thackeray in *Vanity
Fair*. It is the fourth dimension of Time and Memory which
acts like Tolstoy's added dimension of History, to give the
book – despite its odour of corruption – a depth possessed
by no other twentieth-century novel.

Treatments of large numbers of characters, seen in their social connexion rather than in their private lives, were attempted by JULES ROMAINS (b. 1885) in the many volumes of *Les Hommes de bonne volonté* (*The Men of Good Will*), by GEORGES DUHAMEL (b. 1884), in *La Chronique des Pasquier* (*The Pasquier Chronicle*), by ROGER MARTIN DU GARD (b. 1881), in *Les Thibault* (*The Thibaults*), and, more economically, by JEAN-RICHARD BLOCH (1884–1947) in his story of an Alsatian Jewish family, *Et Cie* (*And Co.*). But it is doubtful whether any of these panoramic novels of the years between the wars has great powers of survival. As social analysis, they are interesting, but they lack that additional dimension that makes *War and Peace* and *À la recherche du temps perdu* something more than analyses of an epoch. Romains' broad humanitarianism, Duhamel's subtler and more ironic sense of participation, the disillusioned naturalism of Roger Martin du Gard, and the more hopeful naturalism of Bloch are alike insufficient to carry these vast structures.

More confident of survival are FRANÇOIS MAURIAC's (b. 1885) studies in sin and guilt, which are confined to as small a canvas as those of Ivy Compton Burnett, but which are closer to life, at least as it is lived in the deep South-West of Catholic France. Mauriac's best studies are those early ones written before his conversion to Catholicism. Where most of the other important French writers of the years between the wars take the broad romantic licence of a Balzac, Mauriac reverts to the close classicism of Mme de Lafayette or Constant, and studies a single case. Severely classical also are the two novels of RAYMOND RADIGUET (1903–23), a precocious young man, whose study of adolescent sex and whose retreatment of the theme of *La Princesse de Clèves* have a brilliance and economy, remarkable – despite his youth – for their achievement rather than for their promise. Yet one is left with no feeling that here, had he but lived, was the missing great novelist of the generation after Proust. ANDRÉ MALRAUX (b. 1901), on the other hand, in his single masterpiece *La Condition humaine* (*Storm over Shanghai*) presents a picture of revolution, melodramatic and at the same time acute in its character drawing, which seems to promise major achievement. Malraux has, however, been deflected into politics and art-criticism, and has produced no successor to this singularly spare and moving novel.

Theoretical interests, the illusions of political activity, and the German habit of pseudo-philosophical digression have bedevilled the post-war French novel in France. JEAN-PAUL SARTRE, a master of compression in his pre-war studies in violence *La Nausée* (*Nausea*) and *Le Mur* (*The Wall*), has lately written long novels, too closely concerned with contemporary events and too shapeless to be even readable. Like Malraux, he seems to be too much caught up by action to devote his full talents to artistic creation. ALBERT CAMUS (1913-1960), on the other hand, wrote a single allegorical story of great power, *La Peste* (*The Plague*), which tells more about the atmosphere of the Occupation than a dozen documentary disquisitions. Camus also, however, indulged in deliberate studies of the revolutionary temperament, and involved himself in the politics of existentialism; a philosophical attitude rooted in violence and disillusion, which has presented no writer with any valid criterion by which to measure the disorder of his age. To write as an existentialist is to describe chaos in terms of chaos.

In the Central European breakdown which preceded the overthrow of France by twenty years, the pessimism of defeat was best expressed by an Austrian novelist whose influence has counted for much in the early history of existentialism. FRANZ KAFKA (1883-1924), in his two great but unfinished works *Der Prozess* (*The Trial*) and *Das Schloss* (*The Castle*) defined the situation of the solitary man for whom life was a bad dream, full of baleful significances. Both are expanded nightmares, influenced, perhaps, by the theories of Sigmund Freud, but true to the experience of this bewildered man, hemmed in by his own fears, by disease, and by the lack of any belief that the powers by which the world is governed were anything but hostile. Viewed apart, Kafka has great strength, and succeeds in convincing his reader that his symbols stand for something more than his own fears. Compared with Dostoyevsky, however, his seems a very partial view of man's spiritual world, one that stops short at the boundaries of hell, but gives no glimpse of higher possibilities.

The German novel scored some great successes between the wars. But it is doubtful whether many of the best-sellers of that day are still readable. Of the war books, ARNOLD ZWEIG's (b. 1887) *Der Streit um den Sergeanten Grischa* (*The Case of Sergeant Grischa*) which shows one man overwhelmed by the impersonal forces of a society made up of men who, individually, pity him, owes something to the Russian novelists, but retains a quality of its own, which is absent from such straight war reporting as ERICH REMARQUE's (b. 1898) *Im Westen nichts Neues* (*All Quiet on the Western Front*). HERMANN HESSE (1877-1962), who began with a strong lyrical strain relating him to the nineteenth-century Romantics of Southern Germany, moved steadily in a philosophical direction, to conclude with a large symbolic novel, *Das Glasperlenspiel* (*Magister Ludi*). But it is probably by his early semi-autobiographical novels that he will be remembered. Hesse, like many of his generation, passed under a succession of philosophical influences, and was probably happier in his Hindu legend, *Siddharta*, than as an exponent of Freudianism in *Der Steppenwolf* (*The Wolf of the Steppes.*) A curious novel of the thirties, *Der Mann ohne Eigenschaften* (*The Man without Qualities*) by ROBERT MUSIL (1880-1942) attempts to do for late Habsburg Vienna what Proust did for his aristocratic quarter of Paris. Musil shows a large number of characters brought together by a fatuous scheme for collecting money to erect a statue, and sets them moving, one with the other, in very slow motion.

Other curiosities of the period between the two wars are the light-hearted satire, also of the Austrian régime, by the Czech, JAROSLAV HAŠEK (1883-1923), translated as *The Good Soldier Schweik*. Schweik, the inimitable scrounger and dodger, manages to survive the fall of an Empire, whose last years are also reflected in the novels of ITALO SVEVO (1861-1928), a Trieste business man who wrote, in Italian, sad, garrulous comedies of fatuity, which won him the friendship and advocacy of James Joyce.

A very interesting figure who made no great mark during

the inter-war years, but who now seems likely to be better appreciated, is WERNER BERGENGRUEN (b. 1892), a novelist of great integrity, who works within the German tradition, and is to some extent a disciple of the Swiss historical novelist, C. F. Meyer. But Bergengruen stands in a far closer relationship to his material. For him history is not dead, or reflected in a distant mirror. His *Der Grosstyrann und das Gericht* (*A Matter of Conscience*) and *Am Himmel wie auf Erden* (*In Heaven as on Earth*) are remarkable for the close parallels that are implicit between the age in which they pass and that in which they were written. Perhaps this was a necessary device for a writer working under the Nazi régime. But its results do not appear to be contrived; and the Wendish country, awaiting its prophesied flood in *Am Himmel wie auf Erden,* and the Italian city of *Der Grosstyrann,* fanned by its unhealthy wind, have the immediacy of Camus's city beneath the plague, or of a Kafka nightmare. A Catholic by conversion, Bergengruen possesses a profound sense of history, and of the way in which events and atmospheres may be distant in time but parallel in spirit. His is a far deeper understanding of the Nietzschean philosophy than Gide's immoralism or Thomas Mann's preoccupation with the death of society. For Bergengruen's values are positive, where those of his contemporaries are for the most part negative.

Russian novels after Chehov's death follow the same line of decay as the Russian drama. IVAN BUNIN (1870–1953) wrote impressionistic stories, pessimistic in tone, delicately nostalgic in style and usually sensual in content: while IVAN KUPRIN (1870–1938), a more robust realist, scored his only considerable success with *The Duel*, which showed up the conventions of a Tsarist officer's life. Fëdor Sologub, besides some symbolist poetry and a metaphysical trilogy, wrote a satirical novel, translated under the misleading title of *The Little Demon*, about a schoolmaster in a small town, which is entertainingly destructive, a tale about poltergeists whose author seems to be by a member of the fraternity; and, last of the emigrants, of whom only Kuprin returned to Russia, ALEXEI REMIZOV (b. 1877) is a writer with a great power of language in the descent from Gogol and the folk-tale.

The biggest figure in the transition from Tsarism to social-ism was MAXIM GORKY (1868–1936), a poor man's son who made his way by literature, and finally threw his weight behind the Soviet government in 1928. Gorky's autobiographical trilogy contains his best writing. His novels are too often shrill and propagandist. One alone, *The Artamonov Business* is an objective study of the rise and decay of a middle-class family, and their weaving business. Gorky had experience of working for just such people, was familiar with their violences, their fundamental shiftlessness, and their good humour. In this novel he sees them across the divide of the Revolution with-out rancour, and shows how from their loins sprang the generation of students who formed the first core of the Bolshevik party.

Gorky's social realism was not the only medium favoured by the artistic generation which accepted Lenin. It was, how-ever, the one supported by the country's new rulers, and other kinds did not long survive the liberalism of the New Economic Policy. Of the writers of that brief heyday, BORIS PILNIAK (b. 1894), a fellow traveller, who greeted the revolution, much as the poet Pasternak did, as an elemental event, atoned for his lack of political conviction with a novel of the five-year-plan, *The Volga flows into the Caspian Sea*. But though this book fulfilled the claims both of politics and art, he has long since lapsed into a discouraged silence. LEONID LEONOV (b. 1899), author of the Dostoyevskyan *Death of a Little Man* and the comical New-Yorker-like satirist MIKHAIL ZOSHCHENKO (b. 1895) have also failed, despite efforts, to make any pos-sible compromise with the party's directive, which has in-sisted on forms of naturalism and historical fiction suitable to a public without humanistic education, and without interest in problems of conscience, consciousness, or meta-physics. The resulting production, if sometimes competent, has been perforce on a low artistic level, interesting only for its descriptions of a different world and different ideals from those of the West.

The immediate post-war period in Italy saw a quick

flowering of realistic writing, which synchronized with a parallel development in the cinema. Fascism had not on the whole interfered with artistic production. Nevertheless with its fall, and with the disaster of the lost war in which it had involved its country, the arts received a much-needed fillip; and Italian fiction of the last dozen years is remarkable for its variety, extending from *Il Molino del Po* (*The Mill on the Po*), a historical trilogy by RICCARDO BACCHELLI (b. 1891), which recalls Manzoni, to the brilliant and humane writing of CARLO LEVI (b. 1902), the short, bitter, and poetical novels of the unhappy CESARE PAVESE (1908–50), and the shapely tales of GUIDO PIOVENE (b. 1907), with their echoes of the eighteenth century.

Spain has produced little fiction of importance since the death of Pérez Galdós. A single modern writer, CAMILO JOSÉ CELA (b. 1916), has drawn a grim and disgusted picture of squalor in the country and in the Capital in *La Familia de Pascual Duarte* (*The Family of Pascual Duarte*) and *La Colmena* (*The Hive*). Cela is a master of sordid dialogue, and a writer without a viewpoint, who nevertheless stands out from a generation of charming lady-novelists, who run away with the annual prizes. Several recent novels, all containing veiled social criticism, have lately broken the conventions imposed by the Spanish censorship, which suppressed Cela's two works. Of these the best is *El Jarama* (tr. as *The One Day of the Week*) by RAFAEL SÁNCHEZ FERLOSIO (b. 1927), the account of a long summer Sunday punctuated by a single tragic moment.

The novel has died a victim to the loss of an agreed picture of the Universe, which has faded with the stifling of Christianity by non-dogmatic idealism and crude materialism.

However, the novel is only the youngest of artistic forms, and it is easy to imagine that even its commercial varieties may decay in the next fifty years, destroyed by the competition of television and the televised film. The drama, too, unless it finds its way back to an alliance with poetry and with philosophical ideas – unless it lends itself once more, as in Greece, as in the miracle plays, and as in the Spanish *autos*, to a religious purpose – may yield to more popular mass-produced types of entertainment. Poetry, however, which demands repeated readings and a recollected state of mind before it can deliver its message, must, like music, and like painting, survive in its present forms if it is to survive at all. A reading over the air can do no more than stimulate the desire to possess the printed page.

In poetry, therefore, remains the hope for literature's survival; and since poetry is at present only read by small numbers, it may well remain for some time, as it now is, private in its form and language. *Avant-garde* poetry, however, with its deliberate defiances of the philistine, its unrelated images, its neglect of syntax, and of the rules of typography, probably shot its bolt between the wars. It is plainly absurd for the poet to challenge a society which does not read him rather than accommodate himself to the few who may; and poetry since Baudelaire has clearly failed to increase its readership by provocative methods. That there is some new poetry, concerned on the whole with the serious subject of man's isolation, with his need of a myth by which to understand the Universe, and of some willed change in his own states of mind, is the most hopeful sign at this mid-century. In England there are T. S. Eliot, Robert Graves and a group of younger men who write chiefly on intimate themes; in France there is little that is not obscure and overhung with the last fumes of Surrealism; in Germany the endeavour is to make good the last years of Nazidom and absorb the influences then forbidden; in Spain, however, there is a new beginning with such young men as BLAS de OTERO (b. 1916), JOSÉ HIERRO (b. 1922), CARLOS BOUSOÑO (b. 1923), and JOSÉ ÁNGEL VALENTE (b. 1929) who, despite the rigidity of Franco's censorship, have written poetry of genuine simplicity, deep feeling, and great promise; and in Spanish America not only such poets in exile as Rafael Alberti, but a number of national poets whose work is beginning to show some independence of the European models which American poetry has followed since the days of Rubén Dario.

Whether the poetry of PABLO NERUDA (b. 1904) in Chile, of RICARDO MOLINARI (b. 1898) in Argentina, of CÉSAR VALLEJO (1895–1937) in Peru, of RAMÓN LÓPEZ VELARDE (1881–1921), CARLOS PELLICER (b. 1899) and OCTAVIO PAZ (b. 1914) in Mexico represents the beginnings of something new, or the end-product of European symbolism and naturalism, it is still too early to say. Fiction in Spanish America follows European models, and is remarkable for its social realism, for its portrayal, that is, of life in backward communities and under stresses and clashes of tradition unknown on this side of the Atlantic. But poetry there seems to have returned to elemental subjects, to man's isolation in a hostile world, to the cruelty and garish beauty of nature, and to the melancholy of the Indian clinging to his old way of life, but exploited by his would-be civilizers.

There is little public for this poetry in the South American republics themselves, and no great attention is paid to it abroad. The majority of the poets would appear to adhere only loosely if at all to the Christian faith, but to be strongly attached to the literary tradition of Europe. Whether any new myth will arise in Spanish America – or elsewhere – is the great question, which will decide more than the future of literature. For poetry in the service only of a tiny cultured minority will be as incapable of real achievement as poetry hamstrung by its subservience to a political creed or to the compulsive advocacy of a *way of life*. Poetry and the drama, if they are to be reborn, must express a belief which is shared by the community, as they did for the Greeks, for the Christians of the Middle Ages and even of the Counter-Reformation, and as since the Romantic era they have progressively ceased to do. Imaginative literature in the service of rebellion, or satanism, quickly sinks into exhibitionism or obscurity. Imaginative literature as the expression of a deeply apprehended truth, poetry which interprets to a man the myth of his own age, can in the hands of Dante, of Shakespeare, of Cervantes, of Camões and of Goethe, help to raise the level of a whole civilization.

A NOTE ON TRANSLATIONS

FEW readers who wish to explore the whole territory of Western literature are likely to be equally at home in all the main languages. Everyone must approach some works in translation. It is useful, therefore, to offer a few notes, and make some recommendations for the benefit of those who are going to read the great works in English.

The ideal form of an English version is, to my mind, that of the Loeb Classics, or of the Penguin Books of Verse in various languages, now in course of publication. Here the original is set face-to-face with, or immediately above, the translation. The reader can then follow the work in its writer's language, but help himself out every now and then by recourse to the translator, whose unobtrusive duty then is to present the most literal paraphrase possible. He is there merely to perform the office of a prompter, and supply the missing word. Two or three generations must have read Dante in this way, with the aid of Thomas Okey and Philip Wicksteed, whose names do not even occur on the title page of the Temple Classics edition for which they were responsible. Thanks to them, however, anyone with adequate Latin or French, and sufficient Italian to pronounce the words and recognize the verb-forms, can get nearer to Dante than those who meet him in the equally current Cary translation of the *Commedia*, in cold blank verse, which Coleridge admired. Latterly two new versions have appeared in the original metres, of which Laurence Binyon's (Macmillan) – from which I have taken my quotations – is slightly preferable, for its greater mastery of poetic phrase and its subtler rhythms, to that of Dorothy Sayers (Penguin).

Other great poets have been less fortunate than Dante. C. K. Scott Moncrieff's *Chanson de Roland* is a good modern version, slightly marred by deliberate archaisms. But there is no adequate presentation of the *Cantar del Cid* and the *Nibelungenlied* is still no better represented than in the pre-Raphaelite prose of Margaret Armour (Everyman). Some of the Arthurian romances, and the sagas of Burnt Njal and Grettir, also appear in Everyman, rendered into prose that echoes that of William Morris.

The Renaissance poets were well served by their early translators; both Sir John Harington's Ariosto, of 1591, and Edward Fairfax's Tasso (1600) are readable to the end, though – as Professor C. S. Lewis has pointed out – the *Furioso* is not quite so like *Don Juan* as it appears to be in Harington. Camões, on the other hand, has had to wait until recent times for an adequate poetic version – that of the American scholar, Leonard Bacon. There is an edition of the Portuguese, with English octaves by J. J. Aubertin on the opposite pages, which appeared in 1878 and is hard to find. Failing one of these, the *Lusiads* are easily available in Professor Atkinson's prose Penguin. The Renaissance epic, however, like the contemporary *Faery Queen*, loses almost all its quality when pared down to a skeleton of bare prose.

The same is necessarily true of writing in such highly condensed styles as those of Racine or the Spanish dramatists. Here again, practically no translations exist. Goethe's *Faust*, on the other hand, appears in many forms, most of which capture at least some of the poem's original virtue. Philip Wayne's Penguin of Part One, and Louis McNeice's freer abridged version of the whole (Faber and Faber) are preferable to the complete rendering into Victorian poetic cliché by Bayard Taylor.

Lyrical poetry can be sampled in the Penguin anthologies, and in such collections of pieces by various hands as Sir Maurice Bowra's two books of Russian Verse (Macmillan), and Eleanor Turnbull's *Ten Centuries of Spanish Verse* (Johns Hopkins), which contains Aubrey Bell's Luis de León, and Professor Wilson's amazing recreation of Góngora's *Soledades* (though in excerpts only). Complete successes like these are necessarily rare, but are often to be found on the odd pages of accepted poets, major and minor. Shelley's adaptations of Calderón and Goethe, James Thomson's Heine, Longfellow's excellent version of Manrique's *Coplas* and other Spanish poems, and a few fine renderings by J. E. Flecker are remarkable among these. Valuable too is Stephen Spender's Lorca (Hogarth Press), done in collaboration with J. L. Gili, though this could with advantage be reprinted face to face with the Spanish, and his Rilke elegies – printed in both languages – in which he worked with J. B. Leishman. The best Rilke translations, however, are those of Ruth Speirs, which are to be found in various periodicals, and have never been gathered into a book.

It may be said, as a rough rule, that no work of prose should be tackled in the original unless the reader can take it almost as fast as he would English. This is a personal statement, and no doubt provocative. I will venture another, however, and say that any translation made between Elizabeth's day and 1700 is worth reading for its own sake, even though it be sown thick with inaccuracies. Mabbe's *Celestina*, Shelton's *Don Quixote*, Urquhart's Rabelais, and Lestrange's Quevedo – even Florio's verbose

Montaigne – convey a quality that later and more accurate translations fail to capture. Not only was English then a richer language, but its syntactical possibilities were far less restricted. But readers without first-class knowledge of foreign languages will inevitably get far more pleasure even from impoverished Victorian English than from ploughing through Rousseau or Goethe, let alone Ibsen or Dostoyevsky in the original. The more up-to-date and colloquial translations that are now appearing, however, are infinitely preferable to these. Indeed David Magarshack's Dostoyevsky (Penguin), Kathleen Raine's Balzac (Hamish Hamilton and John Lehmann), C. K. Scott Moncrieff's Stendhal and Proust (Chatto and Windus), and Una Ellis Fermor's Ibsen (Penguin) are, each in their way, as good as translations can be. They may be, as George Borrow said, at best an echo. But the echo of thunder is an impressive sound.

J . M . C .

LIST OF DATES

	CONTINENTAL EUROPE	ENGLAND
c.1100	*Le Chanson de Roland*	
1127	Death of the Troubadour, William of Poitiers	
c.1140	*El Cantar de mió Cid*	
1154	The drama of *Adam*	
1154		*Anglo-Saxon Chronicle* (final version)
1159	First dated Fabliau	
c.1165	Chrétien de Troyes' *Erec*	
bef.1189	Marie de France's *Lais*	
c.1190	Death of Chrétien de Troyes	
c.1196	Death of Bertran de Born	
c.1200	*Le Roman de Renard* (first version)	
	Nibelungenlied (existing late version)	
	Béroul's *Tristam*	
c.1210	*Aucassin et Nicolette*	
	Wolfram's *Parzival* and Gottfried von Strassburg's *Tristan*	
1213	Defeat of the Albigenses	
1215	Death of Hartmann von Aue	
1219 or 20	Death of Conon de Béthune	
1230	Death of Walther von der Vogelweide	

c.1235	Guillaume de Lorris begins *Le Roman de la Rose*	
c.1240	Death of Jacopo da Lentini	
1241	Death of Snorri Sturluson, writer of the prose *Edda*	
1253	Death of Thibaut de Champagne	
1276	Death of Guido Guinizelli	
c.1280	Completion of *Le Roman de la Rose* by Jean de Meun	
c.1284	Rutebeuf's *Miracle de Théophile*	
1300	Death of Guido Cavalcanti	
1306	Death of Jacopone da Todi	
1307–10	Dante's *Commedia* begun	
1325	Death of King Dinis of Portugal	
1327	Death of Meister Eckhart	
1340	Juan Manuel's *El Conde Lucanor*	
1346	Tauler active till this year	
c.1350	Death of Juan Ruiz	York cycle of miracle-plays
1348–53	Boccaccio's *Decameron*	
1354 or after		*Sir Gawain and the Green Knight*
1374	Death of Petrarch	
1375	Death of Boccaccio	
1377		Principal version of Langland's *Piers Plowman*
1381	Death of Jan van Ruysbroeck	

LIST OF DATES

	CONTINENTAL EUROPE	ENGLAND
1384		Wycliffe Bible
1396		Death of Walter Hilton
c.1400	Froissart's Chronicles completed	
1400		Death of Chaucer, leaving *Canterbury Tales* unfinished
1430–65	Charles d' Orléans writes his *Ballades*	
1454–5	Gutenburg and Schoeffer's printing press established at Mainz	
1461	*Le Testament* of François Villon	
1464	*Maître Pierre Pathelin*	
1474	Accademia Platonica founded at Florence	
1479	Death of Jorge Manrique	
1480	Poliziano's *Orfeo* produced	
1485		Caxton publishes Malory's *Morte d' Arthur*
1489–98	Memoirs of Philippe de Commynes	
1492	Death of Lorenzo de Medici	
1494	Death of Boiardo	
	Brant's *Ship of Fools*	
1499	First version of *La Celestina*	
c.1500	First version of *Till Eulenspiegel*	

1501	Publication of Sannazaro's *Arcadia*
1511	Gil Vicente's *Autos of the Four Seasons*
1513	Machiavelli writes *The Prince* and (?) *La Mandragola*
1516	Ariosto's *Orlando Furioso*; More's *Utopia* Latin text
1522	Luther's New Testament
1528	Publication of Castiglione's *Book of the Courtier*
1532	Rabelais's *Pantagruel*
1533–4	Marot in his prime
1543	Posthumous publication of Garcilaso's poetry
1544	Scève's *Délie*
1552–3	Ronsard's first *Amours*
1553	Death of Rabelais
1554	*Lazarillo de Tormes*
1558	Du Bellay's *Antiquités de Rome* and *Les Regrets*
1559	Poems by Wyatt and Surrey published in Tottel's Miscellany
1561	The tragedy of *Gorboduc*
1569	The first part of Ercilla's *Araucana*
1570	Camões's *Lusiads*
1575	Tasso's *Gerusalemme liberata*
1576	Death of Hans Sachs
1580	First two books of Montaigne's *Essays*
1579–83	Saint John of the Cross's *Dark Night of the Soul*

LIST OF DATES

	CONTINENTAL EUROPE	ENGLAND
1582	Death of Santa Teresa	
1585	Death of Ronsard	
1588	Third book of Montaigne's *Essays*	
1590		Spenser's *Faerie Queen* Books I-III Marlowe's *Tamburlaine* part I
1591	Death of Luis de León	Posthumous publication of Sidney's *Astrophel and Stella*
1594		Shakespeare's *Richard II* performed
1597		Bacon's *Essays*
1599	First part of Alemán's *Guzmán de Alfarache*	
1602		*Hamlet* performed
1603	Quevedo's *Buscón*	
1605	First part of *Don Quixote* published	
1606		Jonson's *Volpone*
1611		Authorized Version of the Bible Shakespeare's *Tempest* performed
c.1613	Lope de Vega's *Fuenteovejuna*	
1613-14	Góngora's *Soledades*	
1622	Boehme's *De signatura rerum*	
1623	Marino's *Adone*	Webster's *Duchess of Malfi*

bef.1630	Tirso's *Burlador de Sevilla*	
1631	Posthumous publication of Luis de León's works	Death of John Donne
1635	Calderón's *La Vida es sueño* Death of Lope de Vega Académie française receives letters patent	
1636	Corneille's *Cid*	
1637	Descartes's *Discours de la méthode*	Publication of Milton's *Comus*
1654	Vondel's *Lucifer*	
c.1660	Pascal writes *Les Pensées*	
1664	La Rochefoucauld's *Maximes*	
1667		Milton's *Paradise Lost*
1668	Books I-VI of La Fontaine's *Fables*	
1669	First *Simplicissimus* of Grimmelshausen	
1674	Boileau's *Art Poétique*	
1677	Posthumous publication of Spinoza's *Ethics* Racine's *Phèdre*	
1678	Mme de Lafayette's *Princesse de Clèves*	*Pilgrim's Progress*
1681		Dryden's *Absalom and Achitophel*
1688	La Bruyère's *Caractères*	
1691	Racine's *Athalie*	
1699	Fénelon's *Télémaque*	
1700		Congreve's *Way of the World*

LIST OF DATES

	CONTINENTAL EUROPE	ENGLAND
1715	Lesage's *Gil Blas* vols I and II	
1716	Death of Leibniz	*Gulliver's Travels*
1719		*Robinson Crusoe*
1723	Metastasio's *Didone abbandonata*	
1728		Pope's *Dunciad*
1730	Marivaux's *Jeu de l'amour et du hasard*	
1731	Prévost's *Manon Lescaut*	
1740		Richardson's *Pamela*
1748	Montesquieu's *Esprit des Lois* Klopstock's *Messias* Cantos I-III	
1749		Fielding's *Tom Jones*
1751	First part of *L' Encyclopédie*	
1753	Goldoni's *La Locandiera*	
1758		Swedenborg's *Heaven and Hell* published in London
1759		Sterne's *Tristram Shandy* part I
1764–70	Rousseau's *Confessions*	
1766		Goldsmith's *Vicar of Wakefield*
1767	Lessing's *Minna von Barnhelm*	
1774	Goethe's *Werther*	

1775	Beaumarchais's *Barbier de Seville*	
1781	Kant's *Critique of Pure Reason*	
1786		Burns's first poems
1787	Bernardin de Saint-Pierre's *Paul et Virginie* Schiller's *Don Carlos*	
1789		Blake's *Songs of Innocence*
1790	Goethe's *Faust* part I	
1791		Boswell's *Life of Johnson*
1798		*The Lyrical Ballads* (Wordsworth and Coleridge)
1800	Novalis's *Hymnen an die Nacht*	
1802	Chateaubriand's *Génie du Christianisme*	
1811	Kleist's *Zerbrochene Krug* and death	
1812	Grimm's *Fairy Tales*	
1813		Scott's *Waverley* and Jane Austen's *Pride and Prejudice*
1819	Posthumous publication of André Chénier's poetry	
1820	Lamartine's *Méditations*	Shelley's *Prometheus Unbound* *Essays of Elia*
1823		
1826	Hölderlin's poems De Vigny's *Poèmes antiques et modernes*	
1827	Heine's *Buch der Lieder* Hugo's *Cromwell* and preface	

LIST OF DATES

	CONTINENTAL EUROPE	ENGLAND
1827	Manzoni's *I Promessi Sposi*	
1831	Leopardi's *Canti*	
1835	Pushkin's incomplete *Evgeny Onegin*	
1837	Balzac's *Père Goriot*	Dickens's *Pickwick Papers*
1839	Stendhal's *Chartreuse de Parme*	
1840	Lermontov's *Hero of Our Time*	
1842	Gogol's *Dead Souls*	
1844	Annette von Droste-Hülshoff's poems	
1848		Thackeray's *Vanity Fair*
1850		Tennyson's *In Memoriam*
1852	Gautier's *Émaux et Camées*	
1857	Flaubert's *Madame Bovary* Baudelaire's *Fleurs du Mal*	
1859	Hugo's *Légende des Siècles*	
1860		George Eliot's *Mill on the Floss*
1861	Turgenev's *Fathers and Sons*	
1864		Dickens's *Our Mutual Friend*
1866	Dostoyevsky's *Crime and Punishment*	
1867	Ibsen's *Peer Gynt*	

1869	Tolstoy's *War and Peace*
1871	Posthumous publication of Bécquer's poems
1874	Verlaine's *Romances sans Paroles*
1876	Mallarmé's *L'Après-midi d'un faune*
1880	Dostoyevsky's *Brothers Karamazov*
1883	Nietzsche's *Also sprach Zarathustra*
1884	Ibsen's *Wild Duck*
1885	Jules Laforgue's *Complaints*; Meredith's *Diana of the Crossways*
1885	Zola's *Germinal*
1886–7	Pérez Galdós's *Fortuna y Jacinta*
1887	Rimbaud's *Les Illuminations*
1888	Strindberg's *Miss Julie*
1891	Fontane's *Effi Briest*; Hardy's *Tess of the D'Urbervilles*
1895	Darío's *Prosas profanas*
1896	Housman's *A Shropshire Lad*
1897	George's *Jahr der Seele*
1901	Thomas Mann's *Buddenbrooks*
1902	D'Annunzio's *Francesca da Rimini*
1904	Chehov's *The Cherry Orchard*; First volumes of Rolland's *Jean Christophe*
1907–8	Rilke's *Neue Gedichte*
1907	Bergson's *Evolution Créatrice*
1908	Bennett's *The Old Wives Tale*

LIST OF DATES

	CONTINENTAL EUROPE	ENGLAND
1909	Gide's *Porte étroite*	H. G. Wells's *Tono Bungay*
1912	Anatole France's *Les Dieux ont soif*	
1913	Apollinaire's *Alcools* First volumes of Proust's *A la recherche du temps perdu*	D. H. Lawrence's *Sons and Lovers*
1918	Blok's *The Twelve*	Posthumous publication of G. M. Hopkins's poetry
1922	Rilke's *Duineser Elegien* and *Sonette an Orpheus* Pirandello's *Henry IV* Valéry's *Charmes*	T. S. Eliot's *The Waste Land* Joyce's *Ulysses*
1924	Thomas Mann's *Der Zauberberg*	
1925	Gorki's *Artamonov Business* Posthumous publication of Kafka's *The Trial*	
1927		Virginia Woolf's *To the Lighthouse*
1928	Lorca's *Romancero gitano* Alberti's *Sobre los ángeles*	Yeats's *The Tower* A. Huxley's *Point Counter Point*
1933	Malraux's *La Condition humaine*	
1935	Bergengruen's *Der Grosstyrann und das Gericht*	
1936		Auden's *Look Stranger*

1938	Sartre's *La Nausée*	
1943	Molinari's *Mundos de la Madrugada*	
1944	Camus's *La Peste*	Eliot's *Four Quartets*
1947	Octavio Paz's *Libertad bajo Palabra*	
1949		
1950	Neruda's *Canto general*	

INDEX

Académie française, 176, 177, 180, 183

Academy, Florentine, 96-100, 171

Adam, 85-6

Aeneid (Virgil), 15, 145, 146, 148

Akhmatova, Anna, 311

Aksakov, S. T., 278

alba, 29

Alberti, L. B., 97

Alberti, Rafael, 321, 354

Aldus Manutius, 109

Aleixandre, Vicente, 319-20

Alemán, Mateo, 199-200

Alfieri, Vittorio, 221

Alfonso the Wise, 42, 66

Almeida Garrett, J. B., 304

Amadis de Gaula, 83

Amboise, Cathérine de, 73

Andersen, Hans Christian, 326

Andreyev, L. N., 334-5

Angelus Silesius, 170, 283

Angioleri, Cecco, 49

Annensky, Innokenty, 309

Anouilh, Jean, 336

Apollinaire Guillaume, 317, 319

Arabian Nights, 209

Argensola, Bartolomé de, 152, 222

Argensola, Lupercio de, 152, 222

Ariosto, Ludovico, 103-4, 107, 145

Arnaut de Mareuil, 28

Arnim, Ludwig von, 246

Arnold, Matthew, 251, 304

Ars amatoria (Ovid) 22

aubade, 30

Aubigné, Agrippa d', 125

Aucassin and Nicolette, 35-6

Aufklärung, 224, 226, 228, 231

Bacchelli, Riccardo, 353

Bagritsky, E., 311

Baïf, Jean-Antoine de, 120, 122

Baïf, Lazare de, 123

ballade, 70-1, 110

Balmont, K., 309

Balzac, Honoré de, 258, 268-9, 272, 273-4, 289, 342

Baratynsky, E. A., 262

barcarola, 42

Barnes, William, 292

Barrios, Miguel de, 167

Baudelaire, Charles, 297-8, 299, 301, 302, 340

Bayle, Pierre, 209

Beaumarchais (Pierre-Augustin Caron), 216

Bécquer, G. A., 311

Belinsky, V. G., 277

Belleau, Rémy, 122

Bellman, C. M., 295

Bely, Andrey, 309

Bembo, Pietro, 101

Benavente, Jacinto, 335

Beowulf, 39, 40

Berceo, Gonzalo de, 43

Bergengruen, Werner, 351

Bergson, Henri, 341-2

Bernardez, Diogo, 136

Bernart de Ventadour, 28, 29

Bertran de Born, 28, 30

Bertrand, Aloysius, 255, 301

Bèze, Théodore de, 123

Bhagavadgita, 17, 283

Björnson, Björnsterne, 330

blason, 112, 116

Bloch, Jean-Richard, 348

Blok, Alexander, 294, 309-10

Bocángel, Gabriel, 164-5

Boccaccio, Giovanni, 38, 62-4

Bodel, Jean, 86-7

Bodmer, Johann Jakob, 224

Boehme, Jakob, 169-70, 225, 228, 231, 241-2, 243

Boiardo, M. M., 102

374   INDEX

Boileau, Nicolas (Despréaux), 189
Borel, Petrus, 255
Boscán, Juan, 133
Bossuet, Jacques-Bénigné, 175
Bousoño, Carlos, 354
Boutens, P. C., 308
Brant, Sebastian, 111
Brecht, Bert, 338
Brederode, Gerbrand, 168
Brentano, Clemens von, 246, 247
Brieux, Eugène, 329
Bruno, Giordano, 98, 151, 174
Bryusov, V., 330
Buchanan, George, 122
Büchner, Georg, 324
Bunin, Ivan, 351
Bunyan, John, 198
Bürger, Gottfried August, 230, 238
Byron, Gordon Lord, 243, 254, 260, 261, 263, 264, 298, 301

Calderón de la Barca, Pedro 160-3, 177, 246
Camões, Luís de, 135-6, 146-7, 281, 355
Campana, Dino, 304
Campanella, Tommaso, 98, 150, 151
Camus, Albert, 349
Cancionero de Baena, 75-6
Cancionero geral, 81-2
cantar de gesta, 19-21
Cantar de mïo Cid, 20-1
cantiga de amigo, 42-3, 312
canzone, 30, 45, 134
Čapek, Karel, 337
Carducci, Giosuè, 302-3
Carillo y Sotomayor, Luis de, 165
Carlyle, Thomas, 246
Castiglione, Baldassare, 105, 133, 157
Castro, Eugénio de, 315
Castro, Guillén de, 156
Castro, Rosalía, 312
Cavalcanti, Guido, 48-9, 51, 52

Cela, Camilo José, 353
Cernuda, Luis, 321
Cervantes, Miguel de, 141-4, 153, 198, 204, 355
Chamisso, Adalbert von, 246
chanson, 30, 45
chanson de geste, 12, 13, 15-19
chanson de mal-mariée, 32
Chanson de Roland, 15-19, 25, 145
chanson de toile, 32
chant royal, 70, 73
Char, René, 318
Chartier, Alain, 71
Chassignet, Jean-Baptiste, 126
Chateaubriand, François-René, Comte de, 248-9
Chaucer, 33, 36-7 38, 63
Chehov, Anton, 285-6, 332, 333-4
Chénier, André, 217
Chiabrera, Gabriello, 151-2
Chrétien de Troyes, 22-4, 40
Cino da Pistoia, 52, 58-9
Claudel, Paul, 316-17, 336
Claudius, Matthias, 229-30
Cocteau, Jean, 317
Coleridge, S. T., 238, 239
Colonna, Vittoria, 106
Commedia dell'Arte, 108, 185, 216, 218, 219
Commynes, Philippe de, 72
Compton Burnett, Ivy, 348
conceptismo, 152, 166
Conon de Béthune, 31
Constant, Benjamin, 265, 267
Conversion de l'Apôtre Paul, 87
copla, 30, 78, 312
Corbière, Tristan, 200-1
Corneille, Pierre, 156, 177, 178, 179-81, 190, 195, 226
Corneille, Thomas, 182, 195
cosante, 42
Cowper, William, 218, 261
Crabbe, George, 261
Crébillon, Claude-Prosper de, 207-8, 213
cultismo, 152, 165, 166
Cyrano de Bergerac, 204-5

Dancourt, Florent Carton, 195
Daniel, Arnaut, 30, 53, 57
d'Annunzio, Gabriele, 303-4
Dante Alighieri, 49-58, 65, 355
Darío, Rubén, 297, 312, 314, 354
Daudet, Alphonse, 274
Defoe, Daniel, 200, 264
Dehmel, Richard, 305
Delvig, Anton, Baron, 262
de Quincey, Thomas, 298
Derzhavin, G. R., 260
Desbordes-Valmore, Marceline, 250
Descartes, René, 172-3, 189, 197, 241
Deschamps, Eustache, 70
Desportes, Philippe, 125-6
Dickens, Charles, 281, 342
Diderot, Denis, 214-16, 218, 226, 325
Dinis, King of Portugal, 42
Donne, John, 126, 162
Dostoyevsky, Fëdor, 272, 283-5, 286, 289, 342, 349
Douglas, Norman, 343
Drelincourt, Laurent, 129
Droste-Hülshoff, Annette von, 287, 291, 292
Dryden, John, 195
Du Bartas, Guillaume, 125
Du Bellay, Joachim, 120-2
Du Guillet, Pernette, 119
Duhamel, Georges, 348
Dumas, Alexandre, 256, 269

Eckhart, Meister, 54, 67, 146, 283
Eddas, 39
Eichendorff, Joseph von, 247, 251, 293
Eliot, T. S., 308, 318, 354
Éluard, Paul, 317-18
Emmanuel, Pierre, 318
Encina, Juan de, 90
Encyclopédistes, 205, 212, 213, 214-15, 242
Enríquez Gómez, Antonio, 167
Erasmus, Desiderius, 98, 110-11

Ercilla, Alonso de, 147-9
Esenin, S. A., 310, 321
Espinel, Vicente, 200
Espinosa, Pedro, 165
Espronceda, José de, 257-8
estribillo, 79
Everyman, 88, 89, 307
Evtushenko, Evgeny, 312
Ewald, Johannes, 324

Fabliau, 33-4, 38, 183, 204
Fabre d'Olivet, 242-3
farce, 89
Fazio degli Uberti, 58
Fénelon, François de, 208
Ferlosio, Rafael Sánchez, 353
Ferreira, Antonio, 136
Fet, A. A., 294
Ficino, Marsilio, 96
Fielding, Henry, 200, 218
Flaubert, Gustave, 271-2, 274, 280, 282
Fleming, Paul, 170
Fontane, Theodor, 288
Fontenelle, Bernard de, 209
Fonvizin, D. I., 260
Foscolo, Ugo, 258
Fouqué, Friedrich de la Motte, 246
France, Anatole, 242
Francis Saint, 46
Freud, Sigmund, 342
Freytag, Gustav, 288
Froissart, Jean, 71-2
Fromentin, Eugène, 270
Furetière, Antoine, 205

Gaboriau, Émile, 270
Garcilaso de la Vega, 133-5
Garnier, Robert, 124
Gassendi, Pierre, 173
Gautier, Théophile, 253, 295-6, 298
Gay, John, 189-90
Gellert, Christian Fürchtegott, 224

Geoffrey of Monmouth, 22
George, Stefan, 305-6, 308
Gezelle Guido, 295
Gibbon, Edward, 218
Gide, André, 316, 345-6
Giraldi Cinthio, Giambattista, 107
Giraudoux, Jean, 336
Giraut de Borneil, 28
Goethe, Johann Wolfgang von, 225, 226, 230, 231-3, 235, 238-40, 244, 250, 326, 328, 339, 355
Gogol, Nikolai, 278, 283, 286, 332
Goldoni, Carlo, 220-1, 223
Goldsmith, Oliver, 223, 231
Goncharov, I. A., 278-9
Goncourt, Edmond and Jules, 272-3
Góngora, Luis de, 126, 138, 152, 163-4, 165
Gorki, Maxim, 280, 352
Gottfried von Strassburg, 41
Gottsched, Johann Christoph, 224
Gozzi, Count Carlo, 220, 221
Gracián, Baltasar, 167-8
gracioso, 153, 157, 216
Graves, Robert, 292, 354
Gréban, Arnoul, 88
Green, Henry, 266
Greene, Graham, 284
Grillparzer, Franz, 323
Grimm, Jakob and Wilhelm, 245, 325-6
Grimmelshausen, Johann von, 201-2
Gryphius, Andreas, 170
Guarini, Battista, 108
Guevara, Antonio de, 132
Guicciardini, Francesco, 105
Guillaume de Lorris, 36-7
Guillén, Jorge, 320
Guinizelli, Guido, 48
Gumilëv, N., 311
Günther, Johann Christian, 229
Gutiérrez Nájera, Manuel, 313
Gutzkow, Karl, 323

Hamann, Johann Georg, 228
Hardy, Alexandre, 124, 177
Hardy, Thomas, 281
Hartmann von Aue, 39
Hartzenbusch Juan Eugenio, 257
Hašek, Jaroslav, 350
Hauff, Wilhelm, 326
Hauptmann, Gerhart, 275, 332
Hebbel, Friedrich, 324, 327
Heine, Heinrich, 290-1, 298, 312
Hélinant de Froidmont, 33
Herder, Johann Gottfried, 225, 229, 231
Hérédia, J. M. de, 297
Hernández, Miguel, 321-2
Herrera, Fernando de, 138
Herrera y Reissig, Julio, 313
Hesse, Hermann, 350
Heym, Georg, 307
Hierro, José, 354
Hoffmann, E. T. A., 244-5, 261, 269, 283, 284, 326
Hofmann von Hofmannswaldau, Christian, 170
Hofmannsthal, Hugo von, 305, 307
Holberg, Ludwig, 218-19, 325
Hölderlin, J. C. F., 225, 244, 306, 308, 321
Holthusen, Hans Egon, 308
Hölty, Ludwig, 230
Hooft, Pieter Cornelisz, 168
Hôtel de Bourgogne, 178
Hugh of Saint Victor, 66
Hugo, Victor, 252-3, 255-6, 269, 284, 296, 298
Huysmans, J. K., 274, 303

Ibsen, Henrik, 223, 288, 326-29, 333
Iliad (Homer), 17
Imperial, Francisco, 76-7
Inquisition, Holy, 31
interlude, 89, 153
Isla, José Francisco de, 223
isopet, 33-4

Jacobsen, Jens Peter, 289
Jacopo da Lentini, 46
Jacopone da Todi, 47
James, Henry, 240, 280, 343
James, William, 342
Jáuregui, Juan de, 165, 222
Jean de Meun, 36-8
Jean Paul (Richter), 228, 246
Jerena, Garcí Fernandez de, 76
Jiménez, Juan Ramón, 314-15
Jodelle, Étienne, 122, 123-4
John of the Cross, Saint, 138-40
Joinville, Jean de, 44
Jongleurs, 11, 12, 13, 14, 15, 42
Jonson, Ben, 189, 198, 218
Jouve, P. J., 317

Kafka, Franz, 349-50
Kaiser, Georg, 337
Kant, Immanuel, 237
Kästner, Erich, 308
Keats, John, 329
Keller, Gottfried, 287, 326
Kleist, Heinrich von, 247-8
Klinger, F. M. von, 230, 231
Klopstock, Friedrich Gottlieb, 225
Koltsov, A. V., 294
Krasinski, Zygmunt, Count, 263
Krylov, I. A., 260
Kuprin, Ivano, 351

Labé, Louise, 119-20
La Boétie, Étienne de, 116
La Bruyère, Jean de, 181, 196, 197, 208
La Ceppède, Jean de, 126
Laclos, Choderlos de, 216-17, 264
La Fayette, Mme de, 203, 264, 348
La Fontaine, Jean de, 182-4, 260
Laforgue, Jules, 300-1
Lamartine, Alphonse de, 249-50
Larivey, Pierre 124
La Rochefoucauld, Francois, Duc de, 196, 203, 208
La Tour du Pin, Patrice de, 318
'Lautréamont, Comte de,' 301-2

Lawrence, D. H., 213, 275
Lazarillo de Tormes, 199, 200
Leconte de Lisle, 296-7
Leibnitz, Gottfried Wilhelm von, 224
Lemaire de Belges, Jean, 112
Lenau, Nikolaus, 292, 293
Lenormand, H. R., 336
Lenz, J. M., 230, 231
Leon, Derrick, 281-2
León, Luis de, 137-8, 140, 222
Leonov, Leonid, 352
Leopardi, Giacomo, 259, 298
Leopold, J. H., 309
Lermontov, M. Y., 262-3
Lesage, René, 144, 195, 200, 201, 205-6
Leskov, N. S., 280
Lessing, Gottfried Ephraim, 224, 225-7, 323
Levi, Carlo, 353
Lichtenberg, Georg Christoph, 227-8
Liliencron, Detlev von, 297
Lillo, George, 225
lira, 134-5, 137, 139
Loerke, Oskar, 308
Lope de Rueda, 153
Lope de Vega Carpio, 152-6, 182, 199
Lorca, Federigo García, 320, 321, 335
Loyola, Ignacio, 139-40
Lucian, 115, 204
Lull, Ramón, 66, 172
Lulli, Jean-Baptiste, 188, 195
Luther, Martin, 98, 111

Machado, Antonio, 312-13
Machaut, Guillaume de, 70
Machiavelli, Niccolò, 104-5, 107
Maeterlinck, Maurice, 331
Mairet, Jean, 177-8
Maître Pierre Pathelin, 89-90, 186
Malherbe, François de, 127, 179
Mallarmé, Stéphane, 299-300, 304, 306, 317

Malraux, André, 348
Mann, Thomas, 343-4
Manrique, Jorge, 74, 78
Manuel, Juan, 82
Manzoni, Alessandro, 258-9
Marcabru, 28, 29
Marcel, Gabriel, 336
March, Auziàs, 82
Mareschal, André, 178
Marguerite of Navarre, 113 115
Marie de France, 33, 38
Marinetti, F. T., 318
Marino, Giambattista, 150-1, 170, 183, 184, 224
Marivaux, Pierre, 195-6, 206, 213, 223, 256, 264
Marot, Clément, 112-13, 176, 183
Martin du Gard, Roger, 348
Martínez de Toledo, archpriest of Talavera, 83
Martí, José, 313
'Matter of Britain,' 22-4
Maupassant, Guy de, 272
Mauriac, François, 348
Mayakovsky, V., 310
Maykov, A. N., 293
Maynard, François de, 127-8
Mechtild von Magdeburg, 66
Medici, Cosimo de, 96
Medici, Lorenzo de, 97, 100-1
Mena, Juan de, 77
Mendelssohn, Moses, 225
Mérimée, Prosper, 269-70, 280
Metastasio, Pietro, 219, 259
Meyer, Conrad Ferdinand, 287, 293, 297, 351
Michaux, Henri, 317
Michelangelo, 106
Michelet, Jules, 249
Mickiewicz, Adam, 263
Milton, John, 125, 138, 162, 169, 194, 224
Minnesänger, 41
Mira de Amescua, Antonio, 159
Miranda, Francisco de Sá de, 136
Mistral, Frédéric, 295
Molière (Jean-Baptiste Poquelin), 184-9, 190, 216, 218, 220, 223

Molinari, Ricardo, 354
Molinos, Miguel de, 167
Montaigne, Michel de, 116-18
Montale, Eugenio, 319
Montesquieu, Charles-Louis, Baron de, 209-10, 212
Monti, Vicenzo, 221
Moore, George, 275, 343
morality play, 88-9
Moratín, Leandro Fernández de, 223-4
Moratín, Nicolas Fernández, de, 222
Moréas, Jean, 302
Morgenstern, Christian, 308
Mörike, Eduard, 291-2
Muset, Colin, 31
Musil, Robert, 350
Musset, Alfred de, 253-4, 256-7, 270, 290
Mystère du Vieux Testament, 88
mysteria platonica, 95-7
mystery play, 87

Naharro, Torres, 91
Nekrasov, N. A., 294
Neruda, Pablo, 355
Nerval, Gérard de, 255, 295
Nibelungenlied, 41
Nicolai, C. F., 225
Nietzsche, Friedrich, 340-41
Novalis (Friedrich von Hardenberg), 247

Oehlenschläger, Adam, 325
Opitz, Martin, 169
Orléans, Charles d', 71
Ossian, MacPherson's, 225, 229
Ostrovsky, A. N., 332
Otero, Blas de, 355

Paracelsus, Theophrastus, 169, 243
Parini, Giuseppe, 222
Pascal, Blaise, 173-5, 204-5
Pascoli, Giovanni, 303

Pasqually, Martines de, 242-3
Pasternak, Boris, 310, 321, 352
pastourelle, 30, 31-2, 42
Pavese, Cesare, 353
Paz, Octavio, 355
Péguy, Charles 316
Pellicer, Carlos, 355
Pereda, José María de, 275
Pérez Galdós, Benito, 274, 276-7, 289, 342, 353
Périers, Bonaventure de, 115-16
Perrault, Charles, 196, 325
Perse, Saint-John, 318
Pessanha, Camilo, 315
Pessoa, Fernando, 315
Petöfi, Sandor, 295
Petrarca, Francesco, 59-62, 145, 254
Pico della Mirandola, 97, 109
Pilniak, Boris, 352
Piovene, Guido, 353
Pirandello, Luigi, 219, 335-6
Pisan, Christine de, 71
Platen, August von, 292
Plethon, G. Gemistus, 96
Poe, Edgar Allan, 298, 330
Poliziano, Angelo, 97, 99-100
Polonsky, Y. P., 293
Pope, Alexander, 146, 190, 210, 218
Précieuses, 175-6
Prévert, Jacques, 317
Prévost, l'Abbé, 206-7, 212, 213
Proust, Marcel, 343, 346-7, 348
pseudo-Dionysius, 66
Pulci, Luigi, 101-2
Pushkin, A. S., 260-2, 277, 286, 294

Quasimodo, Salvatore, 319
Quem quaeritis, 84
Quental, Antero de, 304
Quevedo, Francisco de, 128, 152, 166-7, 200, 201
Quierós, Eça de, 277
Quinault, Philippe, 195
Quíntero, Serafín and Joaquín, Álvarez, 335

Raabe, Wilhelm, 288
Rabelais, François, 113-15, 198
Racan, Honorat de Bueil de, 127, 178
Racine, Jean, 181, 190-4, 210
Radiguet, Raymond, 348
Rambouillet, Marquise de, 175-6
Regnard, Jean François, 195
Régnier, Mathurin, 128
Remarque, Erich, 350
Remizov, Alexei, 351-2
Resende, Garcia de, 81-2
Restif de la Bretonne, 217, 268
Reuchlin, Johann, 98, 110
Rhétoriqueurs 110, 112
Richard of Saint Victor, 66
Richardson, Samuel, 206, 218, 224, 232, 264
Rilke, Rainer Maria, 99, 238, 305-7, 315, 316, 321, 347
Rimbaud, J. A., 300, 340
Rivas, Duque de, 257
Rojas, Fernando de, 130-2, 198
Rojas, Francisco de, 163
Rolland, Romain, 343-4
Romains, Jules, 348
Roman de la Rose, 36-8
Roman de Renard, 34, 38
romance, 79-81, 252
rondeau, 70, 71, 112
rondel, 30
Ronsard, Pierre, 120-2, 127, 146, 176
Rotrou, Jean, 178, 182
Rousseau, Jean-Jacques, 197, 212-14, 215, 218, 228, 229, 232, 237, 242, 244, 249, 264
Ruiz, Juan, archpriest of Hita, 74-5
Ruiz de Alarcón, Juan, 159, 182
Rutebeuf, 33, 87
Ruysbroeck, Jan van, 69

Sacchetti, Franco, 98
Sachs, Hans, 89
Sade, Marquis de, 217, 303
sagas, 39-40
Saint-Amant, Marc-Antoine de Girard de, 128, 166, 184

Sainte- Beuve, C. A., 254
Saint-Martin, Claude de, 242, 268
Saint-Pierre, Bernardin de, 217, 249
Saint-Simon, Louis, Duc de 196, 197
Salinas, Pedro, 319
Saltykov, Shchedrin, M. E., 280
Samain, Albert, 302
Sánchez Calavera, Ferrant, 76
Sand, George, 251-2, 256, 270, 280
Sannazaro, Jacopo, 103
Santillana, Marquis de, 77-8
Sardou, Victorien, 329
Sartre, Jean Paul, 337, 349
Scarron, Paul, 205, 206
Scève, Maurice, 118-19
Schiller Friedrich von, 230, 233-5, 238, 239
Schlegel, A. W. von, 245
Schlegel, Friedrich von, 245
Schnitzler, Arthur, 332
Schopenhauer, Arthur, 339-40
Scott, Sir Walter, 230, 252, 258, 260, 261, 263, 264, 269, 288
Scribe, Eugène, 327, 329
Scudéry, Georges de, 177
Scudéry, Madeleine de, 176, 202-3
Sedaine, Michel-Jean, 216
Segrais, Jean Regnault de, 203
serrana, 75
sestina, 30
Seuse or Suso, Heinrich, 68
Sévigné, Mme de, 196, 203
Shakespeare, W., 107, 154, 158, 189, 194, 210, 224, 227, 228, 231, 239, 245, 255, 257, 260, 261, 355
Sheridan, R. B., 223
Sierra, Gregorio, Martínez, 335
Signoret, Emmanuel, 302
Silva, José Asunción, 313
Slowacki, Juliusz, 263
Snorri, Sturluson, 39
Sologub, F., 309, 351
Solovyëv, V. A., 309
sonnet, 46
Sordello, 45

Sorel, Charles, 204
Soto de Rojas, Pedro, 164
Sousa, Francisco de, 82
Spinoza, Baruch, 241
Sponde, Jean de, 126
Sprüche, 42
Stael, Mme de, 248
Stampa, Gaspara, 106
Stendhal (Henri Beyle), 265-7, 268, 270, 289
Sterne, Laurence, 218, 227, 228, 246, 281
Stifter, Adalbert, 287
Storm, Theodor, 287, 292-3
Strindberg, August, 275, 330-31
Sturm und Drang, 224, 226, 230, 233, 235, 243, 324, 337
Sudermann, Hermann, 330
Sue, Eugène, 270
Supervielle, Jules, 317
Svevo, Italo, 350
Swedenborg, Emanuel, 242, 244, 268, 330
Swift, Jonathan, 189, 198, 210
Swinburne Algernon, 303

Tasis, Juan de, Conde de Villa-mediana, 165
Tasso, Torquato, 108, 148, 149-50, 151
Tauler, Johannes, 68-9
Tegnér, Bishop E., 295
Tennyson, Alfred, Lord, 251, 300
Teresa, Santa, 140-1
Testi, Fulvio, 152
Theologia Germanica, 69
Théroulde, 15-16
Thibaut, Count of Champagne, 31
Thomas à Kempis, 69
Thomson, James, 247, 293
Tieck, Ludwig, 244, 245, 247, 326
Till Eulenspiegel, 111
Tirso de Molina, 156-9, 187
Toller, Ernst, 337
Tolstoy, Alexey, 257, 294
Tolstoy, Leo, 272, 275, 280-3, 285, 286, 289, 333, 342, 347, 348

Torga, Miguel, 319
Torres Villaroel, Diego de, 222
Trakl, Georg, 307
Trissino, Giangiorgio, 107, 149
Tristan and Iseult, 25-6, 41
Tristan l'Hermite, François, 182, 184
trope, 84
troubadours, 13, 15, 27-31, 45-6
trouvères, 13, 15, 22
Turgenev, Ivan, 279-80, 285, 332
Tvardovsky, Alexander, 312
Tyard, Pontus de, 120
Tyutchev, Fëdor, 293, 294

Unamuno, Miguel de, 314, 316
Ungaretti, Giuseppe, 318-19
Unruh, Fritz von, 337
Urfé, Honoré d', 202, 204

Valdés, Juan de, 132, 139
Valdivielso, José de, 165
Valente, José Ángel, 354
Valera, Juan, 275
Valéry, Paul, 304, 316, 319
Vallejo, César, 355
Vasconcelos, Jorge Ferreira de, 199
Vauvenargues, Marquis de, 212
Velarde, Ramón López, 354
Vélez de Guevara, Luis, 159, 201, 205
Venevitinov, Dmitri, 262
Verga, Giovanni, 275, 303
Verhaeren, Émile, 302
Verlaine, Paul, 298, 301
Verwey, Albert, 305, 308-9
Viau, Théophile de, 128, 166, 177
Vicente, Gil, 91-4

Vida, Marco Girolamo, 145-6
Viélé-Griffin, Francis, 302
Vigny, Alfred de, 250-2, 256, 269
Villalón, Cristóbal de, 132-3, 199
villancico, 77, 79
Villasandino, Álvarez de, 75-6
Villehardouin, Geoffroy de, 44
Villon, François, 72-3
virelai, 30
Vives, Juan Luis, 132
Voiture, Vincent, 176
Voltaire (François-Marie Arouet) 148, 205, 210-12
Vondel, Joost van den, 169

Wagner, Richard, 325
Walther von der Vogelweide, 41
Wedekind, Frank, 332
Weinheber, Josef, 308
Wells, H. G., 218
Werfel, Franz, 308, 338
Wieland, C. M., 227
William, Count of Poitiers, 27-8
Wolfram von Eschenbach, 41
Wordsworth, W., 238
Wycherley, William, 188

Yeats, W. B., 306, 315

Zabolotsky, Nikolai, 311
Zejel, 27-8, 42
Zhukovsky, V. A., 260
Zola, Émile, 273-4, 275, 341
Zorrilla, José, 257
Zoshchenko, Mikhail, 352
Zuckmayer, Carl, 338
Zweig, Arnold, 350